Rev. Charles Owen Rice

REV. CHARLES OWEN RICE

Apostle of Contradiction

BY PATRICK J. McGEEVER

 Duquesne University Press
Pittsburgh, PA

Copyright © 1989 by Duquesne University Press

All Rights Reserved

Published by Duquesne University Press
600 Forbes Avenue, Pittsburgh, PA 15282

FIRST EDITION
Printed in the United States of America

Library of Congress Cataloging-in-Publication Data

McGeever, Patrick J.
    Rev. Charles Owen Rice: apostle of contradiction / by Patrick J. McGeever.
        p.   cm.
    Bibliography: p.
    Includes index.
    ISBN 0–8207–0209–9
    ISBN 0–8207–0210–2 (Pbk)
    1. Rice, Charles Owen. 1908–   . 2. Catholic Church—United
States—Clergy—Biography.   3. Church and labor—United States—
–History—20th century.   I. Title.   II. Title: Reverend Charles
Owen Rice.
BX4705.R453M38 1988
282′.902′4—dc19
[B]   88–19766
                                                              CIP

Contents

	Introduction	vii
	List of Abbreviations	xiv
ONE.	Poor Wee Charlie	1
TWO.	"Are We Really Radical?"	29
THREE.	Wartime Patriot	70
FOUR.	Redbaiter Extraordinaire	92
FIVE.	Up The River?	136
SIX.	Black Rage, White Conscience	167
SEVEN.	This Time Really A Radical	198
EIGHT.	Keeping The Faith	224
NINE.	A Preliminary Assessment	260
	Notes	281
	Index	305
	Photographs	158–166
		255–259

Introduction

THIS BIOGRAPHY IS SUBTITLED "Apostle of Contradiction" for two reasons. "Contradict" means literally "speak against," and Msgr. Charles Owen Rice for a half century used his voice and his pen time and again to speak out against those who, in his opinion, used their power foolishly or immorally. His targets ranged from antilabor businessmen to labor leaders, from conservatives to communists, from policemen to presidents, and from ecclesiastical authorities to rebels within his church. Rice performed this function of contradiction often enough and ably enough that we can think of it as his particular stock in trade.

But "contradictory" is more often used in the sense of someone or something that contradicts *itself*, something made up of inconsistent tendencies. Charles Owen Rice struck many observers over the years as contradictory in this sense — to the point that those who admired him as well as those who despised him, and those who knew him casually as well as those who thought they knew him well for many years, sometimes wished that the "real" Rice would stand up and be identified once and for all. Is he aptly styled, as he would have it himself, "a simple parish priest"? Or is he better described by the title Pittsburghers attribute to him: "labor priest"? What about the epithets "communist" or "subversive" frequently hurled at him by some of his readers or listeners, or the term "radical," for which he has expressed his own preference? And how much truth is there to the claims of some critics that lurking beneath the surface of what they regarded as various disguises there was yet another Rice, an unprincipled, Machiavellian reactionary who espoused progressive causes only to betray them?

Rice marked his golden jubilee — his fiftieth year a priest — in 1984 at St. Anne's church at Castle Shannon, a suburb of Pittsburgh. At age seventy-five, he was well settled into his most perennial role of parish priest, whether or not simple. The monsignor (he had been elevated to that honor twenty years earlier) was surrounded by that devoted platoon of women who served the physical and secretarial needs of the parish, by younger and generally admiring curates who helped with the spiritual mission of St. Anne's, by a thriving parochial school, and by a parish with a rich variety of organizations and activities, where even the spacious parking lot was crowded each Sunday when Masses were offered. In addition to his varied spiritual and administrative duties, Rice regularly enjoyed his eighteen holes of golf, his afternoon cocktail hours, his somewhat ceremonial "repasts" at the rectory, and the firm ride of his new Volvo. Rice had clearly been a success in the church, and it, in turn, had been good to him. When the bells of St. Anne's tolled the passing hours, they marked as well the comfortable evening of a satisfying ecclesiastical career.

Yet those bells intoned other memories for Rice, dramatically different from his present life. They rang from a tower erected in the memory of St. Anne's most famous parishioner, and chieftain of labor chieftains, Phil Murray. When Rice had first met Murray during labor's early organizing battles, Rice had been a fiery young priest heading up the Catholic Radical Alliance and living in a Depression-era soup kitchen/flophouse that sheltered a small army of unemployed men and a larger army of cockroaches. Murray and his followers had plenty of enemies and too few friends inside the church (or outside it) as they attempted to organize the unorganized workers into industry-wide unions, but he could always count on the young and charismatic Father Rice to put heart back into the men out on the picket line for the CIO. Murray's own mentor, the inimitable John L. Lewis, had passed on to him the leadership of the CIO in 1941, symbolized in the gavel that convened the congress that year. Then, when the great John L. had turned savagely against him, Murray had shared his anguish with his priestly confidant, Father Rice. Over the years their friendship had prospered and now, with Murray in his grave, the gavel rested on Rice's desk in the rectory.

Thus had Rice become known as the "labor priest." But that popular title had been etched in acid in the 1950s when Rice had fallen into ecclesiastical disfavor under "Iron John" Dearden, bishop of Pittsburgh. Then Rice, who had (at least as he recalled it) called New York's Cardinal Francis Spellman a "scab" for sending in seminarians to bury the dead in place of striking gravediggers, was himself "sent up the river" to a parish far removed from Pittsburgh.

But all of that had been many decades ago, and Rice had long since ceased to think of himself as a "fren-a-labor" (his term), at least in the sense of a reliable supporter of labor union leadership policies. He had supported too many union insurgencies over the years, most of them losing causes, and needled too many labor leaders, many of them powerful and vindictive. In the 1960s he had broken sharply with organized labor, with the Democratic Party, and in fact with the liberal New Deal coalition generally, to struggle instead in favor of black rights and in opposition to the war in Vietnam — causes then in disfavor with many unions, Democrats, and liberals. He had proclaimed himself "reradicalized" by a new generation of the young, had worn his hair long, and had generally cut himself off from most of his earlier supporters.

By the 1980s, Rice had mellowed a bit, and resumed some interrupted liaisons with labor and liberals. But his weekly column in the *Pittsburgh Catholic* still regularly brought in virulent letters from readers outraged by Rice's views and anxious to have him silenced. When the U.S.A. invaded Grenada, Rice denounced first the invasion and then the continued occupation of that small island. When Lutheran pastor David Roth and his prolabor followers occupied a church despite ecclesiastical and judicial orders to vacate, Rice was supportive. On the subject of terrorism, Rice submitted that the West owed its dominance in the world to its use of high-tech terror. When P-9, a rebel union of the United Food and Commercial Workers, engaged in a life-or-death struggle with Hormel in Minnesota and with its own international union, it received both a visit and extensive coverage and support from Rice. Local elections provided him with the opportunity to denounce the City of Pittsburgh and the Democratic Party in both the city and county as racist. In 1988, when the cause of the day was the "war on drugs," Rice decried congressional votes to involve the military. He argued that this constituted "another small step away from our system and toward the destruction of our freedom." One week when Rice was away and his column was absent from the pages of the *Pittsburgh Catholic*, the space was readily filled with a collection of letters from readers protesting one or another of his recent pronouncements and ranging in tone from thoughtful discussions of the issues to anguished howls of "communist!"[1]

This charge may have been the occasion for mirthless laughter by card-carrying members of the American Left who recalled quite a different Rice over the years: the one who had driven Catholic pacifists out of the Catholic Radical Alliance when he embraced the New Deal and American entry into World War II; the consummate Red-baiter after that war who struggled to drive communist influence out of the CIO and especially out of the electrical workers' UE; the holder of the purse strings of seeming black grassroots organizations in Pittsburgh's Homewood ghetto around the time of the riots in the 1960s; the opponent of most forms of women's liberation most of the time.

Still others, rebels within the Catholic Church, found in Rice neither a radical nor a liberal but an archconservative on such issues as hierarchical authority, female priests, priests' associations, and even the unionization of parochial school teachers — thus concluding that he was an advocate of radical change only when it was least likely to upset his own applecart. To some of these activists, Rice seemed to be not an agent, but a saboteur, of progressive movements.

Who, then, was the "real" Rice? Was he the one who outraged his readers and listeners from afar, or the one who invariably charmed them close up? Was he the radio priest with the delightful Irish lilt, or the native of New York City? Was he the conservative cleric or the antiestablishment priest? Was he the lefty or the Red-baiter? Was he none of the above, but merely an unprincipled gadfly who never could resist the lure of notoriety? If both casual and close observers of Rice have had difficulty resolving these questions, this was, as the following pages will serve to demonstrate, not entirely without reason.

I first became interested in Rice when I was growing up in the 1950s in western Pennsylvania in a steelworker-union-Irish-Catholic family. Among our political household deities were Franklin Roosevelt, Harry Truman, and Phil Murray. Murray seemed to rank below Roosevelt but above Truman, and Rice was right up there too. My father recalled with pride the time he and Rice had spoken from the same podium at a steel workers' meeting. About the time I was old enough to start reading about politics, Rice, unfortunately, was in disfavor and his column "On the Condition of Labor" had been discontinued.

I next reacquainted myself with Rice in the early 1970s, when I was teaching political science in the Midwest, the U.S. involvement in Vietnam was trudging sullenly towards its inglorious ending, and Rice was again peppering his readership with syndicated columns that punctured with wit and acute insight many of the prevailing assumptions of the liberal American establishment.

Apparently Rice's political thinking had undergone some major changes since New Deal days, as had my own. Eventually I contacted him about putting together a collection of his political writings.

Rice himself was altogether cooperative, but publishers doubted the viability of a collection of *anyone's* writings, and in Rice's case were much more interested in a biography. At first I quailed at the thought of undertaking so ambitious a project as a biography of Charles O. Rice. It was a job not so much for a political scientist as for a historian, or, better yet, a whole relay of them — one for each historical era in which Rice had played a part. Bit by bit, however, my curiosity about Rice's life and my enthusiasm for him as a subject overcame my prudent reluctance, and I reoriented my sights toward a biography.

Thus was I launched on what became a several years-long voyage of discovery. In many hours of taping interviews with Rice, of collating his decades of writings, of studying his massive collected papers at the University of Pittsburgh's Hillman Library, and of talking with some of those who have worked with him, I was introduced to quite a few more layers of what I came to think of as the Rice riddle:

> a small frail boy, deprived at an early age of both mother and father, whose feistiness rendered him better at starting fights than at finishing them;
>
> a young cleric who brought to Pittsburgh the radical Catholic Worker Movement, but there changed it into something quite different from the intentions of its founders, Dorothy Day and Peter Maurin;
>
> a highly improbable but remarkably successful administrator of the New Deal Rent Control Program, who left the bureaucrat's desk at the end of World War II for an even more improbable role of mediator/broadcaster at a time of dangerous labor confrontation;
>
> probably the most overlooked Red-baiter of the post-World War II era, who was instrumental in driving communists out of the labor movement and in offering a preview of the McCarthyism of the 1950s;
>
> a middle-aged man who watched the triumphs of his youth turn to ashes and who struggled to be "born again" as a radical;
>
> a priest who tested over many years the limits of social activism permissible to the Catholic clergy, without ever quite transgressing those limits;
>
> a mature man who could look back over the panorama of his life,

sometimes with amusement or regret, usually with pride, and always with an intense curiosity about how he would be remembered.

To say that at the end of these years of study I have solved the Rice riddle and will now unveil it to the reader would be to claim too much — or too little. For Rice is a deeply complex person, and many facets of his personality remain inscrutable even to the biographer's diligent probings. What this biography attempts to do is to open up to the reader much of the rich complexity of Rice's career, to demonstrate that Rice is truly an important if sometimes overlooked figure in the history of Catholic social activism in this century, and perhaps to pioneer the way for future students of Rice's life.

This biography does not enjoy Rice's approval yet he was not only a cooperative subject, but on many occasions a most gracious host and even a source of encouragement. He has read an earlier version of this manuscript and submitted many corrections of fact, though vigorously disputing certain matters of interpretation. (Of course, the responsibility for any and all interpretations, unless specifically attributed to Rice or to someone else, must rest with me.) Both in his cooperation with me and in the extensive papers he has made available, Rice has offered to posterity a far larger target than most noted figures in history would be comfortable with.

Many other debts of gratitude can hardly be repaid, but must at least be acknowledged. Among them are those to various librarians who have provided essential help: William Spinelli at Duquesne University who arranged access to Rice's microfilmed columns, and Frank Zabrosky and his staff at Special Collections in Hillman Library. Important insights and help were also provided by Mark McCollogh of the University of Pittsburgh Archives of the Industrial Society, and by Charles McCollester. McCollester is a chief steward at UE Local 610 who doubles as Rice's literary executor and is now engaged in the work I had originally envisioned: volumes of selected writings by Rice. I wish him and the project well.

Back home at Indiana University, financial assistance was provided by the Center for American Studies to enable me to travel to Pittsburgh and to the Library of Congress in Washington, D.C. Various versions of this manuscript were ably and speedily typed by Marsha Neawedde, with assistance from Susan Albers, Kathy Collins, and Cathy Hines. Karl Illg at our Faculty Research Laboratory rescued me repeatedly from impending disasters with the computer. John Dowds at Duquesne University Press has ably shepherded this project through the thicket of potential problems to publication, while his expert staff has greatly improved the quality of the manuscript.

Finally, my thanks to my immediate family. Kate, Tim and Brendan experienced enough of their father's absence to realize he wasn't necessary, but had the good grace never to tell him that. My wife Rachel, a native Pittsburgher, not only provided encouragement and expert advice, but repeatedly took time from her legal studies and career to tend the homestead while I worked on the Rice manuscript. To all of you, and to many others I have not been able to mention, my sincere thanks.

List of Abbreviations

AAA, American Arbitration Association
ACLU, American Civil Liberties Union
ACTU, Association of Catholic Trade Unionists (Actists)
ADA, Americans for Democratic Action
AFL, American Federation of Labor
BCC, Black Construction Coalition
CAP, Community Action Against Poverty
CASH, Citizens Against Slum Housing
CIA, Central Intelligence Agency
CIO, Congress of Industrial Organizations
CPUSA, Communist Party, U.S.A.
CRA, Catholic Radical Alliance
CW, *Catholic Worker* (newspaper)
DMS, Denominational Ministry Strategy
FAT, Forever Action Together
HBA, Homewood Brushton Alliance
HBCIA, Homewood Brushton Civic Improvement
   Association
HBCC, Homewood Brushton Chamber of Commerce
HBCRC, Homewood Brushton Citizens' Renewal Council
HISC, House Internal Security Committee
HUAC, House UnAmerican Activities Committee
IBEW, International Brotherhood of Electrical Workers
ICFTU, International Confederation of Free Trade Unions
IUE, International Union of Electrical Workers
K of C, Knights of Columbus
LEAA, Federal Law Enforcement Assistance Administration
NAACP, National Association for the Advancement of
   Colored People
NEED, Negro Educational Emergency Drive
NLF, National Liberation Front (Vietnam)

NLRB, National Labor Relations Board
NN, Neighbors in Need
NORC, National Opinion Research Center
NPAC, National Peace Action Coalition
NSA, National Security Agency
OPA, Office of Price Administration
OSV, Our Sunday Visitor (newspaper)
RAHR, Religious Agency for Human Renewal
SGHOTPA, Soho and Gazzam Home Owners and Tenants
    Protective Association
SNCC, Student Non-Violent Coordinating Committee
SWOC, Steel Workers' Organizing Committee
TWU, Transit Workers' Union
UE, United Electrical Radio and Machine Workers of
    America
UEMDA, United Electrical Members for Democratic Action
UMP, United Movement for Progress
UMW, United Mine Workers
UOPWA, United Office and Professional Workers'
    Association
USWA, United Steel Workers of America
WABCO, Westinghouse Air Brake Company
WFTU, World Federation of Trade Unions

ONE

Poor Wee Charlie

CHARLES OWEN RICE was born in New York City in 1908 to immigrant Irish parents, Michael Rice and Anna O'Donnell Rice. They had left behind the rural past of their native land and were working their way rapidly up the American ladder of success and prosperity. Time and tragedy would interrupt these prospects for young Charlie and his older brother Pat, but for now their lives were comfortably middle-class in one of the world's great metropolises.

The boys' father had come from the bosom of a large Catholic family near Dundalk, Ireland, in County Louth. But he chose to leave that family at quite an early age: born in 1873, he set off in his early teens to pursue a religious career with the Irish Christian Brothers, the schoolmasters of Ireland. He spent ten years in India with them before leaving due to ill health. After clerking at a grocery store back in Dundalk for a year, Michael set off again, this time to the United States. Arriving in New York amid the excitement of the early twentieth century, he capitalized upon his experience in Dundalk to go to work for the P. H. Butler Company, a grocery chain. He also married in New York, and established a family.

Anna Rice had been born an O'Donnell and a Protestant. The fact that she met, dated, and eventually married a Catholic man who had been a Christian Brother, no less, was not without its special irony. For Michael, observing her setting off dressed for church each Sunday morning, assumed she must be a Catholic, and she inferred from his well-kept appearance that he must be a Protestant. Thus did an interdenominational romance begin de-

1

spite, or perhaps because of, narrow sectarian stereotyping of the day! But when the two discovered their religious differences, according to Anna's older sister Jennie, they broke off for a while — to be reconciled later by Anna's decision to convert to Catholicism. They were wed in 1905, with their sons Pat and Charlie being born one and three years later, respectively.

A third pregnancy, begun in 1912, found Anna O'Donnell Rice in much poorer health, the victim of scarlet fever. She managed to give birth to a daughter, Ellen, in March 1913, but died in the process. Ellen survived her mother by only a month. These deaths, as it turned out, not only deprived Pat and Charlie of their mother and a sister; they led as well to the breakup of what remained of their immediate family. For Michael Rice decided that he was not prepared to raise two young boys while pursuing his own career. He therefore made arrangements for his sons to be cared for by their grandmother, aunts, and uncles back in Dundalk.

In the spring of 1913, Charlie and Pat returned to the Irish past that their parents had left behind, and their father resumed his career as a grocer in the United States. How long this arrangement was anticipated to last is unclear, but World War I would soon intervene to make passage of the Atlantic dangerous in any case. As a result the boys would remain in Ireland until 1920, in effect experiencing most of their boyhood there. Although letters and gifts would occasionally make their way across the Atlantic, the boys would not lay eyes on their father during these seven years. How much personal insecurity, and how deep-seated, was instilled in these two young boys by this rapid succession of deaths, separation and displacement to another country, one can only wonder. What is clear is that the two of them came to be very close to one another, and to rely on one another, especially the younger Charlie on the older Pat.

But if Pat and Charlie[2] had been suddenly wrenched away from the family they had known, there was no lack of parental surrogates awaiting their arrival in Ireland. Their parental grandmother, Ellen Rice, had succeeded in raising her own nine children to adulthood and now looked forward eagerly — even somewhat possessively — to having youngsters in her house once again. She was joined in this anticipation by three of her unmarried children, who still lived with her: the boys' Uncle Owen and Aunts Maggie and Sarah. Then there were Uncles Matt, Jem, and Paddy, all of whom lived nearby, and Great Uncle Patrick, a neighbor who often took his meals with the family. This aggregation of elder Rices, all of them single except for Matt, would provide the two boys with a superabundance of adult supervision.

The aunts and uncles, because the boys were not their own children, treated them as if they were made of glass. Charlie and Pat were not allowed to ride bicycles, swim, or row a boat, for these activities were considered too dangerous. Candy was interdicted and the boys' teeth were scoured each week with dental floss and pic to prevent the dental caries common in the Irish. And on the small family farm with its varied crops and animals and endless chores, the boys took the role of observers rather than participants in the work. The lone exception came one summer when their father expressly ordered that his sons were not to be coddled but to "get their hands dirty" by planting and harvesting potatoes, and the like. Charlie hated every minute of it, and quickly drew an important conclusion regarding his future life: manual labor was not for him! In Rice's considered opinion many years later, his father's worst fears had been realized: his sons had been thoroughly spoiled by their doting aunts and uncles.

When the boys arrived in Ireland, they were sporting white sailor suits, the epitome of fashion and gentility in their native New York, but a subject for raucous ridicule by their much more drably clad Irish playmates. Pat rebelled successfully, hiding his suit behind a hedge. Less easy to shed were their clipped Yankee accents, which sounded quite harsh in a land of soft, lilting tones. Ironically, after the passage of seven years and their return to the States, the boys would again be ridiculed for their speech — this time for sounding outlandishly Irish to American ears (Charlie would retain the Irish lilt throughout his life). On both sides of the Atlantic, then, the boys had the experience of being outsiders, of being in a culture but not entirely of it.

The major institutional molder of the culture to which Pat and Charlie were exposed in Ireland was, of course, the Catholic Church. The vast majority of the residents in Bellurgan (the small "townland" outside Dundalk where the Rice homestead was located) was Catholic. A small remnant of the Protestant Ascendancy still perdured, but was now numerically insignificant; no other religious minority was even visible. And of Catholics, almost all were regular practitioners who showed up faithfully for Sunday Mass, holy day observances, and the other sacraments of their church.

One of the most outspoken critics of this Irish Catholic culture in which Rice was reared is the American writer Paul Blanshard.[3] His harsh critiques of that culture are relevant here not merely because Rice underwent much of his early socialization in Ireland, but also because Blanshard argues that emigrants from Ireland carried with them the authoritarian Irish Catholic culture to such an extent that they came to endanger nonauthoritarian, democratic principles of the societies to which they emigrated, most notably that of the United States. Because similar criticisms have been leveled at the adult Rice by at least some of his later critics, it may repay our effort here to examine his recollections of his upbringing in Catholic Ireland in counterpoint with the analyses of Catholic Ireland offered by Paul Blanshard.

Blanshard begins by observing that Ireland is the only predominantly Roman Catholic country in the English-speaking world. Even more significant in Blanshard's opinion is the fact that the Irish take their Catholicism very seriously, much more so than for example the Italians, in the pope's own backyard.[4]

Much of the dominance of the Catholic Church in Ireland Blanshard attributed to the Irish pattern of segregated education: Catholic children were educated at schools financed by the state but operated and controlled by the church, whereas the non-Catholic minorities attended schools likewise administered by their respective churches. Blanshard finds the teaching in the Catholic schools dogmatic and partisan, shunning large areas of modern thought, with little emphasis on freedom of inquiry or scientific curiosity, with no more than a conditional respect for the principles of democracy, and heavily reliant on corporal punishment to keep pupils in line.[5]

Rice attended a small two-room "national school" near Bellurgan run by one Master O'Hare and his daughter. The term "national school" is not to be confused with the concept of "public school" in the United States, because the former was, as Blanshard notes, state-financed but church-run. Even in those days, before national independence, the national school of Master O'Hare began each day with the recitation of Catholic prayers, included regular religious instruction, and otherwise had a decidedly sectarian cast to it. There were too few Protestant families in Bellurgan to merit their own school, so the children of Godkin, the grounds-keeper to the landlord Tipping family, also attended Master O'Hare's school. Rice recalls how these pupils would retreat to the cloakroom when religious instruction was underway, supposedly with ears to the door to pick up any tantalizing papist secrets that might be divulged in their absence.

It is difficult to judge from Rice's latter-day recollections whether the curriculum of the school did indeed, as Blanshard would expect, "exclude large areas of modern thought," or downplay the spirit of scientific inquiry. But it is clear that what Rice took with him from O'Hare's classroom was not a scientific orientation but a love for the great classics of English literature. O'Hare was reputed to have trained for a collegiate teaching post but to have been disappointed in that objective due to an affliction with the "Irish curse," alcoholism. Accordingly, the schoolchildren of Bellurgan had a more than ordinarily gifted pedagogue, who succeeded even in teaching Latin to some of the boys in the upper forms (seventh and eighth grades). He was, in fact, preparing his own son, who was Pat's age, for entrance into the seminary, where requirements were higher than at other schools.

The result was that Pat in particular got quite a rigorous classical education at the seventh- and eighth-grade levels, and would indeed continue to be an outstanding student throughout his years in school. The younger Charlie, however, was not a very bright academic light — partly because of his fidgety disposition, and partly because of an undiagnosed case of nearsightedness. But frequently, while pretending to be reading his slate or transcribing the exercises demanded of him, he would in fact be thrilling to the voice of O'Hare reading passages from *MacBeth* or other English classics.

As for corporal punishment, Blanshard's critique appears to be on target in the case of Bellurgan's national school. Anything from rapped knuckles to full-dress whippings were common, particularly after one of O'Hare's nights on the town. Charlie got into trouble occasionally, but knew better than to complain about it when he got home to his family of schoolteachers and housekeepers. Other pupils like Felix Byrnes, "the Incorrigible," seemed to suffer more severely and more frequently.

Turning to another facet of Irish Catholic culture, Blanshard finds most egregious the Irish approach to questions of sex, chastity, and population:

> What makes the Irish policy on marriage unique is that Ireland is probably the only place of any considerable size in the world today where the entire Catholic sexual code is accepted at face value. The Irish priests and nuns are sincere celibates who accept virginity with

sober enthusiasm. Irish married couples rarely divorce each other, and Irish cities have no licensed prostitution. . . .

Outwardly and officially at least, the Irish Catholics accept their Church's standard of sexual conduct. If there is some rebellion against that standard — and there is not much doubt that Irish young people feel rebellious — it is an unsuccessful rebellion which rarely reaches the level of public protest. The Irish priests have been so triumphant in imposing their sexual standards upon the people that they are now somewhat embarrassed by their own success. They have exalted virginity to the point where it is almost a national catastrophe: they have surrounded the sins of the flesh with such a poignant sense of guilt that they have weakened the Irish mating instinct.[6]

Blanshard goes on to point out that a young woman of marriageable age in Ireland would have less chance of marrying than would a young woman in any other country. Although admitting that the institutions of bachelorhood and spinsterhood had some economic underpinnings (those who were unable to inherit property were correspondingly less likely to wed), Blanshard feels that Irish celibacy had to be explained by Catholic frigidity as well as by agrarian poverty. He points to Ireland's policies on birth control and divorce as creating unhappy marriages, from which many young women, particularly from the countryside, chose to escape by emigrating — first to the cities and then to other countries. What were exalted beyond all reason, he argues, were religious vocations and the celibacy of nuns and priests. All this conspired, Blanshard believes, to render Ireland "an unsuccessful laboratory of love."[7]

It is undeniable that many of the observations Blanshard makes of Irish culture in general applied with considerable force to the extended family of the Rices. Although grandmother Rice, as noted earlier, had raised nine children to adulthood, only three of them ever married: the boys' father Michael and two of his brothers. Neither of the sisters, Maggie or Sarah, ever married, although they were, to judge by their pictures, quite attractive. Thus grandmother, as Rice later recalled, "presided over her sterile brood, forefending any prospect of marriage as a threat to the family."[8]

Attempts at religious vocations were as frequent as marriage in that generation of Rices, with both Michael and Sarah entering religious life and then withdrawing, and another brother Peter becoming a priest, emigrating to the United States and serving out his days as the pastor of a parish in Wisconsin. It is perhaps unsurprising, then, that both Pat and Charlie would eventually opt to become priests, as did another cousin, the son of Uncle Matt. Rice reports that although Pat decided at quite a young age to be a priest, he himself did not make that choice until many years later after graduating from college — and, interestingly, after another vacation back in Ireland.

Were the boys, living in this celibate household, exposed to the Irish prudishness about matters sexual? Most assuredly. Apparently it had not yet come to the attention of young Charlie that certain matters simply were not discussed at home, until one day he came racing back from school with the juicy tidbit that the father of one of his classmates was a bigamist, who had left his family to go and live with his mistress. This announcement was greeted with a frozen silence, and then Charlie was, in his own words later, "cast out upon the cold strand (the house fronted on Dundalk Bay) to contemplate the nature of my offense." By the time the boys returned to the United States, at the ages of eleven and thirteen, they were still unaware that babies were conceived by sexual union between man and woman.

A final relevant aspect of Blanshard's dissection of Irish Catholicism is his assertion that "fanaticism and moral childhood" were the natural products of a hierarchical religion when its pronouncements were accepted at face value as in Ireland. Bishops and priests, he alleged, were authoritarian figures in whose selection the faithful had no voice, but who brooked into interference — and indeed encountered no questioning — as they pronounced upon all matters of faith and morals, and often acted as the only leadership of the common folk in matters that had nothing to do with faith or with morality. The entire Catholic population, argues Blanshard, might troop to see the latest arm of a dead saint or other alleged holy relic, with never a voice of doubt raised in public. The minds of the priests themselves were "wrapped in cotton wool" to protect against any virus of skepticism that might be abroad in the modern world. Immature concepts of sin and virtue were recited and learned by rote, in place of preparing persons to cope as adults with moral dilemmas in which they might find themselves. Whenever any serious problem or doubt arose, it was of course to be turned over to the local priest. All of this was possible, says Blanshard, because of the near total segregation of Irish Catholics from non-Catholic influences, coupled with heavy clerical and lay pressures brought to bear on any whose beliefs or practices showed signs of deviating from the approved norms.[9]

Perhaps partly in response to the sort of critique aired here by Blanshard, the Bellurgan Rices, in Charles O. Rice's recollections, made a point of being loyal Catholics without being priest-ridden or inappropriately subservient to the clergy. The story was often repeated of the time a zealous curate had urged Grandfather Patrick Rice to vote in upcoming elections, and upon being faced with a stubborn refusal had threatened, "If you don't, I'll knock you down!" Patrick's reply, as the story went, was "Father, don't try it." Patrick Rice did not vote and the priest did not try to hit him. The story is illuminating both for Patrick's refusal to follow the priest's orders in political matters, and for the priest's apparent expectation that he would.

This relative independence of the Bellurgan Rices from clerical influence was sometimes contrasted with the behavior of neighbors or more distant relatives. One such cousin was a Barney Rice, nicknamed in the Irish tongue Barney *na Soggarth* or Barney the priest.[10] Apparently Cousin Barney spent as much of his time as possible in the company of a priest, and reached his high point each week when he took up the collection at Sunday Mass.

For the rest, Rice's reminiscences tend to confirm that a high level of moral conformism reigned in Bellurgan, along with strong sanctions on nonconformists. The only person in town known not to be in regular attendance at Mass was an elderly woman whom the children rather feared, and about whom adults whispered that in her youth she had entertained a succession of British soldiers from the garrison across Dundalk Bay. Then there was the blacksmith who was said to beat his small, frail wife. One suspects that wife beating may have met with less in the way of sanctions than nonattendance at church. The point is, in Bellurgan both kinds of offense were carefully noted and regularly discussed.

Such, then, are some of Rice's later recollections of his boyhood exposure to Catholicism in Ireland, as compared with Paul Blanshard's portrait. One need not accept Blanshard's critique of Irish Catholicism as a balanced and objective one (and I for one do not) in order to recognize that he has underscored several troubling aspects of that culture and raised some provocative questions regarding the probable results of transposing elements of Irish Catholicism to a more pluralistic culture like that of the twentieth-century United States. Because Rice's life is something of a microcosm in which Blanshard's theses may be tested out, it is well to note how that life proved similar and dissimilar to Blanshard's expectations.

Although in certain aspects Rice's recollections are at variance with Blanshard's depiction — a school that was not altogether segregated, a family that was not always obedient to clerical authority — still in the main it is clear that Rice was raised to a Catholicism that felt extremely sure of itself, found little need to tolerate other varieties of religious experience or moral persuasion, and succeeded in exalting to a very high level the values of celibacy and religious vocations. Both Rice's later choice of the priesthood as his lifelong vocation, and key aspects of his conduct within that vocation, are without question related to his early socialization in Catholic Ireland.

But the more provocative question is whether Blanshard was correct in believing that this culture, when transposed to American soil, came to pose a threat to the democratic texture and institutions of the United States. This is a question to which I will have occasion to return after traversing some of the later and more public phases of Rice's life.

If life for the Rice boys at Bellurgan was influenced predominantly by the church, it was powerfully shaped by economics as well. The standard of living in rural Ireland hardly compared with what was beginning to emerge in the United States and other industrialized nations: most houses in Bellurgan were still thatched with straw, refrigeration would remain inaccessible for many years to come, and hunger was not unknown in the "blue months" of late winter. But in comparison with these local standards, the Rices fared rather better than their neighbors. Their roof was a modern one of slate, a new barn had recently been erected, and the livestock they kept and the garden crops they grew enabled them to eat quite well. Yet it should never be forgotten — and by Grandmother it never *was* forgotten — that all of this was quite precarious. The farm was a small one of nine acres, hardly enough to sustain the family. Uncle Owen's income as a schoolteacher was needed, as were his many hours of farm work — not to mention the help from the other brothers or the work of the sisters in keeping house. The loss of one more income, or the addition of another family member to support, could make the farm no longer tenable. Later, in fact, it would all be sold off. This situation, as much as anything else, served to convince grandmother Rice that the marriage of her children would be an economic threat.

Although Charlie and Pat would eventually return to the greater affluence of their father's household in America, they would discover there too the precariousness of prosperity, during Depression times. Thus financial uncertainty, rather than material deprivation, would be more or less a constant throughout their years of upbringing.

Years later, when Rice tried to recollect what sort of a boy he had been, he described himself in somewhat unkindly terms as a "rotten little kid, skinny and argumentative who could talk better than I could fight."[11] That a lot of fights occurred and were expected of Irish schoolboys seems undeniable. But what is more, the Rices were nicknamed the "Cock Rices," both to differentiate them from other families in Bellurgan named Rice, and to connote a certain feistiness on which they prided themselves. Treasured family stories included not only Grandfather Patrick's facing down the curate who wanted him to vote, but many other examples of Rices who took on those who were more powerful than they, rather than knuckle under.

Charlie Rice's disadvantage, then and later, was not merely that he was the youngest of the Cock Rices, but also that he remained the smallest and frailest of the group — "poor wee Charlie" his Aunt Jennie had called him. So in order to live up to the family nickname, and to avoid being lost in the shadow of his older brother, and later of his father, "Big Mike," or of Uncle Joe, Charlie did indeed need to project a certain macho quality that may have gotten him into many fights he could not hope to win. And this pattern of taking on the powerful, as will be seen, carried well beyond his boyhood in Ireland.

Perhaps the greatest irony about Charlie's stay in Ireland is that although he was there during the country's revolutionary period, and although he would later be a wholehearted supporter of that rebellion, the politics of his family at the time kept him and the others isolated from and unsympathetic with the struggle that would ultimately lead to Irish national independence. To explain why this was the case, it is necessary to go back to the political scene of the generation before Pat and Charlie's arrival in Ireland.

In the late 1870s, Charles Stuart Parnell, himself a Protestant Anglo-Irish landlord, was beginning to emerge as the head of Ireland's "Home Rule Party" in the British Parliament. Combining tactics of systematic obstruction at Westminster (like the filibuster, which he originated) with massive protest in Ireland, he became chairman of the Irish Party in 1881, and after the election in 1885 he headed a tightly-knit group of eighty-six MPs, upon whom the British Prime Minister Gladstone was forced to rely for support. Gladstone thus introduced a bill for Irish home rule in 1886, but his own Liberal Party split over the issue and the bill was defeated. Successive attempts were made to revive home rule, but in 1890 all forward progress was halted by the disgrace of Parnell himself.

Parnell had conducted a long-standing extramarital affair with Kitty O'Shea, the wife of a British officer. In 1890 Kitty filed for divorce, naming Parnell as correspondent. The Catholic hierarchy and clergy of Ireland turned against Parnell immediately and vehemently, in a struggle that split the Irish Party and Ireland itself from one end to the other.

In the Dundalk area, most residents went against Parnell and sided with the opposing faction that came to be headed by Timothy Healy ("the people's Tim," his electoral slogan had it). But in Bellurgan there were many stubborn holdouts for Parnell, the Cock Rices among them, remaining loyal to Parnell until his death in 1891, and later to his successor in the quest for home rule through parliamentary action, John Redmond. This stubbornness involved definite losses for the family. Grandfather Patrick fell out not only with the local clergy but with many old friends, with whom he was not reconciled until he lay on his deathbed. And Uncle Joe, before emigrating to America, barely escaped with his hide intact the night he led a parade of Parnellites through the opposition turf of Ravensdale. These events had occurred before Charlie and Pat went to Ireland, but they had left scars which, in what some have noted is unfortunately the "Irish way," came eventually to fester rather than heal. (As an example of such festering, there is a field near Bellurgan where visitors to this day may be told that a small boy was onced hanged by British soldiers with a turnip in his hand. His offense: stealing the turnip during the Famine.)

In 1913, when the Rice boys arrived in Ireland, the issue of Irish independence was a burning one, but no nearer a parliamentary solution than a generation earlier. Sir Edward Carson, the MP representing Trinity College in Dublin, was the leader of the largely Protestant anti-home rule movement in Ireland. A cadre of Ulster Protestant officers of the British Army in the north staged a gunrunning operation and a successful military insurrection in opposition to the threat of parliamentary action granting home rule. In the south, Eoin MacNeill, a distinguished scholar and Gaelic enthusiast, launched the Irish Volunteers that year. The volunteers aimed at providing a counterweight to the Ulster military presence in the north, their most obvious deficiency being their lack of weapons.

Resonances of these events were soon picked up by Charlie's developing political antennae. "No surrender" was the slogan of Carson and his Ulster supporters, which led to a rhyme often repeated in the Bellurgan schoolyard:

Sir Edward Carson had a cat
that sat beside the fender,
And every time it spied a rat
it shouted, "No surrender!"

Then too, Charlie would see his Uncle Jem, the mildest of men, marching in the field with the local contingent of Irish Volunteers, most of them carrying hurling sticks on their shoulders as they responded to Jem's shouted commands. Charlie felt very proud.

But another force for Irish national independence was growing, one that the Rices of Bellurgan would not support. This was the *Sinn Fein* ("we ourselves") Party, the political branch of the armed Irish Republican Brotherhood (IRB). *Sinn Fein* had been organized in 1905 out of the conviction that neither the Parnellite-Redmondites nor any other parliamentary party could deliver national independence, but that it would have to be seized by force of arms and by arousing the Irish people from its apparent torpor. Until September 1914, *Sinn Fein* and the IRB upheld an earlier decision not to stage an armed uprising until they had the mandate for it from the Irish people. But when World War I broke out, and the British postponed action on the Redmondite home rule proposal until the conclusion of the conflict, and managed at the same time to secure Redmond's enthusiastic backing for the British war effort, the IRB decided to capitalize on Britain's problems by mounting a rebellion before the war came to an end. The IRB infiltrated the ranks of the Irish Volunteers, without Eoin Mac-Neill's knowledge. Among the leaders who emerged in the rebellion was the socialist James Connolly. He, together with James Larkin, had led the Irish Transport Workers' Union (TWU) in an extremely bitter and ultimately unsuccessful strike in Dublin in 1913.

Charlie went into Dublin with one of his uncles while this strike was going on, and listened to his conservative uncles' fiery denunciations of Connolly, Larkin, TWU, strikes, unions, socialism, anarchism, and so on, and so forth. And he began picking up on these lines and repeating them.

By 1916, the year chosen by the IRB for an uprising at Easter, it was probably apparent to IRB leaders that they had little chance of success in the short run, and could further the cause of Irish national independence only by sacrificing themselves in such a way as to move the Irish people to rebellion. Even those slight chances for success, however, were lessened when a gunrunning scheme with German nationals failed, and Eoin MacNeill learned of the plot and denounced it in public. Plans were thrown into disarray and "the Rising" actually took place on the Monday following Easter. The resistance occurred mostly at several sites in the center of Dublin, including the Post Office and the Inns of Court. It did not last long, and the British military soon killed or captured most of the leadership. They then proceeded, in one of history's great miscalculations, to execute fifteen of the rebel leaders over a ten-day period. Last to die was James Connolly who, because of his wounds, had to face the firing squad strapped to a wheelchair.

Charlie returned to Dublin after the Rising, curious like most others to see the wreckage that had been created. He was particularly struck, as he recalled, by the havoc at the Inns of Court, the Post Office, and Cleary's Department Store.

The next two and a half years saw an about-face of public opinion in Ireland that changed the status of the Rising's leaders from that of fools and brigands to one of heroes and prophets, so outraged were most of the Irish at the British handling of the insurrection.

But not in Bellurgan. When two young *Sinn Fein* representatives came out from Dundalk to speak on a Sunday morning after Mass, they got no further than, "Men and women of Bellurgan," before they were cut off by booing and hissing. Charlie, who had maneuvered himself to the front of the crowd, would never forget the sight of their sensitive and intelligent faces, frozen in tension and surprise at so negative a reception. They shouted back, "You are a disgrace to Ireland!"

Most of Bellurgan and most of the Cock Rices remained with Redmond and his party through the Rising, through the Civil War troubles — virtually until the end. When elections were next held in Ireland it was December 1918. The credibility of the Parliamentary Party of Redmond had been sapped not only by its failure to deliver home rule, but also by the British attempt, in the depths of the World War I, to extend conscription to Ireland. Public sympathy had redounded to *Sinn Fein* as the IRB rebuilt itself and Eamon De Valera emerged as the new leader of the independence movement. At the election *Sinn Fein* won seventy-three seats and the Parliamentary Party was virtually wiped out.

History was being made in Ireland, but the recalcitrant Rices were not on its side. For Charlie Rice, the most enduring memory of that election night was of the lighting of the whins — furze bushes set ablaze on the mountain to celebrate victory. But it was victory for *Sinn Fein*, and a crushing blow to the Redmondites and to the Rices who supported them. Charlie would later change sides, as would his family and Bellurgan, as the Dundalk area eventually became an IRA stronghold. But for them, at that time, the lighting of the whins was an agonizing sight.

In the meantime, many effects of the "war to end all wars" were being felt in Bellurgan. Conscription had not been forced upon the country as a whole, but Charlie remembered a fractious meeting at Bellurgan when it had been proposed. Some Irish sailors, volunteers in the British Navy, were captured and interned into the German Navy. When this happened to a neighborhood youth, Tom Byrnes, the telegram sent to his mother by the British Navy contained a classic spelling error. "Your son," it read, "has been interred." It would take some time before the hysterical mother could be convinced that Tommy still lived.

Less lucky was another of her sons, Felix the Incorrigible. Felix had left O'Hare's school with its whippings and enlisted in the British Navy. He was stationed on a British ship off Dublin at the time of the Rising. He stood on deck at night smoking a cigarette, giving the rebel gunners a target in the darkness, and even as some rebel shots struck the door jamb behind him. "The fools, the fools!", he later called them. He survived his own foolhardiness that night, but later in the war his ship disappeared in the North Sea, never to be recovered.

As the naval war heated up, German U-boats began attacking traffic in the Irish Sea. The two boats that regularly serviced Dundalk were both destroyed. Fishermen would return to town to report seeing colliers (coal boats) one after the other floating upside-down in the water. Day-to-day life was of course affected by scarcities and rationing of goods. Sugar and white bread disappeared. White bread was replaced by the healthier brown, but sugar remained a problem. A common line ran, "How's your mother for sugar?" To which the response was, "She's up to her knees in tay!" Beyond these shortages, the Rices were not greatly inconvenienced. It was a good time to be living on a farm in a more or less noncombatant country.

In November 1918, World War I finally came to its end as an armistice was signed at Versailles. Civilian life and politics would return to something like normalcy, but in Ireland the Time of the Troubles would begin. On the Atlantic, the threat of submarine warfare would pass.

Charlie and Pat were not yet recalled to return to their father, although he had by now remarried and established a household. Another year and a half would pass before transatlantic passage became normalized and the boys went back to America.

During this time Grandmother Rice died, and Great Uncle Patrick not long after. The wake and funeral for grandmother left memories of Aunt Sarah's inconsolable grief, whereas that for Great Uncle Patrick was the joyous celebration that Irish wakes can be. That fall Pat reached the eighth and highest form in Master O'Hare's little elementary school and emerged as a most promising scholar, whereas Charlie dawdled and fidgeted in the sixth form, and still had trouble reading from the blackboard.

Finally, in the spring of 1920, there came word from America: passage had been booked for the two boys and an adult cousin on a ship sailing to New York. Their long stay in Ireland — in some ways like a vacation on the farm — had lasted a full seven years, but now was drawing to a close. When Charlie and Pat went to the steamship office to pick up their tickets, they overheard a man braying out a pronunciation of the English language that was as strange as it was loud. The man, it turned out, was an American.

If the boy's transplantation from New York to Ireland had been a sudden and difficult one seven years previously, this transition from Ireland back to the United States was arguably even more trying. Having grown accustomed to the green fields and leisurely pace of life in Ireland, they were now to be thrust not only into a burgeoning industrial empire, but into the dark heart of that empire, Pittsburgh.

The passage from Dublin to New York had hardly disposed Charlie and Pat to a joyous arrival anywhere: although their father had paid for first-class tickets, they and their cousin, Joseph Rice, had tossed about in steerage during the entire turbulent crossing. At the dock, they did manage to recognize the tall, broad figure of their father, even though he was now seven years older and minus his mustache. Then came an arduous trip overland to Pittsburgh (where their father now worked for the Atlantic and Pacific Tea Company) amid a railway strike. Scant comfort was offered by the benches of the Philadelphia train station, where they slept overnight.

Then came Pittsburgh, the size of thirty Dundalks, glowing at night with the light of a thousand furnaces (one traveler had found it "hell with the lid off"[12] and by day oppressed by the pall of soot rising from a thousand smokestacks, obscuring the sun, dropping powdered filth everywhere, and invading the nostrils and palate with acrid stench. The streets and sidewalks were far broader than anything the boys remembered from Bellurgan or Dundalk, and along them streetcars clanged and pedestrians scurried at a pace that made one think they must indeed be pursued by demons. The finale was a ride up the seemingly 90% vertical rails of the Mount Washington Incline to the boys' new home on one of the more stately streets of Mount Washington.

Before relocating to Pittsburgh in 1916, the boys' father had remarried. Jennie O'Donnell, the older sister of his first wife, was his second bride. Like her sister before her, Jennie had converted to Catholicism and would in Rice's memory turn out to be the most determined and triumphalist in the Catholic faith of all the family. She never bore any children of her own, and was fifty years old (her husband forty-seven) when she undertook the role of stepmother to young Charlie and Pat.

Charlie's later memories of Jennie were an amalgam of affection and frustration: she supported her stepson through many battles; she sometimes started family rows and then headed for cover about the time the others were not speaking to one another; and she was prone to tell what the other males of the family regarded as untruths because, said Rice, "Reality was what she wanted it to be." As he grew older, he said, he took her as she was, but the first years of adjustment had probably been more difficult.

Michael Rice's youngest brother and the helion of the clan, Joseph, had followed Michael to America, into the grocery business, and now to Pittsburgh where he had married and taken a job as warehouse foreman for A&P. Uncle Joe and his wife Ida were invited to share the large house with Michael and Jennie Rice and their two returning sons. Their daughter Eleanor would be a lifelong companion to Rice, often mistakenly referred to as his sister rather than cousin.

This joining of the two families and a variety of personalities under one roof made for a rich, if sometimes fractious, domestic life. Michael Rice appears in his son's later memories as a calm and orderly person, disinclined to push himself forward. Uncle Joe's style could hardly have been more opposed: a hard-charger given to fearsome outbursts of temper, who later left A&P in protest of its strike-breaking activities, to become a pistol-packing organizer for the CIO in many bitter battles around the country, and later still to be eulogized by Alan Haywood as "the most independent man I've ever known." Both of the women in this extended family occupied the traditional at-home role — a fact that led to many a turf battle between them, which might then escalate into a full-blown family feud. Charlie, as the slightest of the male Rices, and for many years the youngest of all save Eleanor, found himself again somewhat in the shadow of the others, with something to prove — and generally more with his mouth than with his fists.

In some ways, then, the family environment into which Charlie and Pat were deposited was similar to what they had known in Ireland: predominantly adult, determinately Roman Catholic, often feisty. But the neighborhood was quite different. The boys found themselves living, for the first time, in a predominantly Protestant milieu. Not only were Catholics in the minority, but as the 1920s wore on with a revival of the Ku Klux Klan and its anti-Semitism and anti-Catholicism, they were in an unpopular minority. The Klan staged a cross-burning one year not far down the road from the Rice home. In 1925 race riots broke out in Pittsburgh.[13] Sectarian rivalries among schoolchildren were commonplace, with the Catholic children — in Rice's memory — giving as good as they got.

By the fall of 1920 young Charlie's vision problem had been diagnosed and corrected with glasses. It is not clear that this led to an improvement in his scholastic performance: he still became bored easily in the classroom and got poor grades as a result. But those glasses caused, according to Rice, a marked deterioration in his street-fighting ability. Taunted for his bespectacled appearance ("four eyes!") or his Catholicism ("filthy papist!") or his Irish accent ("bog trotter!"), he would take on his taunter but pause to remove his glasses. Unfortunately, he might in the process catch one across the choppers from an unsportsmanlike opponent, or be unable to see the next blow coming. Thus he lost quite a few fights.

It seemed never to occur to him to stay out of fights.

The boys were sent, immediately upon their arrival, to local Catholic schools for their education. At St. Mary's of the Mount High School, Pat, who was always to be at the head of his class, was skipped ahead to tenth grade in the fall of 1920. Charlie, however, was held back in the sixth grade at St. Mary's Elementary School. Later that year he would be promoted to the seventh grade, but for a short while he was four full years behind his brother Pat, who was less than two years his senior.

Charlie's school years at St. Mary's consisted mostly of tedium. Still only an average student at best, he did show a decided talent in one field: writing. The year that St. Mary's High School had an essay-writing contest with Ireland as the topic, Charlie Rice, the otherwise undistinguished pupil, walked off with top honors. He finished grade school in 1922, and graduated from high school in 1926.

Under the tutelage of their older and more restrained father, and the younger, irrepressible Uncle Joe, the two boys found their political attitudes undergoing a sharp transformation. The Rices of Bellurgan had been vehemently anti-*Sinn Fein*, but the Rices of Pittsburgh were wholehearted supporters of the rebel cause. (This pattern of stronger *Sinn Fein* support among emigrant families than among those who remained in Ireland was far from uncommon, and would make American cities regular stops along the insurrectionists' campaign trail.) Pat and Charlie argued the Parnellite side for a while, but eventually were "brainwashed," as Rice later put it, into a pro-*Sinn Fein* position.

In American politics, the older Rice brothers were Democrats by inclination and habit, but parted company with that party in 1920, after Woodrow Wilson failed, at the signing of the Treaty of Versailles, to obtain recognition for an independent Ireland. In 1924 they supported Robert LaFollette for president, as did many in the Pittsburgh area. As a teenager, Rice accompanied his father and uncle to hear LaFollette speak at a Moose lodge in Pittsburgh, and would ever remember the hoarse, booming voice that filled the hall without any need for a microphone.

By 1928, the Rices were back in the Democratic column, voting for the Catholic governor of New York running for president, Al Smith. (Rice says they were dismayed to discover later what a conservative politician Smith really was.) Throughout the Roosevelt years, the Rices were staunch supporters of FDR and the New Deal.

In addition to this general background of prolabor Democratic liberalism, Charlie Rice was also being exposed at an early age to a much more radical critique of U.S. society and politics. Ed Volk was a neighbor whose thoroughgoing disrespect for institutionalized power of all sorts would have cast him as the village atheist, had he lived in Bellurgan. He was a socialist who had been involved in antiwar resistance during World War I, believing that the war and America's entrance into it were primarily for the benefit of munitions manufacturers. Fortunately for Volk, he had been able to stay out of jail. He now took an interest in the Rice boys, engaging them in lengthy and serious political discussions and debates after school. So long as he stayed off the topic of religion, this was acceptable to the elder Rices. Volk was then an unabashed admirer of the Russian revolution, although his enthusiasm would abate as information filtered across the Atlantic about the purge trials underway in the U.S.S.R. He was vehemently opposed to U.S. attempts to overthrow the revolution by means of armed intervention in Russia, an adventure that was just coming to an end in 1921.

Volk shared with the Rices a recently published radical critique by former Senator Richard F. Pettigrew of South Dakota, *Imperial Washington*, based on his fifty years in public life.[14] Because this book seems to have had a deep impact on young Rice's political outlook at the time, on his writings decades later, and even on his political recollections more than half a century after reading it, this small volume is worth summarizing at some length.

Pettigrew's themes were, first, that capital was nothing but stolen labor and its only function was to steal more labor and secondly, that the republican institutions of American government had one by one been subverted to serve the needs of capital rather than the needs of the people.

The American public, he began, was consistently lied to and generally confused by leaders who promised to fight big business while actually extending its sway (Theodore Roosevelt), or to avoid war while actually preparing for it (Woodrow Wilson).[15] The U.S. government, held Pettigrew, had in fact done battle with the giant trusts — and lost.[16] Bankers, whom he regarded as parasites pure and simple, worked on behalf of the American plutocracy (that 9% of the population that owned 71% of the wealth)[17] and, by manipulating the currency through the Federal Reserve, regularly engineered panics and depressions in order to drain away from workers the fruits of the prosperity they had created. The way to deal with such economic thievery, urged Pettigrew, was like catching any other thieves and making them return stolen property: public takeovers of the railroads, banks, currency, utilities, and of all property whose value was given by the community, with all of these to be used subsequently only for the general welfare rather than to benefit the plutocracy.[18]

The Constitution, Pettigrew had discovered, had really been written by the economic elite, for the benefit of the few. Lawyers, working for rich clients to preserve the status quo, controlled government and thus perpetuated the privilege of the few. The Supreme Court in particular had usurped the political sovereignty of the people, eviscerating in the process the Bill of Rights. His solution: abolish all the federal courts created by Congress, thus reducing the Supreme Court to impotence.[19] The Democrats and Republicans, in Pettigrew's estimation, differed only on how *best* to rob workers; they both served the interests of big business.[20]

Turning to international affairs, he saw the United States embarking once more on the path of imperialism. This tendency, quiescent since 1846 when the U.S.A. attacked Mexico and took away half its territory, was once more illustrated in the overthrow of the Hawaiian government for the Dole Family in 1893, in the betrayal of Philippine independence by annexation of those islands in 1898, in the U.S.-inspired creation of the state of Panama by secession from Colombia in 1903, and in repeated Yankee interventions in Puerto Rico, Cuba, Nicaragua, Costa Rica and Haiti. But because the citizens of this country were loathe to play the role of imperialists, vital information and understanding had to be withheld from them — so that the republic at home was sacrificed for a big business empire abroad.[21]

Pettigrew's final topic was the Great War (World War I) just recently concluded. This he analyzed as a conflict between advanced European capitalist empires, which the United States had entered only when and only because its industrialists had discovered profitability in it. He felt the right solution had been found in Russia, where the people had conducted a revolution, ended its participation in the war, and forged a new constitution based on its own *economic* rights. But exactly the wrong solution had emerged at Versailles where the terms of the treaty and the makeup of the new League of Nations (exclusion of the U.S.S.R., of the defeated powers, and of the exploited, underdeveloped countries) guaranteed only a pause in hostilities and their resumption at a later date.[22] Looking ahead to the entrenched powers of capitalism and the rising spirit of liberation among the peoples of the world, Pettigrew predicted in 1922 that it was going to be a bloody century.[23]

Several points are worth making about this early exposure of Rice to a leftist critique of American economic and political institutions. First, the exposure occurred when he was still in his early teens — indeed, when most of his contemporaries paid not the least attention to questions of politics or social justice — and it made a lifelong impression. Secondly, Pettigrew's critique, seconded by Volk, was a thoroughgoing one, likely not only to raise a few questions about selected economic and political issues, but to inspire systematic doubt about the goodness of American institutions and the announced motives of American political leaders. Finally, this was not a foreign tract derived from the political struggles of Europe or expressed in a jargon incomprehensible to Americans; it was as American as the plains of South Dakota from which Pettigrew hailed. Rice would later manage to confound both his friends and his opponents as he appeared successively as a "radical," an anti-communist, and a "born-again" radical. Some (but not all) of this ambiguity may be explained by noting Rice's early attraction to the American (as opposed to the International) Left, and his subsequent attempts to reconcile this with his loyalty to Catholic institutions and social teachings.

In 1926, when he graduated from high school, Rice faced the question of what to do next. His brother Pat, who had long since decided to become a priest, had opted not to enter the seminary directly after high school but to take his undergraduate degree at Duquesne, the Catholic university run by the Holy Ghost Fathers across the Monongahela River from Mount Washington. His father's willingness to pay the modest tuition there, rather than have his son embark too early on a religious career as he had done, was doubtless a factor in Pat's decision. This year Pat would be a senior at Duquesne; next year he would enter the seminary. His younger brother, who had thought about becoming a priest too, but had not yet decided one way or the other, chose to follow in Pat's footsteps for now. Duquesne it would be for the next four years.

The course of studies at Duquesne was very much the traditional liberal arts curriculum for which the Rices had been prepared ever since their boyhoods in Ireland. It featured large servings of language and literature, topped with philosophy and theology, and sprinkled with mathematics, the natural sciences, and some social science, including psychology.

At these studies Rice proved himself a middling student, earning as he later put it "a gentleman's 'C' at best." He learned Latin well enough, but never mastered Greek. His love of literature continued, but expressed itself more in extracurricular activities than in anything else.

Beginning in his sophomore year, Rice again imitated his brother's example in writing for the *Duquesne Monthly*, a campus literary magazine. He also wrote for the student newspaper, *The Duke*. He became the sports writer for the latter publication, which led, as will be seen, to some of his more memorable undergraduate experiences. In his junior year, the position of student director of public relations became vacant when the previous occupant was fired. Rice received this plum, which paid what was then the handsome sum of $40 per month. In addition to his high- paying position, Rice had one of the few automobiles on campus — thanks to his father who let him borrow the family car frequently. Rice was able to transport other students to out-of-town football games, and even to provide the gasoline. He was, to judge by pictures from that era, quite the well-dressed collegian, even somewhat of a dandy. Although at the midst of a swirl of social life on campus, he did little dating. He did engage in what he later described as a *very* mild flirtation with a young Catholic lady of *very* high moral standards. Apparently his early training in Irish Catholic prudishness was still operative.

Abruptly at the end of his junior year, Rice was fired from the public relations position, just as his predecessor had been. He turned to the *Duke*, where by an unexpected chance he was chosen editor-in- chief. He was also elected president of the student body for his senior year. What seems to have propelled Rice to the forefront of the attention of the student body's was his writing, particularly as sports reporter for the *Duke*, and most particularly because some of his articles seemed to involve him in potentially violent confrontations with oversized football players and coaches.

On one such occasion, two football players were competing for captainship of the team. One became captain; the other was offered the presidency of the student body as a consolation prize. Rice got wind of this and wrote an article speculating whether someone who was unworthy of being football captain really ought to become student body prexy. The aggrieved footballer the next day grabbed Rice on his way up the steps of Canevin Hall at lunchtime. Apparently bent on Rice's physical dismemberment, he had to be dragged off by a brawny intervenor. Rice, meanwhile, was gripping a pop bottle in his hand and wondering whether he would use it. The episode was captured for readers of the *Pittsburgh Post Gazette* by city editor Ray Spriegel.

Another time Rice reported in his Winchell-like column rumors about an insurrection against the head football coach, little realizing that the insurrection was being quietly fomented by an ambitious assistant coach, Buff Donelli. Donelli caught Rice alone one evening, and Rice found himself doing some very fast talking until some friendly law students happened by.

On still another occasion, Rice had inked some derogatory comments about the head football coach, Leyden. Leyden encountered Rice one day by the fence atop the steep bluff overlooking the Monongahela, and words ensued. Leyden threatened publicly, "Don't get smart, Charlie, or I'll knock you over the fence!" Correctly guessing that he was in the presence of more than one bluff, Rice retorted, "Go ahead and do it!" The coach did not.

In the summer of 1930, after Rice had graduated from Duquesne, he and his brother, who was now only one year short of ordination, returned to Ireland for an extended summer vacation. The trip proved memorable for a number of reasons. It was the finest summer weather anyone could remember in Ireland. The homestead looked as well kept as ever by Uncle Owen and Aunt Maggie, but the farming had become more mechanized and Uncle Paddy had even acquired an automobile. Pat and Charlie visited for the first time the Protestant side of the family — their mother's and stepmother's relatives in County Clare. Charlie was for the first time introduced to IRA operatives, with whom he would be in sympathy — and sometimes in collusion — in the years ahead. Finally, on the trip back to the States, Charlie made up his mind about his future: he would become a priest. He would prepare to take up the service of his God and his church by entering the seminary of the Pittsburgh diocese that fall.

The seminary year had already begun by the time Rice returned from Ireland, and so he had to get special permission from the bishop to enter late. This led to his first meeting with Hugh C. Boyle, bishop of Pittsburgh. The prelate was favorably impressed with Rice's Irish background, his voracious reading habits, and his broad acquaintance with classical and contemporary literature. Once Rice had passed the entrance examination (consisting mostly of Latin definitions of terms used in scholastic philosophy), Boyle gave his permission for Rice's late entrance. (Later, Boyle would give Rice his special protection when others wanted the young priest restrained or disciplined. This favored position would last until 1948, when ill health caused Boyle to be eased out of office. He died in 1950.)

St. Vincent Seminary was only a part of a large educational and religious complex run by the Benedictine monks and sisters near Latrobe, Pennsylvania, some thirty miles distant from the Steel City. The archabby came to include the seminary for the Pittsburgh diocese, a college, a preparatory school, a novitiate, and monastery for the monks themselves, as well as a cloister for the sisters. In this rural setting, a four-year curriculum of theological and related studies prepared seminary students to become priests.

Rice found the intellectual atmosphere at St. Vincent's less than stimulating, but attended to his theological studies in workmanlike fashion. Neither literature nor politics was given much play in the curriculum and reading newspapers was officially *verboten*, but Rice still found time for both literary pursuits and the events of the day. He read widely in Joyce, Faulkner, and other contemporaries ("Just don't say anything to the younger men," enjoined the rector) and regularly kept up with *Time*, *Commonweal*, and later *The Catholic Worker*. This reading kept him abreast of the political drama of the times, as the Great Depression plummeted the national economy to new depths in 1931 and 1932, as Roosevelt was elected in 1932 and took office in 1933, and as the New Deal struggled to be born the next year or so while Rice was still at St. Vincent's, impatiently awaiting his turn to play a role in the great events of the day.

Another event that was to have a powerful formative influence on Rice's career occurred on May 15, 1931. From Rome, Pope Pius XI issued an encyclical letter entitled *Quadragesimo Anno*, which in turn commemorated the fortieth anniversary of another papal encyclical on economic and social issues, *Rerum Novarum* (1891).[24] These two documents, supplemented by other official papal pronouncements and by their application to American circumstances in statements of the American bishops (*Statement on Social Reconstruction* in 1919 being the foremost in this category) would, among other things, help create a new generation of "labor priests" in the United States. Rice would soon become one of them, and arguably the most colorful member in their ranks.

It may be useful at this point to compare and contrast some of these official Catholic teachings both with the prevailing capitalist practice of the day and with the radical analyses of that practice offered by socialists like Pettigrew. Catholic social doctrine was consciously designed to steer a middle road between the extreme individualism that the popes saw in the established order on the right and the emerging socialism of the left. Although the Church's opposition to socialism — which it perceived as a godless program incompatible with its own spiritual mission — was of long standing and well known, a new emphasis in these two encyclicals was a strident criticism of the practice of contemporaneous capitalism and its tendency to impoverish the masses both physically and spiritually. Thus the encyclicals criticized the existing social order, and formulated nonsocialist alternatives to that order.

The concept of private property is a convenient place to begin. Church teaching held that private property was a "natural right" of human beings, with both an individual aspect (ownership) and a social one (use).[25] Capitalism, in its extreme individualism, tended to concentrate ownership in the hands of a few, with no restrictions that mandated the use of property for the common good.[26] Socialism, at the other extreme, would place all property at the disposal of the state.[27] Both programs would deny to most persons the exercise of their natural right of ownership, leaving them instead at the mercy of a small elite.[28]

The limits that needed to be placed on the use of private property, particularly productive property in an industrial economy, were guarantees of just wages and reasonable prices in addition to satisfactory profits. The yardstick for "just" wages was the family. A wage was just if it provided for the needs of the worker and his wife and children, and to some extent for their desires.[29] But the determination of this wage would also have to take account of the condition of the business enterprise, as well as the more general social conditions.[30] Prices were reasonable when they were in accord with the "common estimation" of the value of the good or service in question.[31] And a satisfactory profit would both protect the health of the enterprise and provide for the "station in life" of the owner.[32]

These values were coordinated with the teaching that wealth was produced only through the cooperation of capital and labor, with each making its distinctive contribution. It followed that just as neither capital nor labor could function by itself, so each had a duty to be concerned with the welfare of the other.[33]

Thus the preferred order of society involved neither class warfare à la socialism, nor oppression of the working class à la capital-ism. Instead, the church proposed that guildlike syndicates including both workers and owners be formed in each trade or vocational grouping (as opposed to political representation along geographic lines), to care both for the welfare of the trade itself, and for that of persons engaged in it one way or another.[34] Class harmony, rather than exploitation or class warfare, was to be the result.

The role of the state, as a nonorganic entity (the family was an organic unit), included both positive obligations and negative limitations. The state should, for example, provide relief programs for the poor (although such programs could never substitute for Christian charity).[35] But the state could not resort to excessive taxation, which was only another route to the enslavement of the masses.

Church teaching still held, as its earlier expressions had, that economic inequality was the inevitable result of inequalities in talent, that hierarchy was necessary to the ordering of society,[36] and that the hardships of life were the inevitable result of human sinfulness.[37] The church thus stood opposed to the socialist prog-ram of economic equality, democracy, and the achievement of a workers' paradise on this earth. Such promises, it taught, were deceitful and based on a failure to understand the spiritual as well as the material side of human life. Although noting the split between communists and socialists (whom it found to be more moderate), and although expressing the hope that the latter might eventually evolve to a more acceptable position, the church con-tinued to teach that cooperation with either group was unacceptable.[38]

What was, however, undergoing change was the official stance on unions. Previously the popes had regarded them with consider-able suspicion — particularly when they involved oaths of secrecy — as carriers of godless socialist ideology. Membership in the Knights of Labor had narrowly escaped a papal condemnation in the 1880s, and this only when they had abandoned their policy of secrecy.[39] But now, recognizing the need of workers to protect themselves against the predatory practices of management, and abandoning the earlier insistence on membership only in Catholic unions, Pius XI gave the go-ahead for Catholics to join non-Catholic unions, but strongly suggested that auxiliary organiza-tions be formed for Catholics, in order to protect their faith.[40]

It was particularly this papal teaching that opened the doors for a generation of young priests — "labor priests" they would be called — to go out to the union halls and picket lines with the message that the church was after all on the side of the workers as they struggled for the chance to better their lives and the lives of their families. To many loyal Catholic workers in the United States, the news of the church's blessing would be indeed welcome, perhaps even something of a surprise.

But if the doors had been opened and marching orders issued, those orders contained some very strong caveats as well. Support for non-Catholic labor unions was still rather tentative, and was clearly divorced from support of class struggle as a means or socialism as a goal. The church favored a "third way," its own way.

In the push-and-shove world of labor union activism, however, the choices would not always be so nicely arrayed as they were in the papal encyclicals. Could the popes' notions of "just" wages, prices, and profits hold water in the advanced industrial age? Could social justice be achieved without a struggle that took on at least overtones of class warfare? Were medieval guilds a realistic model for economic organization in the twentieth century? Was the church's social teaching relevant to the modern world, or a mere anachronism? Or, to strike a more sinister note, was the Church genuinely on the side of the workers *in practice*, or was it merely fearful of losing the working class once and for all if it became clear that the Church was part of the status quo against which workers had to struggle? These hard questions would be posed and tested in the careers of young priests then emerging from the seminaries, and by none of them more vigorously than by Charles Owen Rice.

Rice's seminary studies finally reached their end in 1934, and on June 17 that year he was ordained a priest of the Pittsburgh diocese.

To the career on which he was embarking Rice brought with him, as this chapter has attempted to indicate, a bundle of varied and even contradictory tendencies that he had acquired during his first quarter-century. He showed a youthful self-assurance, even flippancy, that covered over deep insecurities going back to his mother's untimely death. His innate likeability and bonhomie sometimes were overridden by the pugnaciousness and stridency of the youngest and frailest of the Rices, striving (with great success, it would turn out) to emerge from the shadows of the others. He possessed a genuine willingness to serve and to take on the problems of others, counterpointed by an aloofness (sometimes manifesting itself in impatience with others) that he had learned as he moved from country to country, from family to family. His love of literature and of the English language, begun in a two-room school in rural Ireland, would continue to blossom throughout his public life. He had become accustomed to living comfortably, yet he was never free of financial insecurity. Perhaps most significantly of all, he felt simultaneously an attraction to the fire-breathing revolutionary and a loyalty to the church that blocked the revolutionary's path.

Pittsburgh, over the next half-century and more, would have ample opportunity to become acquainted with all these aspects of this apostle of contradiction.

TWO

"Are We Really Radical?"

THE AMERICA IN WHICH RICE took up his apostolate in 1934 wore a grim appearance. Emerging from his pleasant pastoral surroundings at St. Vincent's, the young priest encountered a nation shattered by the worst economic depression it had ever experienced, with little confidence as to when, if ever, good economic times would return. Rice would see up close the tragic effects that the Depression had on Pittsburgh in general, on the parishioners he served, and even on his own family. He himself would not escape completely unscathed, although his own suffering was mild in comparison with that of those around him.

Recessions, depressions and panics had swept industrial America at more or less regular intervals since Civil War times (15 times in 57 years, by one count Rice would use), but none had ever plunged the country into such misery or hung on so tenaciously as this one. Worse, the Depression seemed to be marching in cadence with similar collapses in the other industrialized nations of the world, prompting many to conclude that capitalism had destroyed itself and was merely waiting to be buried.

It had begun with the stock market crash of 1929 when magnates and stock brokers leaped to their deaths from office windows. Spreading waves of disaster soon left millions of others suddenly penniless as banks failed and closed their doors. Industrial production plunged and unemployment figures soared: even according to the government, fully 25 percent of workers, and most of them heads of households with only one breadwinner, were out of work. The newest generation of young job seekers had to contend with the seeming impossibility of their quest; many gave up and turned to alcohol or to riding the rails with the hobo population. Hunger stalked the land as farmers lost their holdings or destroyed their unprofitable crops in bids to drive up the cost of food, while city dwellers scavenged for food in restaurant garbage cans or lined up to receive what was made available by municipal authorities or the hastily assembled apparatus of private philanthropy.

The Depression affected Rice himself only briefly: ordained in June, he had to wait until October for the bishop to find even temporary employment for him, at Immaculate Conception church in Pittsburgh. After serving at that parish in late 1934, Rice in early 1935 became assistant pastor at St. Agnes in Pittsburgh, a predominantly Italian-descent parish near the campus of the University of Pittsburgh.

Like other Pittsburghers, St. Agnes parishioners had been traumatized in the early years of the Depression, then had experienced some improvement during the early rush of the New Deal, only to fall into another trough with the "inventory recession" of 1934. This recession had resulted from the steel mills' rushing to fill the new orders that finally trickled in, until they had produced more steel than could be sold, with the result that workers were again laid off while the companies waited to dispose of their excess inventory. Rice estimated that between one fourth and one half of all St. Agnes families were on relief, and for most of them feelings of desperation had to outweigh those of shame before they consented to take the payments to which they were entitled by law.

Another Depression victim was Michael Rice. The elder Rice, now sixty-one, had been forced out of P. H. Butler by a high-level reorganization, and found his age a severe handicap in obtaining alternate employment. He looked endlessly, it seemed to his family, for a job, but without success. (His only employment the rest of his days would be a political patronage job with the Allegheny County Democratic Party, and that only when his younger son began to acquire enough political influence to win preferment for his father.)

Even as "the lowly" of the country — the Michael Rices and the Italian-American workers at St. Agnes — suffered the effects of the Depression, the big interests and political leaders of the nation were locked into a fierce struggle to determine how the Depression would be dealt with, how prosperity would be achieved again, and what would be the shape of that prosperity when it returned, if it returned.

The Hoover administration had been committed to the conservative notion that the best government is the one that governs least. In times of economic difficulties like those of the 1930s the best thing for government to do was wait until the private sector responded — as it must eventually — to the law of supply and demand. In the meantime, citizens should be counseled to fall back on their own resources and to wait patiently for the prosperity that was just around the corner — or at any rate, *some* corner.

The Roosevelt victory at the polls in 1932 signaled the political failure of that conservative approach to the Depression. Roosevelt had insisted that government could not stand idly by as the nation suffered, but must undertake positive steps to secure relief, recovery, and reform — even if those steps flew in the face of conservative notions of the limitations inherent in the laissez-faire state. The "100 Days" of legislative thunder at the outset of Roosevelt's term produced a large assortment of programs that had two things in common: their targeting on the economic woes of the nation, and their propensity to increase both the responsibilities and the powers of the federal government. Many of these key programs were by 1934 mired in court appeals that would lead to their modification or abandonment, and from this struggle would emerge the lineaments of the American welfare state as we know it today: welfare programs, social security, unemployment compensation, a host of regulatory programs and agencies, and government recognition and protection of unions in their quest for collective bargaining.

But as intense and as bitter as the struggle was between the New Dealers and the Old Guard, the two camps were united in seeking essentially the same goal for the country: a business-oriented recovery in which prosperity would return within the context of the economic status quo of capitalism. What chiefly divided FDR and his advisors from their opponents in Congress and on the Supreme Court was the extent to which capitalism would have to be reformed in order to be able to survive. The New Dealers opted for a variety of new programs and powers to be exercised over the economy by government, whereas the Old Guard would have preferred to leave things pretty much as they had been prior to the Depression. But neither group wanted to do away with private ownership and the profit motive as the ordering principles of the American economy.

But by 1934, as the early rays of hope from the beacon of the New Deal had begun to flicker and fade, many other groups were prepared to seek the abandonment of industrial capitalism as it then existed in the United States. Some of these groups or individuals were new to the political scene in the country; others were hardly new, but found that their radical, anticapitalist proposals were receiving much more popular attention than they had previously.

In order to set the stage to examine Rice's earliest social activism, which he insisted was "radical," I will first sketch brief outlines of radical forces in American politics in the 1930s. For some of them the destruction of industrial capitalism was the primary goal of their activism, whereas others were willing not only to modify capitalism (as Roosevelt was doing) but to abandon it if necessary in order to secure the return of prosperity. After surveying these secular political responses to the Depression, I will turn to the Catholic Church, where a similar array of reformist and radical responses will be noted.

The Communist Party and its organ *The Daily Worker* continued to be caught up in enthusiasm for the Russian revolution and advocated a similar workers' overthrow of capitalism in the United States. By way of comparison, the Socialist Party had expelled the communists from its midst and now, behind the leadership of Norman Thomas, advocated a program of national takeovers of various businesses. The Socialist Party also attempted to establish ties with populists in the South by means of its Southern Tenant Farmers' Union.[1]

The League for Independent Political Action (LIPA) had since 1929 engaged such leading minds as those of John Dewey, Lewis Mumford, Archibald MacLeish, and others in formulating pragmatic alternatives to capitalism. LIPA moved in 1933 to create a new political party, the Farm-Labor Political Federation, in alliance with various progressive and radical forces in the Midwest.[2]

What was common to these communists and socialists was their analysis of the Depression as merely another ordinary recession, whose goal, as usual, was to take prosperity from the masses and funnel it into the purses of the few. But *this* recession, they believed, had gone awry and damaged even the capitalists who had spawned it. Speculation and greedy profit-taking had caused the Depression, they argued, so why not take away from capitalists the power to repeat their folly? Why not nationalize the banks and as many industries as necessary to make the welfare of the masses, rather than the profit of the owners, the ordering principle of the economy? Or, as Pettigrew might have put it, catch the thieves and make them give your money back.

Among the midwestern movements to which the eastern radicals reached out, the most successful to date had been the Progressive Party in Wisconsin, established by the younger LaFollettes, Robert, Jr., and Phil, when the GOP had become inhospitable to their father's brand of progressivism. By 1934 the Progressive Party had swept elections in Wisconsin for governor, senator, most of Wisconsin's congressional seats, and a plurality or near plurality in the state senate and house of representatives.[3]

In Minnesota, the Farmer-Labor Party in 1930 had elected as governor a self-proclaimed radical, Floyd B. Olson. Olson's legislative goals of cooperative businesses, environmental legislation, and stricter public regulation of utilities were only part of an evolutionary process away from capitalism.[4]

In western Iowa, Milo Reno's Farm-Holiday Association urged that farmers set the prices for their own products, and staged a farm strike in 1932 of sufficient intensity to gain, if not victory, at least the respectful attention of the national political establishment.[5] Such rebellions and political progressivism on the plains lent fuel to the fire the LIPA intellectuals and the Farmer-Labor Political Federation organizers had ignited in their drive to form a new third party.

Yet arguably it was neither the East Coast nor the Midwest but California that was the seat of the greatest social ferment and the home of the most serious challenges to the economic status quo of America. Novelist Upton Sinclair in 1934 narrowly missed capturing the California governorship when he ran on a socialist oriented platform called End Poverty in California (EPIC).[6]

Attracting still more national attention was another Californian, Dr. Francis E. Townsend, formulator of the Old Age Revolving Pension Plan, or the Townsend Plan. This approach would have paid a monthly pension to all citizens over the age of sixty, provided they spent it as quickly as they received it, thus increasing the velocity of the flow of money in such a way as to create more jobs and lessen the effects of the Depression. It was to be funded by a federal Transaction Tax on all sales, retail or wholesale.[7]

Nor was the South quiescent during this era of intense economic suffering. It produced a new generation of politicians who were either populist at heart or capable of riding populist issues to political power for themselves, and in the process posing severe threats to the status quo distribution of economic power and privilege. Included here were Herman Talmadge, the gallus-snapping governor of Georgia, and Senator Theodore Bilbo of Mississippi, the former governor with a relatively progressive record and a fierce passion in his use of antiestablishment rhetoric.[8]

But the kingfish of them all was Huey Long of Louisiana. Long had been able to carve out for himself a domination of Louisiana politics so total that even after he left the Louisiana governorship for the U.S. Senate, he could still return to his home state and dictate reams of legislation, which was then dutifully enacted by special sessions of the legislature he had cowed, and signed by the governor he had handpicked. On the national scene, Huey Long by 1935 had become a genuine threat to the Roosevelt administration when he publicly and vehemently split with FDR and put forward as his alternative to the New Deal what he called the Long Plan, but was better known as the Share Our Wealth Plan. This plan would have combined steeply graduated taxes on income, inheritances, and wealth itself, so as to make it impossible for anyone to accumulate more than three or four million dollars. The proceeds, thought Long, would be sufficient to provide a basic estate of five thousand dollars per family, which would enable the family to buy a home, a radio, and the ordinary conveniences of life. The proceeds would also yield a minimum yearly income sufficient to maintain the family in comfort. Resentment of the rich and a desire for redistribution had been the cornerstone of Long's political appeal, first in the South and then nationally. As Share Our Wealth clubs proliferated, Long became a politician as feared and hated by some as he was admired by others. It will never be known just how far Long might have gone, had he not been shot dead by the relative of one of his political enemies in Louisiana.[9]

The Catholic Church, meanwhile, was publicly responding to the human tragedy of the Depression. Its degree of political engagement was already a departure for the Catholic Church in America, which in earlier times had concerned itself with institutional survival and preserving the faith of the flood of immigrant Catholics arriving on American shores. What was more remarkable in the 1930s was that the range of Catholic responses, mirroring the diversity of responses in American society at large, would include the populism of Rev. Charles Coughlin, the reformism of Monsignor John A. Ryan and the U.S. Catholic bishops, and the radicalism of the Catholic Worker Movement.

Surely the best known and eventually the most controversial voice from the Catholic Church was that of radio priest Charles E. Coughlin. His broadcasting had begun with the birth of NBC in 1926, and by the 1930s his show was so popular that it was said that in some neighborhoods one could walk along the street on a warm Sunday afternoon and catch the entire broadcast by over-hearing the radios blaring in one house after another. Coughlin would by turns attack capital and labor in his sermons, castigating both the entrenched powers of the bankers and the rising presence of the Congress of Industrial Organizations.

Some of Coughlin's virulent attacks would in the years ahead bring him into conflict with other Catholic spokesmen on social issues, notably Msgr. John A. Ryan of the Catholic Conference (and, in 1937, Rev. Charles Owen Rice).[10] This disengagement from fellow Catholic clergymen interested in social questions be-came all the more pronounced when Coughlin became disen-chanted with the New Deal and inveighed against its "radicalism," and still later when a harsh anti-Semitism began to emerge in his preaching and he became connected with a Nazilike "Christian Front" whose roving street gangs staged attacks on American Jews. Coughlin would eventually be silenced by the church, but in the early 1930s his was indeed a strong voice from the pulpit, raised with a message that was sometimes populist, sometimes radical, sometimes reactionary.[11]

Msgr. John A. Ryan, with whom Coughlin clashed, was the director of the U.S. Catholic Conference. He had succeeded in having the bishops in their 1919 *Statement on Social Reconstruction* endorse his essentially reformist approach to the American eco-nomy. Ryan, in that statement and in a lifetime of writings on social questions, advocated reforming American capitalism by applying principles of distributive justice, derived from church-endorsed natural-law teachings, in order to arrive at an economic order that was both productive and fair. Distributive justice was based largely on human needs; hence a capitalist economy that regularly paid workers less than they and their families needed was unjust. The Depression, he argued, had been caused not by overproduction but by underconsumption brought on by exces-sively low wages. The solution lay in sharply increased wages for workers, which was moral because it was economically expedient (he would, however, resist socialist attempts to apply the identification of morality with expediency more broadly in political action).[12]

Ryan's program for social reconstruction was envisioned to proceed in three stages. The first stage consisted in législation by the federal government ensuring a minimum wage, the eight-hour workday, protection of female and child workers, the right of workers to form unions, unemployment compensation, social security, public housing, some public ownership of enterprises, control over monopolies, progressive income taxes, and control of stock market speculation. A second stage would involve cooperative societies of producers and workers that would in each enterprise share managerial powers, profits and ownership itself. Finally, broad occupational groupings would emerge along the lines of the syndicates proposed in *Rerum Novarum* and *Quadragesimo Anno*. The entire program was based upon Ryan's premise that capitalism, unlike socialism, was not inherently vicious and could be reformed.[13]

Regarding other social and political questions, Ryan held that democracy was the preferable form of government, but monarchy and aristocracy were also morally acceptable. A proponent of individual liberties and a member of the ACLU, he would resign from that organization when it espoused academic freedom in colleges and universities including Catholic ones. Rejecting pacifism and holding the traditional Catholic just-war theory, he favored U.S. entry into World War II. He opposed equal rights for women, arguing that their place was in the home.[14]

As to political involvement, Ryan saw in FDR's New Deal the nearly perfect embodiment of his first-stage reform proposals. He strongly supported and regularly conferred with the Roosevelt administration, thus earning the nickname "Right Reverend New Dealer." Symbolized in Ryan, Catholic support became one of the cornerstones of the political success of the New Deal.

If Coughlin posed a maverick form of social and political rebelliousness from within the Catholic Church, and if Ryan and the Catholic bishops espoused (at least formally, in the case of the bishops) progressive social reform, a third voice — that of Catholic radicalism — was just beginning to reach the ears of some individuals inside the church and outside it. This was the voice of the Catholic Worker Movement. Because Rice believed both then and later that his own activism was inspired by the Catholic Worker Movement, I shall examine its origin and its sources of inspiration in some detail.[15]

The Catholic Worker story begins with the unique blending in 1932 of two already remarkably unique personalities, Dorothy Day and Peter Maurin. Dorothy Day was a recent convert to Catholicism who brought with her a history of social activism. Born in 1897 into a family with no religious affiliation, she was by the late 1920s a young journalist and diarist writing for a variety of leftist publications and working for a number of social causes such as women's suffrage and birth control. A liberated woman of the times, she had had an abortion in connection with a love affair that turned out badly, and had apparently attempted suicide not long thereafter. When a daughter was born to her of a common-law marriage in 1926, Dorothy had her baptized a Catholic in order not to leave her to "flounder" as she had. She soon thereafter followed suit by being baptized herself. The common-law marriage did not last, but her Catholicism did. Her resolute practice of her new religion helped to bring her assignments with the Catholic magazine *Commonweal* in the early 1930s, which in turn resulted in her receiving considerable attention in certain American Catholic circles.

An unforeseeable result of this exposure was a visit to her New York apartment in late 1932 by one Peter Maurin. Peter had been born into what became a huge (24-member) Catholic peasant family in the Languedoc region of France in 1877. As a young man he had been a Christian Brother until that order was secularized in France. He then emigrated — first to Canada, and then to the United States in 1911. Here he began the life of an itinerant philosopher who worked at one job and one place after another, who thought deeply about the malaises of industrial society, who harangued any who would listen to him about his solutions, and who, like most of his listeners, usually looked (and smelled) like a bum.

When Peter met Dorothy, having been directed to her by the publisher of *Commonweal*, he promptly began expounding his philosophy of "gentle personalism" drawn from the life and teachings of Francis of Assisi, and his plan of action. This plan involved four elements: the publication of a newspaper, the establishment of hospices for the poor or "Houses of Hospitality," roundtable discussions, and farming communes. The publication (*Catholic Radical* was Peter's preference for a title, although he explained that the Catholic Workers were "radicals of the right") would disseminate the social teachings of the popes and would oppose Marxism, liberalism and any other brand of collectivism, materialism, or evolutionism with an insistence on a return to individual responsibility and love. Its House of Hospitality would be an intimate, private home, unlike huge municipal welfare operations. It would provide food and shelter to those who presented themselves, without distinguishing between "deserving" and "undeserving" recipients, and without asking anything (even thanks) in return. The roundtable discussions would bring together scholars and workers for the "clarification of thought," along the lines of the Irish universities of the tenth century. Ideally these discussions would commence around the supper table and probably go late into the night. Finally, the farming communes would be organized in such a way that no one would be in charge, but each worker's labor would be a gift to be given, rather than a commodity to be bought or sold.

Dorothy listened, in part because she was fascinated by Peter's vision, and in part because she was too polite to throw him out when he kept reappearing at her door. Some of his ideas she grasped immediately and intuitively; others of them would not penetrate her combative anticapitalist mentality for some years. At length, she capitulated. Peter would become the visionary, and Dorothy the director, editor, and biographer of the Catholic Worker Movement.

The first issue of *The Catholic Worker* was hawked at one penny per copy (which would remain its price) in Union Square on May Day, 1933. It was sold there clearly as an alternative to the *Daily Worker* of the Communist Party, although the Catholic Worker Movement and its publication would take great pains to avoid red-baiting and often had complimentary things to say about well-intentioned communists. By the fall of 1933, twenty thousand copies were being printed and distributed each month, and over a hundred thousand by 1935.[16]

A house of hospitality quickly evolved at Dorothy's apartment, and moved several times in the next five decades to various addresses in or near the Bowery. Although it did indeed remain small in its living accommodations, it sometimes had persons standing in line up to half an hour to receive a bowl of the renowned Catholic Worker soup. By the time of the U.S. entry into World War II, thirty other Houses of Hospitality would be in operation around the country.

Roundtable discussions indeed went late into the night, bringing in many clerics, well-known philosophers like Jacques Maritain, and a potpourri of humanity from the streets of New York. "Gentle personalism" was the dominant philosophy, expostulated by the emphatic forefinger and sometimes horrendous puns of Peter Maurin.

As developed in these sessions and in the Catholic Worker Movement generally, personalism owed much of its origins to three distinct intellectual sources: the journal *L'Esprit* of Emmanuel Mounnier, English Catholic distributism, and the Russian writers Fyodor Dostoevski and Nicholas Berdyaev.

Mounnier, relying on fellow Frenchmen Proudhon, Bloy, Peguy, and Maritain, had sketched out a personalist "philosophy of action" that resisted any reductionism of the human spirit to an immanent order of society, politics, or history; recognized equally the spiritual and material nature of humanity; affirmed that the fundamental freedom of humanity was realized only amid social and historical conditions; and which to unite thought to action, person to community, and community to historical situation.

The English distributists — Belloc, Chesterton, Gill and McNabb — were anticapitalist, antiindustrialist and antistatist. They favored a decentralized economy of property-owning artisans, farmers, and shopkeepers.

Dostoevski contributed, via his Grand Inquisitor and *The Brothers Karamazov*, the insights that all attempts to set up a paradise on earth were profoundly mistaken and that human freedom was fully realized only by taking up the task of love and responsibility for the world. The philosopher Berdyaev added that it was the bourgeois and the Marxist corruptions of true social ideals that created the apparent contradiction in modern society between the transcendent spiritual order and improvement of the social order.[17]

To this intellectual stew were added, particularly in the writings of Catholic Worker Movement member Rev. Paul Hanley Furfey, a radical reinterpretation of Christian morality based not on established natural-law teachings of the church (which formed the basis of Msgr. John A. Ryan's and the U.S. Catholic bishops' call for social reconstruction), but on a literal reading of certain New Testament passages. All Christians, Furfey insisted, are called by Jesus to achieve perfection along the lines of the Sermon on the Mount. Each individual must undergo a profound change of heart away from self-seeking to the self-sacrificing love for others. Only from such profound conversions can solutions be found to contemporary crises of poverty, racism, and war.[18]

As carried into action, these principles of personalism meant that each poor person appearing at the door must be treated as the equal and unique person he or she was, hence the small houses and the intimate atmosphere. To the older Christian values of humility, poverty and contemplation, Catholic Workers united an American optimism, activism, egalitarianism, and libertarianism.

The Catholic Worker Movement houses relied upon free association and cooperation among workers who embraced voluntary poverty in order to carry out the mission of mercy given to them by Christ.[19] Such a revolution, insisting on individual conversions, did not focus primarily on political action or institutional change,[20] but did attempt to undermine the ideological foundations of contemporary capitalism.[21]

Agrarian communes, established in Easton, Pennsylvania, and elsewhere, succeeded rather less well than did the other aspects of Maurin's program — perhaps because there were precious few farmers among those who made up the Catholic Worker Movement, and fewer still who could organize others to the rigors of farming, given the personalist insistence on individual initiative and responsibility. Many of the Catholic Worker Movement's "farms" seem to have served in fact as vacation homes, offering a respite from city life and from work, rather than as a reorganization of work.

As the country continued to agonize in the toils of the Depression, and as a bewildering variety of alternative visions of the country's future, many of them radical, continued to be discussed, debated and struggled for, the young Father Rice was settling into his life as assistant pastor at St. Agnes. He found satisfaction in the ordinary rounds of his parish duties — saying Mass, hearing confessions, overseeing church bazaars, and directing the teenagers' club. But he also discovered that these duties took up only a minor portion of his available time and energy. He began to look for other outlets.

Interestingly, the first avenue he pursued was not in social activism but in academia. At nearby Mount Mercy College[22] he was hired by the Sisters of Mercy to teach undergraduate courses in psychology. This led to his taking graduate work in psychology at the University of Pittsburgh, with the goal of completing a Ph.D. This plan was derailed a year or so later when Rice was called in by the President of Mount Mercy and informed that his services were no longer required. Rice noted, nevertheless, that another priest was soon hired to teach the same courses. He also noted that by then his name was becoming increasingly associated with the Catholic Radical Alliance. Thus originated the somewhat chilly relationship between Rice and the "ladies on the Mount," which was to last throughout his career. And thus did Rice come to believe that, like his Uncle Owen in Ireland before him, he had lost his first teaching post because of his politics. Be that as it may, Rice gave up his plans to pursue a doctorate at the University of Pittsburgh.

Rice later concluded that his firing from Mount Mercy College determined that he would become a labor priest.[23] But also significant in this turn in his career was the existence of earlier models of labor priests, some of them in the Pittsburgh area. Perhaps the earliest pioneer had been Rev. Raymond Dietz, who earlier in the century had gained a reputation for labor activism by allying himself closely with the American Federation of Labor. Rice may have been influenced by Dietz's example, but had little respect for Dietz himself.[24] Closer to home, during the unsuccessful strike for union recognition in steel in 1919, Rev. Adelbert Kazinsky of Braddock had been one of the more prominent priests aiding the beleaguered steelworkers.[25]

But indubitably the premier labor priest in Pittsburgh prior to Rice was Rev. James Renshaw Cox. A native of Pittsburgh with a Ph.D. from the University of Pittsburgh, Cox had been on the labor scene since the 1920s when he aided miners during their strikes and battled for progressive legislation. In 1929 he supported a long and violent taxi strike in Pittsburgh. In this connection he used his radio show on station WJAS (he was a charismatic radio preacher who did a thirty-minute broadcast each week without a script), switching to rival station WMBJ when WJAS cut him off. Early in the Depression he opened a soup kitchen at his church, St. Patrick's, and gave millions of free meals to the hungry. When a shantytown arose near his parish, he became its unofficial mayor.

In January 1932, Cox called a rally at Pitt Stadium to publicize the plight of the unemployed. This led to a march of some fifteen thousand unemployed workers to Washington, D.C., headed by Cox and remaining peaceful throughout the campaign (unlike the better publicized Bonus Army of the same time). He was appointed to the Pennsylvania unemployment commission by Governor Pinchot, and to the state National Recovery Administration (NRA) board by Franklin Roosevelt. In 1936 he was back in Washington, this time leading a group in support of the Townsend Plan. Cox was clearly percieved as an ally of labor, but he came to regard the CIO drive for industrial unionism as little better than "labor gangsterism."[26]

Rice's career as a labor priest would bear striking similarities to that of Cox, but Rice would also come into sharp conflict with the older priest on the issue of the CIO. Rice also felt that Cox allowed some of his well-intentioned initiatives to be manipulated for economic gain by others less well motivated than he.[27]

The first steps Rice took toward becoming a labor priest were in the direction of another parish, St. Lawrence, where the assistant pastor was Rev. Carl P. Hensler. Hensler, then about forty years old, had written articles in the *Pittsburgh Catholic* dealing with social issues in which he showed himself devoted simultaneously to the papal social encyclicals and to the success of the CIO.

Hensler in turn introduced Rice to an older priest (then about fifty) who had provided much inspiration to Hensler: Monsignor George Barry O'Toole. Both O'Toole and Hensler had taken their seminary training at the elite North American College in Rome, the alma mater of many American priests who became bishops. They had then been instrumental in founding the University of Peking [now Beijing] in China before returning to the United States. O'Toole had in the interim served as chancellor to the bishop of Toledo, but now had returned to teaching philosophy at Duquesne.

Time would later report that O'Toole was chafing at the bit in the archconservative atmoshere of Duquesne,[28] but Rice would say that O'Toole's only chafing was at waiting for a professorship at the Catholic University of America in Washington, and that O'Toole was himself extremely conservative.[29] Rice later recalled that although O'Toole's intellectual commitments involved the rejection of capitalism and a search for radical alternatives compatible with church teaching, O'Toole also held a certain fascination for fascist governments.

At any rate, the three clerics initiated a series of discussions on the social questions of the day, and by early 1937 had begun to attract a following of other priests and of lay persons, numbering eventually in the hundreds. One of the earliest priests to join in, and one of the most action-prone as time went on, was Rev. Thomas Lappan, director of the St. Vincent de Paul Society (a charitable organization) of the Pittsburgh diocese. Mrs. Raymond Byrne headed the Catholic Forum, a women's organization that soon drew in a number of young lay persons. Among them was Alan Kistler, long a disciple of Rice's and later the vice president for organization of the AFL-CIO. Other prominent supporters were Lawrence Sullivan, Sam Eannerino, Francis Tassey, Joseph A. Goney, Patrick T. Fagan, Frank Hensler (Carl's brother), Stephen McCarthy, William Lenz, Mary Tassey and Maurice Sullivan (later a married couple), Marcellus Kirsch, Marie Kiefer and Richard Rooney (later a married couple), and others.[30] Rice later observed of those early days: "Of course the young people came out. Ours was the only thing going in those Depression days!"[31]

A reasonably clear picture of the ideology of the nascent organization emerges from accounts of the final lecture series held weekly between April and June of 1937 and reported in the *Pittsburgh Catholic*. The lectures very clearly followed along the lines of the Catholic Worker Movement then being presented in the pages of *The Catholic Worker*, but there was in addition a shared concern among these three clergymen for the institutional well-being of the Catholic Church, which was less central to the lay-organized Catholic Worker Movement in New York. In particular, O'Toole, Hensler, and Rice were horrified at how the Church in Europe had lost the working class to the communists, and were resolved that history must not be repeated in the United States. Thus both the ideology and the program of what came to be the Catholic Radical Alliance (CRA) would attempt to head off the communists by co-opting many of their programs (labor schools and unemployed workers' councils, to name two). Although the clerical trio indeed supported unions, and in particular the idea of nationwide industrial unionism, this was always to be secondary to their aim of saving the worker for the Church.[32].

A sampling of the major themes found in the addresses of O'Toole, Hensler, and Rice in the spring of 1937 would include the rationale for church's involvement in social issues, the failures of Catholics to understand or live up to the social pronouncements of the popes, attacks on both liberalism and contemporaneous capitalism, and a presentation of the pope's alternative vision of society.

Hensler put the case for church enmeshment in social issues simply: "The Church is the boss, appointed by Christ, of the moral law. . . . Low wages, exorbitant prices, and sharp practice are forms of stealing and cheating." He concluded that, while the Church was not interested in the "technical side of [economic] systems," it had to proclaim that the present system could not possibly be run in a decent way, so that changes had to be instituted in laws, in institutions, and in the guiding ideals of American society.[33]

Rice, though insisting that hatred directed at the Catholic Church had to originate from Satan, still argued that Catholics might have brought some anti-Catholicism upon themselves by failing to live by their church's moral code, particularly in their dealings with blacks, the wealthy, and the poor. He stated that blacks must be treated "as our brother in Christ," and that mere toleration was not enough. As to the rich, he offered an apparently literal interpretation of Christ's words, "Blessed are ye poor . . . Woe to ye that are rich," and concluded that unless the rich repented of their greed, they would end up in hell. As to the poor, Rice denounced the belief that they were such as a result of their own shiftlessness. This was "a damnable error . . . that the well-fed, comfortable invented so that the food would not stick in their throats."[34]

O'Toole, meanwhile, excoriated liberalism, the "social philosophy which proposes *unrestricted individual liberty* as the panacea for all human ills." He went on to argue that the insistence on greater and greater human freedom and the overthrow of external authority like that of the church did not produce freedom:

> Exactly the opposite. In every modern State whose political structure is based upon the principles of liberalism we observe *more and more restrictions* upon human freedom. The modern State is becoming increasingly bureaucratic and totalitarian in imposing its authority upon its subjects.[35].

Competitive capitalism was equally condemned in the lectures that spring, partly because "in the new economy competition has all but disappeared." Pointing to the political pressure system rather than economic contribution as determining one's economic rewards, and to the extreme maldistribution of wealth (1% of the population holding 59% of the wealth), and asking whether the capitalist system worked despite these problems, the lecturer answered: "Emphatically, no! In this country we have had 15 depressions in 57 years. . . . In so-called 'good times' national prosperity was not shared by all classes." The reason for these failures? Because the economic system "is motivated by that most ancient of all vices called 'greed.'"[36]

Then listeners were offered the pope's alternative to the capitalism of the rugged individualists and the class warfare of the Marxists: the guild. They were told that the characteristic features of a just economic system were, first, to assure the wide participation in ownership and control of property, by all who take part in the productive process, and, secondly, to give to all persons enough goods and services for "virtuous living." Then it was added that these goals could best be achieved on a cooperative rather than a competitive basis. Finally the conclusion was drawn that the cooperative guild system expounded in the social encyclicals, with government chiefly standing by to keep the guilds from acting unjustly toward consumers, each other, or their own members, would best achieve the goals of justice while avoiding the pitfalls of capitalism and collectivism.[37]

Thus had the fledgling organization elaborated an ideology. What about an action program? Rice tended to take a back seat to Hensler and O'Toole of questions of philosophy, but in the development of a plan of action he came to the fore. In a presentation on April 22, followed by much intense discussion, Rice proposed the formation of a new set of programs to address the needs of four distinct sets of persons. First, a House of Hospitality in the style of the Catholic Worker Movement would be founded to feed, clothe and instruct the poor (whether or not he was serious at the time about "instructing" the poor, it would pretty much disappear from the program at its inception). Secondly, workers would be served by the founding of a Pittsburgh branch of the Association of Catholic Trade Unionists (ACTU). This organization, recently founded in New York City, would come to play a much larger role in Rice's life a bit later. Thirdly, the intelligentsia would be addressed by a Bureau of Catholic Social Information. Finally, instruction would be offered to employers and to the rich — if they chose to listen.

Concrete activities proposed by Rice included "distributing Catholic literature and doctrine at Communist meetings and Capitalist meetings," investigating strikes and encouraging them if they were just, participating in demonstrations for justice, to show that the church was on the side of the poor and down-trodden. Said Rice in conclusion: "We must work the Catholic way which is through love, not hatred; through unity, not disunity; using pure means no matter what the end may be."[38]

But if such were the ideas and such the intended actions of the organization, what was also needed was a name — something that would catch the popular imagination, perhaps even shock it, but still announce the Catholic nature of this new band of social activists. Perhaps Rice's own words best capture the drama of the moment:

"I still think it's the best name" [Catholic Radical Alliance]. Father Tom Lappan, white-haired youngish director of the St. Vincent de

Paul conference, was quite emphatic. I thought it was the best name too, but what of all the people who would not understand? "The word 'radical' is a perfectly good one in its true sense. Monsignor O'Toole can tell you that. You want a label that will both attract attention and tell what your outfit is up to. Catholic Radical Alliance as a title isn't just good — man, it's perfect!"

"Okeh! Catholic Radical Alliance it is. I wonder what the Bishop will say?" So we wrote out the title. Looked at it a number of times in pride and some trepidation and turned to other matters.

We had been holding open forums for some time on the social question. Learned talks had been given by Monsignor O'Toole and Father Carl Hensler and some not-so-learned by myself. At the question period each night people were always jumping up demanding to know what we were going to do about things. Later I found out some of them were egged on by Father Lappan, who wanted action.

We had roundly condemned the present social order. Had made the point that the Church had marvelous remedies to offer. That some type of definite action was necessary, etc. That, however, was as far as we got.

Now we were going to do something. A definite program was to be submitted at the next meeting of the Forum. An organization with a nice name and everything was to be proposed. I, the proposer, was doing a neat spate of worrying and working.

The grand social encyclicals were our ultimate guide of course; and our immediate inspiration and example was the Catholic Worker crowd in New York. The program, as submitted to the forum and approved, called for long range action through education toward cooperatives, farming communes and the distributive ideal in general. For the immediate here and now we had plans for action among the poor, the workers, the intelligentsia. Classes in principles with the object of molding a fully indoctrinated, enthusiastic body of supporters were started immediately. But that wasn't enough.[39]

For someone of Rice's temperament, the name and the plans were indeed not enough. What he and other members of the CRA sought was a cause and an event around which to organize, and perhaps a way even better than their new name to capture public attention.

Such a cause soon presented itself in Pittsburgh at the H. J. Heinz Company. Heinz was known nationally for its ketchup and fifty-six other varieties of canned food products, and locally as the business of one of the city's most powerful families. There the Amalgamated Meatcutters Local 365 of the AFL had been striking for recognition. It was widely recognized that the strike had not been going at all well, and that H. J. Heinz was anticipating a victory. What may not have been so widely recognized, but what Rice says he was aware of, was that the local had communist leadership in its president, Frank Kraycheck.[40]

Undeterred, Rice and Hensler and some of the younger CRA members decided to throw in with the pickets. Rice gives his description of the confrontation:

> Two somewhat worried clerics advanced hopefully on the immense plant of the H.J. Heinz Company, whose workers were out on strike for union (AFL) recognition. As per arrangement, they met two enthusiastic college boys and two charming young female adherents. Signs were produced telling of our support for the strikers, and down to the picket line we marched. As the laity marched in the parade, Father Hensler and I argued amicably with the police and management representatives, who were aghast to say the very least. The Catholic Radical Alliance was on its way.
>
> Some evenings later, the strike over and an N.L.R.B. election scheduled for the next day, with the addition of Monsignor O'Toole we addressed five or six hundred perspiring workers who may not have known much of what we were talking about, but who did know that the priests were with them and they were glad. The union won the election.[41]

These actions, by priests sporting Roman collars, not only set the CRA on its way, but also captured local and national media attention. Reported *Time* of the picket line incident: "Horrified, the pickets begged the priests to cover the word 'radical' on their signs."[42] Rice did not recollect years later whether they had covered the word or not; Hensler's memory was that they had.[43] It should be added that the *Time* coverage had not happened simply by chance; Rice had made sure to alert the media before proceeding to the picket line.[44]

It would be years later before Rice learned of H.J.'s wrath at this clerical interference: apparently Heinz felt the women working at his plant put more confidence in the priests than in their own union leaders, and that the strike for recognition succeeded as a result.[45] Not that Heinz was about to concede the issue gracefully: in a bitter struggle that extended until late in 1938, Heinz took the position that the NLRB could force him to *negotiate* a contract with the union, but it could not oblige him to *sign* that contract (bargaining was apparently an end in itself). It took an appeal to the Supreme Court, argued by Pittsburgh attorney Al Wilner, to negate that position. At length, the struggle, kept alive by the timely intervention of the Catholic Radical Alliance, was resolved in favor of the workers. The CRA had arrived with a splash, recruited some new followers and admirers, and probably had made some powerful enemies in the process.

The action at Heinz was a beginning for the Catholic Radical Alliance; much more was to come. There ensued a summer of swirling controversy and labor union activism whose breathless nature was captured rather nicely by a journalist at the time:

After its inaugural flash of action, the Alliance darted to the South Side plants of the Jones and Laughlin Steel Co. to exhort the steelers to stick by the CIO; followed it up by picketing the Loose-Wills Biscuit factory as a sympathetic gesture toward the strikers; then hurried down to Youngstown to address rallies of the SWOC units at the Youngstown Sheet and Tube and Republic Steel, where Rev. Rice vigorously urged the strikers to employ the Charity of Christ rather than "the naked greed of hell" in their relations with the employers; meanwhile, issued a manifesto violently denouncing the "Workers' Council for Social Justice" at Ford plants as a device of the company bosses; quickly returned to Pittsburgh to feed and clothe the suffering families of the Loose-Wiles strikers; travelled to Johnstown to address a giant labor rally which was later cancelled by the declaration of martial law; found themselves instrumental in settling the biscuit strike to the advantage of the workers; dove into the midst of a long-drawn-out Heppenstall Steel strike where they passed out literature, marched in the picket line, and spoke at meetings of the strikers; ran headlong into a tift with Father Coughlin over the sincerity of the Catholic Worker enterprises; tore down to Canton, imploring the steel strikers to hold fast their position; came back to the city to face a sizzling, two-barreled attack from disturbance-raising Father Cox and headline-maker Father Coakley; raced down to Baltimore to radio-cast that "the CIO is not Godless, Communistic or un-American"; momentarily stopped the League Against War and Fascism — sponsored peace rally by horning in on the demonstration with a sign opposing Communism; invaded the Coughlinite fortress of Detroit to discuss the trade union movement at a Catholic Study Club, and presented a paper which asserted that capitalism and Catholicism are fundamentally antagonistic; sped to Indianapolis, demonstrating to the Catholic Conference on Industrial Problems how to put Christian morals into practice in the labor field; broke into a leading role in the John L. Lewis Labor-Day rally in South Park; and wound up a summer of activity by distributing opposition-literature at a pro-Loyalist meeting on the North Side.[46]

Several observations are in order about this first summer of activism, because it revealed what was to be the modus operandi of the CRA and of Rice himself in the years ahead.

Fist was the willingness to support *any* union struggle against management. The formally adopted platform of the CRA had called for investigating labor disputes and supporting strikes that were just, but Rice and the others apparently found no unjust strikes, if they bothered to investigate both sides at all. About as far as Rice went in this direction was to exhort some strikers to avoid greed. But the unions he supported included not only the long-established AFL units, but the upstart CIO and particularly the Steel Workers' Organizing Committee (SWOC), now engaged in one of the first major tests of the principle of organizing workers along industrial rather than craft lines. Included were unions known by Rice or the others to have communist leadership or significant communist influence, as well as those of a more conservative hue. In short, there was very little picking and choosing of "just" as opposed to "unjust" union struggles; all of them were justified in the view of Rice and the CRA.

But by the same token, there was already evident a strong thrust against communist presence in and influence on the causes Rice and the CRA supported. When Congressman Jerry O'Connell, a Catholic, brought an antiwar rally to Pittsburgh under the auspices of the American League Against War and Fascism, the CRA showed up to picket that event just as it had H. J. Heinz. Rice went so far as to refer to O'Connell as a "self-styled Catholic" because of his communist sympathies, a tactic Rice would use again and again in later years. And when a rally was held in support of the Loyalist side in the Spanish Civil War, The CRA set aside its earlier insistence that it took no position in that struggle, and distributed literature for Franco's side. To Rice and the CRA, of course, anticommunism was perfectly consistent with the anticapitalist bias in their union activism.

Another noteworthy characteristic was that the CRA interventions in labor and other struggles typically consisted of a quick dash into town, a rally or debate or broadcast at which the fundamental message was that the church did *not* disapprove of unions or the CIO, and an equally quick departure. Rice and Hensler were not engaged in the patient, time-consuming work of organization-building. Nor was it their place, as clerics friendly to the movement, to be so involved. But in later years, when Rice would be the object of criticism by union activists, their typical gambit would be the "where-were-you-when" approach. Rice's answer, maddeningly enough, would be, "I *was* there." As the summer of 1937 demonstrates, he was *and* he was not.

This early involvement with labor union struggles would prove to be one of the characteristics that set off the Catholic Radical Alliance from its intended model in New York, the Catholic Worker Movement. Whether it was a matter of timing (the CRA began in 1937, just as labor-management strife was reaching a crescendo), or locale (Pittsburgh was more of a "labor town" than was New York), or personality (Rice was to become the "labor priest"), it is undeniable that the CRA was much more bound up with labor union activity than the Catholic Worker Movement ever had been or would become.

True enough, the Catholic Workers never cold-shouldered organized labor (although Peter Maurin never joined a union, despite many opportunities). The New York House of Hospitality fed and supported Seamen during their long and bitter strike.[47] *The Catholic Worker* in its pages gave strong support to labor over the years.[48] Dorothy Day herself captured national attention when she appeared at the sit-down strike against Ford in Flint, Michigan. Yet for the Catholic Worker Movement, labor union support always seemed to come *after* the four basic principles of charity, discussion, publication, and farming. The movement had run labor schools from its early days, but when a group seeing labor activism as its first goal later evolved within it, that group and the labor schools left the movement in 1937 (still maintaining cordial relations). They took on their own identity as the Association of Catholic Trade Unionists (ACTU).[49]

In Pittsburgh, by way of contrast, labor unionism preceded rather than followed the establishment of the house of hospitality. The Pittsburgh ACTU, with Rice as chaplain, was one of the earliest ones chartered, in 1938. When the organization held its first national convention in 1941, Pittsburgh and Rice served as host. Labor schools, attempting to train Catholic unionists to play leadership roles in courses ranging from labor history to parliamentary procedure, began as early as did the CRA, and remained a major undertaking throughout its existence. Probably it was no accident that Rice became best known not as the "charity priest" or the "House of Hospitality priest," but as the "labor priest." The priorities of the Catholic Worker Movement were reversed in Rice and the CRA, whose spokesman he was. Put another way, the split between the Catholic Worker Movement and the ACTU that took place in New York never materialized in Pittsburgh. The forces that naturally aligned with the ACTU dominated the entire movement from the outset.

Still another fascinating aspect of this summer of campaigns was the willingness of the trio, and of Rice in particular, to take on other Catholic priests and slug it out in public. When Father Cox charged that the seven-state steel strike with twelve deaths had been brought on by labor "racketeers" who were swinging the pendulum of injustice away from the 5 percent rich, only to favor the 15 percent unionized workers, Rice replied:

> If snobbery and propaganda succeed in keeping the white collar people hostile or suspicious of labor in this country, the result will be class war. . . . I regret the day that a religious representative has seen fit to add to the flood of hatred and misrepresentation.[50]

Rice also contradicted Father Coughlin when the latter interpreted the popes' social encyclicals as opposing industrial unionism.[51] Rice's response, itself very moderate, commented that Coughlin's attack used unduly harsh language. Still another well-known cleric with whom Rice crossed swords was Rev. Fulton J. Sheen, when Sheen blamed industrial malaise exclusively on workers.[52].

Although Rice was prepared to go on the attack against fellow priests with whom he disagreed, bishops were another matter. Because the permission of the local bishop was required before a priest could accept a speaking engagement in his diocese, Rice often found himself in the position of explaining to a bishop outside Pittsburgh just why his appearance in the latter's diocese would be useful. To Cardinal O'Connell in Massachusetts, Rice explained:

> My purpose in interesting myself in labor is above all to advance the cause of Catholicity. . . . My technique is to help labor where its cause is just and thus to gain an influence in its councils where I can expound Catholic principles and give advice.[53]

To Bishop Gibbons of Albany, the tone approached the conspiratorial: "It is for us to bore quietly into the unions."[54]

Does this tone of Rice's bear out what some of his later critics would contend, that Rice was not sincerely interested in the good of unions, but merely used them to advance sectarian causes? Or did Rice take such a tack because he anticipated negative reactions from conservative bishops? He in fact got one from O'Connell when the latter refused Rice permission to speak.[55] Still another interpretation, and arguably the one closest to Rice's mind at the time, is that, though he indeed involved himself in labor in order to advance the cause of the church, he perceived no conflict between the cause of the church and that of the unions.

Of major assistance in spreading the word of the Catholic Radical Alliance, and building up its following, was the willingness of KDKA, the foremost Pittsburgh radio station, to give air time to the three clerics. Three or four half-hour programs were broadcast by the CRA in 1937, and a comparable number in 1938. One of the more noteworthy among these was Rice's "The Dynamite of the Encyclicals," aired on May 15, 1937. After discussing the startled reactions that persons had had to the name of the Catholic Radical Alliance, he said:

> The question is asked of us, are we really radical? And the only answer we can honestly make is: Yes, we certainly are. A radical is one who goes to the root of matters; and we count on doing just that. We are dissatisfied with the present Social and Economic set-up: we want to see it drastically changed.

He went on to argue that the popes and prominent Catholic churchmen were all radicals in this sense, and directed a stinging reproach to American Catholics who engaged in Red-baiting:

> Most of these misguided people are being duped. They rant and rave against the menace of Communism, against its godlessness; with never a word about the menace and godlessness of Finance-Capitalism. . . . Worst of all, they are led around by the nose by reactionaries. They brand as Communistic many proposals which are obviously for the common good.[56]

It was in 1939, when the CRA had taken a more settled form (particularly with the establishment of St. Joseph's House of Hospitality, to be discussed below) that Rice followed the example of Coughlin and Cox in becoming a radio priest. Radio station WWSW offered him a choice time slot on Mondays from 9:45 to 10:00 p.m., in a series of programs to go from late May to late October. During this five-month period, Rice used the program mostly to advertise the work and the needs of St. Joseph's House of Hospitality, but he also managed to work in such guests as Peter

Maurin from the Catholic Worker Movement, Rev. Paul H. Furfey, Msgr. John A. Ryan, by then emeritus professor at Catholic University and the preeminent American commentator on the social encyclicals, and others.

Noteworthy for its bluntness was Rice's address on August 7 on anti-Semitism, a prejudice by no means restricted to Hitler's Germany or to the European side of the Atlantic. He began with the words: "As a Catholic, I regret to note that among Catholics whom I know anti-Semitism, as it is called, is quite strong." He then proceeded to upbraid sternly all Catholics who allowed themselves to be swayed, consciously or unconsciously, by such a sentiment. This was a position, along with his opposition to racial prejudice toward blacks, that would mark Rice's entire career.[57]

Also found in this series is an expression of antiwar sentiment that becomes particularly interesting in light of Rice's later reversal on the question:

> What fools we mortals be! We can find countless millions of dollars to prosecute an insane war. We can make sacrifice upon sacrifice to snatch a meaningless military victory. But we grumble and get afraid when it comes to make a courageous effort to solve our social and economic muddle. . . . Let us in America try to keep sane. Let us give to our youth those peace talks that we gave in such profusion during the past quarter century.[58]

When the series ended in October, WWSW was pleased enough with Rice's work to begin another series, this time on Saturdays from 10:15 to 10:30 p.m. Although Rice would sometimes be preempted by hockey games and sometimes switched to other time slots, this series appears to have been a success as well. From then onward for years to come, radio audiences could each week expect to hear the voice with the Irish lilt begin: "Father Rice speaking to you once again on behalf of St. Joseph's House of Hospitality, 61 Tannehill Street, Pittsburgh, Pa. At the House we feed and shelter hungry and homeless men."

The original Pittsburgh House of Hospitality had been at another address in the Hill District, a small store at 901 Wylie Avenue. But after residing there from September 29, 1937, to March 31, 1938, the CRA decided to move the operation to the much larger former orphanage and then foundling hospital owned by the Pittsburgh diocese at 61 Tannehill Street. Underlying this move was a debate between the CRA and the Catholic Worker Movement of which it was part, and between Rice and Dorothy Day, on how best to provide for those in need. Day, Maurin, and the Catholic Worker Movement in New York followed their personalist philosophy and continued to prefer small, intimate houses where the poor could be treated as esteemed guests. Rice and the CRA seemed to be more concerned about the large numbers of poor and how to feed them in the most efficient manner possible. Regular (and according to some insiders, inflated) accounts of the numbers housed and sheltered at the House of Hospitality appeared in the *Pittsburgh Catholic*. A result was the somewhat impersonal, and sometimes even authoritarian, atmosphere that pervaded the larger operation in Pittsburgh.

Ironically, the numbers of men reported in the *Pittsburgh Catholic* as being fed were higher at the earlier address than at the later one. In late 1937, when the house of hospitality was still on Wylie Avenue, some nine hundred men were reported fed per meal,[59] whereas in the summer of 1938 the highest number reported fed was between four hundred and five hundred.[60] What did change in the upward direction was the number of residents at the house of hospitality, which went from a handful at Wylie to approximately forty at Tannehill.[61] Perhaps some of the apparent discrepancy between the intent and the reported results may have stemmed from a tendency to exaggerate some of the earlier figures (at least one staffer thought Rice had such a tendency[62]).

Most of the day-to-day work at the House of Hospitality was carried out by a staff of laymen, headed intially by William Lenz. Lenz, a nurse who had lost all his money in the Depression and whom his co-workers described as "saintly," moved into the house from the beginning. Other workers who contributed great amounts of time and energy at the house of hospitality over the years came to include Stephen J. McCarthy, Charles Francis Barrett, Leon Helfenberg, Lee Platoff Zane, and Daniel Gallagher.

But it seems to have been assumed from the beginning that the house of hospitality ought to have a resident priest as its director. O'Toole was out of the picture: he had received his appointment to the Department of Philosophy at Catholic University. Hensler also left the scene when he joined the faculty at Seton Hill College. This left Rice, who, after some intense lobbying by the laity, requested that the bishop transfer him from St. Agnes to St. Joseph's House of Hospitality. The bishop acceded, and Rice moved in on February 8, 1940.

Rice, in interviews I conducted with him, often mentioned that the financing of so ambitious a project as the House of Hospitality remained a mystery to him. Most of the food was contributed by merchants — notably kosher bakers who regularly gave day-old bread or rolls for the morning coffee lines, and a friendly butcher named Herman Bronder. A truck owned by the Knights of Columbus regularly made rounds picking up vegetables, bread, meat scraps and clothing. Beds and additional clothing were provided through collections by the Knights of Columbus and St. Vincent de Paul Society. A number of women from nearby parishes showed up with blankets and other much-needed items. (They, along with some young women in the CRA and later the Sisters of Charity from a women's residence up the street, constituted the female presence in what was otherwise a man's world at the House of Hospitality.)

Small monetary contributions came in at first on an irregular basis. The bishop, who previously had said the house would be on its own financially, sent in $30 per week. Finances were put on a somewhat more regular basis when Rice began his radio appeals in mid-1939, and when mailed appeals were sent out every Thanksgiving, Christmas and Easter. Open houses were held on the House of Hospitality's anniversary in November and on St. Patrick's Day in March (the latter marked with a spaghetti supper!).

Another source of income was the sale of *The Catholic Worker* by House of Hospitality regulars. Coal for heating was dug by some of the regulars from a property owned by the diocese. Unfortunately, some of the workers saw fit on occasion to sell the coal or *The Catholic Worker* for funds that went to nearby taverns rather than to the general benefit of the House of Hospitality. Rice decided against selling the labor of his clientele, or resorting to professional fund-raising services (a practice he believed Father Cox had erred in using).

The clientele at the house was quite varied, and included, according to Rice, alcoholics, who would belt down their liquor moments before coming in, in order to beat the house rule against consumption on the premises; criminals and escaped convicts who arrived shortly in advance of the police; a group dubbed the "Hungry Hunkies" whose only apparent problem was their lack of food and money, and some skilled craftsmen who stayed on at the House of Hospitality, using their abilities to enhance life there. The regular staff, some long-term and others coming and going quite often, numbered around fifty.

The food, clothing and shelter provided were no more than

adequate, but were free, with no questions asked and no religious observance required. This changed somewhat when Rice moved in as director and regularly said Mass at the house. Those regulars who professed to be Catholics were expected uo be in attendance each Sunday. The house was kept reasonably warm, and enough food was provided to keep a man going, but other problems persisted. One of these was bedbugs or "chinches," still very difficult to control in the days before DDT. Another was dysentery, which affected everyone sooner or later, Rice not excepted. Still another problem was violence among the guests, sometimes occasioning urgent calls to the police. Rice's room was at the end of the heating line, and too cold in winter. An auxiliary heater had been installed but not vented, and he probably escaped asphyxiation only because of the room's draftiness.

On one well-publicized occasion, the House of Hospitality came near to being closed down. An official named Tufts from the Pittsburgh Housing Association visited one night in winter, only to find many men lying on the bare floor. He recommended to the City Inspector that the place be closed as a health hazard. But a second-in-command, Bill Hickey, managed to leak advance warning of the report to Rice, who was thus prepared for the media. He asserted, in a statement that grabbed headlines that day, that he would rather go to jail than see the house closed.[63] No one had suggested jailing Rice, but his pugnacious response was enough to fend off any danger to the house. It was not closed down, and a year later workers at the Sanitation Department held a minstrel show for the benefit of the House of Hospitality, and raised $3,000 to provide more beds. (The irony of staging a minstrel show to benefit unemployed men, most of whom were black, seemed to pass unnoticed.)

As the result of his identification with the House of Hospitality, Rice's public image as a Catholic "radical" began to be modified somewhat. Priests and lay persons who took exception to his politics were in some cases supportive of his charitable work at the house. He received occasional and favorable media attention as the "flophouse father" or "pastor of the poorest."[64] Rice was honored for his work with a splendid banquet at Pittsburgh's Syria Mosque on January 7, 1941. There was a tendency in the public forum to paint Rice as somewhat of a saint, along the lines of Dorothy Day.

Rice himself decided, however, that he was not really cut out for the saintly life of Dorothy Day or even William Lenz. He had to overcome very considerable reluctance before moving in with the chinches and dysentery at the House of Hospitality. And citing, with tongue partly in cheek, the British maxim that "Animals feed, men eat, and gentlemen dine," Rice did not eat with the guests at the House of Hospitality but had his meals prepared and served separately from the others.[65]

An even less reverent view of Rice's presence at and contribution to the House of Hospitality is provided by a series of undated letters, half-teasing and half-serious, written to him by one of the staff members, Larry Sullivan. Sullivan suggested that if some communist — dread figure — were to come snooping around the House of Hospitality, he would find all the following to be true: the prime purpose of the institution was "to further publicize the name of the Director"; the conscious time Rice spent there was "a negligible infinitesimal"; the picture of Rice in the dining room was the object of many obscene words and gestures by staff members; for the publicly advertized "millionth meal" to be accurate, thousands of meals per day would have had to be served, many of them "a watery mess of turnips and pig snouts"; the testimonial dinner at the Syria Mosque nearly had to be sponsored by Rice himself; the "interracial work" of the Martin de Porres Society consisted in chasing neighborhood kids back out the doors and windows by which they had entered unnoticed; Rice was commonly and disrespectfully referred to as "the Reverend," "His Nibs," or "Charlie."[66]

Although much of the above was enjoyable raillery that Rice accepted in good spirit and returned in like manner (even preserving it in his Papers), there was a serious disagreement that underlay the kidding. Some members of the CRA, like Sullivan, wanted the House of Hospitality to be more like the Catholic Worker Movement model in New York and not the large, impersonal operation it had become in Pittsburgh. When this disagreement was added to divisions over the issues of anticommunism and pacifism, as will be seen, it led to an open split at the house of hospitality.

Running the House of Hospitality certainly accounted for a major portion of the time and energies of the Catholic Radical Alliance and this aspect of the organization was perhaps more central than any other save the labor union activism that preceded the founding of the house. But other major aspects of the program must not be omitted from the inventory of its activism.

Interracial work, the sardonic view of Sullivan notwithstanding, was one of these emphases. In addition to the fact that blacks and whites were brought together at one table under one roof, there were formal meetings every week of the Martin de Porres Society. The goal of this group was interracial understanding and harmony, at a time when such a concern was not yet even on the country's political agenda. William Lenz and others offered to black children from the neighborhood religious instruction and occasional visits to the country. Lenz was also active in counseling local families with respect to marital and financial matters. Rice, although less directly involved than Lenz and some of the others, would always take a strong position for interracial understanding and love, and would in later years be able to secure for some blacks from the district the best jobs they ever had.

Discussion and debate of social issues was likewise a regularly scheduled exercise for the CRA, with the lecture format of the formative stages of the organization yielding more to a roundtable approach later on, and rendering the House of Hospitality, in the description of Rice years later, "a beehive of intellectual activity."[67] Synopses of some of these discussions, many of them growing quite heated, would show up in the pages of the *Pittsburgh Catholic*, although the accounts tended to be highly colored by the viewpoint of that week's correspondent.[68]

For these Catholic clerics and lay persons, a closely related concern was with the liturgy of the Church. Discussions with such renowned liturgists as A. H. Reinhold were combined with experimental forms at the Masses Rice celebrated in the chapel of the House of Hospitality, a less visible location than the ordinary parish church. Much of this discussion and experimentation would become familiar to Catholics many years later, in the era of Vatican II.

The CRA did not publish a regular newspaper, as did the Catholic Worker Movement in New York, but it did produce an in-house newsletter, as well as a House of Hospitality column and a CRA column each week in the *Pittsburgh Catholic*, the latter over the initials of S. F. Eannerino, Alan Kistler, or sometimes others. This effort was discontinued by the young laity of the CRA early in 1941 as the war approached, and then picked up for a year or so by Rice in what would turn out to be the beginning of his long and sometimes stormy career as a columnist. But the chief vehicle of communication from the CRA to the rest of the world, and particularly to that portion of the world that was not Catholic, lay in Rice's weekly radio broadcasts. Thus Rice tended to become the unique voice of the movement, perhaps even its personification.

There were other undertakings of the CRA that deserve to be noted simply because they were attempted, rather than because they were successful. One such was the setting up and meetings of a council of the unemployed, in imitation of a similar effort by the Catholic Worker Movement in New York, which in turn seemed to be emulating some noteworthy successes of the Communist Party. The party led rent strikes in those days, and vociferous demonstrations demanding political action leading to job creation. Nothing much seemed to come of the council initiative, at least in Pittsburgh. It was easy enough to set up, difficult to sustain when jobs were not forthcoming, and wiped out when employment did come along — in the form of military and war-related employment.

Another such attempt was the one based on Peter Maurin's romantic agrarianism — to return from the city to the land with a farming commune. As with the New York group, this attempt culminated in failure, except more spectacular. Frank Hensler, the younger brother of Carl, in 1938 led a group to Slicksville, Pennsylvania, in rural Armstrong County, there to establish a commune that would raise poultry. The novice farmers, unhappily, knew little about the poultry business and by fall all the chickens had sickened and died. The attempt was permanently abandoned.

Rice later argued that if there had been more time before the coming of the war, as there had been in the Catholic Worker experiment in Easton, a full-blown commune might have evolved.[69] This is, of course, quite speculative. But the Catholic Worker Movement modified the farming concept so that it served the movement at least as a source of retreat and respite. Might the failure of the CRA to ride out the war or reestablish itself later have had something to do with the absence of such a resource? This, too, is speculation.

Between 1937 and 1941, then, the Catholic Radical Alliance had grown and evolved, partly in imitation of the Catholic Worker Movement and partly away from that model. In New York, the program had begun with the establishment of the Houses of Hospitality; in Pittsburgh, labor union activism had come first. The Catholic Worker Movement had founded numerous small houses; the CRA, one large institution. Introspection and publication had been more central for Dorothy Day and her followers; action was the first priority in Pittsburgh. Discussion for the clarification of thought had been practiced in both groups, but lectures by clergy to laity came first in Pittsburgh. Farming had been tried and modified in Easton, tried and abandoned in Slicksville. Interracial work, liturgical expression, and unemployment councils were features of both groups — with varying degrees of success. The Catholic Workers in New York had dedicated themselves to a life of voluntary poverty in order better to identify with "Christ's poor"; Rice made no bones then or later about his preference for a comfortable lifestyle, and only a few of his followers seem to have dissented. The principles of personalism seem to have been the criteria governing action in New York; in Pittsburgh, these were largely washed out as a concern; the numbers of those efficiently fed and housed came to predominate.

But what ultimately made the two movements part ways seems to have been the composition of the leadership in the two cities, their respective approaches to the presence of communism, and their reactions to the advent of World War II.

Whereas the movement leadership in New York was exclusively lay, in Pittsburgh it was exclusively clerical, with the younger laity for the most part playing supporting roles to O'Toole, Hensler, and Rice initially, and later to Rice alone. This meant that the Catholic Worker Movement had greater freedom to formulate and adhere to its principles without direct ecclesiastical supervision, but a correspondingly smaller certainty about hierarchical backing and approval. Dorothy Day was once confronted with a wholly unanticipated order to cease publishing The Catholic Worker, and had to hotfoot it to the chancery to avoid that outcome (which she would have accepted, had the cardinal insisted).[70]

Rice, by way of contrast, had been stationed at the Pittsburgh House of Hospitality by Bishop Boyle's assignment, and exercised control or significant influence over virtually every aspect of CRA work. Such problems as arose at the chancery could be ironed out long before they reached crisis proportions. Most of Rice's troubles, then and later, seemed in fact to come less from the church hierarchy than from lay persons whose conservative sensibilities he managed to outrage. But in a church where decisions came from the top downward, and the designated role of the laity was to "pray, pay, and obey," such objections were rarely decisive. Thus Rice and the Catholic Radical Alliance were simultaneously immunized from the kinds of ecclesiastical embroilments encountered by the Catholic Worker Movement, and kept under close (if sympathetic) scrutiny.

Although Dorothy Day left communism behind her when she converted to Catholicism, she continued to show sympathy toward her former comrades-in-arms and to defend their right to be heard.[71] Rice, by way of contrast, evolved into an outspoken anticommunist, even when the nation began to look more favorably on the Soviet Union as an ally against Hitler.

Dorothy in 1939 stated that there was "too much agitation about Communism in trade union ranks,"[72] and in the 1940s and 50s would speak up for communists caught in the purges of that era — purges that Rice would have an important hand in fomenting. *The Catholic Worker* ran an article in 1936 entitled "Why I Like the Communist."[73] Although anticommunism was indeed important to some of the early adherents of the Catholic Worker Movement in New York, many of them seem to have split off for that very reason in order to found the ACTU. But in Pittsburgh, as noted earlier, Rice was the founder of the ACTU chapter in 1938 and the host of the Actists' national convention in Pittsburgh in 1941. Thus it was that the early stance of the CRA, which was quite close to Dorothy Day's, came to be modified to the point of becoming nearly unrecognizeable.

An early CRA flier announced, much as Rice had in his radio program, "we are not Red-baiters," and went on to insist that although Catholics must hate the ideology of communism, they must also love the communist. But it was not long until Rice and the ACTU became preoccupied with rooting communist influence out of organized labor in the United States.[74] By the late 1940s, Rice and the ACTU would be leading the charge against some of those whom Dorothy Day and the Catholic Worker Movement regarded as the victims of unjust persecution. This divergence, which never resulted in a personal split between Day and Rice, was only beginning to become evident in the prewar era.

If Day and Rice and their respective organizations differed on the treatment of communists, a still more dramatic divergence lay in their reactions to the approach of war. Dorothy Day and the Catholic Worker Movement began with a pacifist approach in the early 1930s and remained adamantine in their opposition to U.S. entry into World War II, even after the bombing of Pearl Harbor. Although Rice and many in the CRA started out with an apparently pacifist orientation, they would swing over to the side of interventionism long before the Japanese attack.

Back in its first summer of activism, at a rally staged by the Popular Front to advocate U.S. intervention into the Spanish Civil War on the side of the Loyalist forces, the CRA had staged a counterdemonstration. A flier distributed at that demonstration contained the following paragraph aimed at the pro-war sentiment of the Popular Front:

> Once again we are called upon to rally around Democracy, to make the world safe for Democracy. . . . Tonight you will hear the same old clap-trap that pushed the U.S. into the last world war. War mongering about "returned heroes," "Comrades in arms," "Cigarettes for the boys in the trenches." The same old baloney, but this time our "peace loving" brethren of the Popular Front are behind it.[75]

But it would later become clear that the Rice and the CRA debunking of prowar "claptrap" was not a consistent position, and that it had been largely motivated by the sectarian nature of the conflict in Spain, where the Catholic Church was solidly on the side of the forces seeking to overthrow the Loyalists.

In another early statement, the CRA explained in general terms its position on war:

> We are unalterably opposed to unjust wars, profiteering wars of aggression. In accordance with Catholic teaching we do admit the possibility of a just war, though we can't see how such a war would be probable under the present setup. All reasonable men will agree that certain things are worth fighting for.[76]

Thus was a generally antiwar position modified and equipped with an escape clause, unlike the pacifism of Dorothy Day.

Chief among the causes that seem to have precipitated the about-face of Rice and the CRA on the issue of war were their attraction to Roosevelt and his internationalist stance, information about the persecution of Catholics in Hitler's Germany, and outrage at the Ribbentrop Pact leading to Germany and the Soviet Union cooperation in the invasion and the partition of Poland.

As was true of much of the labor movement, Rice and the CRA by the second term of the New Deal had come to see Roosevelt as the chief protector and promoter of the causes that were dear to them. Now Roosevelt was locked in a struggle with tie forces of isolationism, which were usually on the other side of labor and other domestic issues as well. It made sense to support Roosevelt, at least in his policy of giving to the Allied cause all the help possible, short of actually going to war.

Then the German expatriate, Rev. A. H. Reinhold, showed up at CRA meetings, and when Rice expressed anti-interventionist feelings, Reinhold in Rice's recollection "exploded at me, shot me down" with information about what the Nazis were doing to Jews and Catholics in Germany.[77] Although some pacifists within the CRA continued to believe that such persecutions would not be solved by recourse to war, most joined Rice in favoring American intervention thereafter.

Finally there came the shock of the temporary alliance between Germany and the Soviet Union as Poland was attacked, conquered, and partitioned. Rice watched with rising incredulity and disdain as communists in the United States did a flip-flop from favoring intervention against Germany, to a neutralist position during the temporary accord, and back again to interventionism when the accord collapsed and Hitler invaded the Soviet Union. The servile behavior of American communists in toeing the Stalin line throughout these about faces would inform and heighten Rice's anti-communism for years to come. (He never seems to have admitted that he did the inverse flip-flop himself, opposing intervention to aid Spanish Loyalists who were being overthrown by allies of the church, but favoring intervention against the Nazis who were persecuting Catholics.)

At any rate, Rice had now come down solidly on the side of U.S. intervention against Hitler. He became a member of the Committee to Defend America by Aiding the Allies, where he was welcomed for the first time by members of the liberal wing of the Pittsburgh industrial elite. They were delighted to have a representative of Catholics, Irish and unions added to their number, because those groups had heretofore displayed little enthusiasm for going to war on the side of the British.

But Rice did not stop at endorsing the war against Germany as a just war in Catholic doctrine. When Germany invaded the U.S.S.R., he combined his prowar and anticommunist sentiments in the following broadcast message:

I am sure that Germany will beat Russia, and I am all for it. But I want the Nazis to take a long, long time about doing it, and it will be a grand thing for the world if they knock themselves out in the process. This may sound like bloodthirsty talk coming from a clergyman . . . it's a question of preferring the lesser of two evils.[78]

Clearly, Rice had come quite a way from his earlier antiwar sentiments and from his diffident support for the notion of a just war, to say nothing of the Christian injunction to love one's enemies!

Meantime, *The Catholic Worker* continued its total opposition to war, even after the Japanese attack on Pearl Harbor. In so doing, it created a storm of dissent within the Catholic Worker Movement,[79] experienced a 50 percent decline in its newspaper sales (the CRA was among the groups that stopped selling it at this time, although for Rice the reason was economic rather than ideological),[80] watched 80 percent of its young men "betray their pacifism,"[81] and was evicted, because of its antiwar stance, from its store in Harlem.[82] During the war, fifteen of its thirty houses of hospitality would close.[83]

In Pittsburgh, the House of Hospitality remained open during the war, but not altogether intact. A number of members of the CRA had had enough of the direction in which Rice was leading the organization: a large, impersonal institution, preoccupation with the communist menace, and now an abandonment of the pacifist principles of Dorothy Day. As early as March 1940, an account in the *Pittsburgh Catholic* mentioned talk within the CRA of forming a "real" Catholic Worker House of Hospitality,[84] and a year later the announcement was made that the St. Francis House of Hospitality would soon open on the South Side.[85] Led by Lawrence Sullivan, CRA members who felt that Rice's organization had ceased to be a part of the Catholic Worker Movement had parted company with Rice and the CRA.

If the approach of American involvement in World War II had caused a schism in the Catholic Radical Alliance, the actual entry of the United States into that war brought about the ultimate dissolution of the organization. Most of the young men in the alliance would soon be drafted, if they had not already enlisted. The leather-faced men in the soup line at the House of Hospitality would enlist too, some of them, or find wartime jobs vacated by others. Labor-management strife would lessen, as the wheels of wartime production began to turn furiously, bringing enormous profits to industrialists and much more stable employment to their workers. The world of 1942 was a grim one, as had been the world of 1934 when Rice left the seminary, but it was very different from the world that had produced the CRA. When the fighting ceased and the troops came back home, the world would have changed even more. The Catholic Worker Movement would perdure, but the Catholic Radical Alliance of Pittsburgh would not emerge again from its ashes.

In later years, looking back on the brief history of the CRA in Pittsburgh and his own leading role in the movement, Rice would experience both regret and satisfaction. He wished he had been more consistent in following the lead of Dorothy Day, particularly in her downplaying of anticommunism and in her unswerving opposition to warfare. He was embarrassed by some of the more extreme statements he had made in the heat of the interventionist debate. But for the rest, Rice continued to rejoice in his early activism, and to insist that he and the movement had been, as he had proclaimed on KDKA, "really radical."

This insistent claim of Rice's, nearly a half-century after the fact, is no more persuasive today than it was then. In the 1930s, when secular radicals ranging from communists to socialists and from the LaFollettes of Wisconsin to Sinclair of California were actively working for measures to overthrow capitalism and transform American society, the Catholic Radical Alliance must have appeared to them a somewhat silly group of pseudoradicals out to subvert the Left by co-opting its symbols and its programs, only to use them to promote the objectives of the conservative power structure.

The title of the alliance was no doubt quite a useful ploy for attracting public attention — at which Rice was already displaying great adeptness. And he could argue plausibly enough that he had semantics on his side: the popes' proposal of reinstituting the medieval guild would indeed have gone "to the roots" of capitalistic society, if anyone had taken the idea seriously. But despite early lectures espousing this alternative, neither Rice nor any other CRA members seems to have worked for it in practice. Thus, although the use of the term "radical" in the context of the 1930s was perfectly serviceable, the irony is that Rice seems to have defended the title so often that he came to believe it was an accurate description of himself and his organization.

Let us try to get a cleaner fix on political reality and Rice's activism in the 1930s by bypassing for now the term "radical." (Webster's has it meaning anything from "favoring basic change" to conservative European political parties, and teenagers use it to describe skateboards that are especially "cool.") Instead, I turn to three other rather more delimited political terms: "revolutionary," "rebel," and "reformer."[86]

The revolutionary party or individual is one who wishes to alter basically a government in power and the principles by which society is organized, in line with a fundamental theory proposing a new vision of society. Such change frequently implies the use of violence to overthrow existing power holders and to undermine their power bases. Because their goals cannot possibly be accommodated by the present regime or social system, revolutionaries find that system irredeemable and look forward to its demise. Present evils of the system should sometimes by tolerated until they grow so bad and create so much distress that the opportunity for revolutionary action is presented. Revolutionaries are pessimistic about the present system, but they are optimistic in believing that a new society can be achieved. Thus their loyalty and optimism are directed to a future that has not yet begun. France in 1789 or China in 1949 are commonly cited as examples of revolutionary eras.

The rebel, like the revolutionary, is one who uses illegal and perhaps violent means — but for rather different ends. Not seeking to remake society in any fundamental way, the rebel wants to alter the conduct of a regime or perhaps the regime itself, to satisfy certain specific demands. Rebels oppose the current behavior of government officials, but they are more optimistic than are revolutionaries that their demands could be satisfied by those officials, if they so chose. Indeed, rebels' demands are often carefully crafted to be within the power of the government as constituted. Civil disobedience may be violent, or may invite a violent response from a government, with the hope of thereby creating more support for rebellion. If the latter approach is used, it is necessary that the rebels' illegal behavior be punished by arrest and incarceration or other repressive official response. Once their demands are met, rebels would typically be content to allow the rest of society to continue pretty much on its way. The American revolution of 1776 can be cited as a rebellion that led to a new nation, which then largely imitated the mother country in organizing itself. Rebellious movements within the United States include the Whiskey Rebellion, the Bonus March, the labor movement prior to the New Deal, and the civil rights and antiwar movements of the 1960s.

Reformers, also wishing to alter the conduct of a regime or certain of its policies, choose not to do so by violent or illegal means. Instead, they opt to change a regime or its policies by working "within the system" — often because they feel that they either have or can obtain the necessary resources (access, money, votes, etc.) to bring about the desired change without breaking the law. Sometimes reformers work quietly behind the scenes, using the access to decision-makers they already have; at other times they may be obliged to go public with their causes in order to enlist support. But illegal actions, taken in public, would generally be counterproductive to reformer's tactics. Both the optimism and the loyalty of reformers attach to the present order of society, which they seek to reform in order to improve it and ensure its continuation. The Progressive movement of the early twentieth century along with recent drives for the Equal Rights Amendment, environmental protection, and consumer safety are a few examples of reform movements.

To return now to the term "radical," I would suggest that it can most plausibly be attached to revolutionaries. With some stretching, it might also be applied to rebels. But it hardly applies with much meaning at all to reformers. Were Rice and his fellow Catholic "radicals" best described as revolutionaries, rebels, or reformers?

Let us first look at the Catholic Worker Movement from which Rice drew much of his inspiration. In its personalist philosophy and its insistence on carrying literal interpretation of the Sermon on the Mount into social action, were indeed the makings of a revolutionary movement. Although the Catholic Workers did not take direct aim at economic or political institutions, preferring instead to work for the conversion of individuals, one at a time, still the consciousness they sought to inculcate was so fundamentally at odds with the acquisitive ethos of contemporaneous capitalism that they had the potential to undermine the legitimacy of capitalism — if only large numbers of Americans had been converted to their brand of New Testament perfectionism. This potential was a limited one, however, because it depended upon a willingness to adhere to a very demanding standard of personal conduct, which only a few persons (not including Rice) have ever been inclined to do. Even this limited revolutionary potential was less than clear during Depression days, when a rich variety of religious, social, and political movements shared the same turf and the same outrage at capitalism, as they proposed alternatives. It was with the advent of World War II and the Catholic Worker Movement's continued resistance to military service that its radical nature became clearer.

But by this time Rice (and about half the movement nationwide) in effect parted company with the Catholic Workers, after having modified most of their principles of personalism nearly out of existence. More importantly to Rice's own involvement, the personalism of the Catholic Workers was not simply a theory to be embraced intellectually or an ethos to which a romantic attachment would suffice. The Catholic Workers insisted on a day-by-day practice not only of voluntary poverty but of a self-emptying love for others that alone could make Maurin's notion of houses of hospitality work as intended. Rice never chose this degree of commitment, even when he resided at the Pittsburgh House of Hospitality. He lived as comfortably as he reasonably could; he had an ego of considerable proportions, which the staff had to deal with; and he abandoned some of the practices of personalism so readily that one wonders if he understood them in the first place. And all this was in place before going his own way on the question of communists or the advent of World War II.

The plain fact, then, is that Rice and the Catholic Radical Alliance, as distinct from the Catholic Workers, were not revolutionaries: they did not have or certainly did not follow any revolutionary theory. It is one thing to attack the failings of a system — capitalism in the Depression was an easy target — but quite another to advocate an alternative system and to have a plan of how to get from the present system to the next. One looks in vain through the literature of the CRA to find such a sense of direction.

Nor were Rice and his followers rebels. The actions that they took — marching on picket lines, other forms of labor activism, and prolabor, anticommunist advocacy in various public forums — were perfectly legal at the time and would even come to enjoy the sanction of the federal government.

Rather than revolutionaries or even rebels, then, Rice and his followers were liberal reformers who worked for certain modifications of contemporary capitalism along the lines of Msgr. John A. Ryan, the Catholic bishops, and the CIO. But the goal of Ryan, the bishops, and the CIO was never to overthrow capitalism or remake the fabric of American society. They endeavored instead to incorporate certain limited economic reforms into contemporaneous capitalism, in order to humanize it and restore it to health.

Ryan's *Reconstruction of the Social Order*, issued in 1919 in the name of the U.S. Catholic bishops, clearly was a reformist charter. Using the concept of distributive justice, it called for such legislative initiatives as a minimum wage, the eight-hour workday, protection of women and child workers, collective bargaining, unemployment compensation, social security, and a progressive income tax. Such reforms were of course significant ones, and not to be realized without a struggle. But they were hardly revolutionary in the mold of the Bolshevist revolution in Russia or other socialist initiatives of the day. Indeed the very title of the bishops' letter was hyperbolic: the letter advocated remodeling U.S. society, not building it anew.

Viewed as reform efforts, the activism of Rice and his followers is quite consistent, and in the end quite effective within its own parameters. By the 1940s Rice and the majority of his followers jumped aboard the bandwagon of Franklin Delano Roosevelt, jettisoning in the process whatever radical demands they may have once had that did not fit comfortably within the contours of the New Deal. Even if they had once entertained radical notions of implementing guilds in America, they were now prepared to act as staunch advocates of the New Deal and its erection of the modern welfare state.

Thus Rice was not, at this stage in his life, either a secular or a Christian revolutionary or rebel. He was instead a liberal reformer and a priest who got into social issues in order to advance the cause of his church. To describe his activism with the term "radical" would be to paint it in false, misleading colors. It is unfortunate that he has continued to do so.

This is not, however, to say that the contributions of Rice and the Catholic Radical Alliance were insubstantial. They clearly advanced the cause of the CIO and unionism generally in western Pennsylvania, at a time when unions needed all the help they could get. In an age of anti-Semitism and second-class citizenship for blacks, they began to build bridges between gentiles and Jews, blacks and whites. They put food into empty stomachs, clothing onto shivering backs, and gave a night's rest to the homeless street people of their day. Revolutionaries, by transforming society, might have been seeking to remove the causes of these forms of human suffering. Rice and the CRA chose instead to treat symptoms, to relieve the pain. And this they did with great effectiveness. They thus incurred a debt of gratitude not only from the men in their soup line, but from all those who honor the tradition of kindness to the less fortunate.

THREE

Wartime Patriot

DURING WORLD WAR II, Rice's earlier attraction to Franklin D. Roosevelt and the New Deal would become fired with patriotic emotions aroused by the war, alloyed by his gaining a prestigious and remunerative position in the federal government, and steel-hardened when he discovered how useful his anticommunism could be both to allies in the labor movement and to government agencies. World War II was the blast furnace in which Rice was changed from the liberal reformer (not to mention "radical") he had been when he began into a superpatriot.

Numerous facets of Rice's development during the war years deserve our attention, including his career as a radio broadcaster, his years as the "rent czar" of western Pennsylvania, his work as an arbitrator of management-labor disputes, and his clandestine role as informant to the FBI — all of these against the backdrop of his continuing presence at the House of Hospitality. Because these several developments defy any attempt at chronological integration, I will treat each of them separately, beginning with Rice's burgeoning career on the airwaves.

Rice's chief outlet during the early war years was his broadcast slot on WWSW at 9:45–10:00 every Sunday evening — right before the news, hence with a sizeable audience. Here it became clear that he had what was known as a "radio personality" — combining an attention-grabbing voice with an instinct for coming right to the point, driving it firmly home, and leaving listeners in the desired frame of mind, whether informed or intrigued, soothed or out-

70

raged. Such personalities would tend to become fond memories with the advent of television after the war, and its emphasis on the bland, but Rice was one of the truly gifted radio artists of the 1940s.

Each week's installment would begin with the standard appeal for the House of Hospitality, where there was even greater need during the war years than there had been during the Depression. Rice and others had expected that the wartime absorption of excess labor would remove the House of Hospitality's raison d'être,[1]but just the opposite proved to be the case as the unemployed residents and guests were replaced by the unemployable. Rather than the young, able-bodied men of Depression days, the House of Hospitality now had to serve the very aged, sick and crippled — due to the curtailment of programs maintained by charitable institutions and overcrowding at hospitals and other custodial institutions run by the city, county, and state.[2] Thus, although the absolute numbers of guests declined, the total amount of care they required increased. In face of these needs, unfortunately, the available pool of staff members was shrinking. Again and again Rice would tell his listeners that food, though more abundant, was much more expensive, that the House of Hospitality had no rich benefactors,[3] and that various festive occasions previously celebrated at the house had to be canceled for the duration of the war.[4]

Rice made it a matter of conscious principle not to imitate radio gospelers who unendingly asked their listeners for sums of money, but he did appeal for funding for the House of Hospitality and every so often he offered religious medals to any of his listeners who would send in their names and addresses. His purpose in doing this was not apparently to make money (no fee was charged) but to satisfy himself that there was an audience out there, aside from those who called in to complain to the station about his talks.[5]

Then Rice would launch into his message for the evening. Officially, once he became a federal govenment employee, he was "Hatched" — forbidden to engage in various forms of political partisanship. But the practical standards of enforcement seem to have been that so long as he did not get into whether the Democrats or the Republicans should have political power (and Rice did avoid this), then he could advocate any use of political power, so long as it was not in any way un-American. Rice's messages in this era were not likely to fall under these strictures, but many of them were blatantly political.

Probably the commonest of all his themes, aside from religious ones, was support for the Allied war effort. Particularly in 1942 and 1943, Rice appealed to his listeners for patriotism and sacrifice, warning that the Allies could very well lose the war.[6] He urged his listeners to put more effort into singing the Star-Spangled Banner.[7] He assured American mothers that the Armed Forces were turning their boys into men, not bums.[8] He exhorted listeners to double their contributions to the War Fund,[9] and expressed dismay that of a boxing match crowd of fifteen thousand to whom he had appealed for donations of blood for the Armed Forces, only six hundred had pledged a pint.[10] He had special praise for a father of seven who received a draft notice just shy of his thirtieth birthday, and showed up for induction even though he probably could have gotten a deferment.[11] (One wonders whether some of Rice's non-celibate listeners entertained the suspicion that fighting a war might have looked less difficult to the papa than the prospect of raising the seven children he had sired.) One of Rice's more stirring accounts was of the day he marched to Union Station with a group of selectees.[12] Yet that was as close as Rice himself came to actually serving in the war. He explained later that although his brother Pat enlisted as a chaplain, Bishop Boyle refused to allow the younger Father Rice to do the same.[13]

Any pacifist tendencies or debunking of past war efforts that he might once have shared with Pettigrew, Dorothy Day, or early CRA members had vanished. He found "absolutely no jurisdiction in the Catholic religion for pacifism."[14] He regretted that the United States had been so torpid prior to entering World War II that it took a "stab in the back" to awaken the country.[15] He reasoned that the mistake the nation had made in World War I, which must not be repeated this time, was a failure to "carry through."[16] Although warmly praising Dorothy Day on one of her visits to Pittsburgh, he noted his disagreement with her on the issue of pacifism.[17]

As he rehashed news from the front each week, he would often excoriate military actions and treatment of prisoners by the other side, but found Allied attacks, even when they affected civilian populations, regrettable but necessary. Thus he bitterly decried the Japanese attack on Pearl Harbor each year as its December 7 anniversary approached,[18] and joined with the United States Catholic bishops in urging Catholics to use the Feast of the Immaculate Conception (December 8) to pray for victory over the Japanese.[19] He repeatedly expressed concern for death rates among United States military personnel held prisoner by the

Japanese,[20] for the Church and people in Poland under Hitler (and later under Stalin)[21] and for the Vatican when it was surrounded by Nazi forces.[22] His first mention of Nazi concentration and extermination camps came in April 1945: "We are all of us terribly shocked over the news from Germany: the revelation of widespread barbarity and cruelty to the slave laborers, to prisoners of war and above all to Jews."[23] He went on to add: "These are conditions that we knew existed," but there is scant evidence for that statement in any of his previous broadcasts.

By way of contrast, when the Allies bombed Rome (sparing the Vatican), it was regrettable but unavoidable.[24] He defended General George Patton against domestic "bleeding hearts," and offered the opinion that a "shellacking" of Berlin would be necessary.[25] The Allied shelling of the historic Benedictine monastery at Monte Cassino was "unfortunate," but there was some solace in the fact that it had been occupied of late not by monks but by an anticlerical government.[26] When civilian targets in Cologne and Aachen were hit, and when Dresden was subjected to saturation bombing by Americans that caused thousands of civilians to perish in huge firestorms, it was Hitler's fault.[27] Even when A-bombs were dropped on Hiroshima and Nagasaki, Rice, although delivering an eloquent prayer for the children of the nuclear age, did not condemn or in any way criticize the United States for developing or using these fearsome new weapons.[28]

If this double standard for judging Allied and Axis wartime actions seemed to render Rice little more than a propagandist screeching from the sidelines and forgetful of the common humanity that united all the warring nations, there were at least some messages that seemed to play on the latter theme. Thus Rice warned his listeners against hating Nazis or Japanese.[29] When Japanese-American citizens were removed from their homes and their work and herded into concentration camps under Roosevelt's orders, with the eventual approval of the Supreme Court, Rice disapproved.[30] He likewise kept up his attacks on anti-Semitism[31] and various manifestations of racial hatred and prejudice in the United States.[32]

As the end of the war approached, Rice rook a harsh stance toward Germany and Japan, along with a moderate and pragmatic approach toward U.S. allies, notably the Soviet Union. Of the Germans he said: "They have brought two major cataclysms upon the world. It is only the better part of wisdom to draw their fangs."[33]

Generally, Rice approved of the Potsdam and other pacts outlining the postwar arrangements for power in Europe.[34] He also pleaded for American understanding toward its wartime ally, Great Britain,[35] although repeatedly defending De Valera's policy not to involve Ireland in the conflict on the side of the British.[36]

But of all these pleas for understanding, the most intriguing — and perhaps, in light of the anti-communist crusade Rice was soon to launch, the most downright puzzling — was his accomodating view toward the U.S.S.R. and its postwar needs and desires. After reviewing in relatively sympathetic terms the Russian revolution and the success of socialism since revolutionary times, Rice concluded:

> As Americans what does Russia mean to us today? Very few of us consider the problem calmly. We are likely to get enthusiastic or hysterical one way or the other. Well, first we must consider Russia as an ally who has done a tremendous job and who has tremendous power. This ally must be given consideration. Other things being equal this ally has the right to say how things are going to be done in his immediate neighborhood. As far as is consistent with decency and international obligations he must be allowed to call the turn with regard to the countries around him. He must be allowed a major influence in the treatment of the aggressor nations. I say allowed. That is in a way laughable. Try and stop him. But even if Russia could be stopped he has rights in that field.[37]

As Rice and his opinions were becoming familiar to many radio listeners, his had already become a household name to uncounted thousands who never bothered to tune into his broadcasts: he had become the wartime "rent czar" for much of western Pennsylvania.

Rice's involvement in housing and rental policy actually went back to the spring of 1939. Then, as war clouds were gathering over Europe, a smaller cloud but one that probably appeared just as ominous to those under it, was hovering over a section of St. Agnes parish in Pittsburgh, the neighborhood known as Soho-Gazzam. Urban renewal programs sponsored by the federal government were new to the United States then, but were about to make their debut in Pittsburgh with the construction of the Terrace Village project in Soho-Gazzam. Dilapidated housing would be torn down to make way for new apartments.

Dilapidation, like beauty, is often in the eye of the beholder. And although there was a generalized enthusiasm for renewal, there was also fierce opposition among the owners and renters of the housing slated to fall before the federal bulldozer. Tenants were frightened at the prospect of seeking housing elsewhere at a time of shortage; owners found the prices they were being offered for their property inadequate to buy others of comparable quality, and all resented the stigma of "slum" that the Pittsburgh Housing Authority seemed to be applying to their neighborhood. It was an opening skirmish in the sort of war that would be fought out in various American cities for generations to come.

A group of homeowners and tenants decided to enlist the clergy in their battle. Among clergymen they approached was the charismatic young curate at St. Agnes who had been making a name for himself on various picket lines. Their demand, they told Rice, was quite simple: stop the bulldozers, scrap the project, and have the government leave them and their families in peace.[38] In Rice they found both a sympathetic listener and one quick to leap into action. Somewhat later the group would realize that although Rice was able to translate their discontent into action, he also ended up greatly modifying their original demands in the process.

A mass meeting was scheduled for February 21, 1939, and attended by over five hundred persons, "protesting the inhuman actions of the City of Pittsburgh Housing Authority." Rice was the first speaker, and exhibited his flamboyant style when he charged that the housing authority was guilty of nothing less than an assault on the Christian family and on private property when it in effect forced residents to move from their present homes into apartments.[39]

From the meeting emerged an ad hoc organization, the Soho and Gazzam Home Owners and Tenants Protective Organization (SGHOTPA). Rice subsequently represented SGHOTPA in various hearings held by the city, and it was here that the original demand for the abandonment of the project began to be watered down. Rice now departed from his original incendiary charges and argued merely that the housing authority had used high-handed tactics in inducing some owners to sell, had not conducted satisfactory studies to determine whether the relocation of departing residents was working satisfactorily, and had paid insufficient prices to home owners. Still, in a statement on March 15, Rice continued to enunciate the "unshakeable demand" that all tenants be assured of homes to replace their present ones.[40]

An appearance by Rice before the Pittsburgh Housing Authority produced little change, except perhaps in the blood pressure of the participants. An extremely circumspect letter from the authority's head, Bryn Hovde, was answered with the charge that SGHOTPA was being insulted and threatened, and its members called "racketeers engaged in a shakedown."[41] No grounds for such a retort appear in Hovde's letter, but Rice had in fact decided that the real object of his intervention would be not to stop the project or to secure guarantees of equity for the displaced tenants, but to get better prices for the homeowners.[42]

By April, the issue had been decided: the Terrace Village project would go ahead, but owners would be paid better prices — about a thousand dollars more on the average. Thus the owners, most of whom were white, got a tangible benefit from Rice's intervention; the tenants, most of whom were black, did not. On October 12, 1940 Franklin Roosevelt came to Pittsburgh to officiate at the opening of Terrace Village — and to campaign for reelection. Rice was on the platform.

The episode would also prove to have some extremely interesting long-term consequences for Rice. His erstwhile opponent, Bryn Hovde, would become both a fast friend and a colleague with whom Rice collaborated to oppose the Davis Act on federal housing later that same year, and to broadcast information about the Defense Housing Program in 1941.[43] Another principal, Al Wilner (whom Rice already knew from the Heinz strike), would provide Rice with entree to the Fair Rent Committee two years later, which in turn would lead to Rice's tenure as rent czar.

The year 1941, with the approach of World War II and the resultant heating up of the American economy, led to multiple problems with inflation, of which rental increases were one of the most notable. A first attempt was made to deal with the problem on a voluntary basis, by setting up a Fair Rent Committee under the Pittsburgh Defense Council. This panel of ten volunteer members, to be drawn from real estate, labor, and other interest groups, was charged with studying rents in the area and establishing a review process for particular cases where tenants complained of unfair increases. The committee, however, was to have no power to enforce its recommendations; it could only make appeals to public and patriotic sentiment against wartime profiteering.

In September, as the panel was being selected, Al Wilner recommended Rice to Mayor Scully as someone who had been active on housing issues since 1939. Rice was appointed to the committee, and it was not long before he emerged as its head. George E. Evans was the original chairman, but by October was succeeded by

Morris Zimmerman. Zimmerman in turn resigned the following February, clearing the way for Rice to accede to the chairmanship.[44]

The committee's workload proved to be a heavy one: it heard over four thousand cases at its weekly meetings between October 1941 and May 1942. A major reason for the busy schedule was that Rice went public with appeals to renters bring their problems to the committee. One statement he authored was entitled "Stop Rent Profiteering," and promised: "No rents should be raised unless improvements have been made, or unless the landlord can prove additional expense. We can stop the landlord from evicting you if he has raised your rent unfairly."[45] The last statement would appear to be inaccurate in view of the nonbinding nature of the committee's recommendations.

But Rice from the outset had believed that voluntary compliance with the committee's recommendations would not be sufficient, and had beseiged OPA in Washington with requests to invoke federal rent control in Pittsburgh as it had done elsewhere. In 1942 he cued his powers of persuasion to May 1, when most rent leases traditionally expired, urging that unless mandatory rent control was invoked by that date there would be a spree of rent profiteering. Many landlords had already notified tenants that rents would be going up on that date, war or no war and Fair Rent Committee or no Fair Rent Committee. Some tenants had already signed new leases at higher rents; some wished to appeal to the Fair Rent Committee, but hesitated for fear of being evicted in reprisal.

Rice responded to these concerns with a public interest broadcast on WJAS on March 16, in which he dangled before recalcitrant landlords the stick of rent control, urging instead the carrot of cooperation with the Fair Rent Committee:

> If we succeed in keeping the situation under control, there will be no necessity for invoking the "Rent Sections of the Emergency Price Control Act." This "Price Control Act" has teeth in it. It can override landlords who evade its provisions. It will be better all around if we can avoid the "Price Control Act." However, you may be assured that if the committee ever becomes convinced that Act is necessary we will not hesitate to ask Washington to invoke the Act.[46]

It was of course somewhat disingenuous of Rice to strike the pose of believing that application of the act would be unfortunate when he had been asking Washington for exactly that, but his and the Fair Rent Committee's stance became a bit clearer in his next broadcast twelve days later: " . . . two days ago the Fair Rent Committee split 50/50 on whether or not to call for that law."[47] Finally, on April 29, just short of the appointed date, the OPA acceded to Rice's (and presumably now the committee's) wishes and invoked rent control for Pittsburgh.

This action meant that the Fair Rent Committee would be superseded by an office of the Rent Control Division of the OPA, with full powers to freeze and regulate rents as opposed to merely "jawboning" with landlords. It meant that the area to be so regulated would expand from the one-county environs of Pittsburgh to a nine-county area of southwestern Pennsylvania, and later up to as many as twenty counties. And of course it meant the selection of some qualified individual to head the entire operation, a person to be known in popular parlance as the "Rent Czar."

What ensued was a furious campaign between those in favor of and those opposed to Rice's becoming rent czar. In Rice's later recollections, someone else originated the idea, and he was himself at first cool to it — until he found out some local realtors and other powers-that-be did not want him to land the job.[48]

Be that as it may, it is clear that any initial period of hesitation must have been quite brief. As early as June 1, barely a month after the OPA invocation of rent controls, a letter from Rice to Senator Guffey indicated an ongoing campaign when it said that Rice had had the inside track to the job until "local reactionaries" objected to his appointment in view of his friendship with labor and his clerical status.[49]

In the course of the campaign a memo, unsigned and undated but looking very much like memoranda prepared by Rice's typist John W. Rosemonde, alleged among the reasons in favor of Rice's selection for the post his work at the House of Hospitality, his public opposition to communism, his support for U.S. entry into the war prior to Pearl Harbor, his leadership in the Soho-Gazzam affair (circumspectly described as bargaining over prices, rather than opposition to a federal housing project), support by most realtors on the Fair Rent Committee and by various officials, and "the enthusiastic support of his bishop, Hugh C. Boyle." Dismissed as mere sorehead opponents were Harry Noah, the government purchasing agent in the Soho-Gazzam affair, and Irwin D. Wolf of Kaufmann's Department Store where Rice had supported a strike. Likewise dismissed were the arguments that Rice was too close to labor ("whom have we left then") and that he was a priest (covert anticlericalism). Not many stones were left unturned in this vigorous memorandum, which most likely had been authored by Rice himself.[50]

The allegation of Bishop Boyle's support was overstated, to say the least. In fact one of the several alternative candidates in the running was Boyle's own nephew and namesake, Hugh C. Boyle. And the Bishop, who had supported or at least not interfered with Rice on everything else, had grave reservations about the appropriateness of this position for one of his priests. He called Rice in and suggested that his pursuit of the high-paying position ($6,500 per year, as opposed to the $30 per month Rice was then earning) had the appearance of avarice. Rice responded that he had given freely of volunteer time on rent issues already, and that other Catholic priests had been recruited to serve in a variety of New Deal agencies. Then he went straight for the jugular and protested, "Your Excellency, the local opposition has done everything possible to stop me — they even propose your own nephew!" Boyle, Rice remembered later, turned a variety of colors and then concluded, "Well, I won't do their dirty work for them." If Boyle did not become an "enthusiastic supporter" of Rice's nomination, at least he ceased to be an opponent.[51]

Although Rice had demonstrated his ability at infighting with memos, a skill necessary to bureaucrats, other hurdles remained. A report in the *Bulletin Index* claimed that he failed his Civil Service exam. Rice later denied this and stated that he had never taken the exam. At any rate, Rice went to Washington to appeal to the Civil Service Commission.[52] Meanwhile, a letter on June 9 from Civil Service Recruiter W. B. Graves to National Rent Executive A. E. Casgrain recommended Dr. Joseph Loucheim for Pittsburgh rent director, and reiterated an earlier conclusion that "Father Rice does not appear well qualified and we had hoped that the laymen in his church would be successful in calling him off."[53] (Another highly qualified candidate who had been recruited to seek the position, Frank C. McLaughlin, declined to oppose Rice.)[54] Casgrain was convinced that Rice was an inappropriate choice; he was prepared to resign if Rice were selected for the post — which in fact he did.[55] Another civil servant threatening resignation (although he later backed down) was the head of the Civil Service in Philadelphia, a Mr. Hetzell.[56]

On the other hand, a great deal of political muscle was being applied on Rice's side of the contest. On the same day Graves was telling Casgrain that Rice was unqualified, Senator Guffey wrote to

Casgrain that Rice's committee "was the most successful Fair Rent Committee in the United States."[57] But it was probably a strongly-worded telegram from CIO President Phil Murray to OPA head Leon Henderson that carried the day for Rice. Henderson replied with alacrity that Rice would indeed be appointed to the post, but asked Murray to hold this information "in confidence" until the required 60-day period would have elapsed from the declaration of Rent Control in Pittsburgh.[58]

But even that date passed without the anticipated appointment. Daniel Brooks was named acting rent director on July 1, and a rent freeze was decreed, retroactive to March 1.[59] At length, after Murray kept up the pressure at the OPA, and presumably after all internal opposition to Rice had been silenced or eliminated (Hetzell remained, Casgrain departed), Rice was appointed rent director for Pittsburgh on August 3, 1942. He crowed victoriously, "I'm like a fighter who was knocked out of the [ring], broke both hands and came back to win by a knockout."[60] One week later, Rice wrote to Murray asking if he could find employment for Frank C. McLaughlin — whether as part of a prearranged deal or a thoughtful reward for McLaughlin's staying out of the rent director race.[61] At the same time, Daniel Brooks was packing his bags to go to Philadelphia where he was to become chief attorney for the OPA Rent Division. Rice was then sworn in on August 11. He had in point of fact "knocked out" quite a few opponents.

On the surface, Rice's tenure as wartime rent czar appears to have been the calm that followed the storm of his appointment campaign. Even this appearance of serenity, however, was belied by some fundamental and hard-fought struggles going on not far below the surface.

Rice proved to be a vigorous and competent administrator of a sizeable agency, combining a clear-cut bias in favor of tenants with enough savvy to placate most of the landlords most of the time. By one early account, the 43-person staff had handled ten thousand petitions from landlords and thirteen thousand complaints by tenants, well enough that only twenty or thirty tenant complaints went to court (the first one not until 1944), and less than a quarter of the landlords' petitions were appealed — all of this with some five hundred eviction cases to be dealt with each month.[62] It was understandable that organized labor, which was generally critical of OPA performances during the war, would applaud Rice's tenure in office[63] — he was, after all, a labor appointee. But Rice's administrative abilities seem to have been appreciated within the

OPA itself: when another rent control office was to be established in Brooklyn in 1943, it was Rice who was sent there to get the organization set up and running smoothly.[64]

Much of Rice's success, by his own account, seems to have come less from his own attention to the minutiae of administration than from his ability to hire qualified lieutenants and to maintain their morale and allegiance. C. Howard McPeak, an old school chum, was Rice's chief inspector and functional head at the office (he would succeed Rice in 1946). J. W. Rosemonde from the house of hospitality, who had worked for the Fair Rent Committee, was Rice's secretary and shield against a myriad of callers. Rosemonde was also one of a number of blacks who were hired by Rice in a move that raised many OPA eyebrows. (After Rice's tenure, unhappily, many of these college-educated blacks went back to operating elevators or scrubbing floors in Pittsburgh.) Rice's major contribution seems to have been defending the agency in public, and keeping staff members fully and regularly briefed on developments from above.[65]

Rent control, along with the OPA in general, needed plenty of defending. Rice's correspondence with Murray and others reflected a continual concern — eventually justified — that the program would be gutted from within at the insistence of realtor and landlord interests.[66] Locally, one of Rice's more memorable battles with realtors' interests came when one of their spokesmen charged that the rent office, in stopping evictions, was protecting among other things certain houses of ill repute. Rising to the fullest height of clerical indignation, Rice retorted, "If the gentleman says I am fostering prostitution, he is a liar!" The realtor quickly retreated.[67]

An unanticipated and not wholly unmixed benefit of Rice's rent directorship came in the personnage of Bridget Lee. Bridget had come from Galway, Ireland, to Pittsburgh where she and her husband (a childless couple) had over the years saved up their money and become the owners of over a dozen rental properties. Since her husband's death, Bridget had become the sole proprietress, and now she wanted very much to raise the rates for her renters and boarders. To that end she vigorously sought and eventually obtained Rice's presence at her table for dinner one evening. Rice says he discussed her request but told her there was nothing he could do: she had no basis for an increase. But Rice's subordinates may have placed a different interpretation on his dining with Bridget, which became a regular practice, because she was in fact granted the increases she sought. Rice later wondered what the other diners, Bridget's boarders who had just had their rents raised, must have thought of his presence![67a]

Bridget further insinuated herself into Rice's life, accompanying him and his ailing father on a trip to Ireland in 1947 and helping to defray the costs. When she died, she left a bequest of $1,000 to Rice personally, and the bulk of her estate (around $70,000) to a charitable trust to be administered by Rice. She had intended to leave the latter amount to the House of Hospitality, but at Rice's insistence allowed him discretion to use it for whatever religious or charitable purpose he saw fit.[68] This would prove extremely useful to Rice for many years to come.

Another activity in which Rice had become increasingly involved prior to World War II was that of arbitrating labor-management disputes.[69] Although this was a somewhat curious role for one who was publicly identified as an ally of labor, Rice was able to find considerable employment in arbitration; in some local businesses he was even written into labor-management contracts as the arbiter of any disputes that might arise. His interest in expanding this sideline is evidenced by his accepting a position on the American Arbitration Association in April 1941, and by his letter that October to Sidney Hillman at the Office of Wartime Production Management stating his desire to get onto the Defense Mediation Board.[70]

But it would be the position of rent director rather than one on the Mediation Board where Rice found wartime employment, and his case load in local arbitration dropped to only a modest fraction of its previous yearly number. It would increase again after the war in the labor struggles that ensued, and Rice would continue to take some cases until as late as 1965. His compensation for this work would typically be $50 or $100 per case in routine matters, half paid by management and half by the union. He had more success, he later said, in collecting his fees from labor than from management.[71]

The bulk of Rice's arbitration work, then and later, was done in teamster and laundry disputes. It was particularly the latter field that Rice at the time conceived to be the heart of the proletarian labor movement. This would prove to be quite a mistaken conception, for laundry proved to be a dying (no pun intended) area for labor organization. At any rate, laundry was the business where

Rice not only did the bulk of his arbitrating, but also where he engaged in some of his more memorable clashes.

One of his early allies in laundry was Amy Ballinger, a staunch and outspoken unionist whom Rice regarded as something of a proletarian hero. He had walked many picket lines with her and with Local President Sam Begler. Indeed, one of Rice's most ignominious experiences as a labor priest had occurred in nearby Coraopolis in a strike for union recognition, when word spread that the local Catholic pastor, Pat Healey, reputed as an antiunionist and a "madman," was coming down to the line. The young Rice panicked at the thought of confronting a pastor known for tyrannizing over his curates, borrowed Sam Begler's car, and circled the block until Healey had come, engaged in some pushing and shoving with Amy, and departed. Rice returned sheepishly, and apologized for having turned tail. Begler and Ballinger laughed, and consoled him: "That's all right, Father. He's known as 'one-punch Healey': he won't be back!" Thus concluded what may be the only admitted instance in which Rice passed up a fight.[72]

In 1941 a case was presented to Rice for arbitration that offered him the opportunity to strike a blow at the communist presence in laundry unions. Rice, then convinced that a historic struggle between the church and communism was being waged in American labor unions for the allegiance of the working class, and that laundry unions were to be at the very heart of that struggle, would take full advantage of his opportunity.

Amy Ballinger came to Rice to tell him that she was having difficulties with a communist woman in Local 141 at Independent Towel. The woman was Carolyn Burkhart, the daughter of Logan Burkhart, a well-known communist activist in UE Local 601. Carolyn, said Amy, had married a nice young Catholic fellow and taken him away from the church. Rice's services would be required in dealing with a case involving Carolyn Burkhart.[73]

The case presented for arbitration did not involve Burkhart's marriage or her husband's religious practice, at least not ostensibly. Instead it concerned an election for steward at Local 141, which Carolyn Burkhart had won, only to have the election declared invalid by Sam Begler. Begler had invoked his powers under the Laundry Workers International Union constitution, on the grounds that Burkhart was "unacceptable." Undeterred, Burkhart on January 13, 1941, called a meeting of members on the shop floor. Sam Begler and Amy Ballinger appeared, told local members that the meeting was illegal, declared it adjourned, and then departed. But the meeting in fact continued, and Burkhart, in the words of the later Laundry Workers record of the case, made a series of remarks exhibiting "gross disloyalty" toward the local and even the international union. As a result, she was fired by the company, and it was Burkhart's appeal of her firing that Rice was called upon to arbitrate. He upheld the company.[74]

Burkhart subsequently argued that her meeting had been held and concluded in a "completely peaceful atmosphere," that she had later been fired "without being given any reason," and that Rice's hearing on the matter had been a "scandalous, one-sided procedure, with the Company attorney and [Rice] working hand in hand."[75]

A month later, Burkhart convoked a meeting at North Side Carnegie Music Hall, attended by hundreds of people, to attack Rice's handling of the dispute. But far from suffering the attack in silence, Rice entered the meeting himself, to be greeted by the vociferous applause of his adherents. Burkhart was by his account thoroughly defeated in debate. On appeal to the international union, she was expelled from membership.[76]

Looking back on the affair from the perspective of four decades later, Rice admitted to a certain unease at his actions at that time: although Burkhart's behavior probably was a fireable offense, "I think now I might have given a different decision." By 1983 he wondered " . . . if the Lord loves me or the communists; . . . I don't know."[77]

But that sentiment would come many years later. What was clear in the early 1940s was that Rice's opposition to communist influence in American labor unions was enough to prompt him to use his trusted role as arbitrator to push communists out of positions of influence, even at the very lowest levels, and even if it involved overriding the sentiments of fair play for workers that otherwise guided the young labor priest.

Another method that Rice was already using to combat communist influence in labor was that of passing along to FBI agents information on communists or suspected communists on the labor scene, particularly but not exclusively in Pittsburgh. Rice was becoming, albeit in a relatively casual fashion, an informant.

His contacts with the FBI dated from the early days of the House of Hospitality when, as Rice later recalled, some young agents used to come in the evening for a friendly game of ping-pong. Rice would entertain them with ping-pong competition and with bits of information in which they might be interested, trying to extract information from them in turn. But apparently the agents were less forthcoming than Rice, and he felt they were not providing him with the information he would like to have on local communists.[78]

In fact, the one time in these years that Rice did obtain inside information, his injudicious use of it put him in bad odor with his source (and probably with the FBI) for years to come. This occurred when James B. Carey, the recently deposed president of UE, who allegedly worked closely with the FBI, alleged to Rice in confidence that Charles Newell, business agent of UE Local 601 in East Pittsburgh, was a communist. Rice proceeded not only to announce this fact publicly, but to cite Carey as his source. Carey subsequently denied to Newell that he had made any such statement, but was furious with Rice for having possibly blown his cover as an FBI informant.[79] Although Rice consistently supported Carey, Carey as late as 1950, when he was head of the new IUE, would refuse to have anything to do with Rice and even ordered an associate to sever any ties with Rice.[80] It stands to reason that the FBI may have been every bit as apprehensive as was Carey about giving sensitive information to Rice.

At any rate, a partial record of some of his evenings with the agents is contained in the FBI file on Rice, which he would obtain many years later. They show that Rice advised the agents that John Barry, alias Jack Rose, "used to be connected with the Communist Party" (1943), that Harold J. Ruttenberg, a close friend of Rice's, was associated "with liberal groups" (1943), that Stanley Earl Glass was a socialist rather than a communist, that Dr. John Torok had "acquired confidential, inter-office memos of the OPA" (1943), that Cominfil, the infiltration operation of the communists, had penetrated the CIO (1944), that Rev. Casimir Orlemanski was not a communist (1944), and that Lee Pressman, whom Rice would like to get out of the Steelworkers and the CIO, had communistic tendencies (1946).[81]

Is it appropriate to describe Rice as an informant? He vigorously rejects the label, arguing that he was never paid for his contacts, that many of his conversations had the effect of exculpating rather than incriminating those under discussion, and that he was telling FBI agents only what they already knew. We shall return to this question later.

What Rice did not know at the time was that the FBI was not only using him to keep tabs on various communists, but was keeping tabs on Rice himself. Thus the number of entries in Rice's dossier between 1937 and 1946, in which he gave information to the bureau, is only about half the number of entries in which information about Rice was recorded — beginning with an appearance by Hensler and himself at a Telegraphers' convention in New York City in 1937.

Rice recalls that toward the end of the war (to judge by the FBI dossier it was late in 1946), the group of young and friendly agents was moved out and replaced by others with whom he never developed the same contacts.[82] This impression is corroborated by a drop, after 1946, in the number of entries in Rice's dossier where he passed on information to the FBI.[83] But if this was the end of Rice's informal collaboration with the bureau, it did not, as will be seen in the next chapter, bring to an end his practice of delating suspected communists to the agency.

In 1945, World War II began drawing to its close, and with it this phase in Rice's life as rent czar and as the radio preacher who had helped to fuel the fires of patriotism on the home front. It might have been expected that Rice's wartime prominence would give way to a quiescent obscurity. But such an expectation could hardly have been further from the truth.

Perhaps as a curtain-opener on the postwar era of labor-management strife in Pittsburgh and the United States generally, a nasty confrontation was brewing at the Pittsburgh electric utility, Duquesne Light. This confrontation would command Rice's credentials as friend-of-labor, arbiter, and broadcaster, and would in the process catapult him into public view throughout much of 1946 in the sort of dramatic context that would etch Rice's image unmistakably into the consciousness of those Pittsburghers who had not hitherto known of him.

The Independent Association of Employees of Duquesne Light and [five] Associated Companies was, as its title suggested, affiliated neither with the CIO nor with the AFL — a fact that had been of considerable solace to the antiunion management there for some years. Now, however, the "motormen," as they were dubbed by the local press, were, like many other workers, intent on gaining substantial wage increases after the stagnant war years. Unlike many other unions, of course, the motormen by striking could inflict immediate and serious damage on the entire city.

When an impasse did in fact lead to arbitration, Rice was asked by the union's strong-willed president, George Mueller, to act as the union's arbiter on a three-arbiter panel. The arbitration fizzled, and in early February 1946 a remarkably successful shutdown was called by George Mueller. Pittsburgh stopped in its tracks, shivering in the cold and dark. Other labor leaders in Pittsburgh were fearful of the bad press for unions in general that the strike might occasion, not to mention the economic losses imminent for many of their own members. They tried to get together with Mueller to pressure him to call off the strike and submit the case instead to binding arbitration. But the balky Mueller (subsequently portrayed in the local press with mule's ears) sensed their purpose and refused even to meet with them. Meanwhile the new mayor, David Lawrence, was appealing to President Truman to invoke his powers under the recent Taft-Hartley Law to issue a back-to-work order and declare a cooling-off period. No success was forthcoming at the White House. Finally, it was Rice who was able to turn the trick: he induced Mueller to meet with the other labor leaders, after which Mueller bowed to their collective pressure and called off the strike in less than twenty-four hours.[84]

The next week, the union met and concluded that the company was being intractable in offering a settlement even less attractive than its original offer, and set midnight February 26 as the new strike deadline. In this crisis atmosphere, and in view of his familiarity with and involvement in the dispute, Rice was asked by all the major radio stations of Pittsburgh to broadcast daily developments over all their airwaves for fifteen minutes during the noon hour. He accepted.[85]

On these broadcasts, the daily drama of the battle was depicted: Lawrence appealed for arbitration; the union lowered its asking price; the company agreed to arbitration; the union remained silent.[86] On February 26, twenty-six minutes before the strike deadline, the union voted to postpone the strike one more week.[87] On March 2, it voted to go to arbitration. The city breathed a sigh of relief; Rice's broadcasts came to an end.[88]

In April the arbitration process resulted in a compromise settlement of an 18-cent-an-hour pay increase.[89] But the company was bent on phasing out one of its divisions, the construction unit, and this Mueller felt he could not allow to happen. In July another strike was voted for, then postponed, then rescheduled for September 10. Bad press for the union resulted: Mueller, who was now promising a 100 percent power stoppage, was accused of being "drunk with power."

Rice again became the "point man" for the media as the crisis resumed. Although he had generally taken the line that the company was to blame for the poor state of labor relations at Duquesne Light, he now editorialized in a broadcast on September 8:

> The people have a right to be furious about the whole business. Whichever side gives in before the strike, will deserve the deep and lasting gratitude of the people of this community. If neither side gives in, they both deserve public anger and punishment. There is no call for this controversy. It should not be. It is ridiculous that we should have to have this strike threat every few months. It is an evil thing, a wrong thing. This community deserves better from both.[90]

But neither side gave in and the strike commenced on September 10, this time to be halted almost immediately by a temporary injunction and the arrest of Mueller when the motormen violated the order. On September 21 the membership voted 1,035–309 to reject arbitration, to attend en masse the court hearing scheduled for Mueller, and by so doing to recommence the strike at 9:30 a.m. September 24.[91]

As the new deadline approached, Rice, who would later be praised in the press as the only cool head in the dispute, correctly predicted that a strike was inevitable this time. It began as scheduled: some fifteen hundred or so workers showed up at the court in what Rice later described as a mob scene organized by communists.[92] (Never in his coverage up to that time had Rice alleged communist influence on the motormen.) Mueller was sentenced to one year in prison. In front of the City-County Building one demonstrating worker, presumably angry at Rice's apparent swing away from the union, spat at him.[93]

The strike came close to paralyzing Pittsburgh, but never reached its earlier 100 percent effectiveness.[94] On October 1, after a tentative agreement had been reached in Mueller's absence and the initial fury of the demonstrating workers apparently spent, Mueller was released from jail. He promptly repudiated the tentative settlement. Rice reported public sentiment as shifting against the union. But the motormen on October 5 followed Mueller's lead and voted 635 – 362 to reject the agreement and stay out.[95]

At that point the major labor affiliations succeeded in scheduling an NLRB-sanctioned representation election in a bid to undercut Mueller's independent leadership. But in the vote taken on October 14 and announced on October 16, Mueller seemed to triumph by a wide margin over all the opposition: Independent, 958; AFL, 261; IBEW, 116; CIO, 80. On October 15, however, a membership meeting had been held from which Mueller had been ejected and at which a back-to-work vote had passed 430 – 128. Nevertheless the strike continued.[96]

On October 18, in a gambit increasingly employed against un-cooperative union leaders, Mueller was summoned to appear before the House Un-American Affairs Committee (HUAC) on charges of communism (which Mayor Lawrence went on record to denounce as unfounded).[97] This pressure, combined with some shift in rank-and-file sentiment, may have been what crushed the strike. On October 21, after a 27-day strike that had idled more than a hundred thousand workers and caused losses estimated at $300 million, union members voted 1,197 – 797 to return to work and submit the dispute to arbitration.[98]

Throughout the strike, although Rice had expressed anger at both sides, he had publicly spoken of Mueller as a solid labor leader who was following the will of his rank and file.[99] Privately, years later, he would charge that Mueller had deliberately de-ceived him several times. Perhaps because of his refusal to make Mueller the public scapegoat of the affair, or perhaps because of the communist involvement, which he admitted years later, Rice's broadcasts were all subpoenaed by HUAC — which, understan-dably, had a chilling effect at WWSW. Rice would continue to broadcast there, but would in the future incorporate much more religious content and much less political commentary into his weekly talks. Thus did his exposure to the full glare of publicity turn out to have its darker aspect as well.[100]

Meanwhile, with the end of the war and the return of those who had been fighting it, the environment in Pittsburgh and the coun-try had been undergoing deep changes, some of them obvious and others more subtle in their manifestations. For Rice, there was a whole new generation of workers coming into the labor union movement — some of them coming to seek advice and help from Pittsburgh's now famous labor priest. It was a heady time for Rice, in some ways reminiscent of the early days of the Catholic Radical Alliance.[101] Another less happy symptom of the change was evi-dent in the soup line at the House of Hospitality: younger and able-bodied men were showing up once more, some of them war veterans, some of them newly unemployed by defense industries that were receiving no new orders.[102]

As the country returned to a peacetime footing, life as rent director was becoming distinctly less satisfying. On February 1, 1946, Rent Control had itself been "evicted": it was transferred from the handsome Fulton Building, replaced there by the Veterans' Administration, and moved to shabbier headquarters. What was worse, the pressures of pent-up capitalism prepared to sweep aside controls of all sorts. As most OPA controls were being dismantled, Rice took one parting shot at his foes on this issue:

> I don't condemn the people who removed the controls, but do condemn those responsible for undermining the program — pressure groups and stupid people outside. They may have done irreparable harm.[103]

Later, Rice also mentioned that during a vacation in 1946, he was thinking ahead to the inevitable ending of his tenure in Rent Control when he wondered, "What will I do then without the big money?" His salary now stood at $7,200 and Bishop Boyle's concern about the corrupting possibilities of so large an income for a priest came back to haunt him. Abruptly, he decided to get out.[104] On October 29, 1946, just eight days after the end of the Duquesne Light strike, Rice resigned as rent director, effectively bringing to an end this era in his life.

So far as concerns the public visibility of Rice's image, the war years had proved to be the springtime of rapid growth. From first taking up residence at the gaunt, gray House of Hospitality, Rice had become something of a media myth in Pittsburgh and even nationally as the "flophouse father," "pastor of the poorest." From an occasional stint on radio for the Catholic Radical Alliance, he had become first a regular fixture as a radio priest, and then for a time a voice heard daily by nearly every radio listener in Pittsburgh. From being an assistant pastor trying to help some of his parishioners with a housing problem, he had become the federal "rent czar" of western Pennsylvania. From limited visibility in labor union halls and on picket lines, he had moved to a wide acceptability to labor and management alike as an arbiter of their disputes. And throughout the war years of alliance with the Soviet

Union, Rice had remained one public figure unflinchingly determined to do battle with domestic communist influence.

All these developments, remarkable at an age when most curates were busy trying to keep on the good side of their pastors, were placing Rice in a position to play an altogether crucial role in preparing the way for the dramatic, sometimes violent, reaction against communism that would sweep the United States in the next decade. The wartime patriot would soon emerge in the national consciousness as the scourge of communists in American labor.

FOUR

Red-Baiter Extraordinaire

HARDLY HAD THE GUNS OF WORLD WAR II stopped firing in Europe or the bombs stopped falling on Japan before important forces within the United States began preparing for the next major national confrontation, this one with the Soviet Union and this time along the ideological lines of the capitalist-communist divide. Some of the lines had been drawn at Potsdam. Now, skirmishing would take place in Eastern Europe. Before long, the cold war would heat up with military confrontations in Asia, and wars of national independence throughout the Third World. And ineluctably the conflict would become global in scope, not only drawing in many nations from around the world, on one side or the other, but threatening all nations with the prospect of nuclear annihilation.

But at home in the 1940s, the turnaround that transformed the Soviet Union from a wartime ally into the preeminent cold war foe would be reflected primarily in a preoccupation with and persecution of American communists or communist sympathizers, a persecution that one of its foremost historians has dubbed "The Great Fear."[1] This purge, David Caute points out, was neither unique in the history of the United States (the "red scare" during Wilson's second term was quite similar) nor was it on the whole a bloody one like corresponding episodes in France, Italy and Germany.[2] But although communists or suspected communists were not tortured or executed, they were fired from their jobs, socially ostracized, refused credit, denied both unemployment and retirement benefits, and in some cases imprisoned or driven to mental breakdowns or suicide.[3] As for any credible threat posed by domestic communists to the American government or way of life,

Caute points out that membership in CPUSA constituted one-twentieth of 1 percent of the population[4] and that to this day there has not emerged one documented case of a direct connection between that party and espionage, sabotage, or attempted sabotage during the postwar years up to and including the conflict in Korea.[5] Thus Caute concludes that the anticommunist purges of the 1940s and 50s constitute a "dark and discredited" chapter in American history, and demonstrate that "American liberalism had itself taken on the coloring of latent hysteria."[6]

Although it is true that the anticommunist purge of the postwar era would become a major chapter of national history, invading every walk of life and every kind of employment, and reaching from the halls of Congress to virtually every town and village in the country, it was in the labor movement that the early battles — and some of the most intense ones — were to be fought. And it was Pittsburgh that was to earn the title of the "violent epicenter of the anti-Communist eruption in post-war America."[7] Here it was, in the labor union halls of Pittsburgh, that Rice would attain his greatest renown as an anticommunist, here that he would play his most important role in weakening the American left in the labor movement, prior to the onset of McCarthyism in the 1950s.

He would counsel mighty union leaders of the day to disavow any apparent leftist entanglements and to drive the communists from their midst. He would write a pamphlet on anticommunist strategy and tactics that would become a classic. He would conduct labor schools, revive the ACTU in Pennsylvania, and give information to the FBI — all to drive communists out of labor's house. He would pen hard-hitting columns, broadcast radio attacks each week, and establish and maintain a nationwide anticommunist network. He would amass, in his own words, "a dossier on every Communist in the U.S., a bigger anti-Communist file than anybody else had."[8] Nor would he stop with advice offered from the sidelines, but would himself plunge headlong into the battle to purge the largest left-led union of them all, the UE. His leadership of an otherwise motley crew of union oppositionists would transform their wrangles into an anticommunist crusade that, together with the attack on UE by Phil Murray, would lead to the virtual destruction of that huge union. His battles would take him to distant cities in the dark of night and would even on occasion break out into rioting and scuffles that produced black eyes and police records for some of his associates.

Historians like Caute have treated Rice as a minor figure in the postwar persecution of American communists, and understandably so. Major figures in Washington (McCarthy, Nixon, et al.) were doubtless more important in the later, decisive stages of the struggle to discredit and destroy the American Left as a political force. But it was in the earlier episodes of that battle, when the communists were stronger and the eventual outcome more in doubt, that Rice and others in American labor played a significant role.

There are two other reasons why Rice may not yet have been accorded the full credit (or blame, depending on one's perspective) he deserves in this struggle. The first has been the difficulty of assembling a complete picture of the many facets of Rice's anticommunist crusade — a task which this chapter is meant to bring closer to completion.

The second is that Rice himself, due to a later change of heart which prompted him to view the purge more as a tragedy than a triumph, became quite modest about the full extent of his own role in breaking the left in American labor.[9] There is of course considerable irony to the fact that Rice attained his greatest national fame for that activism about which he later entertained the greatest misgivings. Yet history should record that Rice, more than any other single individual, fomented the crusade which expelled the left from the CIO.

A question that has occurred to some observers of Rice's anticommunist crusade in the late 1940s, particularly when viewed from the perspective of some decades later, is: Was he serious? Did he really believe that the small leftist presence in the union movement of the day constituted a deadly danger to that movement or to the religious faith of its Catholic members? Or did more selfish motivations like the sheer love of public attention motivate Rice, as later they seemed to motivate politicians who advanced their careers at the expense of the communists?

Rice always insisted that anticommunism, far from being an expedient to advance his career, had long been a deeply and intensely held conviction. There is much evidence in his life to bear out this assertion. To his early anticapitalist orientation had been added a corresponding dread of socialist totalitarianism, when he read such works as Koestler's *Darkness at Noon*.[10] His anticommunism had been evident even in the heady days of the Catholic Radical Alliance. In 1938 in a debate with *Daily Worker* editor Clarence Hathaway (who substituted for CPUSA head Earl Browder), Rice had replied to the question "Can a Catholic accept the outstretched hand of Communism?" by saying, "We will accept the outstretched hand of Communists only when it ceases to be Communist and relinquishes the doctrines and tactics that have put it beyond the pale of morality and ethics." He had gone on to argue that "Communism, while it remains Communism, is an even greater menace than Fascism." Hathaway's suggestions that Catholics need not fear communists, because of their small numbers, and that progressive Catholics ought to join with communists to fight the common enemies of fascism in Europe and profascists in the United States, seemed to have no effect on Rice.[11]

A more personal sense of loss and threat had been added to this ideological position around the same time, when Rice received a telephone call from a likeable young man named George Meyers. Rice had met Meyers while talking to striking Celanese workers in Cumberland, Maryland, struck up something of a friendship, and later was aghast to learn that Meyers was headed to New York to join the Communist Party. Rice predicted that Meyers would become disillusioned and quit; Meyers never did, and eventually became the secretary of organization for the CPUSA.[12]

It likewise appears that Rice's chief reason for distancing himself from the early Catholic Worker Movement, and throwing in instead with the Association of Catholic Trade Unionists, was precisely his desire to offer active opposition to communists in the labor movement. Early in 1938, Rice had written a letter to the editor of the ACTU *Labor Leader* arguing not only that communists should not be allowed to hold public office but also that any concern for their civil rights in such a case was misplaced:

> A Communist is not as other men. . . . When you say a Communist should hold public office you say that a man who is sworn to use every means in his power to overthrow a state to put up a monstrous caricature in its place should be given the tremendous aid of public office in carrying out his plan. A bit mixed up, a bit Hearstian, but nonetheless true. If your treat the Reds as a normal American political party, they have won a point.[13]

His activism in the 1930s on behalf of labor, and particularly of the CIO, had served to make him more, rather than less, fearful of the impact communism might have on American labor. The historic achievement of the CIO — the establishment of industrial unionism — was in Rice's opinion imperiled by the wrong-headed but not always totally inaccurate charges of communism against which he often found himself defending the organization.[14]

With the approach of World War II, as noted earlier, Rice's anger and scorn for American communists had been heightened by their steadfast adherence to the Soviet line: Hitler came to power amid violent street brawls with German communists and then menaced Europe and the Soviet Union, American communists expressed alarm at the ascendancy of the Nazis; with the conclusion of the Molotov-Ribbentrop Pact, they became antiwar and supported strikes in American defense industries; when Germany invaded Russia, they were once more for an all-out defense effort — including industrial peace and a no-strike pledge. Thus, Rice concluded, the communists and their allies put the well-being of the Soviet Union ahead of that of the United States, and certainly ahead of the good of the workers whose allies they merely pretended to be.[15] Throughout the war, even when Rice appeared resigned to the hegemony of the U.S.S.R. throughout much of Europe after the conflict, his sympathy and understanding seemed not to extend to American communists and fellow travelers.

In 1945, as World War II came to its end, Rice believed that American communists controlled between one-fourth and one-third of the labor movement in the United States. Although he admired the organizing abilities and the militance of many communists, and although he had walked their picket lines at Heinz, at West Penn Hospital, and with the Newspaper Guild, their very determination convinced him that whatever gains they made, they would never allow to be taken away from them.[16] Better, then, to prevent those gains from occurring in the first place.

It was also in 1945 that the Pope condemned the Christian Left, formerly the Communist Party of Italy; later, he would condemn even those who cooperated with communists.[17] These papal pronouncements came at the same time news was beginning to arrive about Soviet expansionism in Eastern Europe in the wake of the war. Pittsburgh was a city with a heavy flavoring of ethnic groups from Poland, Czechoslovakia, Yugoslavia, Rumania, the Baltic states, and so forth. As these lands fell under the domination of the U.S.S.R. during and after the war, their intelligentsia muted, their churches closed, and many of their other freedoms curtailed, word of these repressions began to seep into the homes of relatives in Pittsburgh and to reach the ears of the local clergy. Rice began to pick up on these events and their implications quite early, even before the trial and life sentence of Cardinal Mindszenty in Hungary brought the confrontation between the church and the communists to front-page attention in the U.S. media.[18]

Thus Rice had an early predisposition against the communists and personal resentment at some of the adherents they had been able to win, the fear that their presence might well bring down the house of the CIO, a contempt for their sometimes slavish adherence to a pro-Soviet line, a belief that they already controlled much of American labor and might in time be able to dominate most of it, and a rising indignation at the anti-Catholic Soviet hegemony that was overtaking ancient Christian lands in Eastern Europe. A certain thrill of battle and of celebrity may indeed have accompanied his anticommunist crusading, but it is hardly necessary to postulate such motivations to explain that crusading in the first instance.

By the end of World War II, Rice had developed personal ties with a number of powerful labor leaders, particularly those who were Catholics, and he now began to use these relationships to urge strenuously the expulsion of communists from organized labor. He worked on quite a number of labor leaders in this way, but on none of them so persistently — or arguably with such dramatic effect — as Phil Murray, now the chief of the Congress of Industrial Organizations.

Rice's acquaintance with Murray went back to the very early years of the CIO, when it held its first convention at Pittsburgh, in 1938. But the relationship became a close one at another CIO convention, the one at Atlantic City in 1940, the year when Murray accepted the CIO presidency from the hands of the departing John L. Lewis. Lewis, though relinquishing the leadership of the CIO, nevertheless sought to keep a foot in the door by having his daughter Katie Lewis stay on as director of organization. But Murray, despite his very sincere admiration for Lewis, could not accept this condition. The resultant friction between the two men seems to have affected Murray deeply — so much so that he could not even discuss it with his wife — and it was to Rice that he turned for a sympathetic ear.[19]

Rice's new status was perhaps best captured later in the descriptions of two foreign observers of American labor. Britain's Lord Halifax referred to Rice as "a sort of chaplain to the CIO," and French critic Daniel Guerin took this dim view of Rice's prominence:

The very fact that the CIO had organized these immigrants, that is to say the workers in the basic industries, made it much more vulnerable to Catholic influence than the old AFL. Its late President, Philip Murray, belonged to the Church more than to Labor and represented the hierarchy within the working-class movement. God always came into his speeches, and he did nothing without taking the advice of a Pittsburgh clergyman, the Reverend Charles Owen Rice.[20]

But labor insiders even more than foreign observers were quick to pick up on Rice's access to Murray's ear. As early as the 1940 CIO convention, Rice was visited in his hotel room by Frank Hughes, an old Lewis loyalist from UMW District $6 in Greensburg, Pennsylvania. Said Hughes to Rice, "We know Murray brought you here and that he talks things over with you. Remember this: Lewis is a strong man who has broken people before. Don't cross him."[21]

Murray nevertheless stood his ground on the Katie Lewis issue and her father eventually relented. When Murray inherited the CIO mantle, there were many who thought it would not be worth having: the industrial unions would depart one by one and reaffiliate with the older AFL, and the CIO would be unable to navigate the financial straits it was encountering. Murray's own skills at holding fractious labor chieftains together, along with the war and the postwar prosperity, would give the lie to all these predictions. But Rice remained one person who always supported Murray wholeheartedly.[22] For this he was rewarded with regular access to Murray's inner counsels.

Thus in early 1941, when a group at Heinz applied for a CIO charter, Rice wrote to Murray warning him that this group was the company union that he and the CRA had opposed back in 1937. Murray quickly responded, "I shall be governed by your advice in this situation."[23]

As early as 1942, Rice broached the issue of communism in the CIO, even though he realized the matter was a prickly one with Murray. Rice felt, although he was not yet prepared to say so openly, that leftists in Murray's office, among whom he numbered general counsel Lee Pressman, were a formidable threat to Murray and the CIO. Murray had recently issued a statement condemning "witch-hunting" for communists, and Rice wrote to Murray that the statement had "aided the Reds." He went on to express the misgiving that when the present generation of labor leaders had passed (Murray, Lewis, Hillman, et al.) their places might be taken by unionists whom Rice regarded as leftists, like Emspak, Curran, Robinson, and Bridges. But having so written on January 28, Rice sat on the letter until February 26 — perhaps partly out of fear that it would be received by the wrong hands in Murray's office.

Murray in the meantime had issued another criticism of the communist-hunting Dies Committee, and now Rice penned a second letter saying that Murray's newest statement was "chock-full of typical Communist jargon" — although he quickly inferred that someone else at headquarters must have drawn up the statement and merely gotten Murray's signature under it. Rice then mailed both letters, not to Murray directly, but to his niece and secretary, Mercedes Daugherty, asking her to show them to Murray when she thought it opportune. Murray replied on March 5 that Rice's suggestions were "quite pertinent" but of "dubious authenticity."[24]

Rice had not enlisted Murray in the crusade to rid the CIO of communists, at least not yet. But he had raised the issue early on, probably in more blunt language than most others would have dared use with Murray, and he would keep up the pressure for years to come. For the most part, however, Rice's communications with Murray would come not in the form of letters exchanged but in conversations they would share over lunch every two weeks or so.[25]

Of the next rank of labor leaders whose friendship Rice cultivated and used to combat communist influence, surely the most colorful was Mike Quill. Quill was the Irish-born-and-reared head of the Transport Workers Union (TWU) who had for many years been known as "Red Mike." He was the consistent target of criticism by the ACTU for his support of the communist line on all issues foreign and domestic, a criticism perhaps sharpened by the fact that Quill was himself an Irish Catholic. Rice long considered himself a friend of Quill's and the two kept up a regular and amicable correspondence. But Rice once warned him that "he was a prisoner of the Communists and they could break him as they had made him."[26] Still, Rice supported Quill in a crucial battle within the TWU when Rice's ACTU confreres were begging him to disavow Red Mike.[27]

Whether such admonitions-cum-friendship caused Quill to see the error of his ways, or whether he correctly calculated that there was little future in left-wing alliances in the late 1940s (the communists were unwilling to compromise on the five-cent fare in New York subways, which Quill believed had to go), or whether because of some combination of both, Quill split with the CPUSA in the spring of 1948 over the twin issues of the Wallace presidential candidacy and the Marshall Plan (the CPUSA supported the former, opposed the latter). He also sent an operative to steal his own membership record from party headquarters.[28] Even more significantly, Quill brought with him the TWU, which then enabled Murray to wrest control of the New York City CIO away from the communists.

As news of these developments reached Rice, who was quite familiar with Quill's ability to camouflage almost any position with his native blarney, he reacted cautiously. Initially he thought Quill was engaging in some "artful dodging"; [29] a week later "playing a double game";[30] and only in the third week "honestly trying" to break with the communists.[31] But thereafter Rice welcomed Quill back into the fold and sympathized with his further struggles. A generation later, Rice officiated at Quill's funeral Mass in New York.[32]

Still another Irish Catholic leader of an international union whom Rice was pleased to see break with the communists was Joseph Curran of the National Maritime Union, who split in 1947 and then won reelection in what Rice termed a "stunning victory" in 1948.[33] Unlike Quill, however, Curran never became close to Rice, and developed, in Rice's opinion, into an autocratic and high-living labor leader.[34] As Rice would have occasion to note more than once, allies in the anticommunist struggle were not always the best labor leaders — nor necessarily the most honest.

Encouraged by the return to the flock of two major labor leaders, Rice attempted the conversion of still another black sheep, Albert Fitzgerald, president of the left-led UE. In the fall of 1948, Rice invited Fitzgerald to join "the smallest, most exclusive club in the world" — namely that of Irish Catholic presidents of CIO unions who had formerly been "held in thrall by the Communist Party." This club, of course, consisted of Quill and Curran.[35] Fitzgerald could join, Rice suggested, because "the Communist hatchet men in his union live in fear of the day when Albert Fitzgerald will remember his heritage and will smash his fist into the grey but dominating face of the Communist control apparatus of UE-CIO." But Fitzgerald, who had only recently been castigated in Rice's column as someone who "will swallow just about anything" and who would break with the Left only because "he will think he can make a break without losing his job as kept president of the UE," somehow never saw fit to accept Rice's gracious invitation.[36]

Yet the printed abuse Rice heaped on Fitzgerald's uncooperative head was as nothing compared to that directed at two other candidates for the smallest, most exclusive club in the world: James Durkin and Bernard Mooney, officers of another CIO affiliate, the

United Office and Professional Workers of America (UOPWA). Rice had characterized the UOPWA as communist- led, to which Durkin replied not only that Rice lacked proof for such an allegation, but that both he and Mooney were themselves practicing Catholics. Rice responded in a letter reprinted in his column, an attack reaching a new zenith of vitriol even for Rice:

> You say you and Mooney were reared Catholics . . . the Reds picked you because of your Catholic and Irish sounding name and you played it for all it was worth. *You* introduced religion into this by claiming to be a good Catholic. So far as I can find out, you may have been reared a Catholic, but you no longer live up to your faith. I do not know about Mooney and I do not care; he is merely another Irish-monickered half-man who has been produced at the proper time to front for the real Communist operators who stepped down when they did not dare to swear that they are non-Communists. . . . You say you have deep respect for the cloth. The only cloth you men respect is the cloth of the Red flag of Moscow. You are washed up, all of you Communist fronters, washed up in the American labor movement. Say goodbye and go quietly.[37]

Another "Irish-monickered" opponent of Rice's, CPUSA National Committee member Elizabeth Gurley Flynn, shot back in the pages of the *Daily Worker*:

> That's an argument on a high political level, isn't it? What should we do with our good Irish names? Are only cops, politicians and priests allowed to use them, according to Father Rice? Somebody like Durkin has to prove that "fighting Irish" has some real significance.[38]

Still another prominent leftist Irish Catholic labor leader (by way of Australia) was Harry Bridges, head of the West Coast longshoremen. But aside from calling for Bridges' conviction and deportation, Rice knew Bridges only casually and considered him beyond the pale.[39]

Thus had Rice developed warm personal relationships with a number of key leaders in the CIO and its international unions, and used those relationships as best he could to further the anticommunist cause in the late 1940s. But if the common ties of Irish ancestry (Rice always insisted that Murray was Irish, and not a Scot) and the Catholic religion cemented working relationships with those labor leaders who took up the cause, they decidedly exacerbated Rice's opposition to those who refused to be converted.

While Rice was using counsels with the mighty to wage his anticommunist battle, he was spending even more time on correspondence with the humble (most of them) in seeking to end communist influence in the unions. The most widely-read Catholic newspaper in the country at the time was *Our Sunday Visitor*, published in Huntington, Indiana. Because of its highly conservative coloration, Rice had until now stayed away from appearances in its pages. But in 1947, as a major step in his anticommunist crusade, Rice proposed to *OSV* editors that he do an article in their columns attacking communism in the unions and offering assistance to those who wished to oppose it in the union movement. The editors agreed, and the article appeared on March 23, 1947. The response was overwhelming, with more than a thousand letters pouring in, most of them from union members all over the country who feared that their unions might be infected with the virus Rice had described.[40]

Rice and a crew of undergraduate students at Duquesne, where he was now teaching some courses, struggled to answer this flood of correspondence, much of which would go on for years, and which consumed hour upon hour of working time every day. But it soon became apparent that something more efficient — and more substantial — was needed to guide those who sent in the myriad requests for information and advice. Thus was born the idea of a publication to provide anticommunist union members with strategy, tactics, and information about which unions were or were not communist-led. The result, which Rice wrote in 1947 and, on May 9, 1948, offered to send to *OSV* readers, he entitled "How to Decontrol Your Union of Communists." [41] (See Appendix).

This twelve-page pamphlet, typed and offset at Duquesne and containing all sorts of hard-headed advice on how to battle the Reds in one's own local, proved to be a smashing success with *OSV* readers. A typical passage urged anticommunists to keep communist union officers off balance at meetings by "yammering" like infielders in a baseball game. Again the requests poured in, sometimes for one copy and accompanied by the requested dime, sometimes for hundreds of copies for mass distribution in union halls or churches.[42] Rice later estimated that between thirty and forty thousand copies of the pamphlet were printed,[43] but thirty-five years later, an ABC television news team preparing a documentary on the McCarthy era would find copies of the pamphlet all over the nation.[44]

Reading through the resulting correspondence years later, it is clear that the typical request came from a loyal Catholic who had had or was now beginning to have some doubts about his or her local union, and wanted advice. But other inquiries came from less ordinary persons: a company president, a national research bureau, public libraries, and even the Military Intelligence Section of the Army's Far East Command! Some writers made it clear that a person's job would hinge on Rice's reply (a union's executive council had agreed to fire its attorney if he had any communist connections; did he?), or that someone's standing in the community could be jeopardized (a Chicago priest wondered if Saul D. Alinsky was a communist; Rice disliked Alinsky's tactics, but no reply is preserved in the file). Perhaps most unnerving to observe in many of the letters is that almost any kind of unusual behavior noted then or previously might have given rise to an inquiry to Rice, who had in effect set himself up as an authoritative judge of communists throughout the country.[45] It was, to say the least, an awesome power.

Did Rice use this power to finger as communists those he knew were not or those he only suspected of communism without knowing for certain? Such charges were leveled at him by Durkin of the UOPWA and others. Rice always maintained that he drew careful distinctions between genuine Stalinists and those who merely had certain leftist leanings. The files of correspondence from his crusading days do not provide a definitive answer, due to their incompleteness. But what can be said is that Rice did take inordinate pains to familiarize himself with the internal affairs of a great array of unions, and the presence or absence of communist influence in their locals.

An impressive indicator of his research is provided today by a mere listing of those unions on which Rice kept files, including copies of their publications, their internal minutes, and his own correspondence with anticommunist members. Here is the index to his files from the postwar era, which are today preserved in his Papers in Hillman Library at the University of Pittsburgh:

Aluminum Workers	Office Employees
Auto Workers	Oil Workers

Clothing Workers
Engineers and Architects
Farm Equipment
Farmers
Fur and Leather Workers
Glass Workers
Hotel/Restaurant Workers
International Brotherhood of
  Teamsters
International Jewelry Workers
International Ladies Garment
  Workers
International Longshoremen
International Moulders and
  Foundry Workers
International Photo Engravers
International Typographical
  Workers
International Union of Electrical
  Workers
International Union of Elevator
  Constructors
Machinists
Marine and Shipbuilders
Meatcutters
Mine and Mill Workers

Plasterers
Railroad Brotherhoods
Rubber Workers
Shoe Workers
Sign, Pictorial and Display
  Workers
Steel Workers
Teachers
Telegraphers
Telephone Workers
Textile Workers
Transport Workers
United Food and Tobacco Workers
United Furniture Workers
United Gas Coke and Chemical
  Workers
United Mine Workers
United Office and Professional
  Workers
United Packing House Workers
United Public Workers
United Salary Workers
Westinghouse Federation of
  Salaried Employees
Wood Workers

Whether Rice was always precisely on target with the information and advice he passed on to his nationwide and even international network of anticommunist correspondents may be impossible to discover. What is clear is that he had put a great amount of research into the advice he gave.

By July 1948, Rice was offering the pamphlet in his *Pittsburgh Catholic* column and noting with a "Haw!" that since the UE leadership had issued a criticism of the tract, the number of requests for it had increased.[46] In September he noted that hundreds of letters had been received from those who wished to oppose communists, but feared to do so openly, and that an attempt had been made to use the pamphlet in the trial of Harry Bridges then underway in Hawaii.[47]

In 1950, following the expulsion of communist unions from the CIO, Rice would make one more follow-up in the pages of *Our Sunday Visitor* to proclaim that "Catholics lead in labor's anti-Communist drive," in which he reiterated the offer to send his pamphlet to those interested, along with a one-page update listing unions that had been purged, and those that still remained to be mopped up. But interest had fallen off considerably by this time, and only about eighty requests were received.[48]

In addition to his leverage with prominent labor leaders and his endless correspondence with anticommunists around the country, Rice in the postwar years had acquired another power base in his struggle: directorship of the Institute of Management-Labor Relations at Duquesne University. Early in 1945 Rice had been approached by Rev. Raymond V. Kirk, C.S.Sp., president of Duquesne, about starting up a labor school in some ways reminiscent of those conducted by the Catholic Radical Alliance in prewar days. But there would be differences. As the title suggested, these classes were to be conducted not just for workers but for management as well. The nominal tuition of the old labor school would be replaced by a larger fee of ten dollars. And the operation would move from downtown Pittsburgh up to the campus of Duquesne University. Rice agreed.[49]

His directorship of the institute was significant for a couple of reasons. First, it was one of only two labor schools in the country sanctioned by the USWA. As a result, much of the future leadership of the Steelworkers would pass through its classes, along with those who led or aspired to lead other major unions in the Pittsburgh area. Rice later estimated that at one time as many as 50 percent of all local union presidents and business agents in Pittsburgh had attended his classes.[50]

In addition, these classes, together with undergraduate classes Rice was also instructing, would produce for him a whole generation of recruits to assist in his struggle against the communists. As noted earlier, it would be the undergraduates who would use the facilities of the institute to do the typing, mimeographing, and much of the research that made it possible for Rice to maintain what his targets could only describe as a whirlwind of activity directed against them. The institute would continue as one of Rice's power bases until 1950, when a rapid shuffle would ensue.[51]

Another power base that was significant to Rice in his crusade was the Association of Catholic Trade Unionists. After the war, he took the logical step of resuscitating the Pittsburgh chapter — henceforth termed rather more grandiosely the "Pennsylvania"

Chapter — of the ACTU, which had been suspended shortly after U.S. entry into World War II. The New York City chapter, which had founded the ACTU, had remained active during the war, publishing the *Labor Leader*, so that it was simply a matter of reaffiliating. This was accomplished in April 1947, as the chapter elected William Hart and Lawrence Sullivan (who had led the rebels out of the House of Hospitality) its leaders and Rice its chaplain. It began by passing three resolutions, the first opposing communism and the other two addressing the problems of displaced persons and the housing shortage.[52] In July that year the first postwar ACTU convention was held, in Cleveland, and the Pennsylvania ACTU was represented (as were a total of ten other chapters) by a full delegation.[53] Michael Harrington has referred to the Pennsylvania chapter as a "one-man ACTU" during this period, the one man of course being Rice.[54] If we add that a few confederates like John Duffy were also, as will be seen, intensely involved in the struggle against communists in UE, Harrington's description can be accepted as accurate.

It was noted earlier that during the war Rice had had a relatively informal relationship with local FBI agents who fraternized with him at the House of Hospitality and with whom he exchanged information and gossip. That relationship had ended when the agents in question were transferred after the end of the war.

Evidence from the files the FBI kept on Rice indicates that during the postwar era he made attempts to replace the previous informal relationship with a more official one, and one tied to higher levels of the FBI hierarchy. The attempts seem to have unsuccessful, but are indicative of the lengths to which he was prepared to go in his crusade against communists.

In April 1948 Rice told conservative labor columnist Victor Riesel that he wanted to sit down and have a talk with FBI Director J. Edgar Hoover. Riesel used his influence with the bureau to try to set up such a meeting, but without divulging what the topic of the conversation was to be. He told officials that Rice might be "seeking to satisfy curiosity by associating with people in important places," or seeking help in his fight against the communists, or even acting as an intermediary from Murray. Whatever the purpose, the FBI was not enthusiastic about such a meeting, and Rice subsequently demurred.[55]

In 1950, at a luncheon engagement with an FBI agent, Rice made accusations against two individuals he believed were tied up with communist elements. One of them was William McCabe, chairman of the Brotherhood of Locomotive Engineers in Homestead, Pennsylvania. The agent recorded that Rice "was unable to give any specific information showing the relationship between McCabe and the communists," aside from McCabe's having publicly expressing sympathy for eleven CPUSA leaders then on trial in New York under the Smith Act.

The other object of Rice's discussion that day was an official at Westinghouse Air Brake Company who, Rice said, had been instrumental in bringing about a cooperative labor–management relationship between WABCO and the left-led UE. This led Rice to think there was some sort of tie-in between the official and the communists, but the most he could state definitively was that the man had a mistress, whom Rice proceeded to name.

Rice requested the opportunity to discuss, with an FBI agent familiar with the labor situation in Pittsburgh, other information he had relative to communists in the labor field. But a follow-up by the Pittsburgh office concluded that he could furnish no information it did not already have.[56]

It would appear from these excerpts that if a working relationship was not established between Rice and the FBI, it was not because of a lack of effort on Rice's part. Perhaps the bureau was mistrustful of Rice despite his anticommunist record: it had on file a statement from a socialist who had been told that his or her politics would not make membership in ACTU impossible.[57] On the other hand, Rice in 1947 was able to produce photostated copies of CPUSA membership cards for Thomas Fitzpatrick, George Poblich and Clyde Johnson, all of UE.[58] But if we ask the key questions of whether Rice willingly passed information to the Bureau, whether some of this information could be used against the individuals being discussed, and whether those individuals were unable to defend themselves against what Rice said about them, the answers are yes, yes and yes.

Of all Rice's activities after the war, perhaps the clearest barometer of his resolve to become pretty much a full-time anticommunist was his column in the *Pittsburgh Catholic*. It was noted earlier that for a period of about one year — from the summer of 1941 to that of 1942 — Rice had written and initialled the ACTU column appearing in the *Pittsburgh Catholic*, which earlier had been authored by Lawrence Sullivan, Alan Kistler, and others. But in 1947 Rice became the regular correspondent for a feature that would evolve from the ACTU column into the Charles Owen Rice column, and that would last, with one very notable hiatus, from 1947 to the 1980s. Thus on June 26, 1947, Rice was relaunching what was to become his most prominent and ongoing form of communication with the public for the rest of his days.

The most obvious change in the column from its earlier version was the increased frequency and intensity of its attacks on communists in American labor unions. This is not to say that such attacks had been a minor feature in the 1941–42 editions: an item count of 55 columns written during that period shows that 33 of them, or fully 60 percent, had contained hostile references to "communists" or "Reds." In 1941, for example, when Harry Bridges of the Longshoremen was under orders to be deported because of his communist sympathies (orders that were later overruled on constitutional grounds), Rice had offered this opinion:

> We are inclined to sympathize with Bridges because of his good labor record. However, he has brought his troubles on himself and since he had the audacity to take orders in domestic affairs from a foreign-controlled group, he must now take his medicine.[59]

Although Rice frequently took potshots at his sometimes hysterical fellow columnist Westbrook Pegler, he had felt bound to admit that, "In his castigation of Communists in the [labor] movement, Peg, has . . . done good."[60] In the spring of 1942, when CPUSA leader Earl Browder was released from prison, where he had been held for leadership of the CPUSA as proscribed under the Smith Act, Rice had applauded. But this was not because of any concern for Browder's civil liberties: Rice simply had not wanted Browder to become a martyr.[61] At the same time, Rice had been using the communist issue to praise Phil Murray and attack John L. Lewis, then his rival. Rice insisted that it was Lewis who had brought communists into the CIO, and Murray who would put them out — when the time was ripe.[62] In these columns, and in many others where he closely followed the fortunes of the anticommunist minority in UE 601, Rice had already been advocating hostile activities towards communists in 1941–42.

But from 1947 onward the pace was accelerating and the temperature was decidedly rising. Of the nineteen columns that appeared that year, only two were devoid of aggressive references to communists. Rice still distinguished his own opposition to the Reds from that of the "loud, undisciplined orator against Communism," when he attacked a speech given by a fellow cleric, Rev. Frank M. O'Reilly. O'Reilly had claimed that the postwar wave of strikes had been inspired by communists, that the CIO Political Action Committee was tied to communists, that Joe Curran of the Maritime Union was a "Browderite," and that Walter Reuther was "Moscow-trained." All lies, responded Rice, lies that mostly succeeded in giving the communists credit they did not deserve.[63] In a similar vein, he hailed Walter Reuther, who had triumphed over the communists in the UAW, as an exponent of "native American radicalism . . . a good thing." He also suggested that the UAW might now want to take over some communist locals in the UE and the FE (Farm Equipment) unions.[64]

Rice said he didn't believe in seeing communists where there were none, but he was prepared to advocate quite an array of tactics to stymie and drive out of the union movement those he thought were there. Thus he liked the idea of putting communist labor leaders in prison on "federal raps," although he noted ruefully that contemporaneous communists were not making the same indictable errors with union treasuries that their predecessors had a generation earlier.[65] He observed with satisfaction that the "steady squeeze" begun by the CIO in 1946 on leftist unions was pushing them out of the limelight at the national convention.[66] He decried "campus commies" in Pittsburgh and he applauded the work of Victor Riesel in exposing communists in Hollywood, and urged that there be a follow-up.[67] He even hesitated to join in attacks on the Taft-Hartley Bill, passed that year to limit labor's power, for fear of being manipulated by communists like Lee Pressman at CIO headquarters.[68]

In fact Rice and other anticommunists had very mixed feelings about Taft-Hartley. It permitted states to pass laws banning the closed shop, and in other ways hamstrung the drive to organize more of American labor. But it also provided a useful tool against communists, when it required central union leaders to submit affidavits swearing under pain of imprisonment that they were not communists. Should a union not file these affidavits, employers could refuse to bargain with them, and new NLRB elections could be held, possibly resulting in the selection of new bargaining agents. Rice and his allies spoke against Taft-Hartley, sometimes on the basis that it merely drove communists underground, yet they repeatedly used its provisions to challenge communist leaders in the unions.[69]

When a strike occurred at the Oak Ridge A-bomb plant, for

example, Rice wondered whether it was appropriate to invoke Taft-Hartley to fire government workers merely for admitting membership in a union that supported strikes against the government, or to deprive government employees of their civil rights in loyalty probes. "All this is justified," he nonetheless concluded, "by the necessity of weeding Communists out of government service."[70]

Thus quite early in the game, when Rice was struggling, with varying degrees of success, to avoid subordinating his own principled labor-unionism to the crusade against communism, he was ready and almost eager to subordinate the civil rights of others to that battle.

Another interesting theme that had surfaced as early as 1947 was a certain disillusionment with some of his allies in the anticommunist struggle within the UE. Thus Rice noted that some of the right wing in 601 were not terribly bright[71] (or terribly well motivated, he later conceded),[72] and he watched in dismay as anticommunist leaders elected in that local repeatedly fumbled the ball.[73]

Finally there emerged in 1947 the two issues that would become the litmus tests of loyalty within the CIO, and for which communists would be expelled after failing them. These were the third-party presidential candidacy of Henry Wallace, liberal politician and former vice president under Roosevelt, and the Marshall Plan. Support for Wallace became a capital offense within the CIO, and seemingly an odd one, given Wallace's excellent relations with labor earlier, and his unchanged stance at this time. It is interesting to note how Rice saw this issue emerging in 1947:

> The Reds want Wallace to run, so that they can ensure the defeat of Truman and the election of a reactionary. The non-Red liberals want Wallace to stay out of the race, so that they can either elect Truman or stimulate the Republicans to run a half decent candidate. Non-Stalinist liberals and labor men have no stomach for four years of reaction. Four years of triumphant reaction would kick big holes in the labor movement. It would give an opportunity for a lot of demonstrations, political strikes, parades and rabble rousing, but that sort of thing will not help true social progress. It would destroy the firm basis which we need to achieve a just, orderly and progressive social order. The Reds don't want us to achieve such stability. Labor men, true secular liberals and humanitarians and, above all, Catholic social leaders, want it.[74]

The Marshall Plan was the proposal, soon implemented, of reviving the capitalist economies of Europe with massive infusions of foreign aid from the United States. This the Left opposed as a measure for setting up an American-based capitalist empire. The Right had no such objection, and saw the leftist stance as disloyal.

In 1948, Rice's preoccupation with communists increased: forty-nine out of fifty-two columns (94%) contained attacks on them. He exulted as the Wallace candidacy proved a loser for the Left in the face of Truman's last-minute win over Dewey.[75] Although Rice expected Truman to get Taft-Hartley repealed (which did not come about), he was impatient with the Left's insistence that Truman redeem *all* his campaign pledges.[76] He repeatedly noted that the Reds were losing power,[77] and simultaneously expressed regret that some good unions were being broken in the process.[78] Still he argued that the pitting of Red and anti-Red factions against each other could be healthy for labor unions,[79] and admitted that in any case he was himself unable to stop pursuing the topic.[80]

Also in 1948, the issue of communist workers at defense plants took on a new seriousness as Rice supported Atomic Energy Commission head David Lilienthal's refusal to use UE labor at atomic plants.[81] Rice also began to attack "campus commies" by name now in a running battle with Dr. Marion Hathaway at the University of Pittsburgh.[82] He kept up his steady drumfire against Harry Bridges, urging his deportation.[83]

Amid these anticommunist pronouncements, he managed to get in only one bad word for capitalism. In a piece headlined "Goodbye, Capitalism," he announced: "The free enterprise system is on about its last trial anyway. It is done in Europe, where it started."[84]

But if 1947 and 1948 were the first two movements of Rice's anticommunist concerto, 1949 was the crescendo. In that year, every single column he wrote for the *Pittsburgh Catholic* took at least a passing swipe at the communists, and more typically excoriated them at length. Most of his ink that year was spilled on the climax of the UE battle at Local 601 (to be reviewed later). Beyond that, and beyond some of the themes already mentioned above, Rice now found it necessary to insist that he and the ACTU were not seeking power in the union movement, despite their obvious leadership in the anticommunist purges then in progress.[85] He refused to criticize the anticommunist hearings then being conducted in Washington by HUAC[86] (in fact, as will be seen, he was secretly trying to manipulate that probe to his advantage at Local 601). Nor did he have any words of criticism for the conviction of eleven top CPUSA leaders under the Smith Act,[87] and demurred when another priest suggested clemency for them.[88] He also complained that the local chapter of the American Civil Liberties Union, though not a communist front, had of late been offering assistance "all for one type of person" (leftist).[89] In a broadcast that year he offered his thoughts on the FBI, loyalty boards, and J. Edgar Hoover:

> The FBI is a terrific organization. It is an investigative body that is no danger to Democracy. It is a model of what a Democracy can do to protect itself from spies and other subversives without sacrificing or injuring any of our freedoms. . . . [loyalty boards] have been set up and the government has been pretty well deloused. A certain amount of injustice was done in the process. That was inevitable. . . . It was necessary to clean out the Communists by procedures other than those used in the courts. . . . [On rumors that Hoover was in disfavor at the White House:] I hope they leave Hoover alone, he has done a good and necessary job. He has shown that he knows how to care for the safety and internal security of the country.[90]

If Rice seemed to have lost nearly all concern for the civil rights of accused communists, and if his attacks on them seemed to have gone beyond the boundaries of fair play and moderation, he defended his behavior as being the result of a conscious decision carefully taken:

> In a balancing of the books we figured out, a couple of years ago, that the calculated risk had to be taken. The anti-Commie fight could not have been well begun, even, without plain speaking. The Reds thrive on oblique talk and soft handling. Call a spade a spade, a rat a rat, and a Red a Red![91]

Of all the battles that Rice undertook to combat the influence of the Left in American labor, none involved him so personally and passionately, and none, arguably, had so much significance for the future of the labor movement, as the struggle going on in the United Electrical, Radio, and Machinery Workers of America (UE).

The UE had been founded just about the time Rice was becoming politically active, in 1936. Its fundamental principles included a commitment to industry-wide unionization, along with its sister unions, in what was to become the CIO, and a firm opposition to what it saw as the "business unionism" of the older AFL affiliates. To forestall the drift toward plutocracy, it prohibited its top officials from earning more in salary than its best paid skilled workers on the shop floor.[92] The youthful spirit of the UE leadership, combined with workers' resentments at being cold- shouldered by the AFL, led to a period of remarkable growth for this fledgling organization in the late 1930s. It enabled it to become the third largest of the CIO unions, eventually representing over a half million workers in their contests with General Electric, Westinghouse, General Motors Electric, and other corporate giants. One of the early locals to be formed was Local 601 at Westinghouse in East Pittsburgh, which was chartered in April 1937.

Like many other CIO unions, the UE was regularly accused of harboring communists within its ranks. The newly formed HUAC, chaired by Rep. Martin Dies, in 1938 heard sensational testimony from John P. Frey of the AFL that the CIO was in fact a communist conspiracy to overthrow the government of the United States.[93] But unlike its sister unions, the UE clearly adopted party- line resolutions on war-related and other international affairs.

The charges and the reality of communist influence did little to retard the organizing successes of the UE or the CIO prior to World War II. But they did become an internal issue for the UE beginning in 1941. That was the year when a small Pittsburgh local wrote to national headquarters to inquire whether a local could refuse union membership to communists, fascists or nazis. UE President James Carey took the position that it could, but was outvoted on the issue by the two other national officers, Frank Emspak and James Matles, then by the General Executive Board, and finally by the national convention that year, all of whom interpreted the union charter to forbid exclusion of an otherwise qualified union member on the grounds of any political adherence whatever.[94]

At the same convention, Carey, the only one of the three national officers to be opposed for reelection, was defeated by Albert Fitzgerald from Lynn, Massachusetts. Carey insisted that the reason for his ouster (he did remain as secretary of the CIO, at UE recommendation) was his opposition to communism.[95] In the years ahead, Carey and the opposition that formed behind him would argue that UE had become dominated by communists, whereas the UE leadership would claim that the only real issue was freedom for members to hold whatever political preference they chose, whether Left or Right.[96]

Rice, meanwhile, had gotten his feet wet in UE politics in 1941 when a probationary worker named Joseph Baron had been fired at Westinghouse for founding a local antiwar third party at a time when the CPUSA opposed U.S. intervention in World War II, and

Local 601 was trying to have him reinstated. Rice mobilized a network of nearby parishes to convince workers, from the pulpit, that Baron should not be reinstated. Rice triumphed on a vote at a membership meeting. He would be less successful when a group of UE 601 members approached him later that year prior to the national UE convention to seek his help in electing a slate of delegates who would support Carey against what they saw as the leftist domination of their national union. Rice obliged them, but they were not able to elect a pro-Carey delegation. What they did stir up were charges of clerical interference in the affairs of a labor union, and allegations of dual unionism.

Carey, after being defeated for the presidency, was able to remain a force in UE politics due to Murray's decision to retain him as secretary of the CIO. A pro-Carey and anticommunist faction remained in the minority, but regularly contested for power in many regions, including western Pennsylvania. The leader there of the Carey minority, who worked hand-in-glove with Rice for many years, was John Duffy.

Rice recalls that he was still rent director when he was first approached by Duffy, a red-faced, Catholic, conservative Republican coal miner from Scranton. Duffy had emigrated to Pittsburgh from the anthracite region of eastern Pennsylvania and had found employment as an electrical worker at Allis-Chalmers. He was a fierce unionist, but an even fiercer anticommunist. He once confided to Rice that what he would like to do would be to find some small but profitable company (perhaps like Allis-Chalmers) and "bring it to its knees." But what he would like even more was to drive the communists out of District 6 of the UE.[97]

District 6 at that time encompassed western Pennsylvania, along with some sections of West Virginia and Ohio. Duffy's own local, of which he soon became vice president and in effect the leader, was the relatively small Local 613 of Allis-Chalmers. Other locals were scattered over a wide geographical area, including Erie in northwestern Pennsylvania, Fairmont in West Virginia, and others in between. But the center of gravity in the district was located in eastern Pittsburgh and along the heavily industrialized Turtle Creek. There were located the huge Westinghouse plant represented by Local 601, and the somewhat smaller Local 610 representing Westinghouse Air Brake Company (WABCO) as also Union Switch and Signal of Turtle Creek. Duffy's leadership of Local 613 put him onto the Executive Council of District 6, and it was this position that he would use to wage relentless guerrilla warfare against the dominant left faction. Rice believed that his hooking up with Duffy by 1946 involved him more deeply and longer in UE politics than he otherwise would have chosen, but Duffy's goal of cleansing District 6 of communists was one that Rice could hardly have resisted.[98]

It was also in 1946 that Rice's pressure on Murray, doubtless in combination with many other pressures, appeared to have the effect of initiating a tilt against the Left in the CIO. Whereas Murray had previously simply dismissed charges of communism in the CIO as unfounded or a ploy of big businesses to break the power of the new labor alliance, now he had instructed a committee at the 1946 CIO convention to prepare a resolution on the topic of communist attempts to intervene in internal CIO affairs. The final resolution, which Murray had the convention adopt without debate, did not deny the existence of such attempts, but warned the Communist Party against continuing to make them: "[We] resent and reject efforts of the Communist Party, or other political parties and their adherents, to interfere in the affairs of the CIO. This convention serves notice that we will not tolerate such interference."[99]

Had Rice, the close confidant and spiritual advisor to Murray, had a hand in creating this turnaround on the part of the CIO and its leader? Certainly it is clear that Rice had been warning Murray about the danger of communism to the CIO since at least 1942. He would also in his columns begin hinting at or openly suggesting various expedients that Murray could — and eventually did — employ against the communists and their power: lessening the influence of Lee Pressman, [100] permitting other CIO affiliates to raid communist-dominated locals,[101] expelling disloyal unions from the CIO,[102] and issuing alternate CIO charters to set up new unions.[103]

Yet Rice's own later depiction of his relationship to Murray had himself much more the pupil at the knees of the master, rather than the Svengali at the ear of the monarch.[104] And there is evidence to support this view in Rice's columns and correspondence of that era. He heaped praise on Murray at intervals.[105] He expressed to a third party an awed gratitude at being able to participate in a testimonial dinner to Murray.[106] And there were indications, as will be seen, that Rice was unaware of some pivotal decisions that Murray had made to take action against communist influence.

But perhaps the key question is not how Rice viewed his relationship with Murray, but how Murray viewed the counsels of Rice. To the extent that Murray listened to Rice's views as the voice of the Roman Catholic Church — and Rice always presented his social teachings that way — this deeply loyal Catholic may have been more influenced by Rice's repeated diatribes against communists in the CIO than even Rice himself realized. At any rate, it would be impossible to disregard the influence of Rice, albeit in combination with numerous other factors deriving from internal CIO politics, in assessing why Murray apparently decided in 1946 to begin moving against the communists, though cautiously.

Murray began by turning a blind eye to various raids on UE locals' memberships, conducted by other CIO affiliates, sometimes with help from central CIO staff. UE officials complained repeatedly about such infractions, and Murray assured them that he would not permit such practices. But the raids continued.[107]

Meanwhile, Murray's hand against the UE was strengthened by external political events. On March 5, 1946 Winston Churchill had in effect declared the cold war by announcing at Westminster College in Fulton, Missouri, that an "iron curtain" of repression had fallen over eastern Europe and the Soviet Union. He called for a military buildup by "English speaking peoples" to contain communism. Harry Truman had been sitting beside Churchill at Westminster, and by March 22, 1947, had implemented the cold-war resolve by issuing a "Loyalty Order" allowing the firing of any of over two million workers in plants with government contracts. The UE, with over half its workers in such plants, was clearly a prime target for Executive Order 9835.[108]

Working in tandem with the Loyalty Order later in 1947 was the newly enacted Taft-Hartley Act, and its proviso that allowed employers to refuse to negotiate with unions whose leaderships had not signed noncommunist affidavits, and to initiate new NLRB elections in which a Red-tainted union would not be allowed on the ballot. Employers now had the power either to throw out the UE or to coerce the workers, by the threat of firings, to throw it out. At first, all CIO affiliates pledged not to sign such affidavits; but within the year all the major affiliates had reversed themselves and signed up, save the UE and the Steelworkers. This left other unions, notably Walter Reuther's UAW, a free hand in conducting membership raids of UE locals — which they did with increasing audacity and impunity.[109]

Meantime, the presidential year of 1948 had arrived and with it the third-party Wallace candidacy. Murray not only had the CIO adopt a resolution against third party candidacies that year, but construed the resolution as binding all member unions to support Truman. Because the UE refused to abide by the resolution, it dropped out of the CIO Political Action Committee that year, and ended up endorsing no candidate for president.[110] Clearly Murray's authority had been defied. And as it would turn out, the days were few in number before he would strike back with everything he had.

While the above events were transpiring at the national level, Rice had taken a personal hand against the UE leadership in District 6. With Duffy at his side, with the ACTU organized into subunits at the parish level, with what inside information could be gleaned from his nationwide network of anticommunists and from the FBI, Rice now took aim at UE District 6, and in particular at two of the largest locals in the entire Left-dominated union: 601 and 610.

Rice re-entered Local 601 politics in late 1947, interestingly at a time when the local had actually elected a noncommunist leadership to office. Unhappily for Rice, this leadership was split with internal dissent and had been unable to hang onto office for more than one year at a time. Its emerging leader was Mike Fitzpatrick, brother of the head of the left faction, Thomas J. Fitzpatrick (not to be confused with Tom Fitzpatrick, the son and second of Mike). To the fires of union factionalism was added the fuel of sibling rivalry! By December 1947, the right-wing leadership faced poor prospects of reelection against a united Left and its own mediocre trade union record.[111]

At Local 610 the situation stood much as it long had, with a noncommunist majority at "Switch" outweighed by the communist majority at "Brake."[112] What was different in the elections held in October 1947 was that an anticommunist slate made a reasonable showing, whereas in the previous election there had been no such slate at all.[113] By the close of the year, it was clear to Rice that what had to be done in both locals was to convince members that communism was not only an issue, but *the* issue that overrode all others, even those of traditional bread-and-butter unionism. He had been selling this line in his column for years, but the membership obviously had not been buying.

By early 1948, some of the problems that were to haunt Rice and his followers through the campaign ahead were already taking shape. Charges were made that Rice and the ACTU were outsiders who had no business meddling in union affairs, or alternatively were seeking to advance Catholics in the union at the expense of good trade union practice. (The group tried to steal the administration's thunder by naming itself "Rank-and-File," and was subsequently referred to by the leadership as "Rank and Foul.") Divisiveness persisted: Rank-and-File went up against the progressives but had much support pulled away by Mike Fitzpatrick and his son, running independently.[114] At first count, the result appeared to be a tie on the six-member Executive Board, but when the final tally was in it was five progressives to one Rank-and-File.[115] (Of another election, Rice intoned: "Those UE recounts are really something."[116]) At other times, an anticommunist Executive Board would be elected, only to have the progressives win a victory in subsequent stewards' elections, thus gaining membership again on the Executive Board.[117] Still other times when shopwide elections had favored the Right, the Left would win at small membership meetings or in elections, held on summer Sundays, of delegates to the national convention.[118] Clearly, Rice and his confederates were up against a firmly entrenched leadership that knew how to play hardball at union politics.

But there were some victories. A membership meeting voted to instruct the UE national officers to sign the Taft-Hartley noncommunist affidavits (the UE leadership would do this, but not until another year had passed).[119] When the Left in Local 601 attempted to get the vote reconsidered, the membership instead reaffirmed it and further voted to communicate their decision to all other UE locals.[120]

One event that would etch Rice's image permanently on the consciousness of the national UE leaders occurred on January 29, 1948, when Fitzgerald, Matles, and Emspak came to Pittsburgh to address members assembled from throughout District 6 on prospects for contract negotiations facing the union. The gathering at the Fort Pitt Hotel was part of a national speaking tour the officers were making, and so far everything had gone smoothly enough. But after the first speaker, Emspak, finished, John Duffy arose to ask some questions. District 6 President Stan Loney ruled that questions were out of order until all three speakers had finished, whereupon another ACTU adherent, Tom Nolan of Local 638 (who Rice says had consumed a pint of gin beforehand),[121] according to a District 6 memorandum on the affair issued the next day, "leaped to his feet and yelled for about 20 minutes."[122]

The meeting was then adjourned and the ACTU group headed for the hotel lounge, only to have the meeting reconvened in its absence. Getting wind of this, the Actists returned to discover that the doors to the conference room had been locked and the police summoned. Nolan proceeded to kick in the glass door, and both he and the District 6 representative who had been guarding the door were taken into custody.

It was later noted that the director of personnel at Allis-Chalmers, Frank Michaelowicz, appeared in a press photo of the incident. District 6 leaders inferred from this that the disruption was planned and executed jointly by ACTU and Allis-Chalmers management.[123]

At the conclusion of the event, Rice left the hotel with Duffy and the next morning bailed Tom Nolan out of jail. Later, both Duffy and Nolan were brought up on charges stemming from the Fort Pitt incident and expelled from membership in District 6 and the UE, in lengthy proceedings that Rice likened to the purge trials then underway in the U.S.S.R. and "a foretaste of the totalitarian regime the Reds want to fasten around us all."[124]

Nolan would react by leading his local out of the UE and into the UAW, but Duffy was now unemployed (by Duffy's own choice, Rice noted). He turned to Rice, who in turn contacted Phil Murray. Apparently Murray was still unwilling to oppose the Left in the UE openly. But he now began secretly subsidizing — presumably with CIO funds — Duffy's living and travel expenses as Duffy and Rice traveled the length and breadth of District 6 and beyond, trying to stir up, motivate, and organize opposition to the administration. Not until Murray was in his grave would Rice reveal that Murray for two years sent Rice $1,000 per month, which Rice put into an account to subsidize both Duffy's travels and his own anticommunist file. When UE leaders complained to Murray, he repeatedly disavowed Rice's activities even as he secretly funded them.[125]

Although the funding of these anticommunist forays may have been kept secret from the unions paying for them, the probability is that it was well known to the FBI, which had Rice and the revived ACTU under close surveillance from 1947 onward. One report received by the bureau related that George Sadler, division steward at Local 601, stated that "Father Rice will furnish the money [and] the literature" for running an entire anticommunist slate of officers in Local 601, and that if any ACTU operatives got into trouble, "he, Father Rice, will furnish them with an attorney and this attorney will be Charles Margiotti, former State Attorney General."[126] Rice dismissed this allegation as pure fiction. Thus the source of funding for the campaign in general, and for Rice and Duffy's travels in particular, may have been less of a secret than Rice supposed at the time.

Some feel for the arduous and nerve-wracking nature of these travels may be gleaned from Rice's contemporaneous columns. He described sorties to St. Mary's, Pennsylvania, where a 100 percent Catholic town had a communist-led UE local;[127] to Sharon, Pennsylvania, where a turn-around vote against the communists and action taken against leftist delegates brought in the district council "with a vengeance";[128] to West Virginia, where the leadership of the Fairmont local soon began being "ACTU-baited" because of Rice and Duffy's visits;[129] to Erie, where there was little opposition to the leadership of Catholic leftist John Nelson before Rice and Duffy hit town, but a "boiling cauldron" afterward. Rice accused Nelson, an extremely popular union leader, of being a bad Catholic. This charge appears to be absolutely without foundation, if not positively malicious: Nelson had studied for the priesthood for two years at Rice's alma mater, St. Vincent's, sent his children to Catholic schools, attended Mass frequently, belonged to the Holy Name Society, and astounded his secular UE colleagues when attending meetings in New York City by heading first not to UE headquarters, but across the street to St. Patrick's Cathedral.[130]

Standard operating procedure on these forays was for Rice to drive Duffy (Rice's large automobile was an object of invidious comments by his opponents even this early) to the city where a UE election was in the offing. There Duffy would head for the bars and Rice for the Catholic rectory. Rice would work on the pastor to get him to urge his flock at Sunday mass or the UE portion of his flock, to turn out at the union election to vote against the communists. Duffy, meantime, would conduct an unscientific sample of union opinion in as many taverns as he could reach before closing time. The two of them would attempt to cement the right-wing opposition, perhaps conduct a practice meeting (not unlike earlier days in the labor schools of the CRA), and then hit the road back to Pittsburgh. It was, Rice reflected later, "hard-dog, back-breaking work."[131]

Along the way, the duo discovered that the allies they were able to enlist in the struggle against communism were not always the best trade unionists. A prime example was Mildred Turner, the president of a small local in a Sylvania plant that did sensitive work on radar in Huntington, West Virginia. As the story was told by the District 6 administration, Turner's uninspiring leadership had left her members with hourly pay thirty cents less than the national norm for Sylvania plants, a grievance procedure that she declined to utilize, and a series of other complaints that members were unable to take action on because of Turner's practice of conducting local meetings without even the required 10-member quorum.[132] When members took their complaints to the District 6 offices, they were helped in preparing an alternate slate of officers for the next union elections. Turner, who had never before expressed any disagreement with union policies at higher levels, suddenly became an avid anticommunist and called in John Duffy and other ACTU adherents to rescue her from defeat.

Formal charges were filed against Turner in December 1948, including charges of financial irregularities, failure to permit elections of stewards, failure to conduct elections according to the local constitution, and failure to follow democratic parliamentary procedure at meetings. At the meeting held to hear the charges, Turner attempted to introduce Duffy, but when matter was put to a vote of the membership, two or three hundred raised their hands in opposition, to thirty or forty in favor. She then declined to appoint tellers and announced that her proposal had passed. Upon the demand of the members, another vote was taken with a court stenographer recording Turner and Duffy in an "obvious minority." Turner refused to go on with the meeting and Duffy attempted to speak. Eventually he was shouted down and the meeting resumed without Turner. When two weeks later a secret vote was taken on the charges against Turner, she was expelled, 96 to 1.

In these events, the District 6 leadership saw a "welding of local corruption and 'ideological' attacks on the UE [which] is the ACTU's Carey-Block Clique favorite device."[33] Rice never discussed the details of the battle in his column, but inferred that the District 6 interest in the little local sprang not from a concern with good trade union practice, but from subversive designs on the sensitive defense work done at the plant.[134]

Back in Pittsburgh, another confrontation was shaping up that would again pit Rice against the Left, and would help establish, as had the Fort Pitt brouhaha, Pittsburgh's reputation as a "violent epicenter" of the anticommunist drive. Carnegie Hall, on the city's North Side, had been rented by the Communist Party for a rally on April 2. National party leader Henry Winston was to speak against the Smith Act criminal trials then in progress against him and other national leaders of the CPUSA. The event was given a great deal of publicity, and unsuccessful attempts were made to have permission for it rescinded. The gathering went ahead as scheduled.

While a group variously estimated between one hundred seventy and four hundred assembled inside the hall to hear Winston, a hostile crowd of about five thousand gathered outside. Prominent in the crowd were right-wing members of Local 601, who proceeded to set up a picket line. The line was crossed by Thomas J. Fitzpatrick, leader of the UE progressives, on his way into the hall. Rice showed up on the Local 601 sound truck, and proceded to address the crowd, urging calm. He stated then and later that his only reason for coming was to urge demonstrators to refrain from violence.[135] This insistence did not prevent the CPUSA newspaper, *The Worker*, from naming Rice as an "inciter" or from claiming that "each time Rice made a speech denouncing the meeting and calling upon the crowd to be disciplined, more hoodlums arrived and more violent became his pickets."[136]

As the meeting inside concluded, the crowd outside surged out of control of the one hundred police officers then present and struck, kicked, and jostled men and women leaving the hall. No deaths or hospitalizations resulted, but one rioter was arrested for attempting to overturn a taxi with passengers from the meeting. *The Worker* reported:

> Father Rice's "peaceful pickets" carried in paper bags bricks wrapped in tissue paper and threw them at those who came out of the meeting. They also had nails at the ends of the sticks to which their signs were fastened. They were hitting people with those sticks and driving the nails into automobile tires.[137]

Rice's next column reiterated his position that he had been present only as an observer and had urged refraining from violence. Then he added: "I was sorry that there was any violence, but not sorry that there was a demonstration."[138]

An aspect of this affair that became known to CPUSA leaders only later is that one of the party members who had been inside Carnegie Hall planning the meeting was also a paid FBI informant who was simultaneously passing on information about the gathering to the leaders of the crowd outside. This was Matt Cvetic, who would become famous a year later when he published an account of his activities in three installments in the *Saturday Evening Post* entitled "I Posed as a Communist for the FBI,"[139] which was subsequently turned into a film and serialized on radio. Rice later conceded that Cvetic's own motives both in playing the informant role and later going public had more to do with money than patriotism, but still insisted that Cvetic accused no one falsely of communism. Cvetic was later committed to a mental hospital as an incurable alcoholic.[140]

As 1949 wore on, Rice's personal battle with the communists and with UE District 6 was headed for its climax, but the outlook did not appear favorable to Rice and his followers. Shortly before the CIO purges of 1949, Rice had to report in his own column that "Sharon, Erie, Fairmont, and Wilmerding [Local 610] have all been won by the Reds."[141] The Erie local had followed the leadership of Nelson, whom Rice accused of "going through the motions of leading the life of a practical Catholic," by a margin of 3–1.[142] Rice and Duffy had given it all they had, had driven hundreds of miles, and harangued hundreds and thousands of union members that communism in the UE was *the* issue. But they had not succeeded in winning the majority of members to their viewpoint, at least not so far as evidenced in union elections for local control.

What was perhaps worse from Rice's perspective was a series of secession decisions being taken by some of the locals. Rice had been fairly consistent in advocating that members stay in the UE and try to wrest control of it from the Left. One alleged exception to this line, claimed by the District 6 leadership to have been written by Rice in a confidential letter to a prospective "fifth column agent," said, "The author's advice to stick in [the UE] and fight rather than pull out . . . is to be modified where some unions are concerned. In the UE at present it is good advice, but circumstances may change anytime."[143] In his printed columns, at any rate, Rice was consistent in opposing secessionism.

By 1949 the ACTUs organ *Labor Leader* had become more ambivalent about the "stay and fight" strategy,[144] and in District 6 Tom Nolan had led his local into the UAW and even Duffy's old Local 613 had gone the same route. This gave fresh ammunition to Rice's critics who claimed he really meant to destroy the UE, and simultaneously made it more difficult to achieve the original objective of taking it over by democratic vote of the membership.

The tide in the nation, if not necessarily in District 6, had begun to run against the UE leadership. The UE Members for Democratic Action (UEMDA), which Rice had been instrumental in forming in August 1946, when the UE had met in Pittsburgh, had succeeded in uniting ACTU and two other quite diverse opposition groups into one cohesive bloc. UEMDA was now coordinated even to the point of holding its own national caucus well before the 1949 UE national convention in order to name its own slate of candidates for national office. And a total of thirteen locals with an aggregate membership of seventy thousand had crossed from left to right by the end of 1948.[145] The feud between the UE and Murray was still simmering. And by the time the Steelworkers decided in 1949 to sign the Taft-Hartley affidavits, the UE would be the only major CIO affiliate exposed to takeovers for its refusal to comply — unless convention delegates were able to force the leadership to reverse its position and sign the affidavits.

Rice was convinced that the key to success for the right wing lay in the election of national delegates from the vast Local 601. He called it "probably the most important election ever held in a labor union in the Pittsburgh district."[146] Correspondingly, he began pulling out all the stops in a drive to snatch victory from the jaws of many defeats in the district.

One ploy Rice had already used repeatedly and now used afresh was condemnation of UE leadership from Catholic pulpits just prior to the election. One classic in this line appeared in the St. Regis church bulletin (Trafford, Pennsylvania) for Sunday, August 14, 1949:

ATTENTION MEMBERS OF UE LOCAL 601. In view of our Holy Father's recent announcements on Communism it is of the utmost importance that YOU VOTE in the important union election this after- noon. This election of delegates has resolved itself into a fight between *communists* and *anti-communists*. The right wing and anti-Red slate has on it Charles Copeland, Michael Fitzpatrick and Al Pefferman, etc. It is your duty, your Moral duty to vote against those who uphold commun- ism. The people behind the Iron Curtain cannot vote against Commun- ism, YOU CAN — YOU MUST.[147]

Moral strictures from the pulpit were not new to Rice's crusade, but working behind the scenes to instigate an investigation by HUAC, immediately prior to an election, was a novelty. This Rice did as the crucial date approached, traveling by train to Washing- ton with Duffy and Ernest Vida of Local 601 to arrange with Rep. Ernest Walter, a Democrat from Easton, Pennsylvania for HUAC to come to Pittsburgh to conduct hearings into communism in Local 601 just before the elections. The counsel to the committee even arranged to have subpoenas issued to progressives in Local

601 without the knowledge of HUAC members.[148] Rice noted approvingly in his columns that the investigation was to take place, but did not reveal his own role in arranging for it.

The scheme may have backfired, because the national UE got wind of the arrangement and published a scathing broadside prior to the election, which read in part:

> The Un-American Committee's present interference in the affairs of Local 601 was arranged in Washington by the Reverend Charles Owen Rice who makes a career meddling in the affairs of labor unions. He is the national coordinator of the affairs of the Carey-ACTU group in UE, providing them with the brains they are not able to muster among themselves.
>
> In a spree of red-baiting hysteria fomented by Rev. Rice and his associates something less than a year ago, a group subservient to Rev. Rice took control of a number of important offices in Local 601. Since that time the membership of Local 601 has lost confidence in that group and Rev. Rice is in immediate danger of losing his grip on the Local's affairs.[149]

Rice later argued that Fitzpatrick had given him rather too much credit, that it was not he who had engineered the idea, but that he had been "suckered in" to going along on the delegation to Walter.[150] Go along he did.

At length, after all the guns on either side had been wheeled out and fired, it was time for the members to vote. Inasmuch as both factions were represented in the local leadership at the time, the results bade fair to represent overall union sentiment after hearing all the arguments and pleas from Rank-and-File on the Right and Progressives on the Left. As the results became public, Rice at first hailed them as a victory, admitting that the HUAC spotlight had helped.[151] The next week he pronounced it "not a complete victory," and criticised election procedures as "slipshod."[152] Still later he predicted — correctly, this time — that the UE national leadership would win again at the convention.[153]

At the national convention that year, Fitzgerald and the national leadership prevailed as they had in the Local 601 delegate elections. Fitzgerald defeated UEMDA candidate Carey by the comfortable margin of 2,235–1,500. The convention did vote, however, to sign the Taft-Hartley affidavits, now that all the other CIO unions had done the same.

The crusade was now at a standstill. The three-year campaign of Rice, Duffy, ACTU, UEMDA, and all their supporters had produced storms of controversy, had polarized some locals and greatly strengthened and organized the right wing of the union, had even won some elections and made other significant advances. But the final victory as spelled out in "How to Decontrol Your Union of Communists" — namely, control of the international union — remained nearly as elusive as ever.

Then events overtook both the Right and the Left in District 6. The UE, incensed at the continual raiding by CIO affiliates and Murray's refusal to put an end to it, voted at its national convention to boycott the 1949 CIO convention. Murray retaliated on November 10 by "expelling" the UE from the CIO (UE leaders retorted that Murray was like the boss who says to the worker, "You can't quit in this place. You're fired").[154] Murray then proceeded to charter an alternate union, the International Union of Electrical Workers (IUE), under the leadership of James Carey, to replace the UE. Left-led Farm Equipment (FE) was ordered into the UAW, where presumably Walter Reuther would control it. (FE defied this order, and united with the UE instead.) Initiatives were announced that would within the year begin the expulsion of the other left-led unions in the CIO. The purging of communist elements from American labor was now in high gear.

As noted above, the role that Rice played in moving Murray to undertake this wholesale expulsion of the Left from the CIO is difficult to evaluate. The kinds of initiatives that Murray now took were exactly the initiatives that Rice had been advocating for seven years, first in confidential notes to Murray and conversations with him, and more recently in his published columns. On the other hand, Rice was not privy to the inner councils of the CIO prior to the convention, did not correctly predict the dramatic events of 1949, and was in all likelihood as startled as everyone else by the sudden turn of events. Influence he had had, but it had been a subtle influence exerted continually over the years, rather than a single dramatic intervention that produced the expulsions.[155]

There now took place a series of representation elections between the UE and the IUE across the nation and throughout District 6 that would in effect tear this large union to shreds. James Matles in his book on the subject has described vividly and bitterly the strategy arrayed against the UE in the typical election: the company would cancel its contract with the union at the behest of the CIO, then file for an election with the Taft-Hartley board.

HUAC hearings would be held, and UE workers fired under the Truman Loyalty Order. Banner headlines about communists would accompany ACTU operatives as they went house-to-house urging a vote against the UE. Dignitaries from the Truman administration and the CIO would come to town, accompanied by reformed communists like Mike Quill and Joe Curran. Matles concluded:

> An operation of this scope and strength, conducted in the general atmosphere of cold war and Korean War hysteria in the country, and directed at a single independent and embattled union, was bound to take its toll upon the UE. It did.[156]

By 1955, UE, formerly representing over a half million electrical workers, would see its membership shrink to approximately ninety thousand. It would survive, but not as its old self.

In District 6, Rice and Duffy would win some quick victories. Sharon, Fairmont, and St. Mary's joined the IUE, and Duffy emerged as the director of District 6 of the new union.[157] A mass meeting of Local 601 workers at East Pittsburgh Stadium endorsed the IUE and James Carey; the Left enacted a seizure of Local 601 headquarters.[158] The battle would drag on, Rice and Duffy's travels would continue, but essentially the issue had been decided: except for a what Rice termed "surprising" victory at Local 610, the UE would come out the loser. Rice, Duffy, and the ACTU had emerged on the winning side, and were appropriately jubilant.

It is important to recognize, however, that their victory had not come through the union ballot box, and not with the strategy Rice had long advocated of standing and fighting the leftist opposition. It had come instead via an authoritative pronouncement from CIO headquarters, which fit better with the secede-and-purge tactics Rice and Duffy had long opposed. But they were prepared to accept a victory over the Left on whatever terms it was offered, and had likely forgotten Rice's judgment of less than a year earlier, when Duffy and Nolan were being voted out of District 6: "The business of purges is the last resort of desperate men."[159]

How important a force was Rice in initiating the purges of communists in labor, which presaged the advent of politicians like Senator Joseph McCarthy who would make anticommunism into a major chapter in American history in the 1950s?

Perhaps the most dramatic answer to this question is provided in the attacks leveled at Rice by members of the American Left, who felt the full fury of his anticommunist crusade. Even allowing for a certain tendency to exaggerate the strengths of one's enemies in battle, and for a predilection to name an outside clergyman rather than internal union forces as "the mastermind" of a union rebellion, we can see in the howls of Rice's adversaries much evidence to suggest that he was indeed central to the forces that initiated the purge of domestic communism in the United States in the late 1940s.

I will thus conclude my review of this era in Rice's life by examining the charges hurled at him during his anticommunist days and by later scholars of those days. Some of the charges, particularly those carried in *ex parte* publications during the heat of battle, may shed more heat than light. Others should be taken into account by those wishing to understand more clearly what kinds of motivations drove Rice throughout his career as an activist priest. All of them serve to demonstrate that Rice was, for good or ill, an extremely potent force in the formative stages of the anticommunist movement of the post World War II era in America.

First there was the charge, originally articulated by the leadership at Local 601 and District 6 and later echoed and amplified by the *Worker* and *Pravda*, that Rice and the ACTU were in fact reactionary forces using the Catholic faith of many workers and the trumped-up issue of communism as a cover for their real agenda: weakening labor and the CIO at a critical time — when it was under increasingly sharp attack by capital. Emphasis was placed in this analysis on the fact that the Rice and ACTU attacks on communism came not in the 1930s when the Left was in fact expanding its influence, but after the war, when the minority presence of the Left was more stable, and when employers along with reactionary forces in government and the press were making determined assaults on labor and particularly on the CIO. HUAC was called in to investigate unions when those unions were in vulnerable contract-negotiating periods. Movements to secede were not made when unions were strong, but when they had been weakened by prolonged strikes. Secession was often followed by back-to-work movements led by Reuther or lesser supposed champions of militant unionism like Nolan or Duffy or William Hart of the Steelworkers. The coordination of anticommunist activity with the local, often reactionary, press was further cited as showing that these crusaders had more in common with the old guard in America than with the idealists of the CIO.

At the national and international level, this approach concluded, the purpose behind the purges was not to rid the unions of the tiny presence of the Left, or to forestall genuine threats to sabotage America's defense capabilities (not one criminal indictment was ever handed down, despite years of investigations), but simply to housebreak the CIO at home and to render it an acceptable vehicle for U.S. imperialism overseas in the decades ahead when many other unions around the globe would have to be brought to heel. By the time the CIO merged with the AFL in the mid-1950s, it had lost its original militance and threat to the American ruling class anyhow. In short, the big winners from these years of anticommunist crusading were not the workers, but the owners, and it was for them and with them that Rice and his confederates put forth their strongest efforts.[160]

The reason this critique did not succeed very well in the late 1940s, and why it still rings hollow today, was that Rice was simply too well known in the Pittsburgh area as a friend of the worker, and a militant friend at that. He had walked too many picket lines and engaged in too much acrimonious debate with the forces of conservatism, for many to buy the line that he was a reactionary disguised in a friend-of-labor costume. The charges against Duffy, Nolan and Hart were controverted at the time by the ACTU. Whether they were simply invented out of whole cloth as the ACTU claimed, or exaggerated interpretations of hard judgment calls in isolated instances, these allegations hardly convinced many unionists that these men, whose lifework had been in their unions, were antiunion conspirators.

The criticism that the ACTU was splitting labor unions at a crucial time was of course correct. The real question is one of motivation: Did the ACTU wish to destroy the CIO by splitting it, or to save it by purging it of what the ACTU conceived to be a mortal danger? It is much easier today than it was in those hysterical times to conclude that communists had too small a presence in labor to pose a credible threat either to the CIO or to the American defense establishment. Certainly the allegation that Rice and the ACTU intentionally and maliciously worked for the triumph of the bosses was an ill-calculated one.

As to international ramifications of the CIO purge, Rice argues that it was the AFL more than the CIO that became the conduit for

CIA funds pumped into the effort to influence labor unions abroad after World War II.[161] By the mid 1950s, with the reunion of the AFL and the CIO, this rebuttal of course had considerably less force.

A second charge, rather less laden with ideological suppositions than the first, was that Rice and the ACTU were either inventing the communist issue, or exploiting it, or both, in order to gain power and position for themselves. Rice's role as a cleric of course made him relatively immune to the allegation that he was seeking for himself a place in the CIO hierarchy. About the closest that I have come to finding an allegation in Rice's voluminous papers (or outside them) to the effect that he was in labor activism for the money, was a 1953 letter to the bishop from a pseudonymous "Sacerdos Pittsburghensis" who referred to Rice as "anything for an extra dollar Charlie."[162]

Yet Rice regularly had to defend other Actists from the charge of seeking self-advancement at the expense of communists, real or invented. He consistently retorted that once the ACTU had completed its anticommunist mission, it established no separate unions or enduring power centers within existing unions, but went gently into the good night of oblivion.[163] This argument does not quite wash. It must be pointed out that Duffy became director of District 6, other Actists secured positions for themselves, and even as sympathetic an observer as Michael Harrington has concluded that "one can find evidence . . . that Actists tried to advance their own people within the new [IUE] union."[164]

A related consideration, and one that Rice himself has admitted has some merit, is that some of the allies whom the original core group of Actists picked up along the way were not the best or the brightest unionists, and may even in some cases have had some fairly self-serving motives for coming aboard.[165] Mildred Turner was perhaps a dramatic case in point. Nevertheless, the charge that the core group of Actists around Rice, as opposed to some of those who jumped on the anticommunist bandwagon later on, fought the communists simply or even predominantly in order to advance themselves, appear to be overdrawn.

Still another vein of criticism saw Rice and the ACTU as sectarian zealots who sought to expand the power of the Catholic Church in American labor unions, no matter what the benefit or disadvantage might be to union members whose friends Rice and the Actists claimed to be. This charge, interestingly, came from both the Left and the Right. On the Left, *The Worker* argued that Rice, like Father Coughlin before him, had started out claiming that he was interested in social justice, but in later diatribes tipped his hand: the desire to have Catholicism prevail over other religions.[166]

Of particular note to this line of criticism was the interest that the ACTU and its *Labor Leader* were at that time expressing in having the CIO establish relations in Europe not with the socialist trade union federation, the World Federation of Trade Unions (WFTU), but with its Catholic rival, the International Confederation of Free Trade Unions (ICFTU).[167] Also along these lines it was argued that the real reason Murray, Rice, and the ACTU so opposed the Wallace candidacy of 1948 was that the creation of a third party in the United States would have diluted the influence that the American Catholic hierarchy then enjoyed within the Democratic Party.

Finally, a somewhat related charge came from noncommunist Kermit Eby, a former Protestant missionary who served as a CIO staff member and then went to the University of Chicago. Looking at the travail plaguing the CIO, Eby concluded that there were two authoritarian systems, communism and Catholicism, locked in deadly combat for control of the CIO, and that American Protestants had better wake up to this fact.[168]

These criticisms are the more understandable in Rice's case because of his readiness to engage in heated apologetics defending his church against all comers. He was wont to insist in the triumphalist fashion then commonplace among American Catholics that Catholicism was the truth and all other churches were heretical. He even had to be reminded from time to time that not all his radio listeners were Catholics.[169]

Rice replied that in fact one of his great idols in the labor movement was the Protestant Walter Reuther, that what he and his generation of labor priests accomplished was not so much to extend church influence in the CIO as to make the CIO acceptable within the church, and finally that he was indeed seeking to expand the *religious* influence of the church, not its *political* power.[170] It is of course understandable that Rice would view his own sectarian motivations in this light; it is equally understandable that others might not see the distinction that was so clear to him.

Aside from criticisms that Rice and the ACTU pursued unworthy goals (reactionism, self-promotion, or sectarianism), there were also charges that the methods they routinely used against communists were unsavory. Among the unethical methods attributed to Rice and the Actists were: *misuse of a trust*, as in the Carolyn Burkhart affair; *lies* (CPUSA writer George Morris once said of Rice that he "tells more lies in one column than you could detect");[171] *violence* (the CPUSA noted of the Fort Pitt Hotel incident that a "goon squad" and a "riot" had been organized under the direction of Rice, who afterward "walked out of the hall arm-in-arm with the ring-leader of the goons and later appeared to bail out one of the gang who was arrested");[172] *blackmail* (an early letter to Bishop Boyle had charged that Rice kept switching his "communist" targets, and had offered to let one of them off if he "would do certain things");[173] *electoral fraud,* in the 1947 delegate elections in Local 601;[174] *protecting corruption,* in the case of Mildred Turner;[175] *stool pigeon tactics,* in the use of parish census forms that invited the faithful to declare their anticommunism and instructed the census-takers to point the finger of suspicion at those who "seemed pro-Communist";[176] *union raiding,* which Rice advocated the UAW do to the UE and the FE; *secession,* which in fact occurred in UE locals 613 and 638; and *disregard of the civil rights* of those accused of being communists. Of course, the CPUSA at the time was not aware of Rice's informing the FBI about communists, real and suspected, so that its list of charges against him was shorter than it could have been.

Some of these charges appear to have little or no basis in evidence (violence or secessionism, for example). Others Rice either admitted later or had second thoughts about (he regretted his disregard for his adversaries' civil rights; was not sure that he did the right thing in the Burkhart affair). Most of the rest grew out of highly charged adversarial situations in which the inflammatory rhetoric on either side made widely divergent interpretations of the same actions not only possible, but inevitable. But perhaps the clearest conclusion to emerge from these charges is that Rice was indeed an adversary whom the Left came to fear as one of the most effective enemies it had.

A final criticism directed at the ACTU and in very considerable part at Rice is rather more subtle than the preceding ones, and comes from a recent scholar of the Actist movement. Douglas P. Seaton argues that Catholic social teaching had little to offer to unionists, apart from a hard-edged opposition to socialism and to the concept of class struggle, accompanied by certain vague notions of "fair" wages, prices, and profits. But he believes that these notions of fairness reduced in practice to little more than slogans, precisely because the church insisted they must be achieved by voluntary labor-management cooperation rather than by confrontation. And because management had little motivation to compromise in ways that would reduce its powers or profit unless confronted with unacceptable losses, the *effect* of church social teaching, whether or not its conscious *intention*, has been to veto the one real power workers have, and thus to rob workers of the militance they need in order to achieve the goals the church seems to find worthy. Thus, argues Seaton, the effect of the work of labor priests like Rice was to purge from the CIO not so much the communist element, but the early spirit of independent militance that American labor greatly needed. So the ACTU did in fact weaken American labor by its preaching of class harmony, and by its anticommunist crusade. The ACTU was *in effect* a force of reaction.[177]

For his own part, Rice did not believe that his activities made union members less militant, but that his unswerving support of strikes gave them more heart. Catholic social teaching may have preferred cooperation to class conflict, but not everyone could have inferred that fact from the picket-line homilies of this member of the Cock Rices. And he noted that even after the purge of the CIO, which he later came to regret, American unions went on to greater rather than lesser successes, at least in terms of bread-and-butter unionism.[178]

Yet Seaton's thesis, as applied to Rice, has at least some validity. Seaton notes that although the ACTU started out with a "straight down the middle" stance that rejected communism and capitalism equally, arguing that neither of them properly understood or provided for the spiritual dimension of human nature, it soon shifted its ground to attack communism almost exclusively, rarely going on the offensive against capitalist abuses. Such a pattern is abundantly clear in Rice's writings and activism of the late 1940s.

In the 1980s, moreover, two generations worth of hindsight raise more doubts about the direction of Rice and the Actists, and about the results of their activism, than they likely entertained at the time. In the age of Reaganism, as one watches labor unions struggle feebly against the tide of plant closings, corporate disinvestment, worker give-backs, and the shrinkage of the unionized sector of American labor, one is tempted to think it might have turned out differently if the CIO had not been purged two generations ago of its most militant elements. Even if the forces arrayed against labor are so powerful as to overcome even UE-style unions or their European counterparts, the weak state of American labor is a cause for concern to many observers in the 1980s. Rice would not admit that his anticommunist crusades of the 1940s helped prepare the way for the waning of unionism in the 1980s. But the possibility should not be dismissed out of hand.

Nor is it clear today that the Catholic Church is still seeking a middle ground between capitalism and communism. True, the Vatican upholds Solidarity in Poland at the same time that the U.S. Catholic bishops trenchantly criticize American capitalism. But today many Catholic thinkers have given up on the notion of a practicable "third way."[179]

I return finally to the epithet most frequently hurled at Rice during these years: "Red-baiter." The term is often used to describe an employer or official who does not wish to deal with troublesome demands put forth by workers, and so distracts attention from those demands by calling the workers or their leaders "communists," perhaps without the smallest shred of evidence. In that sense, Rice was not a Red-baiter. He spent large amounts of time researching communism in American labor; when *he* called someone a communist, he generally had a good basis for doing so.

But if he did not cry "commie!" as a distraction or when he knew better, he certainly did engage in myth-making about the extent and nature of communism in American labor. He convinced himself that the relatively few communists in labor were capable of taking over the whole movement. He endowed those mostly ordinary men and women with superhuman determination, cunning, ruthlessness, and of course perfidy. He insisted that so vile was their political preference, it vitiated whatever other good they might have done — whether on the job, in the union, or in church.

Particularly distasteful in retrospect was his branding of communists who were Catholics as "bad Catholics," frequently inferring that they were in bad standing with the church because of divorces or other marital irregularities (and this in contrast to the divorce of David McDonald of the USWA, to which Rice never alluded in public).

Moreover, Rice was willing to subordinate the principle of democratic trade unionism to the pursuit of communists when he was unable to persuade unionists by other means that communism was the issue above all other issues. He was willing to acquiesce knowingly in the destruction of once great unions if that was the price for extirpating communism.

In short, he had made the communists into devils, and poor devils they were when the Reverend Charles Owen Rice came after them.

Abandoning his originally balanced critiques of capitalism and

communism, and the apparent realpolitik of wartime radio broadcasts when he had seemed resigned even to Soviet hegemony over
eastern Europe, Rice struck more blows and more effective ones
against the Left in those years, arguably, than he would ever be
able to strike against the Right throughout his life.

It was in all these senses that Rice was a Red-baiter. There were
many other Red-baiters in the late 1940s, but what set Rice apart
from many others was that he passionately believed in what he
was doing, that he generally knew whereof he spoke when he
leveled the charge of communism, and — if the testimony of James
Matles, national secretary of the UE is any indication — he was as
effective in the battle as any opponent the Left in America ever had
to face. Says Matles:

> [He] had few rivals in hostility toward the UE and few who could be
> said to have helped more to weaken and split the union. If Father Rice
> were to be awarded an honorary degree as masterplanner of the red-
> baiting war upon the UE in the late 1940's and through the fifties, it
> would be difficult to discover anyone knowledgeable of the period who
> might dispute his title.[180]

When we cumulate all the evidence, we come to realize that to
call Rice a Red-baiter is to say too little; he deserves a more
distinguished title. Perhaps "Red-baiter Extraordinaire" will do.

FIVE

Up The River?

THE DECADE FROM THE EARLY 1950s to the early 1960s was perhaps the most curious one in Rice's life. Triumphantly concluding his crusade against communists in labor, Rice himself next passed into the twilight of public oblivion. He would attribute this result to a conscious vendetta by the hierarchy for his outspokenness on behalf of labor, but that explanation, as will be seen, is far from adequate. When he emerged from his "exile" in the 1960s, he would no longer appear as the patriotic anticommunist he had been in the late 1940s and early 50s, proclaiming himself instead a "radical" as he had in the 1930s. Even if that was a fairly dubious title, clearly Rice would become an activist in causes where he often found himself the ally of some of the very persons he had crusaded against earlier. If we were to conceive of Rice's life until the 1950s as his caterpillar stage, and the later years as his reemergence as a gaudy butterfly, then the decade between constitutes his curious chrysalis stage, spent in the cocoon of obscurity.

Just about the time Rice was reaching the height of his fame and his powers, his bishop ("Iron John" Dearden, who had succeeded Boyle in 1950) reassigned him from the House of Hospitality first to a nearby parish, and a bit later to Natrona, Pennsylvania, a steel town on the Allegheny River, about a 45-minute auto trip away from Pittsburgh. Rice was also informed at Duquesne University that his services were no longer needed in undergraduate teaching, and he opted to drop his work at Duquesne's Management-Labor Institute as well. Finally, somewhat later, the previously independent *Pittsburgh Catholic* was taken over by the diocese of

Pittsburgh and Rice was not invited to continue his columns in the newspaper's pages.

Why had Rice fallen so fast from notoriety to obscurity? The quasi-official "exile theory" that grew up among Rice and his close friends, and which he repeated frequently,[1] attributes Rice's decline to a statement he had written in the *Pittsburgh Catholic* calling Cardinal Francis Spellman of New York a "scab." But this quotation, perhaps the most frequently cited one in all Rice's columns, simply does not exist.

What happened in New York was that the gravediggers for the archdiocese were turned down for wage increases and went on strike in the spring of 1949. Rather than negotiate with the strikers, Spellman denounced the union as communistic and ordered a corps of seminarians to cross the picket lines bearing shovels to bury the dead. Coffin upon coffin was stacked up in the cemetery. His action had the effect of breaking the strike. The grave diggers subsequently returned to work after a less favorable wage package was handed them.[2] Such an event was obviously an embarrassment to Catholic unionists throughout the country, and particularly to the ACTU, attempting as it was at that time to convince workers that the church was on their side and that its anticommunism was not merely a ruse to disguise favoritism to the management side.[3]

Rice later claimed that "he wrote in an article in the *Pittsburgh Catholic* that a scab was a scab whether he wore 'cardinal red or denim blue.'"[4]

In point of fact, Rice wrote no such thing in his column. Instead, after supporting the cardinal by repeating the charge that the union's international was communist-controlled (but denying that the local was), Rice stated:

> Your writer does not consider himself competent to comment on the moral issues involved; they will have to be worked out on a higher level.[5]

Both here and in his broadcasts at the time, Rice's reaction to Spellman's strike-breaking was a model of circumspection and indeed servility, rather than defiance.[6] (This, by the way, stood in marked contrast to his position, which he had just announced in the *Pittsburgh Catholic*, of plain speaking when it came to communists. His adversaries on the left may have been howling in derision at Rice's double standard when it came to a Red-baiting cardinal rather than the presumed Reds.)

But even if Rice had, in the spring of 1949, taken on the redoubtable Spellman (and there is no evidence that he did), the chronology of Rice's subsequent removal from public visibility hardly fits the interpretation that the rug was pulled from under him in retaliation for his outspokenness, with Dearden acting as Spellman's hatchet man. It was in June 1951, more than two years after the gravediggers' strike, that Rice was appointed to the parish of St. Brigid, near the House of Hospitality, as its administrator. His assignment as pastor of St. Joseph's in Natrona came in December 1952, nearly four years after the incident. And his columns continued to appear in the *Pittsburgh Catholic* until September 8, 1954 — five and a half years after the "scarlet scab" had swung into action!

The only incident, in fact, that chronologically might appear to be a direct result of the gravediggers' strike was Rice's removal from Duquesne University, in 1950. And that incident, as Rice would learn only much later, probably had more to do with his own Irish temper than with a banishment order from the new bishop, John Dearden.

The then-president of Duquesne, Rev. Francis Smith, C.S.Sp., had quietly entered into negotiations with U.S. Steel regarding the future of Rice's Management-Labor Institute. An agreement resulted, stipulating that U.S. Steel would provide extensive funding, and the institute would become more "balanced" (as its title for four years had suggested) by the addition of a co-director with a promanagement orientation, Rev. William Hogan, S.J. of Fordham University. At the same time a decision had been reached to discontinue Rice's undergraduate teaching, so that his only work at Duquesne would be at the reorganized Management-Labor Institute. Unfortunately for these plans, Fr. Smith was reassigned at about this time, and apparently left Duquesne angry. Rice was called in by the new administration, informed that his services to the undergraduates were no longer required, but was asked to stay on at the Management-Labor Institute. Incensed at losing the undergraduate work he enjoyed, Rice immediately resigned both positions. Bishop Dearden later told Rice that he wished he would have stayed on at Duquesne. And later still, one summer at a labor institute at Penn State University, Rice ran into a U.S. Steel executive who finally let him in on a fuller version of the story. "You never really knew what happened to you, did you?" asked the executive, who then went on to describe the arrangement Smith had cooked up with U.S. Steel before his own hasty departure, and explained that Rice had ruined the whole deal by taking his hasty walk.[7] At any rate, it is reasonable to infer that Rice's departure from Duquesne had not been Dearden's plan, but if anything the frustration of that plan.

If Rice's removal from public view was too belated and leisurely to fit well with the theory of swift hierarchical retaliation, could it have been that the bishop was slowly putting the squeeze on Rice for his (undocumented) slur of Spellman? This notion too fails to hold water when we look at Rice's own motivations in leaving the House of Hospitality, where he had resided as resident director since 1940. Rice frequently noted that he never felt called to the sort of voluntary poverty that Dorothy Day and her fellow Catholic Workers elected; he would rather live as comfortably as was reasonably possible after satisfying his charitable obligations toward others. He had moved to the House of Hospitality simply because there had not been another CRA priest to do so, he had dined separately from the guests, and in general had put up with the inconveniences of life there as best he could. But after a decade of such a life, away from the normal parish existence of a priest, he had had enough. Rice himself went to Bishop Dearden to say that if a parish vacancy should occur, he would be happy to fill it.[8]

Thus when the pastor died at St. Brigid's, near the House of Hospitality, Rice was appointed administrator there. He informed his radio listeners that he would continue to reside at the House of Hospitality,[9] but in fact he moved out soon thereafter.[10] So when Rice officiated at his last Thanksgiving dinner at the House of Hospitality in 1952, amid others' lamentations and expressions of sadness at his being involuntarily taken away from them, he had in truth already been living elsewhere, by his own choice, for about eighteen months.[11] It should also be noted that Rice went to Natrona not as an assistant but as a pastor. Such promotions were generally given to priests at about the age of forty; for Rice to be assigned as administrator at age forty-two and pastor at forty-three, was therefore not terribly out of line from the career paths of other priests who were his contemporaries.

Finally, it should not escape our notice that Rice's radio broadcasts were permitted to continue — something that Dearden surely could have quashed if he had really wanted to — and that Rice was invited, after departing Duquesne, to continue his labor classes at the Adult Education Institute of the Pittsburgh diocese, which he kept up for years.

All in all, then, the theory that Rice was exiled because of his effrontery toward Spellman is not persuasive, even if the effrontery could be documented — which has not happened.

An alternate form of the "exile theory," and one that has at least the advantage of prima facie chronological credibility, is that Rice was sent to Natrona for his part in a wildcat strike of bakers at Pittsburgh's Liberty Bakery in 1952.

At his adult education classes in labor, Rice had come in contact with a group of young unionists who were convinced that the leadership of Sam Wehofer at Liberty Bakery was a corrupt and useless one, which could be eliminated only by a wildcat strike without Wehofer's approval.[12] Wildcat strikes are of course viewed with distaste by union leaders generally, and one that had as its proximate goal the overthrow of an existing union leadership was even more likely to cause the local leadership, other labor leaders, and their allies all to close ranks — perhaps even in combination with management — against the wildcatters.

The bakers at Liberty nevertheless walked off the job in the spring of 1952. While the strike was delayed by a Taft-Hartley injunction, Rice proclaimed in his column that it was a just strike.[13] He was even able to persuade USWA District Director Bill Hart to support the action, albeit most grudgingly.[14] The strike recommenced in May, and was deadlocked by June.[15] Rice was away during part of that summer, visiting his uncle, Rev. Peter Rice, who was seriously ill in Wisconsin. In his absence, as Rice tells the story, Dan Gallagher, a friend who happened to be a professional boxer, borrowed Rice's car and visited the strike scene. Confronting strikebreakers on their way in to take the bakers' jobs, Gallagher suggested to the strikers that they "take care" of the strikebreakers. They did so, Gallagher ended up in front of a magistrate, and a picture showing Rice's car parked at the scene of the fracas showed up in the newpapers the next day. When Rice, back in Pittsburgh, asked Gallagher if it really had been his car, Gallagher replied, "It's a g.d. lie, Father, I parked it three blocks away!"[16]

Beginning in August, the city, the bakery and especially Wehofer's union combined forces to arrest scores of strikers, crush the strike, get strikers fired and removed from the union, and in some cases even denied unemployment compensation.[17] Rice defended the insurgents throughout the whole struggle, saying that they had chosen him as their spokesman because they had no one else to whom to turn.[18] But during court proceedings he was additionally accused by the union's counsel, Nick Uncovic, of actually being the leader of the insurgency.[19] If this was accurate, some of the strikers had been led to economic ruin by a cleric who escaped any such outcome himself.

This episode may have embarrassed John Dearden, and it was the next set of assignments after the strike finally flickered out in late 1952 that sent Rice to Natrona. What is missing is any link between the wildcat strike and Rice's reassignment in the correspondence between Rice and Dearden during this period.[20]

If, then, the Spellman quote is doubtful, and the chronology all wrong, and even the nexus between the bakery strike and Rice's assignment at best speculative, and if his new assignment was in fact a promotion, then why did Rice persist over the years in referring to this period as his "exile"?[21]

First of all, there is at least some truth in this interpretation. When Rice retired from labor classes at Duquesne, he asked Dearden's permission to reactivate the ACTU — presumably as an alternative forum — but was refused. When Dearden purchased the *Pittsburgh Catholic* from its previous independent owner in 1954 and reorganized it as a diocesan paper, it was surely no accident that Rice was not invited to continue his column there. Nor was it by accident, probably, that the parish selected for Rice's first pastorate was at a 45-minute remove from the city (his next would be still more distant). Dearden certainly liked a minimum of controversy in his diocese. Rice was told by one senior Pittsburgh priest that his broadcasts were the only spark in an otherwise darkened landscape.[22]

But perhaps more significant than the facts of the case was Rice's own subjective interpretation of them. It would become comfortable years later to picture himself during this era as the champion of labor, banished for allowing his valor to outstrip his discretion. This tendency of Rice to romanticize his past appears in his "exile" interpretation of the 1950s, in his insistence that he was a "radical" in the 1930s, and in other instances that I will have occasion to examine.

But even before the process of romanticized reinterpretation had a chance to set in, the years when he was assigned to Natrona were very clearly a "down" time for him, for reasons having little to do with Natrona or St. Joseph's itself. His beloved Bishop, Hugh C. Boyle, had become ill in 1948 and died in 1950. Harry Truman, for whom Rice had campaigned vigorously in 1948, left office in 1953, succeeded by Republican Dwight Eisenhower. His landmark election in November 1952 was closely followed by the death of Phil Murray.[23] Meanwhile the bakery workers' strike, largely inspired by Rice, was dragging toward its tragic conclusion. In 1953, his uncle, Peter Rice, died in Wisconsin. And Rice himself had to undergo surgery for a hernia, from which he convalesced slowly and painfully. To Rice in 1952 and 1953, it must indeed have appeared that his early allies were dead, his recent battles lost, that Iron John was firmly in the saddle, and that he himself was being sent up the river.[24]

By the end of his decade in "exile," Rice would have seriously rethought much of his Redbaiting activism. But in the early 1950s, his opposition to the Left remained steel-hardened and remorseless. It was only with regard to some of the politicians who were making careers for themselves out of anticommunism that Rice was beginning to entertain certain doubts.

In a message reminiscent of his days as the patriotic World War II radio priest, Rice proudly broadcast his support for U.S. entry into the war in Korea.[25] In his weekly columns he followed the news of campaigns against communist unions and of various hearings and proceedings against individual communists or suspected communists. As hundreds of them lost their employment or were sentenced to prison terms, Rice applauded.

One notable case in point was that of Steve Nelson, chief organizer for the CPUSA in Pittsburgh from 1948 until his arrest in 1950. Charged under a Pennsylvania sedition law (later invalidated by the United States Supreme Court) for his party membership, Nelson faced Pennsylvania Supreme Court Justice Michael Musmanno as both his chief investigator and accuser; he faced a nephew of Musmanno's as the prosecuting attorney; and he faced Judge Harry Montgomery appointed to the case by none other than Musmanno himself! Both Musmanno and Montgomery were running for higher office, and apparently did not want the vote-harvesting proceedings against Nelson to be delayed by any legal maneuvering beyond the dates of their upcoming campaigns. So when Nelson was unable to find a member of the legal profession in Pittsburgh who was willing to handle his defense, he was required by the court to defend himself — notwithstanding his lack of legal expertise and a recent automobile accident that had left him seriously debilitated. Nelson had to try to counter over a month's expert witnessing on the evils of communism by Musmanno, along with testimony by the recently uncovered Matt Cvetic. After several of the jurors who were leaning toward an acquittal had been intimidated, and one of them beaten up, according to Nelson, he was found guilty on all counts in January 1952, and sentenced to twenty years in prison the following July. He would spend one year in prison and one in court before the sentences were finally overturned.[26]

While these proceedings were underway in Pittsburgh, Rice made no mention of them in his column, although he later said that the judge had disqualified him from participating in the trial (perhaps Nelson should have been grateful for this small favor).[27] But as the trial concluded, Rice took occasion to praise the work of informer Matt Cvetic.[28] When Nelson was imprisoned at the workhouse in Blawnox, Pennsylvania, remanded to solitary confinement, and circulated international appeals for help, Rice responded to an inquiry from an acquaintance in Europe that it was not clear Nelson had really been denied counsel and that the situation was in fact "muddled."[29] Not one word from Rice expressed any reservations about the treatment accorded Nelson by the court or the prison.

Steve Nelson in 1953 was only a minor example of the justice accorded to accused communists by American courts. The proceedings that dominated the headlines were those against Ethel and Julius Rosenberg. They and some associates had been arrested on charges of passing the secret of the atomic bomb on to the Soviets, who had exploded their first one in 1949. In 1951 the Rosenbergs, still protesting their innocence, were sentenced to die. On June 19, 1953, after a variety of appeals and delays, they were executed.

Rice discussed the Rosenberg case on a radio broadcast early in 1953 as the execution date began to approach.[30] He had said much earlier that the "secret" of the A-bomb was at once a thousand secrets and no secret at all, inferring that the Soviet research establishment would in time produce its own atomic weapon.[31] He made no mention of this truism in 1953, but joined the chorus of those demanding the Rosenbergs' deaths. As the scheduled electrocutions drew closer, with even Pope Pius XII pleading for clemency, Rice remained adamant. He discussed a visit from someone hoping to get his name on a petition for clemency, but said he could not bring himself to sign.[32] Two weeks later, after the twin executions, Rice observed for his radio listeners, "Well, that problem has been settled by the highest authorities in the land."[33]

Although Rice remained very much the "cold warrior," there were signs that he was preparing to exit the anticommunist platform as the Nixons and McCarthys took center stage there. Thus late in 1935, addressing the Tarentum Lions Club at the Brackenridge Heights Country Club, Rice argued that while communists must be fought, they should be convicted in the courts only after due process had been followed. Of Sen. Joseph McCarthy he said, "[He] is cynical and ruthless . . . one of the most influential men in America; but his influence is for evil, not for good." He also took strong exception to the suggestion that the current USWA demand for a guaranteed annual wage was communist-inspired. The story was headlined in the local newspaper: "Red Hysteria Grips Nation, Priest States."[34] In 1954, when an item in the *Brooklyn Tablet* appeared to Rice to link his name with favorable mention of McCarthy, he wrote a protest letter, which the *Tablet* did not see fit to print.[35] On the other hand, in a 1953 broadcast on the subject of communist influence in churches, Rice had said:

I don't mind admitting that in the early days in my labor activity I was fooled more than once myself, and I am afraid that if I were asked the question, Did I ever belong to a Communist front, I would have to say, "Yes." If I were asked, Did I ever knowingly belong, I would say "No."[36]

This statement, of course, glossed over the fact that Rice had regularly lent assistance to unions that he knew to be communist-controlled. Had Rice, as he claimed in the 1950s, been "fooled"? Hardly. His "admission" thus stands as a good index of the pressure for conformity that Rice himself was experiencing in the mid-1950s — the victim, arguably, of a paranoia he had been instrumental in creating.

Just as Rice remained very much the anticommunist during his years at Natrona, so he managed still to keep a hand in labor affairs, particularly with the USWA. His new parish was quite near the office of his long-time ACTU ally, William Hart, who by now was Director of District 17 for the USWA. It was also in the bailiwick of Allegheny-Ludlum Steel, whose president, Ed Hanley, was rumored to have lamanted upon hearing of Rice's new assignment, "With all my other troubles, now I've got this rabble-rousing priest to contend with!"[37]

Hanley's foreboding turned out to have some truth to it. One year when a major national strike in steel had already been settled, Hart decided to keep the Allegheny-Ludlum workers out a bit longer, in hopes of winning a more attractive settlement. He used Rice as a stalking-horse at a meeting of workers at Harbrack High School. When Rice led off the meeting with the slogan, "Don't let them take it away from you!" the workers responded with a throaty roar. Hart tugged on Rice's coat from behind and said, "That's it, Father; we've got them."[38]

More than once during these years, Rice also managed to involve himself in the internal politics of the USWA, typically with something of a conspiratorial flair. When David Rarick mounted a national campaign against David McDonald for the presidency of the USWA, a district director like Hart of course dared not associate himself publicly with the insurgency. But Rice arranged for Rarick and Hart to meet secretly at night in his rectory kitchen. On one such occasion, as the election approached, Hart was able to provide Rarick with a detailed accounting of the locals in which he would be allowed an honest count, and those where the ballot boxes would be stuffed to his disadvantage. These projections proved remarkably accurate, and Rice later estimated that in a completely honest election, Rarick might have defeated McDonald.[39]

In addition, Rice continued to make the rounds of various union conventions, meetings, banquets and the like, although his visibility at USWA conventions was greatly reduced (which he attributed to McDonald).[40] (Rice would continue to support a succession of USWA insurgents over the years, including O'Brien and the "dues rebels" in the 1950s, Sadlowski in the 1970s and, up to a point, Wiesen in the 1980s.) In a 1957 letter to Henry Maggiolo, Rice also expressed interest in expanding his work as an arbiter by being designated for such work by the American Arbitration Association (AAA).[41]

Thus it was not the case that during this period Rice had been separated from his labor constituency by his "exile," but it was true that his involvement was receiving rather less note than during the 1940s.

A generation earlier, Rice's compatriot in the early CRA, Rev. Carl Hensler, had observed that politics in the church was sometimes like the streetcars in Toledo, Ohio, where he had lived. When the streetcar got to the end of the line, it simply reversed its direction without turning around, so that those who had been sitting in the back now found themselves in front and viceversa. As the 1950s neared their end, Rice was sitting in the back of the Pittsburgh diocese streetcar, but would soon be in front.

At his small, working-class parish of St. Joseph's, Rice carried out the normal duties of a pastor — at the church, the parochial school, and in the community. Pastors in those days often won recognition for brick-and-mortar projects — building new churches, convents, or parochial schools. No such achievements were in the cards those days for St. Joseph's or Rice, although he did oversee various remodeling projects and conducted appropriately festive celebrations for the parish's seventy-fifth anniversary.[42]

Beyond these ordinary activities, and his now largely ceremonial presence at various labor union functions, Rice's life was now a relatively quiet one. His enormous energies, fully occupied in the early days of the CRA, during the war by Rent Control, and in the late 1940s by his anticommunist crusading, now found no comparable outlet. Rice insists that he took naturally to the job of pastor, and vigorously denies that he was "a discouraged, bored, do-nothing, golf-playing priest in my days at Natrona."[43] He did, however, have time to play long rounds of golf at a local country club with his brother Pat.[44]

But at least Rice was proving his loyalty to the institutional church by doing his duties, such as they were, and by being a model of conformity on all issues dealing with clerical comportment and obeisance to the local bishop. At the Adult Education Institute of the Diocese, Rice no longer taught labor, but scripture.

Even his radio broadcasts from 1954 to 1958 showed a marked trend away from the political and polemical, and toward the pastoral and the pious. Fewer than a fifth of them contained major references to political issues, and most of these were approached only in relation to the institutional church: relations with communists in France, Italy and Argentina; the imprisonment of Cardinal Mindszenty in Hungary; persecution of Catholics in China and Russia; aid to parochial schools in the United States, and the like. He would also get in the regular plug for American labor around Labor Day each year. In partisan politics, he took a dim view, interestingly, of John F. Kennedy's run for vice- president at the

Democratic Convention in 1956 and a cautious approach to his presidential ambitions thereafter. At regular intervals, Rice still took up the cudgels to attack racial segregation.[45]

But for all his dutiful work, clerical conformity, and circumspection on the airwaves, it still remained clear to Rice that with Dearden in office he was not "in the plan" or "on the team" and therefore had the status nearly of a nonperson in the Pittsburgh diocese.[46]

It was in 1958 that this ice floe, as Rice saw it, began to show the first signs of cracking. The diocese had agreed with radio station KDKA to provide a spokesman to represent the Catholic position in a broadcast debate on birth control. But as the date approached, it proved impossible to find a suitable debater among the ranks of those close to Dearden. As a result, word went up the river: Would Rice do the job? Rice accepted this episcopal invitation with alacrity, handled himself well in the debate, as was his wont, and earned the bishop's gratitude.[47] Later that year, Rice received what may have been his reward in the form of an appointment to a larger and more affluent parish, Immaculate Conception in Washington, Pennsylvania. Rice was appropriately grateful for this sign of official favor, but he could hardly have helped noticing that in his new assignment he was at an even greater geographical remove from Pittsburgh than he had been at Natrona. He was no longer the pariah he had felt himself to be in 1953, but he still was not on the team.

Meanwhile, larger changes had been taking place in the Catholic Church. Pope Pius XII died in 1958, ending his nearly two-decades-long reign. The College of Cardinals, apparently unable to agree on a suitable successor to lead the Church for an equally long period, settled instead on an affable but elderly Italian prelate who took the name John XXIII amid widespread speculation (shared in by Rice) that he would serve the office of Peter only in a caretaker capacity. But the youthful octogenarian had some surprises in store for the Church and the world, as he announced plans for a Second Vatican Council, and then speeded up its convening when his subordinates at the Vatican appeared to be dragging their feet. The council would introduce sweeping changes in the church, which would leave it still in turmoil a generation after John XXIII's accession to the papacy. The era of aggiornamento, or updating, was underway in the ancient Roman Catholic Church.

The Pittsburgh diocese got an early taste of this era of change when at the outset of 1959 John Dearden was transferred to

Detroit. "This week our Bishop *finally* leaves us," said Rice in a broadcast (emphasis mine, although perhaps not exclusively so).[48] Two months later, in March 1959, the new bishop arrived from New Orleans: His Eminence John Wright. Wright would prove to be the most distinguished holder of the Pittsburgh episcopacy to that time, particulary in retrospect, when he was elevated to the rank of cardinal, assigned to the Vatican, and rumored (before his health began to fail) as a possibility to become the first American pope. When this rising churchman and politically liberal sophisticate arrived in Pittsburgh, he knew the names of only two priests in the diocese. One of them was that of the veteran labor priest, Rev. Charles Owen Rice.[49]

Almost immediately, Rice was appointed to the diocesan Board of Consultors. Under canon law, the bishop was required to have such an advisory board, and to submit to it major administrative matters of the diocese. But although he was required to seek his consultors' advice, he was not bound to follow it. In Wright's case, he met regularly with his Board of Consultors, and consistently followed its counsel. Rice would remain a member of that body, with one significant hiatus in the early 1970s, for over a generation.[50]

Just as quickly, Rice's column, which would later become syndicated, made its reappearance in the *Pittsburgh Catholic*. It was now headed the "Father Charles Owen Rice Column," rather than the earlier ACTU "Condition of Labor Column." It would continue to the 1980s.[51] The freedom given Rice was reflected in the fact that on average more than four out of every five columns would treat explicitly political themes.

Wright also decided to improve relations between the Pittsburgh diocese and organized labor, using Rice as his representative. Thus Rice each year for the next decade organized a Labor Day communion breakfast at which some labor leader or friend of labor was designated recipient of an annual award. In addition to this formal activity, Rice became Wright's trusted advisor and representative on a whole range of labor, civil rights, and political issues, and he was in turn able to induce Wright to take an activist role in quite a number of circumstances, as we shall see.

Thus Rice was not only a member in good standing of the team in the Pittsburgh diocese; he was nearly an assistant coach. At the very least, he was seated in the front of the streetcar.

As Rice took up his new parish in "Little Washington," Pennsylvania, in 1958 and then received strong backing from Wright beginning in 1959, he also attained, arguably, more civic respectability than he had at any time in the past (and certainly more than he would enjoy a decade later).

In this medium-sized city (population ca. 30,000) and county seat, Rice soon showed up as a participant, and an active one, in quite an array of civic organizations and worthy causes. He was a vigorous fund-raiser in a 1961–62 drive for the local hospital.[52] In 1962 he became a board member in Washington's Industrial Development Corporation, which sought to lure industrial investment to the city.[53] He served on a committee of ten to raise $150,00 for expanding the local library (they succeeded, then had to raise more money to utilize the new capacity).[54] He was appointed to an indefinite term on the Youth Commission by unanimous vote of the city council in 1965.[55] He became a member of the local NAACP — a relationship that would have major consequence in Rice's life later on.[56] On a wider scale, he became a board member of the Pittsburgh chapter of Americans for Democratic Action [ADA] in 1962.[57]

Rice conducted delicate and ultimately successful negotiations with the YMCA and YWCA in Pittsburgh to facilitate Catholic participation in these recreational centers formerly boycotted by the Catholic Church.[58] He was moving into the age of ecumenism, rather in advance of the rest of his church.

In 1960 Rice became director of the Washington Country Chapter of the Pennsylvania Association for Retarded Children, and in 1965 of the Washington County Mental Health Association.[59] He served on the Washington Community Chest, and even on the Washington Chamber of Commerce — a far cry from his earlier antagonistic relations with businessmen![60]

As is often the case with membership on a wide range of civic groups, this went hand-in-hand in Rice's case with significant interlocks with the local political establishment. Through a good friend, Judge David Weiner, Rice entered into the inner councils of the Washington Democratic Party, and enjoyed his presence there enormously.[61] It no doubt helped his longstanding friendship with Mayor David Lawrence of Pittsburgh (Rice had often ghosted speeches for Lawrence and written to him for political jobs for various applicants, including Rice family members) had now parlayed itself into a tie-in to the statehouse, where Lawrence was serving as governor.[62]

In short, whereas Rice had appeared to some members of the local power structure in Natrona to be a dangerous, "rabble-rousing priest," he was now a well-entrenched member of the corresponding power structure in Washington.

Rice was also reaching out in new directions to pursue some of his literary and cultural interests. From late 1958 to 1960 he conducted a weekly half-hour program on WWSW called "Literary Varieties," in which he interviewd various literary critics (mostly academics, often from the University of Pittsburgh) about recent books of note, with the accent on making literature interesting and comprehensible to the average person.[63] In 1964 Rice celebrated his twenty-fifth anniversary of weekly broadcasting on WWSW, expressing surprise and satisfaction that his career there had gone on so long (it would continue 45 years altogether).[64]

It was also in 1964, at age fifty-five, that Rice received his highest mark yet of ecclesiastical approval. In March he was elevated to the rank of "domestic prelate" with the title of Right Reverend Monsignor. Congratulatory notes by the hundreds poured in from around the country and beyond.[65]

As Rice's career within the church prospered, he began to develop ties with certain elements in the international church that he would later denounce as reactionary and conspiratorial.

The Pro Deo movement was at that time headed by Rev. Felix A. Morlion, O.P. and headquartered in the mansion in Rome formerly occupied by Benito Mussolini. The Pro Deo University stated its purpose as the education of Catholic laity in a procapitalist alternative, "Democracy Under God," to socialist tendencies then manifesting themselves in Third World nations. Morlion apparently decided that the United States was the most promising source of funds for his movement, and began contacting members of the hierarchy there. Bishop Wright named Rice as his representative, and Morlion on August 16, 1965, wrote to thank Rice for "having accepted membership on the Pro Deo board at the suggestion of Bishop Wright, as his man of confidence."[66] Rice later wrote to Wright to deny that he had ever become a member of the board, and to suggest that Morlion was a money-gatherer who was promoting an undesirable alliance of the Vatican with high-finance capitalism.[67] But there is no record in the Rice Papers of his having given a negative response to Morlion. Perhaps what also helped to sour the relationship was Morlion's insistence to Rice that in order to gain the intellectual respectability in Europe necessary to advancing within Pro Deo, he would have to write a book — good, bad or indifferent. Rice never chose to do so.[68]

Perhaps a better example of Rice's usefulness to those who needed to raise money in the United States came in the form of a testimonial dinner in his honor at the Pittsburgh Hilton on May 3, 1964. Press clippings accompanying the event stated that labor was honoring Msgr. Rice and that a variety of labor leaders were in attendance. The real nature of the event, however, was rather different. The dinner had been organized not by labor but by the local Israel Bonds organization. Unions were invited to attend not merely in order to honor Rice, but also to buy bonds for Israel with their treasuries, strike funds, and pension funds — which they did to the tune of over $700,000 that evening.[69] For his part, Rice not only graced that very successful evening, but promoted purchases of the bonds in his column,[70] and subsequently went on the road for a series of similar events around the country.[71]

The national Israel Bonds organization, prompted by David Lawrence, rewarded Rice's outstanding salesmanship with an all-expenses-paid trip to Israel.[72] Rice traveled there in the spring of 1965 and returned to write additional columns praising the Israeli experiment.[73] Only one voice had been raised in the *Pittsburgh Catholic* to question the appropriateness of Rice's throwing in on the side of the Israelis and against the Palestinian Arabs, and that had been the voice of a priest from Jordanian Jerusalem, Rev. George E. Saladna.[74] But Rice, even though he had spoken to an Arab in Israel who looked forward to wading through ankle-deep Israeli blood, in his writing at the time tended to downplay the plight of the Palestinians.[75] It would be later that his support for Israel would decline, caused in part by the Palestinian question and in part by his observation that the labor leaders lining up to buy bonds were not always of the most respectable sort.[76]

It is ironic that even as Rice's usefulness as a labor union symbol remained ascendant, his own familiarity with the inner workings of the USWA, with which he had been most closely associated, was in his own estimation slipping.

Thus when I.W. Abel, USWA secretary-treasurer, announced his campaign for USWA presidency against incumbent McDonald in late 1964, Rice was caught flat- footed.[77] (In fairness, so were many others on the inside of USWA.)[78] Although Rice's relationship with McDonald had been on the cool side, he nevertheless came to the embattled president's defense in articles praising

McDonald with faint damn, characterizing the Abel campaign as a power play rather than the advertised attempt to return union control to the rank and file, suggesting that it be called off, and criticizing Abel for not employing the AAA to insure an honest ballot count.[79]

If this spate of pro-McDonald articles was designed to enhance Rice's standing with the USWA leadership, it had been poorly calculated. Rice's misestimation of the rank and file sentiment became clear when Abel defeated McDonald in the ballot count. Thereafter, Rice praised McDonald for his graceful exit,[80] and in private moved to mend his fences with the new administration.[81]

A few years earlier, in 1961, Rice's long-time ACTU and USWA ally, William Hart, had written to Rice, upset over the latter's advocacy in the *Pittsburgh Catholic* of a tax measure Hart believed would discriminate against workers. Citing their long history of struggles shoulder-to-shoulder, Hart wondered: Did his old ally now intend to become "respectable"?[82] Their differences of the moment were soon patched up and Hart the next year was as usual driving Rice to the USWA convention in Miami.[83] But a broader reading of Rice's life in Washington, Pennsylvania, from 1958 to 1965 indicates that Hart's question may indeed have found its mark.

As Rice's personal circumstances and his standing in the community became more comfortable and secure, one might anticipate that his political perceptions and pronouncements would become correspondingly more conservative, and that he would, like many other before him, pass from a "radical" (or at least liberal) youth to a mellow and conservative middle age. Rice's tentative involvement with Pro Deo seemed indeed to presage just such an evolution. Yet it would be in the opposite direction that Rice's politics would change. His most dramatic turnabout was to occur later in the 1960s on the twin issues of race and war, as I shall have occasion to examine in subsequent chapters. But already in the 1950s and early 1960s Rice was reexamining his past social activism and reinterpreting its significance in ways that in retrospect presaged the militance he would return to in the struggles for black civil rights and against the war in Vietnam.

First of all, Rice was reevaluating the work of the ACTU. Beginning when he was being interviewed on the subject by Michael Harrington, a prominent socialist and former editor of *The Catholic*

Worker, Rice wrote several pieces that downplayed the impact of the ACTU on communism in the labor movement in the 1940s and argued that the importance of the ACTU had been exaggerated by the opposition.[84] Harrington's article when it appeared in 1960, reinforced this conclusion to some extent when it argued that the ACTU had had little national coordination in its anticommunist crusade and that other groups had played roles as significant or even more so than ACTU's. On the other hand, Harrington brought Rice's own activism into sharp relief, referring to him as a "one-man ACTU" in Pittsburgh, and noting his significant friendship with Murray.[85]

Rice then went one step further in his own thinking: while continuing to admire the anticorruption work stil being done by the ACTU in New York where it still survived, Rice concluded that the anticommunist work of the ACTU had been "good, but not entirely positive."[86]

As the 1960s progressed, Rice also became stridently critical of HUAC, including in his condemnations even the early investigations of the committee into communism. In 1962 he wrote:

> The record of the Un-American Activities Committee is not very good, beginning with its earliest clumsy Red hunting. It has often used its power of subpoena to bedevil and smear non and anti-Communist political opponents. Its "findings" have been misused by others, and what good it has accomplished seems to have been done by accident.[87]

This attack is little short of astounding when one recalls that, at the time of the early investigations in question, Rice not only had not criticized them but had even been one of those who "misused" the investigations to try to win a union election in UE 601. Moreover, he had defended the HUAC investigation of the largest UAW local, #600, as late as 1952.[88] A decade later, it seemed as if another person was speaking.

In 1963, when HUAC was investigating college students who had traveled to Castro's Cuba, Rice was back on the attack:

> Oscar Wilde described the English fox hunting gentry as the "unspeakable in pursuit of the uneatable." One might say that his has been going on in our nation's capital. The unspeakable House UnAmerican Activities Committee sighted what looked like a juicy morsel heavy with the delicious fat of publicity. The morsel, the young people who had gone to Cuba in defiance of State Department rulings, turned out to be uneatable.[89]

In a related attack, Rice recalled the time when HUAC had subpoenaed his own WWSW broadcasts after the Duquesne Light strike of 1947. He reflected that had he been making his living as a broadcaster in those days, he would soon thereafter have become unemployable.[90] This sounded like an empathy with the victims of those crusades, including ironically some of his own victims.

If Rice had been unable to bring himself to petition for clemency for the Rosenbergs in 1953, his thinking on that case and on capital punishment in general had clearly changed by 1960. Writing on the pending (later carried out) execution of Caryl Chessman, who had lived under a death sentence for eleven years, Rice not only pleaded for a reprieve for Chessman, but noted that the Rosenberg executions had induced "neutral intellectuals all over the world [to become] skeptical of American justice, seeing something barbarous in us."[91]

In the international arena, Rice in summing up the 1950s exhibited a great deal less assurance about the goodness of United States intentions throughout the world than he had a decade or two previously. Addressing the nuclear shadow within which humankind now lived, Rice noted:

> We in the United States can never forget that we used the bomb on a couple of undefended Asiatic cities. We had all manner of reasons for using it, chief of which was fear, and we *have* tried to make amends. In the post war world we have honestly tried to be good to the rest of the world, to use our wealth and power decently and properly. We have been willing to share, we have been conscious of our brothers — but we *did* use the A bomb.[92]

Rice's references to communism, particularly to American communism, during these years had pretty much of a pro-forma quality about them, reminding his public that communism was still worse than capitalism, but not conveying any sense of a genuine domestic threat. Only when the UE decided in 1960 to have another run at recapturing Local 601, by then for a decade affiliated with the IUE, did Rice rise to something like his old form to remind his readers that the UE leadership still remained "tainted."[93]

An interesting addition to Rice's political vocabulary in the late 1950s and early 60s seemed to come from his reading of sociologist C. Wright Mills, a non-Marxist critic of American capitalism who would soon become one of the inspirations for the New Left in the United States. Mills and other exponents of what came to be called the Elitist School were then arguing that the United States was not really governed by an open, pluralistic, and democratically elected political leadership, but by an essentially closed power elite based on wealth and privilege.[94] Rice as early as 1959 described such a group controlling the steel industry:

> This control group is a new combination of lawyers, bankers and engineers, who are skilled managers of money, machinery and systems. They are "operators" rather than genuine handlers of men. There is little warmth among them, but, much skill, some intellect and tremendous calculation. . . . They are something cold, new and fearsome. They ride high at the moment.[95]

Of local elite establishments, he said:

> Aristocracies or upper classes, call them what you will, are founded on money and privilege. These days the money and the privilege are tied very close together; in other times and climes they were not so close but they have never been strangers.[96]

Then he went on to outline the Pittsburgh establishment as he saw it: iron, oil, and real estate money; Scotch-Irish, English, Scotch, and Welsh ethnicity; Protestant religion (certainly not Irish Catholic). He argued that that aristocracy had done a poor enough job on Pittsburgh universities, intellectual development, and the arts. Only in music did he find the record respectable, and here only because of the Jewish counterpart to the Protestant aristocracy.[97] But he added a counterpoint to this essentially Elitist analysis when he insisted that the "upper echelon" in America was not a class based on wealth and birth, but was determined more by education and intellectual activity.[98] He was using parts of a ruling class theory, but he was not buying the theory whole.

As the mid-1960s approached, and the free speech movement of students at the University of California, Berkeley, battled for the right to dissent on that campus, Rice took the side of the students when he proclaimed:

> In America there is less tolerance of deep political dissent than in other countries of the free world. . . . We Americans are suffering from our intolerance of basic internal disagreement.[99]

This was yet another breathtaking reversal for one who had thought so little of the right of dissent when utilized by communists in the 1940s that he had applauded their being hounded out of employment, and perhaps even into prison for the beliefs they held. But now, Rice was one of those doing the dissenting, so he had a rather different view of the question of the rights of those who held and expressed unpopular opinions.

Interestingly, Rice did not extend his analysis on the usefulness of dissent to include the Catholic Church. Thus when Pope Pius XII had shut down the French worker-priest experiment (it had been designed to recapture the French masses from communism, but sometimes had resulted in priests being converted instead to communism), Rice accepted the verdict without murmur.[100] And even by the mid-1960s, when the Catholic Church was in the midst of Vatican II ferment, and obedience to the hierarchy was undergoing intense scrutiny both by theologians and the laity, Rice declared:

> I am not and do not intend to be in the vanguard of the present Catholic revolution because I do not know where it is going.[101]

Thus Rice, in the early 1960's, was reexamining much of his activist past. Although not yet breaking decisively with that past, he was weighing it in rather different scales. Unafraid now of American communism, he was insisting on much wider latitude for political dissent, and was beginning to occupy much of the new elbow room himself when he made statements that once might have been caused him to wonder whether they came from a communist or fellow traveler.

On matters of church discipline, however, he remained, in his own view, a loyal soldier. It would be this combination of an increasingly antiestablishment viewpoint with a strict ecclesiastical orthodoxy, that would delineate Rice's significance to American Catholicism in the years ahead.

In 1963 one of the more perceptive pieces yet written about Rice appeared in the Catholic magazine *Ave Maria*. It had been authored by someone who knew Rice well: John Deedy, a former colleague at the *Pittsburgh Catholic* and later a writer for *Commonweal*. Deedy generally gave Rice good reviews for his past social activism, but added:

> But more and more he is content to let the younger priests take over. Father Rice is a healthy 5-foot-10 and 165 pounds; he has no hair, but he still has all his teeth; he is a fine physical specimen. But age is beginning

to be a factor, and the sidelines (where one can coach and call the shots) at times have the lure that the actual playing field once had.[102]

On his depiction of Rice as a hairless elder hankering for the sidelines, Deedy could hardly have been more mistaken. In fact, one wonders whether Rice read the above paragraph and set out to refute it with the next phase of his life.

Anna and Michael Rice, his parents, 1905.

Michael, Charles Owen, Anna and Patrick Rice, ca. 1909.

Charles Owen Rice, ca. 1912.

Meeting Local #325 canning and pickle workers during its strike at Heinz, summer of 1937.
Rev. Charles O. Rice, Rev. Carl Hensler, Msgr. George Barry O'Toole. Note employee in rear — giving communist salute.

Right, Rice watches moving of furniture on House of Hospitality CRA truck, March 1939.

Rice addresses mass meeting of steel workers and families at Youngstown sheet and tube plant, June 6, 1937.

CIO founding convention, December 1938. Left to right: Phil Murray, Mayor Scully, John L. Lewis, Sidney Hillman, Rev. Charles O. Rice.

Hubbard strike – Rev.
Charles O. Rice at police
station where strikers were
held. 1938.

Right, Early House of
Hospitality. To the left of
Charles O. Rice, Alan
Kistler, later director of
organization of AFL-CIO.
October, 1939.

Franklin D. Roosevelt at opening of housing project, city of Pittsburgh, 1940.

Pat Fagan, Charles O. Rice, Eleanor Roosevelt.

1941 hospital workers' strike, West Penn Hospital.

Truman visit to Pittsburgh, October, 1952. Taken at Union Station, Pittsburgh, PA. Phil Murray, David J. McDonald; Foreground, Governor Lawrence, President Truman, Arthur Goldberg, Supreme Court Justice, Charles O. Rice. To the right, Patrick Rice. Barely visible above head of Charles O. Rice, Jock Yablonski.

Alan Haywood, Adlai Stevenson, James Carey, Rev. Charles O. Rice. CIO convention, Atlantic, City, 1952.

25th anniversary of Charles O. Rice, 1959. Mike Quill, President TWU, New York speaking. Seated: David Lawrence, Rice, (unident.), William Hart, J.A. Wilner.

SIX

Black Rage, White Conscience

IT WAS LATE IN 1965 AT HIS AGE FIFTY-SEVEN when Rice decided to give up his comfortable pastorate in Washington, Pennsylvania, in order not only to return to Pittsburgh, but to dive headlong into the city's black ghetto and the black struggle for freedom and equality. That struggle was moving from its early emphasis on nonviolence to years of riots, backlash, and bloodshed, from the demand that blacks receive their rights within the American system to attempts to destroy that system, and from fighting Jim Crow in the South to confronting the more subtly corrosive racism of the North.

Rice signed on in a struggle when its early years were past, and when white allies would be greeted with more suspicion than welcome. He would try at first to play a noticeably paternalistic role, but would be jolted out of that posture by the furious disdain of angry blacks from the streets of Pittsburgh. He would soon make common cause with the more militant among them, laying aside in the process any apparent claim to the mantle of nonviolence. He would thus put himself on collision course with many of those groups and individuals who had been his allies in the past: organized labor, white liberals and Democrats, police, judges, attorneys, the FBI, and even some significant institutions within the Catholic Church. Before many years had passed, he would be a pariah to most Pittsburgh Catholics just as he had been a pariah to certain of the hierarchy there. He would nevertheless remain faithful to his church when other priestly militants were leaving it, and he would be supported consistently by Bishop Wright. It would not be far off the mark, in fact, to suggest that Rice remained Wright's ambassador to the angry, disenfranchised blacks of Pittsburgh's ghetto — and not always to the ultimate advantage of those blacks or their cause. If these were the years when Rice became an angry militant, they were also the years when he proved himself a *Catholic* militant.

The opening gun of the black civil rights movement of modern times was fired when the NAACP finally succeeded in getting the United States Supreme Court in 1954 and 1955 to declare racial segregation in the public schools unconstitutional, and to call upon local and state authorities to dismantle that system with all due speed (*Brown*). As the states of the former Confederacy proved defiant, blacks began to take things into their own hands with successful boycotts of the local bus system in Montgomery, Alabama, and then in other cities throughout the South. A new generation of black religious leaders emerged, including Martin Luther King, Jr., and other members of the Southern Christian Leadership Conference. Black college students added impetus to the movement with sit-ins that desegragated lunch counters beginning at Greensboro, North Carolina in 1960. More collegians joined in, now many of them white, in the freedom rides on interstate buses going south in 1961. The protesters were met with white violence time and again, but their adherence to the principles of nonviolence as espoused by King, Gandhi, and Thoreau won them the respect of much of the country. Under this sort of moral pressure, the old facade of official southern segregation slowly began to crack and crumble.

But American racism did not survive exclusively in the South, nor were all its opponents wedded to the doctrines of nonviolence. The Kennedy administration had been unable (or unwilling) to achieve anything more than minor legislative milestones in civil rights, and many of them had been vitiated by Kennedy's racist appointees to the federal bench throughout the South. Under Johnson the battle was again joined, but southern resistance hampered the passage of meaningful legislation until the later 1960s, when the logjam was finally broken.

New voices of angry blacks began to be listened to in the North, where blacks had been officially equal for over a century, but in fact remained second-class citizens both economically and socially. Stokely Carmichael called upon blacks to be proud of their blackness; Malcolm X and the Nation of Islam preached against the sins of the white devils and in favor of black separatism; many residents of urban black ghettoes came to believe that revolution and the destruction of the prevailing social and economic system, beginning with local white-owned stores, were their only route to freedom from repression. Tensions mounted as police forces were beefed up but experienced more difficulty in maintaining the status quo. The tide of black activism, now roaring with indignation, was rolling toward the North.

Rice's own concern with black rights went back, as we have seen, to his earliest days as a priest. At Soho and Gazzam, he had taken up the cause of black as well as white tenants and homeowners. At the House of Hospitality, guests were admitted irrespective of race, and on Tannehill Street that generally meant a black predominance. As rent czar, Rice had obtained good jobs for qualified blacks. On his radio broadcasts, even during his relatively quiescent 1950s he had attacked racism in churches, [1] in Little Rock, Arkansas, [2] and in the South generally. [3] While at Natrona, he had taken successful action against the police practice there of jailing white girls who dated black boys. [4] Early in the 1960s he had addressed in his column the problems of blacks in finding work and in dealing with the unions. [5] He had advocated boycotts of local private clubs that practiced racial discrimination — notably at the University of Pittsburgh. [6] He had hailed the bus boycott in Montgomery by saying: "The meek Negro population has caught the freedom fever and the South can never be the same again. . . . I confess to finding Martin Luther King, his followers and his tactics, a profound Christian inspiration." [7]

He extended his concern for racial equality to the North as well, and to his home in Washington, Pennsylvania, where his was the first name of fifteen hundred signed to a white "Declaration of Conscience" on racism in that city. [8] He went further than most white liberals were then prepared to go when he declared that interracial marriages were not morally bad but neutral, and that "only when those who want to marry members of other races are so free to do so that it becomes routine, will our race problems be close to solution." [9] Thus had Rice established very clearly his credentials as a white pioneer on the matter of American racism.

Yet despite the strong positions he took, Rice had few illusions that progress toward abolishing white racism would come easily or quickly. The black tenants of Soho-Gazzam had been displaced, black men still stood in the soup line at the House of Hospitality, Rice's college-educated black colleagues from the Rent Office had gone back to mopping floors or operating elevators. He himself had once had a bond posted in West Virginia as the legal surety he would not perform an interracial marriage there.[10] When the *Pittsburgh Post Gazette* published a piece on black unemployment in Washington, Pennsylvania, Rice confessed: "The statistics in the story are shocking, as the naked truth is generally shocking. They shocked me, I admit."[11] Years later he reflected that although he had for years visited patients at Passavant Hospital in Pittsburgh, he had failed to note the absence of blacks at that institution.[12] Pioneer though he was, he was also immersed in a racist society whose symptoms sometimes remained invisible to him.

In an article for *Commonweal* that received considerable national attention, Rice examined a racial blow-up that had occurred at a U.S. Steel plant in Birmingham, Alabama, when blacks sought equal treatment. He laid much of the blame for the failure at the door of the parent corporation, which refused to become involved in any more than a minimal fashion, despite its enormous power in the southern probusiness climate.[13]

When he was pastor at his comfortable parish in Washington, Pennsylvania, Rice had already moved beyond words to activism on behalf of blacks. He was a key member of the NAACP chapter in Washington, which was more than once cited by national headquarters as the "most outstanding" chapter in the state, and which had played a key role in getting the Washington school board to end racial segregation in 1962 — a practice the superintendent just one year previously had claimed did not exist.[14] And late in 1965, Rice participated in the first of what would prove to be many marches for civil rights — this one a relatively tame affair in Harrisburg.[15]

But as the mid-1960s arrived, and cities in the North began to heat up for racial confrontations, Rice could not remain content to play out his role on the small stage of "little Washington." His frustrations were compounded because, despite the modest progress that had been made in desegregating Washington's schools, finding good jobs for qualified blacks remained a flat-out impossibility there. Rice's political connections, his assiduous cultivating of a steel mill owner (who Rice discovered could find a building to donate to become a black social center, but no jobs at his mill for blacks), and Rice's atypical and increasingly strong pronouncements on racism from the pulpit at Immaculate Conception, seemed to him to have failed.[16]

In late 1965 a fascinating opportunity presented itself. Msgr. Henry Carlin, pastor of Holy Rosary parish, passed away. Holy

Rosary, with a huge and beautiful church building, but a declining population of mostly white Catholics, was the major Catholic parish in Homewood, the section of Pittsburgh with the largest concentration of blacks. There was rich irony in the fact that Rice now wanted Carlin's previous parish, for he had suspected for years that Carlin had been badmouthing him to Bishop Dearden, with the result that he had been sent up the river and had stayed there. Now, with the progressive and friendly Bishop Wright in charge, Rice decided to make his move.

At the very funeral of Msgr. Carlin, Rice approached Wright in the church sanctuary to discuss the vacancy. He sought to defuse any reaction to his apparent presumptuousness with a story. It seemed that a priest on a similar quest had once come to Irish Bishop Canevin at a funeral and said, "Milord, I'd like to take this man's place." "It's fine with me," Canevin had replied, "if only the undertaker doesn't object!"

Rice went on to explain that he wanted to take over Holy Rosary in order to pursue the church's interracial apostolate. After some hesitation, Wright consented. Later he always insisted that Rice had *accepted* an assignment, as opposed to lobbying for one. Rice insisted, not necessarily to Wright's face, on the opposite.[17] So in January 1966 Rice returned to Pittsburgh from what he saw as a 13-year exile (although a rather comfortable one) to take up a challenge in some ways reminiscent of his early days at the House of Hospitality. Mayor Joseph Barr proclaimed Friday, March 11, "Monsignor Charles Owen Rice Day." A testimonial dinner was held to welcome back one of Pittsburgh's sons (whether prodigal or not).

Although Rice would once again be dealing with some of society's victims, as in his 1940–1953 Pittsburgh assignment, the differences in his own position would far outweigh the similarities. The weatherbeaten men who had lined up at the House of Hospitality had been glad to have a handout, and had regarded a priest with something approaching reverential awe. Although living on the first floor at the House of Hospitality, Rice had never barred his window and had rarely feared for his own safety. But at the more comfortable Holy Rosary, he would sometimes have to barricade himself and his staff from the local population, and in this age of militance, blacks were beginning to demand not a simple handout but self-respect and indeed control of their own fortunes. Whites were at risk in the mostly black streets of Homewood, particularly from the teenage and preteen "wolf packs" (Rice's term) that governed the turf, and a Roman collar made scant difference to them.

Rice would frequently find himself caught between the outrage of whites who despised his association with the black militancy they hated and feared, and some blacks' mistrust and derision for the honkey priest who kept butting into their affairs. Only by carefully presenting himself not as a leader of blacks but as a gadfly to white conscience could Rice hope to have any effectiveness with this generation of black leaders. And only by walking the thin line between black rage and white backlash could he maintain any peace of mind, or even assure his own physical survival. For Rice, this would be no easy assignment.[18]

To judge by the articles Rice was writing for the *Pittsburgh Catholic* during his early months in Homewood, he was feeling his way cautiously, and was torn by an inner struggle as to what sort and how large a role he would be able to play in the black community there.

He billed his coming to Pittsburgh as the "return of the native," pointed out that Holy Rosary "presents an opportunity to return to a work resembling that of my youth." But he concluded, "It is all new ground. New insights are needed. No one has the answers, and we are all humbly searching for the right way."[19]

That was in January. By May, Rice was lamenting, "I wish the American Catholic Church had more right to speak to the American Negro. I wish we had done more for him in the past."[20] By late summer, commenting on the advice of black power prophet Stokely Carmichael to the effect that the white "friend" was not needed to work among blacks but among whites, Rice said, "Stokely speaks the truth and frankly, I feel that he has a message for me and other could-be helpful Whites."[21] He further counseled other white liberals, who had jumped ship at the Student Non-Violent Coordinating Committee (SNCC) after being rebuffed by black militants, to return to the organization because "they had to be told that for the Negro's own good, and for the good of the whole nation, the Negro had to be forced to develop his inner resources."[22]

Notwithstanding all these sound words to white liberals like himself, Rice's *actions* indicated that deep down he was not yet convinced that there was no room in Homewood for a white clerical leader along the lines of Rev. James Groppi in Milwaukee. If his purpose was to preach racial justice to whites, then why relocate to Holy Rosary where there were far fewer of them than there had been in Washington? A clear example of Rice's proclivity to become a spokesman for disadvantaged blacks came in his response to the plight of the jitney drivers.

The jitney drivers in Homewood operated unlicensed and unaffillated taxi cabs, which were both cheaper than regular taxis and more convenient than the city buses which operated only on axes radiating out from the city center. Licensed taxi drivers often refused to pick up passengers headed for Homewood at all, and most blacks had at least once stood at a bus stop waiting for their bus, only to have it roar by without even slowing down.

In 1966 transit authorities began pressuring the city to enforce existing criminal penalties ($100 or 30 days) against jitney drivers and thus put this illegal competition out of business. Rice in his column argued that jitneys provided a necessary service not usually in competition with public transit, and that police should continue to wink at them, because "we need a super patrol on the jitneys about as badly as we need additional cranial orifices."[23]

Authorities nevertheless went ahead with the arrest and prosecution of jitney drivers. A Jitney Defense Committee was thereupon organized with Rice listed as its head. But defending apprehended jitney drivers was no easy task in the face of summary proceedings that handed down sentences before the committee could even learn of the arrests. As a minimum, arrested drivers were going to have to spend one night in jail unless someone first came up with $100.

One Friday evening in March, Rice received a call from the wife of jitney driver John Scott. The 64-year-old black man had been arrested that day, could not pay the fine, and stood to spend his first night in jail — indeed, his first night out of his own home. "Father Rice," asked the soft voice on the other end of the line, "are you all goin' to help the jitney people?" Rice headed down to the precinct station with his own check for $100; John Scott spent the night in his own bed.[24]

By April the Pennsylvania Public Utilities Commission was using what Rice called "bounty-hunter" private investigators to expose jitney drivers. Rice in his column not only attacked this law- enforcement scheme, but went on to argue against unionizing jitney drivers on the grounds that unionization would make them less "careful, courteous and accommodating" — quite a departure for Pittsburgh's labor priest![25] Thus had Rice, within a few months of his arrival in Homewood, become the leader and spokesman for a black interest group. As had been true with the Liberty Bakery in the 1950s, the cause was a losing one.

Another evidence of Rice's search for his own niche in Home-wood was the number of organizations in the area that he joined, or had significant relations with, or in some cases quietly arranged for their funding. The luxuriant undergrowth of the grassroots organizations that he encountered in Homewood, and on which he kept careful files, is not susceptible of any very logical ordering. I list them here in alphabetical order.

ACTION Housing, Inc. A group of local merchants and property owners seeking to renovate large blocs of housing through the Allegheny Housing Rehabilitation Corporation (AHRCO); funded by the Ford Foundation (and by the Mellons, according to Rice). Rice at first praised this group, but later attacked it as being insensitive to the real housing needs of blacks.[26]

Black Panthers. Rice once denied that this militant black organization, which would be attacked often and eventually neutralized by the police, even existed in Pittsburgh. But in fact he cooperated with the Panthers in a breakfast program for poor children, as a result of which he came under renewed surveillance by the FBI.[27]

Catholic Interracial Council. A voluntary organization of laity and clergy in the Pittsburgh diocese concerned with interracial justice. Rice was a long-time member and on the Board of Directors from 1966, but rela-tions between him and the Council cooled after 1967 as the group chose to confront the diocese of Pittsburgh, including its bishop.[28]

Citizens Against Slum Housing (CASH). A local grassroots organization funded by the Pittsburgh Area Religion and Race Council and at odds with ACTION Housing over a rent strike, housing rehabilitation, and other issues.[29]

Community Action Against Poverty (CAP). A federally funded agency with over a dozen offices in the Pittsburgh area. Rice emerged as their premier, if unofficial, spokesman early in 1967 when he coordinated a mass rally to protest scheduled funding cuts.[30]

Forever Action Together (FAT). An all-black organization of mostly young, mostly militant residents of Homewood. Quietly funded by RAHR (see below), it dropped its blacks-only makeup in 1969 by adding Rice to its advisory board.[31]

FORWARD, Grassroots. An amalgamation of two previously indepen-dent organizations. It had generally compatible relationships with other militant organizations in Homewood, and strongly opposed ACTION Housing.[32]

Headstart. A federally funded summer educational program for young children from disadvantaged backgrounds. It was held at Holy Rosary, among other places, in 1966, 1967, and 1968, until federal funding was cut.[33]

Homewood-Brushton Alliance (HBA). The new name adopted by RAHR (see below), in 1967 as part of the strategy [later revised] of creating an all-black local organization.[34]

Homewood-Brushton Chamber of Commerce (HBCC). The merchants' association in Homewood, with close ties to ACTION Housing, HBCRC and HBCIA (see below). Rice served on its Board of Directors from 1966 to 1969.[35]

Homewood-Brushton Citizens' Renewal Council (HBCRC). Funded by Neighbors in Need (see below) and associated with ACTION Housing, it met regularly and concerned itself with a range of issues including education, employment, health and housing. Rice became a member of its Executive Board in 1969 and served there for a year or two.[36]

Homewood-Brushton Civic Improvement Association (HBCIA). A group of local merchants and property owners, it was criticized by Rice as being even more establishment-oriented and less sensitive to black needs than was ACTION Housing.[37]

National Association for the Advancement of Colored People (NAACP). Oldest of black civil rights organizations and characteristically functioning in the courts rather than in the streets. The local chapter moved closer to its constituency when it relocated at 2203 Wylie under the militant leadership of Byrd Brown. Rice, who had belonged to the NAACP Washington chapter, contributed to and worked for the Pittsburgh Chapter, later becoming a Life Member.[38]

Negro Educational Emergency Drive (NEED). A group seeking to raise money for college scholarships for blacks. Rice worked extensively for it in 1966.[39]

Neighbors in Need. A fund established in the Pittsburgh diocese under Bishop Wright to provide funding for various non-Catholic organizations with social significance. Rice played a key role here as advocate, when funding was given to (among others) FAT, HBA, HBCRC, RAHR, and UMP (see below).[40]

Pittsburgh Area Religion and Race Council. An interdenominational (mostly Protestant and Catholic) race council with links to the Catholic Interracial Council. It supported CASH, among other groups. Rice became active in it in 1966.[41]

Religious Agency for Human Renewal (RAHR). A key agency set up in 1965 with $60,000 donated by Pittsburgh Presbyterians, the Catholic diocese of Pittsburgh, and Methodists. It in turn funded many other groups, as noted in this list. Rice was its vice president even before moving to Holy Rosary, where RAHR regularly met from 1966 onward.[42]

Student Non-Violent Coordinating Committee (SNCC). One of the more militant organizations of young blacks and often critical of the NAACP, the Urban League, and other black organizations it viewed as "Uncle Tom" in nature. Rice particularly admired its charismatic leader, Stokely Carmichael, who received favorable mention in Rice's writings.

United Movement for Progress (UMP). Largely coterminous with the personality and activism of Bouie Haden, Rice's "main man" on the streets of Homewood. Funded by the City of Pittsburgh, RAHR, and a special grant from Neighbors in Need.[43]

Urban League. An established civil rights organization concerned with such urban programs as CAP, but prohibited by its funding regulations from entering the political arena. The Urban League recruited Rice to head the protest against CAP funding cuts in 1967, and then retired from the scene.[44]

This mere listing of organizations with which Rice was involved in one way or another yields a number of important conclusions. The first is that despite his protestations to the contrary, Rice was moving rapidly into a position of leadership or influence in numerous civil rights and neighborhood organizations, including some that had set out to remain exclusively black but decided to make an exception in Rice's case. Rice's influence would be particularly significant in matters of funding. Because many of the neighborhood organizations, particularly those of a "grassroots" nature, were long on enthusiasm and even militance, but short on money, the fact that Rice could provide them with regular funding from Neighbors in Need, the Religion and Race Council, or RAHR undoubtedly enhanced his standing with many otherwise fiercely independent black militants. Whether this sort of aid was ultimately to the best advantage of the organizations the militants represented is quite another question.

Another conclusion to emerge is that Rice, faced with a variegated and sometimes even warring series of organizations, initially chose the expedient of joining all of them! However well-meaning such a strategy may have been, and however much Rice might try to become the cement bringing various factions into contact and harmony, it simply would not work — not in the long run. Thus

Rice was forced after a year or so to pick and choose among these various organizations. Generally he chose to side with the more militant ones and to downplay or drop his relationships with the more establishment-oriented ones. Nowhere was this choice more evident than in the person who became Rice's closest ally in the struggle at Homewood for black rights, William "Bouie" Haden.

Bouie Haden, with his leonine head, his no less leonine roar when aroused, and with what some saw as his fancy cars, leather apparel, and armed body guards, was to many whites the very epitome of the black violence they feared. To Rice he was one of a few great men, together with Phil Murray and John Wright, whom he knew and worked with in his lifetime.

Haden recalled a tough childhood in Virginia, when he noted that Santa Claus forgot him or ran out of toys year after year, but the same thing never seemed to happen to the rich white kids. When grown, he had served in the army, where he proved a serious discipline problem to white officers. Remanded to solitary confinement until he would bow to their authority, Haden remained there, stiff-necked, so long that he was finally released for fear he would otherwise die.

A job at U.S. Steel later brought him to Pittsburgh, but he was fired in a seniority dispute involving blacks, and was not reinstated by the union (after Phil Murray's time, notes Rice). That left Haden on the streets of Homewood, with few financial resources. Fortunately for him, he had a remarkable ability to hustle a living on the streets: by night, he ran a craps game, and by day a small grocery store. His nighttime business of course left him vulnerable to the police he allegedly had to pay off as a business expense. And he was continually rushing out of his grocery store during the day, whenever a new crisis arose in the neighborhood — leaving the cash register in the care of anyone at hand. By night or day, then, Haden lived and dealt with predators of one sort or another, and it showed. The police version of Haden was that of a petty criminal continually making trouble for them, but Rice insists that Bouie was quite honest according to his own lights. When he bought a stolen credit card, for example, he would only run up enough on that card to cover the purchase price. When Bouie was indicted for the theft of cigarettes and fined $300, Rice, Byrd Brown, and another ally, Doc Greenlee, each chipped in $100 to spring him from jail.

It was during Rice's era in Homewood that Haden metamorphosed from a petty criminal into a civil rights activist. His organization, UMP, began in 1967 with quiet funding from RAHR, which Rice had been able to arrange. What Bouie had that civil rights activism needed in Homewood was a combination of an intimidating presence in confrontations and ability to bargain cagily in negotiations. He was able to wrangle many jobs for young blacks by going one-on-one with employers.[45]

Another important community ally of Rice's and Haden's (and who helped pay Haden's fine) was a local physician, Dr. Charles "Doc" Greenlee. One issue on which Rice, Haden and Greenlee teamed up quite early was that of birth control. They believed that when birth control clinics were placed in black neighborhoods but not in white ones, this was evidence of a white establishment plan of genocide for blacks — "death in a douche bag" was Greenlee's term. When Planned Parenthood tried to establish such a center in Homewood, Haden and Greenlee as board members of the new Homewood Brushton Health Center, with Rice's vigorous backing, opposed the plan. Bouie used his power to intimidate when he flat out forbade the Health Center council to even *consider* the idea, and it did not. He accompanied his instructions with some very ominous-sounding predictions of what would happen to Planned Parenthood if its workers circulated through Homewood inducing black women to come to their downtown headquarters.

That he was not merely bluffing is indicated by an episode two years later, when two hundred sticks of badly deteriorated dynamite were discovered near Holy Rosary. Rice, fearful that militants had now turned against the church, called the police (an Army detail disposed of the dynamite in heavy crankcase oil), and Bouie. Bouie laughed and explained that the explosives were not directed at Holy Rosary at all: it seemed the brothers had been fixing to blow up that birth control clinic, then didn't do it, and later had forgotten all about the dynamite![46]

Hardly anyone knew about Bouie's dynamite at the time, but many Pittsburgh whites thought they knew enough about Haden from his frequent press coverage to justify their fear and loathing of him. So their amazed indignation can be imagined when they learned in 1968 that the diocese of Pittsburgh was giving him a grant of $12,000, of which $10,000 was to be his salary for a year.

The story behind the headline was a somewhat complex one, in which Rice figured prominently. Haden had been promised the use of a city-owned building in which to conduct a street academy for youths, along with a number of other UMP programs. But no funds for the programs had been forthcoming from the city. Rice therefore approached the diocesan Neighbors in Need and asked that a $5,000 grant be slipped quietly to Haden. But Neighbors in Need was having no under-the-table deals, and suggested instead that Haden submit a formal proposal to them for whatever he really needed. Haden thereupon upped the ante to $12,000 and a majority on the Neighbors in Need board went along.[47]

As a direct result of the attendant publicity, hate mail and abusive telephone calls poured into the chancery, church contributions fell off noticeably, and an effigy of Bishop Wright was hung in front of the cathedral with the legend around its neck "Bouie's puppet on a string."[48] Had the lynchers been more familiar with what was going on behind the headlines, they might have suspected that Wright was closer to being the puppeteer than the puppet.

Whether the diocese caved in to the adverse reaction, or whether, as claimed at the time, it was merely following its normal funding routines, the grant was not renewed the next year. Bouie would continue as an activist a while longer, but learned in the early 1970s that he had incurable cancer. At the prospect of an early death, he at first reflected that he "had lived long enough to see that we weren't going to make it." But he revised his thinking to a more positive note of hope as his death approached, and Rice at his funeral in 1974 (Haden, although not a Catholic, was buried from Holy Rosary) said: "Your career was constructive, and we are all in your debt and we thank God that you lived and led when you did."[49]

Rice later maintained that Haden did not get rich from his activism, but died as poor as he had lived. But at a banquet back in Washington, Pennsylvania, held in 1975 by the NAACP, whose respectable members were what Bouie had called "necktie niggers," when Rice invoked Haden's name, there was no applause but only silence throughout the hall.[50]

Back in 1967, Rice's second year in Homewood, frustrations were gathering for Pittsburgh blacks, even as they were reaching the breaking point in other American cities with large concentrations of blacks. Widespread and prolonged rioting broke out in the black ghettoes of Newark and Detroit. Governor George Wallace of Alabama, symbol of southern resistance to integration, mounted a vigorous campaign for the presidential election of the next year. Significant civil rights legislation cleared Congress, but Adam Clayton Powell was denied his seat in the House of Representatives on charges of payroll padding and other irregularities, which he retorted were permissible enough when practiced by his white colleagues.

Rice accepted Powell's interpretation of the affair and wrote that the real crux of the problem lay elsewhere: "Southerners are infuriated by his swagger. They dislike uppity Negroes, and to them Adam Clayton Powell is the essence of uppityness."[51]

When George Wallace came to Pittsburgh in the spring, Rice expressed dismay that the popular Amen Corner provided him with a platform from which to speak. But Rice was on hand with a militant crowd to march around Wallace's hotel, singing and clapping, for two hours.[52]

In a field report for a Catholic magazine in April, Rice was asked to speculate whether Pittsburgh was likely to experience a racial outbreak that summer. He replied that Pittsburgh's poverty, declining population, relatively small percentage of blacks (20%) and relatively small black concentrations (Homewood's was the largest with 30,000 at most) made rioting unlikely, even though the plight of the black minority was no better than in other cities. His conclusion: "The Pittsburgh Negro is hurting in soul and body, but not enough to take to the street unless some new stimulus to violence appears."[53] This prediction would make fascinating reading a year later when Martin Luther King, Jr., was assassinated and much of Homewood went up in flames.

Meanwhile, Rice himself had been active enough on the streets of Pittsburgh. Congress in 1967 was in the process of cutting back the neonatal War on Poverty, and CAP funding was scheduled to be reduced by 25 percent in Pittsburgh as across the nation. When the Urban League needed someone to organize and lead a mass demonstration against the cuts, it recruited Rice, who carried out the assignment with his usual thoroughness and showmanship. He began by defending in his column the CAP programs and the federal Office of Economic Opportunity (OEO) which funded them.[54] Then, on what turned out to be the coldest day of the year, Monday, January 16, Rice led a gathering estimated variously at from six hundred to four thousand strong to Pittsburgh's Gateway Center at precisely 5:00 p.m. as rush-hour traffic plodded by. He invoked his famous line from the steel strikes of the 1950s: "Don't let them take it away!" He then introduced a succession of speakers from Pittsburgh area CAP offices, topped off by Bishop Wright himself delivering the benediction. Mayor Barr and at least one county commissioner showed up to listen, and USWA President I. W. Abel telegraphed his support and urged steelworkers to attend. After some haggling with police, a coffin representing the War on Poverty was heaved from a wharf into the water off Point Park and floated away to oblivion.

So did much of the demonstration. Letters to members of Congress got polite, concerned answers, but no action. Promises of going after private money in Pittsburgh ("there's plenty of it around") to replace the lost federal funds were apparently fruitless. The cuts stood.[55]

But if the demonstrations did not save CAP funds, they did produce a whole new host of enemies for Rice after his prime-time appearance on television news that evening. The venom of their hatred can perhaps be gauged from the obviously extreme response of one correspondent, who reminded Rice in a perfectly lucid letter that "Germany solved the Jewish problem in Europe . . . in the not too distant future people will demand the same solution to our Negro and Jewish problem."[56]

Undeterred by the avalanche of opposition, Rice next plunged into the housing issue where his own expertise was long-standing. On February 7 he testified before the Pittsburghs City Council in favor of the most comprehensive possible statute to forbid racial discrimination in the sale or rental of housing.[57]

Back in Homewood, meanwhile, a confrontation was shaping up over the issue of housing rehabilitation, between Bouie Haden's militant UMP and the well-connected ACTION-Housing. ACTION wanted to rehab relatively large blocs of housing and offer them to renters at rates high enough to make the project a profitable one. UMP favored smaller projects at rents affordable to those residents of Homewood who fell below the middle class. Rice took sides by needling the profit motive which ACTION sought to combine with the do-good instinct:

> Tightly controlled by its unique executive director, Bernard E. Losbough, ACTION digs money and, most keenly, the monied. Bernie shows them how to save their souls (which, as a priest, I must assume are worth saving) while at the same time treating their lovely money with respect.[58]

That August, when UMP insisted to the Mayor's Commission on Human Rights that the UMP's version of housing rehabilitation was the better one, and that UMP rather than ACTION or HBCIA was the sole legitimate voice of the Homewood people, Rice was there to back up that position.[59]

In April, Rice attracted national attention when he spoke at the Spring Mobilization in New York City from the same platform as Martin Luther King, Jr., Stokely Carmichael, and Floyd McKissick, after marching arm-in-arm with King at the head of three hundred thousand demonstrators (Rice's estimate; the police said 150,000) to the U.N. building.[60] What onlookers did not know and what Rice learned only after the fact was that he and Benjamin Spock had been positioned on either side of King to shield him from any would-be assassin who might hesitate to shoot down a well-known white.[61]

On a more comic note, William Buckley's review of the event included a nameless reference to "an old Irish Monsignor from Pittsburgh who said he knew Pope John, had he lived, would have approved the proceedings." Rice responded that he had no idea he looked so old at fifty-eight, or sounded so Irish.[62] Forty-six years away from Ireland, he still had a bit of a brogue!

Still another issue that was gathering a head of steam in 1967 involved Pittsburgh Hospital, run by the Sisters of Charity in the Homewood vicinity. Relations between this Catholic hospital and the blacks of Homewood had for years been unhappy. After serving the mostly white population of earlier times, the hospital had become estranged from the neighborhood as blacks moved in. Doc Greenlee said he had for years experienced difficulties in getting his patients admitted, even in emergencies. Although admissions policies were seen by residents as improving over time, by 1966 most blacks who were admitted were treated in the wards rather than in private or semiprivate rooms.[63]

In the face of this perceived discrimination, Greenlee, Haden, and other Homewood activists had formulated a plan for a neighborhood clinic to be set up and run by Pittsburgh Hospital right in the Homewood-Brushton neighborhood. In 1967, after considering this proposal, Pittsburgh Hospital offered its own counterproposal. But so antagonistic were local sentiments toward Pittsburgh Hospital, and so suspect did the militants find the "community representatives" with whom Pittsburgh Hospital had worked, that the UMP called a mass meeting to expose the following alleged facets of the Pittsburgh Hospital clinic proposal: (1) black patients would be exploited to train medical students; (2) only "Jim Crow leaders" had been consulted; and (3) there was to be no citizen involvement, even in the form of an advisory board. Pittsburgh Hospital insisted that these charges were groundless.[64]

This was one situation where Rice was well placed to play the role of mediator, as a close friend of Haden and Greenlee, and as pastor of the largest Catholic parish in the environs of Pittsburgh Hospital (Holy Rosary gymnasium each year was the site of the hospital's Nursing School graduation). Such a position he managed to play, to an extent. By the fall of 1967, regular, if stiff, negotiations were going on between UMP and Pittsburgh Hospital, and Bouie Haden was calling upon the neighborhood for moderation lest the proposed $1.7 million center be lost altogether. It was built and functioning by 1968, and Greenlee for a time served as its director. But divisions remained from the struggle: Greenlee and Haden would fall out over the former's directorship, and Pittsburgh Hospital decided to hold its nursing graduations elsewhere. Later Pittsburgh Hospital would move away from the neighborhood altogether, and into the nursing home business.[65]

Rice saw to it that the St. Joseph's Labor Day Award in 1967 was given to the most prominent black in the American labor movement, A. Philip Randolph of the Brotherhood of Sleeping Car Porters. The award took on additional noteworthiness when Rice mentioned in his column that Randolph had become a socialist and had never disavowed that identity.[66]

A final conflict worth noting from 1967, but of quite a different character, was one that Rice had with a younger priest, Rev. Donald McIlvane. Their acquaintance had begun years back, when Rice had been at the House of Hospitality during World War II and McIlvane, then a seminarian at St. Vincent's, came by to help. That was unusual for a seminarian in those days, and it came to an end when McIlvane's father, a prominent steel executive, raised objections — not to the House of Hospitality, interestingly, but to Rice. Since returning to Pittsburgh, Rice had regularly worked with McIlvane on the Catholic Interracial Council and they had been together at many marches and demonstrations.

The older and younger priests were allies on many issues, but there were sharp differences between them on matters of style, perhaps arising from the fact that Rice had become an activist in the 1930s, McIlvane in the 1960s. McIlvane's confrontational approach landed him in jail time after time, whereas Rice never had been arrested and never would be. More significantly to Rice, McIlvane tended to identify the institutional Catholic Church as the enemy on a number of race-related issues — which violated Rice's sense of loyalty as a priest. Rice wrote an admiring piece on McIlvane early in 1967, entitling it "How flows the Don?" (not smoothly, Rice concluded).[67] But by December of that year, when McIlvane publicly criticized the church for failing to rally for the religious sponsorship of housing in Pittsburgh, Rice broke with him openly.[68] The next year, they would disagree even more pointedly when McIlvane and the NAACP brought suit against the Pittsburgh diocese for failing to offer black students scholarships to its high schools.[69] Rice, as a member of the diocesan Board of Consultors, was a member of the party being sued.

These issues did not cause a permanent rupture between Rice and McIlvane. But, looking at the sweep of Rice's career as an activist, it is interesting to speculate whether he was not seeing in McIlvane a younger and more militant version of himself, much as Rev. James Renshaw Cox had seen a younger and more militant labor priest in Rice back in the 1930s.

By the end of 1967, then, Rice had pretty well carved out a niche for himself in Homewood. Although more of a moderate than a militant in person, he could generally be counted on to understand and side with the Bouie Hadens and other more militant activists in the neighborhood, attempting at the same time to explain those militants to a white audience that, as often as not, appeared not to want to understand. If such a role was difficult in 1967, it would become all but impossible in 1968, which for Rice would be the year of bullets, bombs and Bouie.

The year began badly enough with racial disorders in Miami, which Rice commented on his column. The Miami police department, he said, seemed bent on handling the disorders not with sensitivity and moderation, but with a program of "Peace by Terror."[70] Such armed confrontations would soon occur elsewhere, including Homewood.

In the spring, straws in the wind seemed to be pointing in contradictory directions as the country reacted to the rising tide of black impatience. In one direction pointed the blue-ribbon Kerner Commission Report, which examined the racial disorders of the previous year and concluded that in a society split in two along color lines, the problem was one of white racism. It advocated a panoply of measures to heal that split, and Rice seconded them.[71]

On the other hand came the well-publicized work of Nobel laureate Dr. William B. Shockley, arguing that blacks had not been proved to be "genetically equal." Responded Rice:

> What a rotten thing to say at this moment of history. Genetically equal to what, and whom? Can race be so sharply defined scientifically that we can compare races? The American Negro is such an admixture that to discuss his genes is nonsense. What racial impertinence for a white man to say, let us see if these people are equal to us. Who the blazes are we, and what are we genetically? To wonder if Negroes are genetically equal, and to speak publicly of preliminary research as if there were some golden nuggets of knowledge, is dirty and dishonest.[72]

On April 2 a disturbance occurred in Homewood, whose handling Rice believed offered hope that local militant organizations might be able to play a more central role in handling local problems than previously. It all began at the "Jolly Red Wiener," a white-owned eatery frequented by local residents and police officers. There a husky black youth on his way out one day was stopped by some officers and questioned — for no obvious reason; he had no police record. The young man blew up, had to be restrained, and was arrested as many additional patrol cars sped to the scene.

Two local organizations took up the cause of the incarcerated youth: Bouie Haden's UMP, and a group of younger militants named Forever Action Together (FAT). FAT organized protests against the restaurant and for the young man, protests held on the sidewalk and in the magistrate's court. UMP supported the demonstrations. Rice commented in his column that the incident had led to constructive organization of the neighborhood, which would actually reduce the likelihood of rioting there.[73]

But history was not going to allow this seedling of hope any time in which to grow. Hardly was the ink dry on Rice's words before the news flashed from Memphis around the world: Martin Luther King, Jr., the apostle of nonviolence, had fallen victim to the violence of an assassin's bullet.

Spontaneously, rioting broke out in so many black urban ghettoes as to make preceding long, hot summers look tame by comparison. In Homewood, Rice found himself living in a battle zone as forty-seven hundred National Guards and State Police were called in to back up Pittsburgh's fourteen hundred police in their attempt to restore order. But despite thirteen hundred arrests, order could not be quickly restored, and the police and military forces proceeded to seal off four blocks of Homewood Avenue. The sight of National Guard jeeps by day and the sound of hovering helicopters at night became commonplace.

Rice himself, whose life was now very clearly at risk on the streets of his parish, played only a muted role during the turbulence. A downtown meeting of clergymen to memorialize King convened inside a church rather than outside, with the understanding that there would be no public march. Rice felt that such an outside demonstration, in the presence of police officers who were already tired and edgy from long hours on duty, would likely lead to injuries not of the white clergymen, but of hapless blacks on the streets on whom the police might vent their frustrations. At the end of the service, however, one young clergyman suggested they depart from the plan and defy the ban on public demonstrations to conduct a march. As the young cleric prepared to lead the way out of the church, it was Rice who took to the podium to insist in the strongest terms that there be no march. He persuaded some of those in attendance, but one sign carrier and thirteen clergymen who congregated outside were arrested.[74]

For the rest, Rice left events on the street to the militants, the police, and the media. He reserved his strongest praise in his columns for FAT (Bouie Haden was away at the time), gave the police generally good marks for their restraint, and directed most of his criticism at the media, which he felt did not understand Homewood because they could not be bothered spending the necessary time and effort.[75]

On the Fourth of July, an incident occurred that appeared grim at the time, but in retrospect provided a touch of comic relief to the tragedy enveloping Homewood. The St. Vincent de Paul Society of the Pittsburgh diocese operated a used clothing and furniture store in Homewood, on shabby rented premises. The afternoon of the Fourth, a blaze was discovered there, which partially gutted the store. Worried whites, including the media and the fire chief, were bent on attributing the fire to black militants. Rice was equally vehement in insisting it was a case of spontaneous combustion.[76] The truth of the matter, Rice said he was told later, was that both theories were off the mark: it was alleged that the fire had been set by arsonists hired by the owner for insurance purposes. If that version is true, some mobsters had a good laugh at Rice's and the fire chief's expense.[77] But they may have laughed too soon: the store and its contents, after sitting there the rest of the summer, were set ablaze again in October, perhaps because the job had not been performed satisfactorily the first time.[78]

As the situation on the streets deteriorated in Homewood, Rice would find himself increasingly in conflict with police and other authorities of the law enforcement system. Already back in 1966 when he had been new to the neighborhood, he had learned a lesson as to how justice worked in the ghetto as opposed to other neighborhoods. A black parolee one evening publicly knifed a woman, with no particular provocation, and was pursued by an incensed black crowd to the Holy Rosary rectory, where he sought refuge. Rice assumed the thing to do was to call the police, which he did. Officers dutifully took the assailant into custody, and just as dutifully released him the next morning because no one had come to the station to prefer charges. His victim was in a poor position to do so: she nearly died of her wounds.[79]

By the summer of 1968, Rice no longer expected the criminal justice system to arrest and prosecute criminals in Homewood as it did elsewhere, but he was incensed at the wholesale arrests and detention of civil rights activists who, in his view, were trying to reestablish law and order. One of Rice's targets was Judge David Olbum who was liberal enough to defend the principle of "nominal bail" for the poor so they could be free while awaiting trial, but now in the heat of 1968 was setting very high bail for some of Rice's activist friends. A spirited, if respectful exchange between the two took place in the pages of the *Pittsburgh Catholic*.[80]

Less respectful was Rice's attack on Robert Duggan, district attorney and close friend (later in-law) of the Mellons. Rice accused Duggan of trying to conduct "legal lynchings" of every black militant by his high-bail policy for all those arrested in civil rights disturbances.[81]

But by October, the problem in Homewood was less with the unfair administration of the law by officials than with those who took the law into their own hands. An elderly Italian grocer had been killed "callously and casually," as Rice put it, by a young black.[82] The local community had turned in the killer to the police, but others apparently decided to avenge the crime themselves. Shortly after midnight one night, a bomb was tossed from a passing car by a white hand into a crowd of blacks two blocks from Holy Rosary, injuring twelve and throwing Rice, he said, out of his bed.[83]

Fearful that white backlash might now be on its way in wholesale lots, Homewood girded to protect itself. At Holy Rosary, Rice instructed his curate to disarm the hunting rifles the younger priest kept there, and insisted that they would offer no resistance if violence came.

Quite different was his stance toward militants at the Black Power Center nearby. There, Rice contributed funding for the militants to provide themselves with rifles against the expected onslaught.[84] The militants, armed with these weapons, proceeded to post lookouts on the roof to watch for any approaching white mob. This maneuver only made them sitting ducks for the police who soon arrived after getting reports of guns at the center. After they had descended, two of the militants were shot in the back, each by a black police officer, according to official reports. The police never were prosecuted or disciplined for their conduct, but a year later the militants were convicted by an all-white jury. In his column, Rice had decried the entire incident as "unnecessary."[85] Had he contributed to this "unnecessary" event himself? His silence on his financing of the armaments kept his readers from speculating about that aspect of the affair.

As 1968 lurched toward an end, Rice seemed to be getting his answer from the white conscience he said he had set out to address. Bishop Wright had been hanged in effigy, presumably by white Catholics who could not abide the thought of helping Bouie Haden. Hubert Humphrey was defeated for the presidency by Richard Nixon in an election accompanied by a remarkably good showing by segregationist George Wallace. He not only carried much of the South, but did well in many northern industrial cities, including Pittsburgh. Running up 8.1 percent of the vote throughout Pennsylvania, Wallace took 11.6 percent in Pittsburgh.[86] If this was what the white conscience had to say, it gave few glimmers of hope to Rice.

During Rice's next years in Homewood, after the bloody climax that was 1968, positions were hardened all around: by the police, by the white establishment (including its religious leadership), and by Rice. Black militancy, by and large, was the victim.

The grant to Bouie Haden and UMP, as already noted, was terminated in 1969.[87] (His building had mysteriously burned down.)[88] The same thing happened to RAHR, which had been funded for an initial period of three years beginning in 1966. The Presbyterian, Catholic, and Methodist church bodies, perhaps unnerved by the events of 1968, and continually worried that the RAHR orientation was too much along the radical lines of the Chicago neighborhood organizer Saul Alinsky, declined to renew the $51,000 grant in 1969. RAHR thereafter converted itself into the all-black Homewood-Brushton Alliance, but continued to exist only as a paper organization, and with it went FAT. FAT director Nick Flournoy (who had been chosen by the Presbyterians, who put up more of the money, over Rice's preference, Charles Howard) was terminated in 1970.[89]

It was also in 1969 that Bishop Wright went to Rome, first, in March to be made a cardinal, and again that summer to begin service at the Vatican. His replacement was to be his former assistant, Rev. Vincent Leonard. Rice would be quite comfortable with Leonard, who had come through Duquesne and St. Vincent's one year behind him, but Rice would not play the unique role he had enjoyed during Wright's tenure. When Wright returned briefly to Pittsburgh to officiate at the 1969 Labor Day Mass, McIlvane and others in the Catholic Interracial Conference staged a walkout, bitterly resented by Rice, to protest Wright's record of not taking a hard enough line against racial discrimination in some unions.[90]

Violence continued in Homewood, but the rest of Pittsburgh was largely unaware of it due to concerted attempts to keep it out of the newspapers. One evening at Holy Rosary, a meeting of lay parish leaders was held to discuss plans for salvaging what remained of a declining parish membership. As the gathering broke up, departing parishioners were drawn to the front porch by shouts and banging sounds in the street. They saw a crowd of young blacks beating on a car containing several whites. The young whites were deaf men who frequently came to Holy Rosary to visit with Rice's assistant pastor who worked with the deaf. The blacks had recently returned from a white neighborhood where they had been attacked and beaten up for no apparent reason. They had resolved to take revenge on the first whites they saw, and these turned out to be the terrified deaf men now trapped inside the car. As the horrified white parishioners watched, the blacks appeared bent on dragging the whites out of the car and killing them.

Rice was summoned, and insisted on calling not the police (whose presence, he argued, could only cause a riot) but Bouie Haden. Haden came quickly and began negotiating with the young blacks. At length, a compromise was worked out: the deaf whites were permitted to get out of the car with no further molestation; they and the white parishioners departed quietly from the back of Holy Rosary; but the car was left behind and then torched. Firemen came later, in the dead of night, extinguished the smoldering remains, and towed them away. It was an unusual measure in Homewood where wrecked or abandoned cars littered the landscape, but one absolutely necessary, in Rice's opinion, to keep the event out of the news media and not allow it to turn into a more general conflagration. The only whites aware of the incident were those involved and the onlooking parishioners, whose hopes for reviving Holy Rosary could hardly have been cheered.[91]

Another dead end came in the form of a black business venture that Rice funded. A young black man who ran a florist shop in nearby Homewood had for some time had his eye on a well-located grocery store, which he thought he could run successfully. The owner of the building was willing to offer him the store rent free, but the sum of $700 was needed to stock the shelves. Rice put up the money out of his own savings, only to see the business go under in less than a month. Second-rate merchandise had been sold to the novice grocer, a clerk he hired was unable to count well enough to make change, and members of the neighborhood "wolf pack" stole from and intimidated the black shopkeeper just as they would have a white.[92]

It was in 1969 that Rice's revision downward of his previous admiration for police officers themselves (as opposed to their bosses, whom he had already criticized) became apparent. Looking back on the Homewood disorders of 1968, Rice argued that most of the excesses could have been avoided if only the police had accepted the cooperation offered them by the local militants. The police as an outside presence could not have controlled the ghetto, but the militants could. What made cooperation impossible, he reasoned, was police machismo.[93]

But the court system, in Rice's view, was even worse. After the trial and sentencing of the militants shot in the back at the Black Power Center the previous year, Rice was of the settled opinion that justice for blacks was not available in Pittsburgh's white courts:

> From this and other cases I know first hand, I am convinced that a black man cannot get a fair trial from a jury in Allegheny County, and until there is a change in the method of empaneling our juries there will be no justice where it is a case of black versus white or black versus police or DA.[94]

A year later, reflecting on a tragic case decided by a panel of judges rather than a jury, and a case in which he had been deeply involved, Rice reached conclusions even more negative about white justice. Billy Hines, a mentally-retarded adolescent member of a "wolf pack" near Holy Rosary, had attempted to rape a white girl, the daughter of an associate of Rice's. The clumsy attempt had ended in the girl's death. Not only was Rice called upon to console the bereaved family; Billy Hines asked for Rice while he was awaiting trial, and Rice went to counsel him. At the trial, Billy was found guilty and given a life sentence. Rice denounced the sentence as unduly long, said that sexual crimes by blacks against whites called forth the white majority's paranoia about black sexuality, and proclaimed:

> Such trials are, in a sense, political trials in which the white system is on trial in the eyes of all black people. Every case of this sort either promotes or impedes reconciliation between ruling white and alienated black.[95]

Judge Fiok, one of the panel of three who had heard the case, shot back that Rice's charge of a "political trial" was unworthy of response, that the choice before the judges had in fact been between a life sentence and a death sentence, and that Rice's supposed concern for Billy Hines and for justice had not motivated him to testify on behalf of Billy or even to sit and hear the trial. Rice was thus, in Fiok's view, a "parologist" — someone who relies on word-of-mouth rather than hard evidence.[96]

It was also in 1969 that Rice would burn his bridges with organized labor. He had already taken a stand that won him no gratitude from labor leaders when he had defended the nonunionized jitney drivers. And he had gone even further when he faced the racial exclusivity of unions in the building trades. Back in 1966, when a spontaneous walkout of building-trades workers occurred in St. Louis because non-AFL-CIO black workers had been hired, Rice went so far as to say that if such an effective measure were legal, as the building trades claimed, then there was hardly any need for situs picketing legislation, long advocated by those unions as necessary for their preservation.[97]

But by the summer of 1969, with over $200 million of new construction going up in Pittsburgh, the issue of racism in the building trades was about to come home to roost. As the face of

downtown Pittsburgh was being remade with new corporate headquarters for U.S. Steel and a new stadium for the Steelers and
Pirates, the only black faces visible on the construction sites
seemed to be behind wheelbarrows.

The Black Construction Coalition, headed by Nate Smith, was
preparing to challenge the whites-only composition of the building
trades in Pittsburgh, and at his side was Rice. Various courses of
action were considered. When someone suggested marching right
onto the construction sites, Rice pointed out that the workers
would simply drop metal objects on their heads, from high enough
up to kill them. An alternative more likely to gain the workers'
respectful attention, he suggested, was to blow up a gasoline
tanker on the premises. But there were no takers on that one,
which tended to confirm Rice's opinion that most blacks were
simply too gentle to make real militants.[98]

In his columns before Labor Day 1969, Rice looked with equa-
nimity upon the possible dissolution of the building trades unions
if they refused to abate their racism: "I have to confess that I shall
shed no tears if their bungling arrogance in the race crisis leads to
their destruction."[99]

Then began the marching. On the Monday before Labor Day,
Rice and other white sympathizers marched in protest and the
Black Construction Coalition staged its own public demonstration.
Mayor Barr ordered the construction sites closed (thus denying
work to the construction workers) to prevent escalation into violence. Violence occurred anyhow as the police used their trunc-
heons on protesters assembled at Manchester Bridge, arrested 180
demontrators, and then pursued jay-walking activists around the
Golden Triangle. White construction workers and their families
staged countermarches after the sites were shut down Monday
and again Thursday and Friday; their relations with the police
were much more amicable.[100]

Rice marched with white and black protesters but refused to
accompany the building trades countermarches. To one woman
who telephoned to inquire about this seeming inconsistency, Rice
retorted, "I marched with them because they are right; I will not
march with you because you are wrong."[101] He looked wistfully at
their parting of the ways in his next column:

> I must say that I am not happy over the probable loss of my erstwhile
> title of "Labor Priest" and I regretted the absence of labor chaps from
> our Mass. I appreciate those men and I wish I could be on their side.

Sorry I cannot be with you, men; you may not miss me but I shall miss you![102]

As it would turn out, the Labor Day Mass of 1969 would be the last in a decade-long series. With Wright gone, and after some Catholic Interracial Council activists had walked out on his last stand, and with Rice on the outs with much of organized labor, there seemed little point in throwing a party to which only a few came and at which many of them misbehaved.

Early in 1970 an understanding was signed between the Black Construction Coalition and the building trades, and progress on the construction work proceeded. But Rice feared that the Black Construction Coalition had traded in its activism for toothless promises which relied upon the good will of construction unions, in which he had scant confidence.[103] It is interesting that on this issue, unlike many others, Rice was enlisting a great deal of white support (more whites than blacks marched on Labor Day), but he was simultaneously alienating what had once been the core of his own support, the trade unionists.

Looking back on Rice's decade in Homewood, from 1966 to 1976, it is clear that the height of his involvement in the black struggle for equality came in 1968–69. His would be a friendly presence there for years afterward, but one only occasionally invoked on specifically black issues. The struggle itself would greatly abate as the 1970s progressed.

During these crucial years, then, what was accomplished, what failed to be accomplished, and what were the costs of the gains that were achieved?

Rice's years of close involvement with the black civil rights movement, as noted earlier, were not the heady ones of the early 1960s when the movement was young, all allies were welcomed, and all things seemed possible. He came to Homewood instead at a time when white "friends" were viewed with suspicion and distaste. When the going got tough, blacks discovered, these allies could simply move on to more pleasant pastures, whereas blacks would have to deal with white racism all their lives. Rice stayed at Homewood long enough to see death, destruction, white backlash, and the evaporation of the early appearances of black unity. These were not exactly years of pretzels and beer.

Yet looking back from the perspective of the 1980s, Rice for one saw certain very real gains for blacks emerging from the struggles fought in the late 1960s. Pittsburgh police a generation later no longer routinely treated blacks as if they belonged to a subhuman species; professional conduct toward blacks as toward whites was the expectation and usually the practice.

In economic terms, some job opportunities had been opened up for some blacks: by the 1980s they commonly worked in stores, hospitals, and other places of employment that formerly had been lily-white. This is not to allege that "equal opportunity" had become an economic reality. Particularly during the Reagan years, as the differential between average white and average black employment rates and earnings grew greater instead of smaller, it became clear that the dream of equality remained a dream. But improved economic opportunity, if still far short of the opportunities available to whites, had been opened up for the black middle class, in Rice's opinion.

What had not been gained, in Rice's observation, was a better life for those at the bottom of the black barrel, who in the 1980s lived lives as hopeless and helpless as ever. The Homewood to which Rice had come in 1966 had been littered with winos, junkies, and unemployed young men living on the streets; in the 1980s that remained as true as ever. The young militants with whom Rice worked, who raised fundamental questions about the economic system of a country that routinely consigned Homewood residents to lives of economic destitution, would, in the 1980's, find their questions no nearer to answers than a generation earlier. Their fundamental thrust, which in the 1960's had the potential to develop into a radical and revolutionary one, had been blunted or destroyed.

Even the gains that were made, then, had their cost. Some improvement in status and in economic opportunity was achieved for some blacks, but the price that had been paid was the extinguishing of the spark of black militancy that seemed in the 1960s to offer hope not just to some of Homewood's blacks, but to all of them.[104]

Did Rice have anything to do with extinguishing that militant spark? This is perhaps the most difficult question to answer about his decade in Homewood.

It must be observed first of all that just as Rice's first commitment in the 1930s and 1940s was not to labor unions but to the Catholic Church, so in the 1960s that loyalty was still primarily to the church, not to blacks. As an emissary of the church and particularly of Bishop Wright, Rice's mission in Homewood was to try to soften rather than exacerbate the lines of class and racial conflict, and to uphold insofar as possible the prestige of the institutional Catholic Church. The institutional church had not always been an ally of blacks, and was often enough perceived as part of their problem. Although Wright was a more concerned and liberal prelate than most in the church, still there were times when the church's needs as he perceived them, and the needs of blacks as the militants saw them, did not coincide. Thus Wright was adamantly opposed to any attempt by black militants to tell *him* which priests or nuns were acceptable in Homewood, or to stipulate that only blacks be stationed in black neighborhoods.[105] And Rice himself in a letter to Wright suggested the tenuous nature of the alliance between the diocese and black militants in Homewood when he observed that "the militants have their day and while that day will not last forever we have to avoid confrontation."[106]

But by the same token, Rice more than most whites or even most white liberals exhibited a sensitivity to the need of blacks and particularly black militants to be in control of their own movement and of their own turf. He therefore advised Wright not to reject outright the demand for black say-so in the assignment of Catholic priests and nuns to Homewood.[107] And by 1970 Rice was noting in his column the disturbing effect on black leaders sometimes exercised by well-meaning white organizations:

> Around here, the lower echelons of black leadership have been weakened by helpful white organizations absorbing scores of natural leaders into positions which, for the most part, are meaningless. Would it not be better to have black leaders occupying normal jobs and supporting their own activities by their earnings?[108]

Besides providing employment for black leaders, there were other ways that well-intentioned white efforts could in fact hurt blacks. One of these Rice had noted in a private letter to Wright that brought into question not only the effect of his work in Homewood but of his earlier work at the House of Hospitality:

> The Howze family were our special pets when I was in the Hill [at the House of Hospitality]. Bill Lenz and the sisters thought they were wonderful and did everything they could for them. *This kindness may have destroyed the family*: Sam is one of the very youngest of them. He is convinced that anything that makes, or encourages, Negroes to try to be

white is a deadly influence; he is convinced that it causes mental illness. I suppose you know that he works as a community person in Negro areas for Western Pennsylvania Psychiatric Hospital. I think that Howze is more right than wrong and that we have to be very careful lest we corrupt Negroes with our whiteness [Emphasis added].[109]

Despite the cautionary note with which he approached blacks in Homewood, despite his opposition to putting black leaders on white payrolls, it is arguable that Rice, by arranging to bankroll black organizations with church monies that blacks could not control, was preparing the way for the collapse of black activism in Homewood more effectively than policemen, prosecutors, or unsympathetic trade unions ever could have. Bouie Haden, Nick Flournoy, and other leaders with whom Rice worked were not being absorbed into "meaningless positions," but neither were they supporting their activities by their own earnings. Although RAHR, the Council on Race and Religion, and Neighbors in Need seem to have given the militants grants with no explicit strings attached, still when the churches experienced backlash from their own support bases, they yanked the funding from under the militants quite unceremoniously. The militants were left to ponder again the truism that whatever the white power structure or any part of it gives, it can just as easily take away.

But in fairness to Rice, the choice at that time was not between offering the militants funding that was revocable or irrevocable; it was between offering them some sort of financial help or none at all. Rice seems to have done his utmost to offer financial support in ways that would not compromise either church prestige or militant integrity. That such a strategy would not work in the long run is perhaps more obvious in retrospect than it was at the time.

For the rest, Rice marked out his position and defended it against all comers — of whom there were many. This position was not that of some early white liberal supporters of black civil rights, who pulled out when they did not receive that measure of black gratitude to which they thought their magnanimity entitled them. Nor was it that of a Rev. James Groppi, who led the black struggle in his city, and later left the priesthood and the Catholic Church to continue to serve the cause of justice. Rice always saw his social activism as an offshoot of his priestly office, and hence his insistence on having a *parish* in a black neighborhood to serve.

Rice's position entailed losses to himself that were very considerable. He was not so much bothered by the crank mail he received with regularity; he was used to that. Nor was he dismayed when the FBI began looking over his shoulder; he was much less enamored of that agency than he had been in his anticommunist days. But the loss of his labor alliances, of his ties to the Democratic Party, and even the strained relations with his own family (partly in connection with his antiwar activism, which I shall examine next) — these hurt him deeply.

Years later, looking over the many years and many aspects of his activist past, Rice found some things to regret. But of his work for the rights of blacks in America, from his earliest years to his latest, he regretted nothing.[110]

SEVEN

This Time Really A Radical

IF ONE IS STRUCK WITH THE TOTAL RANGE of Rice's activities against the communists back in the late 1940s, one must be even more amazed at his social activism in the late 1960s. For side by side with his work for black equality discussed in the previous chapter was his even more strident opposition to American involvement in the war in Vietnam, the topic of this chapter. And whereas Rice was reaching the age of forty amid his anticommunist crusading, at the height of his procivil rights and antiwar advocacy, he turned sixty. If age was slowing him down, it was hardly obvious to most observers. Dr. Benjamin Spock, a fellow antiwar activist, said of Rice during this era: "He was this priest, not many years younger than I, who all his life had been doing what I had come to only a year or two before."[1]

Rice's work for civil rights for blacks had engaged him deeply at a visceral level and had cost him many erstwhile friends, but it would be his opposition to the Vietnam War and his alliance with young radicals struggling against it that would convert his basic political viewpoint from that of liberal optimism, holding that the policies of the American political and economic establishment either were good ones or could with some effort be improved, into a deep cynicism and near despair, holding that many American policies were fundamentally evil and not amenable to change.

One difference between the issues of race and war was that, whereas it was not respectable for liberals to oppose civil rights for blacks in the early 1960s, it was still quite fashionable for them to support the American military presence in Vietnam. Another was that, whereas many other priests were working in black ghettoes, few were hitting the streets to oppose American militarism in Southeast Asia. It is true that Rice's increasingly alienated viewpoints on race and war would feed one another as the years went on, but war more than race seemed to force a rethinking of his previous positions, and to produce the feeling of being at odds with those around him, even with his own family. Years later, comparing his days in the Catholic "Radical" Alliance with the years spent opposing American involvement in Vietnam, he would tacitly concede that the former use of the tag was less than fully appropriate when he said, "Now [in the 1960s]. . . I mean really radical."[2]

In an earlier chapter, I argued that Rice's use of the term "radical" was a misleading cover for liberal reformism. Whether his use of the same term in the 1960s is any more accurate, is a subject to which I shall return a bit later. But what is clear for now is that his political outlook was indeed undergoing a profound change rom his earlier liberal optimism that the United States in world affairs was invariably the "good guy."

The war that would "reradicalize" Rice had its roots in the French colonial empire of pre-World War II days. The French had been able to subjugate the subcontinent of Indonesia and to extract from its land and peoples a very considerable wealth from natural resources (especially rubber) and trade advantages. But that favorable position was interrupted by World War II, as the French were thrust out of Southeast Asia as from much of the rest of their colonial holdings, and then forced to struggle simply for their own national survival in the grip of Nazi Germany.

Into the political vacuum created by the French retreat from Vietnam, one of the ancient lands of Indonesia, came the forces of national independence and self-determination, headed by the man who would become the George Washington of his country, Ho Chi Minh. An admirer of American democracy and particularly of Abraham Lincoln, Ho Chi Minh several times petitioned the United States for diplomatic recognition of his regime on the grounds that he merely wanted to gain for his nation the same postcolonial rights that the United States had secured when it broke loose from British rule. But neither the Roosevelt nor the Truman administration found his case a persuasive one, and when the French, struggling back to their feet after World War II, moved to reestablish their colonial empire in Indonesia, the United States quietly backed its wartime ally with economic and later military aid.

The French returned to their capital in the south of Vietnam,

Saigon, where they installed the puppet regime of Ngo Dinh Diem, a Catholic, to begin the reconquest of Indonesia's bread-basket. Guerilla warfare broke out with Ho Chi Minh, who by now was countering French militarism not only with the support of many peasants in the countryside, but also with military aid from the Soviets and even the Chinese (ethnic enemies of the Vietnamese) in what he proclaimed to be a socialist struggle. The war grew through the early 1950s and then escalated by 1954 to a conventional battle at Dien Bien Phu in which the forces of Ho Chi Minh, headed by General Giap, surrounded the French army, moved from guerrilla hit-and-run tactics to a set-piece battle with large mortar pieces, and forced the French to surrender. (The Eisenhower administration briefly considered nuclear intervention at the behest of Secretary of State John Foster Dulles, but abandoned the idea when faced with the opposition of the Senate majority leader, Lyndon Baines Johnson!)

The French phase of the Vietnam war was concluded with the Geneva Accords of 1956, which provided for (1) withdrawal of the forces of Ho Chi Minh north of a newly created demilitarized zone (DMZ) across the middle of Vietnam; (2) withdrawal of the French and Diem forces to the south; (3) French evacuation from Vietnam; and (4) nationwide elections throughout Vietnam to choose a new government. These arrangements were agreed to by the French, by the forces of Ho Chi Minh, and by numerous other nations in the region and throughout the world that had taken an interest in resolving the conflict. The two exceptions were the regime of Diem and the United States. Very soon, the Diem regime would refuse to hold national elections (knowing very well that it would lose overwhelmingly) and the United States would provide Diem with military support in his attempt to hold the forces of Ho Chi Minh at bay.

It was from this point forward, then, that the United States, motivated by its view that socialism backed by the U.S.S.R. must not be allowed to succeed in Southeast Asia, and by some American corporations' interests in the assets of the land, stepped in to fill the place of the departing colonial power of France. That policy, although rife with enormous implications for the course of the United States in the postcolonial world, would remain invisible to the American public. By the early 1960s, when the pretense of backing an independent Diem had worn so thin that the United States had to send in its own soldiers to counter the growing power of Ho Chi Minh, many U.S. citizens had little idea of where

Vietnam was, or what American forces were doing there. Most Americans thus began their phase of the Vietnam conflict with little awareness of or interest in the struggle, combined with a hazy approval of whatever their political leadership was doing to fight the spread of communism throughout the world. A painful education awaited them.

Rice's own writings and pronouncements on world affairs in the 1950s and early 60s were remarkably parallel to this state of American public consciousness. He mentioned international events only infrequently — two or three times out of fifty columns a year in the early 1960s. When he brought them up at all, it was usually in defense of church prerogatives somewhere in the world, or with the unspoken assumption that in international conflicts the United States represented truth and justice, with its opponents invariably in the wrong.

Thus his first mention of Asian problems came when Rice attacked the elected communist government of the state of Kerala in India for its pressure on Catholic schools there.[3] When Gary Powers, pilot of the U-2 spy plane shot down from Russian skies, pleaded for his life, Rice said that Powers had been "on a noble and useful mission" and regretted the pilot had not "defended our country's policies and record," at whatever hazard to himself.[4] Closer to home, Rice applauded the resolve of Munoz government in Puerto Rico to maintain its friendship with the United States, despite the temptation to gain popularity by "Yankee-baiting."[5] When the Kennedy administration carried through Eisenhower's plans to sponsor the invasion of Castro's socialist Cuba by Cuban emigres at the Bay of Pigs, Rice agreed that the Castro regime there was intolerable. Interestingly, he noted the heritage of United States imperialism in Latin America, and feared that subversive activity there might be a threat to freedom and democracy in the United States. But his solution to this quandary lay not in tolerating Castro's Cuba, but in an aboveboard invasion of that island![6]

After the bungled invasion, Rice saw the young President Kennedy conducting himself more successfully against the Soviets in Berlin, and argued that to win the cold war, America would have to make many adjustments, external and internal.[7] He still continued to view Israel as a symbol of the free world, which the United States should continue to support in the Middle East.[8] Even as late as 1964, when the Diem regime in Vietnam had been overthrown and Diem assassinated by his associates who could no longer support his tyrannical ways, Rice continued to praise the record of the toppled regime. Arguing that Diem's Catholicism had made him a target for sniping by the United States press, Rice discounted stories of Diem's repressiveness, said that Buddhists there were wont to burn themselves to death for trivial reasons(!), and predicted that Diem's assassination would lead to a loss of vitality [sic] for Vietnam.[9]

But even as some of Rice's writings in the 1960s were supporting the projection of United States power throughout the world, whether by cooperation with friendly governments or by the use of unadorned military might, other columns of his began to express doubts about the invariable rightness of American positions and goals in world affairs.

An example of this tendency, cited earlier, was his reflection in 1960 that the United States had, after all, been the first and only nation to use nuclear weapons in warfare.[10] That particular broadcast had brought Rice into contact with Robert G. Colodny, then a junior faculty member at the University of Pittsburgh's History Department. Colodny, who had served in the leftist Abraham Lincoln Brigade in the Spanish Civil War, had occasion a year later to benefit from Rice's broadcasts and columns — when his own academic future was in doubt, apparently because of such connections. Rice did not exactly rise to an impassioned defense of Colodny's academic freedom, but he did not conclude that the case against granting him tenure was "not very strong."[11] This public mention of the case, plus the intervention of Pitt's Chancellor Litchfield, apparently saved the day for Colodny, and this in turn established a significant tie between Rice and Colodny, and with some of the latter's students of a radical persuasion.

Among the young radicals coming to Rice would be Paul Le-Blanc, Jimmy Ferlo, and Bob Nelson, the son of Steve Nelson. Rice took part in a number of teach-ins on the war before he returned to Pittsburgh in 1966, but the way he tells the story, it was he who was being educated by the young (and by a variety of radical publications) more than the other way around. He was sometimes taken aback by the sexual openness of these young persons, and their disdain for many established middle-class values, such as personal cleanliness. But for the most part he simply gulped down his shock and kept on going — quite a change for this product of Irish prudery and Catholic seminaries! He even let his hair, or its remaining fringe, grow to collar length.[12]

In his writings at this time, Rice's changing assessment of U.S.

overseas intervention first became evident, interestingly, with respect to Latin America rather than Vietnam. In 1963 he reversed himself on going to war against Cuba, recommending coexistence instead.[13] In 1964 he flatly advocated getting out of Panama, long before the United States was ready for that step.[14] And even in 1965 his loss of trust in the Johnson administration seemed to be caused as much by its invasion of the Dominican Republic and quelling of an uprising there (on the pretext of "protecting American lives") as by anything else.[15]

Meanwhile, American economic and military aid to Diem and his successors was working no better than French fighting forces had in holding back the advance of Ho Chi Minh in Vietnam. Lyndon Johnson had opposed nuclear intervention there in 1954 and had run as the peace candidate against Barry Goldwater in 1964, promising not to lead American boys into an Asian land war. But by 1965 he faced losing prospects in Southeast Asia and was preparing to do almost everything the hawkish Goldwater had advocated the year before. Informed that the only two U.S. options were to watch the little men in black pajamas triumph over American allies, or take over the war with direct military intervention, Johnson now departed from the tentative deescalation of his predecessor, John F. Kennedy, and announced in July 1965 the massive deployment of U.S. land forces in Vietnam. This step was accompanied by an official insistence that it was not United States but the forces of Ho Chi Minh that were escalating the war, and not the United States but the communists of North Vietnam who were invading the south. This view implied that the DMZ of the Geneva Accords was a permanent international boundary between nations rather than a temporary dividing line between armies.

Proponents of the "domino theory" reasoned that if one Asian nation were allowed to fall to communism, all of the rest would follow, and insisted that now was the time to resist just as America had resisted in Korea — and unlike the temporizing of a Chamberlain at Munich in the face of Nazi aggression prior to World War II.

Even prior to Johnson's americanization of the war in Vietnam, Rice the preceding April had come out in favor of U.S. disengagement from that war, first in a radio broadcast and then in the pages of the *Pittsburgh Catholic*. Because this column staked out the position Rice would continue to defend when it was extremely unpopular, when it became more accepted, and until its final vindication in another April a full decade later, it is worth reproducing here in its entirety;

DO WE BELONG IN VIETNAM?

Vietnam is a dirty and dangerous business and we have to get out. The dirt and the danger lie not so much in what may happen to the United States but in what is being done by us against other people and in what additional evil we may be led to inflict.

Long before we got directly into the conflict we supplied our allies with truly dreadful weapons and directed their use. Napalm and phosphorous bombs are an inhuman product of modern technology. While they are not so bad as the nuclear bomb and not so nauseatingly destructive as bacteriological weapons, they are murderous and should be outlawed. It was bad enough to use them against technologically advanced peoples such as the Japanese and the Germans, but to use them against jungle fighters is unclean. The anti-personnel shell with its cruel needles of death is no better.

It is said that the enemy is unfair because he has used terror to get support and respect. What are we doing? What is the jellied gasolene which clings, burns and tortures? What of the phosphorous which eats into the bone? What of the miserable victims of napalm, phosphorous and steel splinters who continue to live in unbelievable agony and helplessness? Is this not terror and are we not guilty?

Are we repelling an invader? No, we are not. The Viet Cong are not invaders. They may be Communists but they are native to Vietnam. We are invaders and we are the only invaders who are there in force. The Chinese Communists are not present in force nor are the Russians.

The North Vietnamese do not want Chinese domination, but we may force it on them.

We have misunderstood the facts and have misread the past every step of the way. We have seen, and we see, parallels where they do not exist and we draw foolish conclusions.

The situation now does not parallel the European situation during the rise of Hitler. Appeasement is not the danger here.

The situation now does not parallel Korea because North Vietnam is not the Chinese puppet that North Koreas was and is. The terrain in both countries is different and the local population is different. How we fought or did not fight in Korea is not relevant here.

The situation does not parallel Malaya where the English won a long jungle war because the people, the culture, the geography and past history are different. The Vietnamese are an ancient people who have always fought foreigners and are a culturally unified people.

Democrats deny that they bungled in not attacking China during the Korean war, but they, strongly and foolishly, are determined to avoid the alleged mistake again.

Some Americans worry about the war merely because it may involve thousands of American casualties and might escalate into a conflict where we would get hit ourselves. We should worry about the miserable and courageous, however misguided, peasants who are defending their country.

Some say, it would be awful to let all Vietnam and Laos and Cambodia slide into Communism. I say, let the people decide. If the Communists can win their allegiance we cannot really do anything about it. We who do not understand their ways. We are growing more hated every day as we kill more and more of them.

I do not fear that we will lose. I fear what we will do in order to win. It looks as if we are ready to destroy the industry of North Vietnam. That industry was built up with sacrifice and heroism, however misguided. What right have we to destroy it even if we intend to build it up again?

So this was done under Communist control, so what? It was done and the people like it.

Is it not better to de dead than Red? Let the Vietnamese decide that for themselves and we will decide it for ourselves.

Finally: We will lose face if we leave. Which is worse? Lose face or lose your soul?[16]

Having come out in opposition to the U.S. war effort at a time when it still enjoyed broad popular support, Rice insisted in 1965 that it was possible to be both antiwar and patriotic,[17] that Johnson was, tragically, in a political position where he could not simply call the troops home,[18] that the trade unions were falling in line behind administration policy, but that the young who burned their draft cards, though they might be "immature," were certainly not "treacherous."[19] It seemed as though Rice, having mutinied and departed from the establishment's fortress, was now preparing for a prolonged siege against those battlements. Such a resolve would prove altogether necessary.

Rice had already participated in some teach-ins and demonstrations while living in Washington, Pennsylvania, but it was after his return to Pittsburgh that he became a significant presence in antiwar activism both in Pittsburgh and on the national scene. It is true that Rice became a member of various groups that were planning and organizing marches and rallies in New York, Washington, and elsewhere. Two such were the Spring Mobilization, which organized a huge march and rally at the United Nations headquarters on April 15, 1967, and the National Mobilization which coordinated the march and the program of civil disobedience at the Pentagon on October 21 of that year.

Although Rice would sit in the company of such antiwar luminaries as Rennie Davis, Dave Dellinger, Jerry Rubin, Abby Hoffman, and H. Rap Brown, he would be there not so much as a mover and shaker himself, as a symbol of support to those who did most of the work and planning. For one thing, many of the strategy meetings were scheduled for weekends, which was fine for students and other academics, but inconvenient for members of the clergy. For another, Rice recognized that the leadership of a movement composed mostly of the young belonged naturally to the young.

But he always showed up for marches or demonstrations in his clerical garb, and early discovered that the Roman collar and his own presence provided a certain welcome aura. From the perspective of movement leaders, the presence of the elderly Monsignor with the Irish accent no doubt gave the proceedings a touch of theater and of legitimacy that was quite useful, especially in the early days. Thus Rice's participation in the huge national rallies was less important for what he had to say (the audiences were polite but not enthusiastic, by Rice's own account) than for the totemic value of his presence.

An incident that illustrated rather neatly Rice's own view of his clerical presence at antiwar activities took place soon after his return to Pittsburgh in 1966. Dave Kelly, the news director at WIIC-TV, in a televised editorial for that station suggested that the appropriate stand on involvement in Vietnam should be "my country right or wrong." He drew attention to Rice as a clergyman involved in opposing government policy, and invoked the separation of church and state to conclude that if Rice must demonstrate, he should do so in civilian rather than clerical garb. In the ensuing debate, which went on for several days, Rice replied that he had not surrendered his civil rights when he became a priest and that on issues of war and peace the clergy must speak up *as clergy* — unlike the unfortunate example in Nazi Germany, where the silence of too many good persons had made atrocities possible.[20]

Rice began showing up quite prominently at a long series of marches, demonstrations, and rallies to protest the escalating American takeover of the war in Vietnam. The following chronology, though far from complete, illustrates some of the scope and nature of this work:

March 26, 1966. At a Pittsburgh antiwar rally, Rice was the only speaker to escape the catcalls of onlookers.[21]

July 11, 1966. Rice led an interfaith march of rabbis, ministers and priests from Rodef Shalom Temple to Ascension Episcopal Church and to St. Paul's (Catholic) cathedral, and at the last stop was one of those who read scriptural antiwar passages.[22]

September 5, 1966. Rice left Pittsburgh's Labor Day observance early to appear with folk singer and antiwar activist Paul Ochs at the annual Bucks County World Peace Fair near Philadelphia.[23]

November 4, 1966. Rice was the last of eight speakers to address fifteen hundred listeners at Pittsburgh's Carnegie Hall, and concluded the antiwar program with the prayer: "Please God, we'll come to our senses before we destroy the world and ourselves."[24]

April 12, 1967. Rice joined Pittsburgh Area Students for Peace in picketing the offices of the *Pittsburgh Press* for what they regarded as its unfair reporting and editorializing on the organization's activities.[25]

April 15, 1967. Rice, marching with Martin Luther King, Jr., Benjamin Spock, and others, led a huge antiwar march from Central Park in New York to the U.N. Building where he was one of those who "greeted" the rally.[26]

May 17, 1967. In a follow-up to the Spring Mobilization, Rice was one of the twelve representatives who led a smaller contingent of two hundred fifty or so persons to the White House, to present a formal protest to President Johnson. As onlookers booed and hurled eggs, Spock read a statement through the locked White House gate to a presidential assistant.[27]

October 11, 1967. A "peace torch," lit at the Hiroshima memorial to A-bomb victims and being carried across the country to the Pentagon, passed through Pittsburgh. Rice led the march and addressed the crowd in a period of quiet unlike the chanting and scuffling that marked most of the occasion.[28]

October 21, 1967. At the March on the Pentagon, which Rice had helped plan, he was one of the leaders who had committed themselves to civil disobedience in an attempt to obstruct operations inside the building. But by the time the leaders got to the Pentagon steps, massed lines of MPs were already keeping out thousands of demonstrators. Dave Dellinger first introduced Rice, who proceeded to lecture the MPs on the evils of war. When the soldiers advanced, with Rice in front of the protesters, the helmeted MPs "flowed around" them rather than push them back. Many were then arrested, some physically roughed up or teargassed, and some would languish for days in jail and engage in a hunger strike. Rice remained untouched, and later walked away with poet Robert Lowell.[29]

That encounter was both climactic and revelatory. Rice, unlike other anti-war activists with whom he worked, including some priests, never was arrested in all his activist days.

After the march on the Pentagon, Rice kept up the activism with a speech to antiwar trade unionists in Cleveland (there were some),[30] a napalm-related protest of Dow Chemical recruiters at

Pittsburgh,[31] and an address to the Ohio Conference on Action for
Peace, in Columbus that December.[32] In 1968 Rice was considerably less prominent in antiwar activities, largely because he was
busy trying to keep the lid on the overflowing cauldron that was
Homewood that year. From 1969 on, Rice kept up with the established rhythm of spring and fall national demonstrations, but with
a greater accent on events in Pittsburgh. Both the nature of his
activities and his choice of alliances were, as we shall see, undergoing some change.

Thus it was in the early years, when the antiwar cause was still
relatively unpopular, that Rice was of greatest prominence in and
usefulness to that movement. It is interesting to compare this with
his prominence in the civil rights movement, which was in these
years no longer new, but newly unpopular with many whites.

A significant aspect of Rice's opposition to the war was his
participation in draft resistance. From 1967 through the early
1970s, he was active both in Pittsburgh and at the national level in
counseling young men who sought to avoid being drafted, in
urging refusal to be inducted into the armed services, in collecting
the draft cards of those who chose to surrender them, and in
helping with the defense of resisters who were caught in the
entanglements of courts or military tribunals. In so doing, he
worked out a Catholic position on conscientious objection to the
draft remarkably at odds with what he had taught during World
War II when had found no authority under the Catholic faith for
conscientious objection to war. Indeed, he almost became a pacifist
himself. But not quite.

His public record of opposition to selective service dated from as
early as December 1967 when Draft Resistance Week in Pittsburgh
began with a religious ceremony at the interdenominational United Oakland Ministry at the University of Pittsburgh, where Rice
collected five draft cards (nine, according to FBI files) and numerous other statements of support.[33] When the FBI sent agents to
interview him a few days later, he consented to answer questions,
described the event in detail (but said he could not recall the name
of the individual to whom he had submitted the cards), and
"stated that he was fully aware that he was committing an illegal
act under the Selective Service Law when requesting and accepting
the draft cards."[34] This and other pieces of evidence were considered at length by the FBI with regard to possible prosecution of
Rice. Many letters went back and forth between the Pittsburgh
field office and national headquarters in Washington, D.C. A final

decision, not to prosecute, was not made until April 1969.[35]

During that time, the number of draft resisters being imprisoned continued to mount in Pittsburgh, just as throughout the nation, and Rice continued to aid them. Their cases ranged from draft card burning to resisting induction to going AWOL or deserting after induction, and from brief brushes with the law to prolonged imprisonment. Rice's work with them ranged from brief correspondence to extended counseling by mail and in prison.[36]

One of the better-publicized incidents of draft resistance in Pittsburgh began when a group of resisters decided to "serenade" a draft board member at home one evening. They were summarily arrested and arraigned the next morning. But sympathizers had managed to pack the courtroom for that proceeding, and met the judge's order for silence with raucous disdain. The judge thereupon ordered the numerous policeman in attendance (the court was in the same building as police headquarters) to clear the courtroom. The police apparently complied with considerable relish, chasing some protesters all over the building and outside, and making numerous arrests in the process. As a result of the incident, a legal defense fund was established to provide bail money for draft resisters, and Rice acted as its chief collector from March to November 1970.[37]

Rice received national attention as an antidraft activist in 1970, when he went to Washington, D.C., on March 9, to plan a national draft resistance rally, and at the demonstration itself where draft cards were collected and placed in a coffin.[38] The pitch of Rice's opposition to conscription, as well as an interesting duality in his analysis of why the draft was permitted to continue, may be gathered from two press releases he prepared for these occasions. The first was for the planning session on March 9:

> Selective service is contemporary slavery and the victims of it are legally kidnapped; the system is not at all necessary for *the prosperity of the military imperialists who dominate us* [emphasis added]. . . .
>
> If there be much of a history, men of the future will marvel that we yielded up our children like so many cattle for no good purpose. They are being killed and corrupted and we lack all perspective. We as a nation have lost our way and our mind that we take the non sequiturs of Richard Nixon at all seriously and permit him to expand the war as he promises to curtail it, to keep on sucking up our lads as he promises to end conscription. We get the government we deserve, God help us and the world that we dominate.[39]

The second was for the rally itself on March 19:

> Selective Service, that simpering euphemism for conscription, is the crime of our generation, a crime upon which other crimes depend for their working out; even conscription is a euphemism because what we are talking about is slavery, involuntary servitude.
>
> In a situation in which we will not even control prices or wages, or come too close to confiscation of property we think nothing of enslaving human beings in the military.
>
> The silent majority is at fault because it silently hands over its young men to the dirty war machine sending them to be whipped into shape, given zombie minds, and herded like expendable animals thousands of miles away only to kill or be killed.
>
> That evil silent majority, that stupid silent majority, is making a greater offering to the god of war than ever did any other empire in history.[40]

In the first statement, President Nixon and the "military imperialists" were identified as the perpetrators of evil; in the second, the majority of American citizens was berated for permitting the president and the military to work their will. Rice seemed to be accepting to a great extent Nixon's notion of a silent majority, which acquiesced in the administration's policies in Vietnam merely by remaining silent — not rising in protest in the streets as were Rice and his allies. This duality of blame — power structure plus silent majority — permeated much of Rice's thought on the whole war in Vietnam.

In 1971, as the war continued and many draft resisters wound their weary ways through the courts, Rice prepared what appeared to be general position paper on the question of whether a Catholic could be a conscientious objector. Its central thesis went as follows:

> To be a conscientious objector is quite consistent with the Bible, one of the sources of the Catholic Faith. Furthermore, it is quite consistent with modern Catholic social teachings, see. *Mater et Magistra, Pacem in Terris,* "The Church in the Modern World" of the Second Vatican Council, and the latest teaching of Paul VI: "The Development of Peoples." The whole thrust of these documents and their implications for the modern world and its problems would certainly encourage a Catholic to be a conscientious objector. Most recently the Catholic Bishops of the United States encouraged the government to respect the conscience of the person who objects to all war on the basis of his conscience.
>
> It is also the teaching of the Catholic Church that a person is compelled to follow his conscience. The person should try to have a well

formed and informed conscience and look to the Bible and the social teachings of the Church. If more Catholics had informed consciences there would be many, many more Catholic conscientious objectors.[41]

Note that Rice was not arguing that conscientious objection was necessary to the Catholic faith (with hawkish hierarchy like Cardinal Spellman in evidence, that would hardly have been a tenable position), but that objection, whether to all war or to particular wars, could reasonably be adopted by a Catholic conscience, and the person in question would then be obliged to follow his or her conscience on the matter.

This was as close as Rice ever came to adopting the pacifism of a Dorothy Day, with which he had flirted briefly in the 1940s before parting company. But even in the depths of his anti–Vietnam war opposition, Rice remained a believer in the use of force when appropriate, and this at two levels.

At the national level, he continued to advocate the use of violence in Northern Ireland to bring about the end of British domination — and such use of force was flaring up there once again, with Rice's support and encouragement.

Secondly, at a personal level, Rice believed in the use of force to repel force. Thus at a demonstration at Pittsburgh's Point Park around the time when construction workers in New York City had attacked and beaten up antiwar demonstrators, Rice noted a group of perhaps thirty unfamiliar men assembling near the speakers' platform. He quietly circulated among the antiwar crowd, and asked any husky young man he spotted whether they would be willing to "rumble", and if so would they please gather near the podium. About the time fifteen of them had done so, the larger group simply melted away.[42] Rice, the leader and inspiration of many conscientious objectors and total pacifists, could never really claim to be one of their number.

During the years of Richard Nixon's first term as president (1969–72) the war continued, but the shape of the American commitment to it changed appreciably. Rice and his allies continued their efforts to get the United States out, finding hope in some developments, darkest despair in others.

Nixon had been elected in 1968 with what he had said was a "secret plan" to end the fighting; to some observers the plan remained a secret four years later. One of Rice's strongest objections was answered when the draft was eliminated and the number of American military in Vietnam began to be reduced toward the end of the fourth year. But the use of firepower increased: much of the south became a free-fire zone, bombing runs were initiated against the northern capital of Hanoi, the major northern port of Haiphong was mined, a ground incursion into neutralist neighboring Cambodia was mounted in hopes of eliminating "sanctuaries," and a heretofore "secret war" being waged by the United States in Laos was revealed to American citizens and Congress. Public opinion had already turned against the war; two-to-one majorities in favor of the war effort in Lyndon Johnson's early days had reversed to equally large majorities in opposition under Nixon. National Guard troops at Kent State University in Ohio fired upon students protesting the war and killed four of them. this, together with the Cambodian incursion, brought the antiwar movement to a new fever pitch.

For Rice, these were years of unquiet desperation and alienation, not only from American ruling circles but from most of his fellow Americans. This alienation did not cease when opposition to the war became a majority sentiment in the country.

Rice never shrank from supporting the antiwar cause in front of the most hostile of audiences. In 1966 he had gone to Duquesne University to debate the issue against the conservative Rev. Daniel Lyons, S.J., at the invitation of the local Young Americans for Freedom — who overwhelmingly sided with Lyons.[43] At the seminary high school of St. Fidelis, he had been roundly booed by the young men preparing for the priesthood, and by their parents.[44] Later he took on a former ally from his red-baiting years, Judge Musmanno, who now differed with Rice on Vietnam.[45] But Rice's adversaries were not always seated opposite him on the platform or even in the audience: often he found himself arguing heatedly with reporters during interviews or taping sessions, and sometimes with the camera crews after the television lights had been turned off.[46] Rice gave as good as he got, however, and by 1970 was condemning the news media of America for failing to tell the whole story of Vietnam, and the national organs in particular for being cowed by the Nixon-Agnew administration.[47]

One constituency from which Rice was becoming alienated both in his civil rights and his antiwar activism was that of labor, and particularly the Steelworkers. Aside from some rapport in Cleveland,[48] Rice had had litle luck in budging the prowar position of the national leadership or of the locals in Pittsburgh. In a contemporaneous interview, he gave his analysis of why labor unionists were mired in prowar sentiments:

> Their sons are going to War [*sic*]. And the sons of the management are not going to war. But instead of being angry about it, they're defensive; they don't want to admit that their boys are going to war just because their boys are dumb or can't get into college or haven't got the money to send them. Instead, they are defensive in another way. They are superpatriotic. I would say, at the executive boards of these locals, it would be hard to figure out whether you were talking to their leading men in an American Legion club, or an Elks club or the Steelworkers.[49]

In 1969 Rice was asked by the New Mobilization to solicit funds from some of the international unions to support the march on the Pentagon scheduled for November. Rice sent many requests, but not a penny came back — not even from Walter Reuther.[50] And Rice confided in a 1968 letter to Alan Kistler at AFL-CIO headquarters that when he had gone to address the USWA Local 1272 executive board, a husky young man had barred his way into the union hall. Rice left without an argument.[51]

Another rupture at this time — fascinating in view of Rice's record as an informant — occured between him and the FBI, and particularly its Director, J. Edgar Hoover. Rice had in his anticommunist days cooperated with the FBI and heaped praises on Hoover, as has been seen. But now he viewed that agency and its head in a very different light, as became evident on a call-in show on radio station KDKA one evening. One caller asked Rice if Hoover was not right when he said that the CPUSA was participating in civil rights and antiwar demonstrations. Replied Rice: "John Edgar Hoover is completely unreliable on this score. He is a punch-drunk old man who doesn't know what he is doing." This attack initiated an FBI investigation as early as 7 a.m. the next morning. The bureau in Pittsburgh decided not to approach Rice himself, in view of his "complete irresponsibility" and ready access to radio and newspaper outlets, but did make a protest that day to Bishop Wright, asking that he take appropriate action against Rice. The whole of Wright's response is blotted out in copies of FBI records of the incident,[52] but Wright did warn Rice to stay off the topic of Hoover, because it could be very dangerous.[53]

The alienation that lay closest to home, and no doubt affected Rice much more profoundly, was from some sectors of the institutional Catholic Church, from his fellow priests, and from members of his own family, most notably his brother Patrick. Rice examined the war relief efforts the church was conducting in Vietnam, and discovered that all the relief was being given to one side. This he compared with the supposedly humanitarian work of the Red Cross in Ireland a half- century earlier, when it dispensed tea and crumpets to British soldiers, but nothing to the Irish rebels the British had come to hunt down. He concluded sternly: "missionary teaching and charity cannot serve an imperial master and a divine master at the same time."[54]

Such an analysis of Catholic missionary work in Asia had already gotten Rice into some vitriolic exchanges with Catholic missionaries there who still saw the communist presence and their own efforts against it in terms he might have accepted back in the 1940s. Rev Frank J. White had written to Rice bidding him to button his lip about a situation (Vietnam) of which he was ignorant. Relied Rice, bluntly if not brutally: "You are too close to the situation and too deeply involved to see it all. As an active missionary, you were part of a system that did not work."[55]

Back in the States, Rice was chagrined and embarrassed to find Catholic priests underrepresented in the peace movement, not only when compared with younger activists, but also relative to their counterparts in the Protestant and Jewish clergies. There were exceptions, to be sure: Rev. Donald McIlvane was probably as active as Rice in antiwar work in Pittsburgh, and Daniel and Philip Berrigan he regarded with close to reverential awe. But on the whole he found the church leadership and clergy a disappointment on the Vietnam issue.[56]

Most upsetting of all, his own family, which had backed him on everything else throughout his career, now disagreed with him somewhat on his very strong pronouncements on civil rights, and profoundly on the war question. This did not lead to a formal rupture, but Rice now found that even with his brother Patrick there were more and more matters that had to be left in silence for civility to be preserved. Nor would the situation change before Patrick's death, which was now not far distant.[57]

By 1971, then, Rice had formally broken with or become marginally estranged from labor unions, the Democratic Party and liberal New-Deal politics in general, Jews (over his new anti-Zionist stand), much of the institutional Catholic Church, the majority of his fellow priests, and his own family and brother.

It was at this time of Rice's greatest alienation from former allies and power bases, at the time of his heaviest involvement in the antiwar cause, and at the time of his deepest immersion into the struggle for black equality, that he began to refer to himself once again as a "radical," or as being "reradicalized." Thus we come to the controversy over whether Rice was any more a "radical" in the 1960s on the issues of race and war than he had been on labor questions in the 1930s and 40s.

When examining Rice's earlier claim of radicalism (chapter 2, above), I had recourse to three relatively more clear-cut political descriptives: reformer, rebel, and revolutionary. I concluded that Rice was at most a liberal reformer in the earlier era. Applying these three terms to the issues of race and war in the 1960s, the reformer would be one who tried to advance the well-being of blacks or to get the United States out of Vietnam by working within the system, using legal means of persuasion to those ends. The rebel would choose to defy the system and use illegal tactics to create support for the two causes, which would still, however, be limited to policies the government had the ability to adopt (opposing racism or withdrawing troops). A revolutionary, by way of contrast, would have concluded that the United States government and the social system from which it sprang were *irredeemably* racist and *necessarily* imperialist, such that antiblack racism and waging a postcolonial war in Vietnam were merely manifestations of these deeper maladies, which in turn could be cured only by eliminating or fundamentally altering the system itself.

In trying to sort out whether Rice was still acting as a reformer of the system, or had evolved into a rebel or even a revolutionary, we need to examine (1) the kinds of tactics he did or did not employ; (2) the alliances he formed or attempted to form; and (3) the extent to which his own analysis of the causes of racism and war had led him to conclude that the American politico-economic system was evil not just in some of its actions but in its fundamental makeup.

First, as to tactics, Rice exhibited the same preference he had in the 1930s for peaceful and legal tactics, but now moved in some cases to civil disobedience, which left him liable to arrest and prosecution. Most of his civil disobedience was centered around resistance to the draft, but also included the march on the Pentagon. Rice himself, as we have seen, had agreed to participate in civil disobedience likely to lead to his arrest there. But he had not carried through to the point of being arrested. He never engaged in tax resistance, not even in the comparatively widespread refusal to pay the tax on telephone service — a tax explicitly enacted to raise revenues for the Vietnam war effort,[58] And when it came to the use of violence — against persons, property, or even against the symbols of American nationalism — Rice was usually standoffish in comparison with some of those around him. When the American flag was burned at the Spring Mobilization in 1967 and the NLF flag displayed on many such occasions, Rice kept silent on the matter — at least in his columns. When H. Rap Brown, seated beside Rice at a press conference, and under indictment on charges of inciting to riot and transporting a weapon across state lines, was asked whether he would bring a gun to the next rally, he responded, "you all took my gun last time. I may bring a bomb, sucker."[59] Rice's reaction, unfortunately, was not recorded.

At the trial of the Chicago defendants in Judge Julius Hoffman's court, resulting from the demonstrations at the 1968 Democratic convention that had led to violence, Rice was brought in to testify that Dave Dellinger had said he expected the demonstrations to be peaceful. On cross-examination, he was asked whether he approved of the deliberate causing of violence in a demonstration. He said he disapproved. Question: "You wouldn't have anything to do with anything like that, would you?" Answer: "I would not, no."[60]

By 1971, when the National Peace Action Coalition (NPAC) had parted company with the New Mobilization of Dellinger, Davis et al., Rice sided with the NPAC, emphasizing that "peaceful, legal demonstrations represent the only hope there is for those who want to end the war. The ballot box has failed and we don't want an urban guerrilla uprising."[60] The only exception to this pattern of preferring legal to illegal means, and opposition to the use of violence (which one would of course expect from a clergyman), came in Rice's clandestine advice to and sometimes financial support for the Black Panthers, which remains undocumented except in Rice's own later recollections.

Secondly, regarding Rice's choice of allies on the issues of race and war, I have pointed out that in both causes he allied himself with some of the most militant-sounding leaders of the day. Yet, as already noted, some of these militants were fearsome enough in their rhetoric but rather pragmatic and moderate in their actions, and in the case of black militants their involvement with Rice sometimes had the effect, intended ot not, of undermining their own independent ability to act. Interestingly, Rice was at this time revising upward his estimation of the CPUSA, not because of its radicalism, but because he found that in the various discussions preceding antiwar events, it was the communists who consistently gave mature, level-headed advice, whereas younger and hotter heads were insisting on greater militance.[62]

There were other alliances in which Rice appeared to be relatively uninterested. As the antiwar movement grew, a debate developed within its ranks (perhaps "ranks" implies far more uniformity than there ever was) as to whether it should remain a single- issue cause, or reach out to establish linkages with other antiestablishment constituencies and movements. If the United States was waging a genocidal war against brown Asians, was there not a link with what it was doing to American blacks, native Americans, Puerto Ricans, and Latinos? If the war represented American machismo gone berserk, did that not imply the need for liberating American men — and women — from dangerously confining sex roles? Could opposition to the war usefully be allied with the critique of industrialism found in the ecology movement? And if the U.S. war machine was built and maintained for the profit of the military-industrial complex, was not socialism a possible avenue to a lasting peace? Rice's answer to most of these questions was an indifferent shrug. His primary interest in the Vietnam war lay in getting the United States out of it. Although he supported many of the issues mentioned (especially the race issue), he was opposed to others (women's liberation, at least insofar as it related to abortion rights), and in general felt that the more issues were added, the less vital the movement would become.[63] This may have been an additional reason why he sided with the NPAC from 1971 onward: it emphasized conducting huge national demonstrations against the war, and against that only.

Thirdly, we need to look at the way Rice was seeing American behavior in Vietnam as a manifestation of a more fundamental imperialism likely to show up elsewhere in the world as well. Clearly, Rice was extending his analysis of U.S. imperialism to include a variety of issues, domestic and foreign. He pointed to the symbiosis of military leaders and industrialists in the U.S. economy, a profitable arrangement that he said had been fed by the Marshall Plan (his communists enemies should have lived so long as to hear this!), by Korea, by Vietnam, and by the ever-handy umbrella crisis, the cold war.[64] On a related issue, he proclaimed, "We might as well face up to it: we are a spy-ridden nation," and then argued that the U.S. control and spy apparatus had helped set up military dictatorships in Greece and Latin America, and that the same thing was not impossible at home.[65]

When the USSR invaded Czechoslovakia, Rice reflected that the Soviet Union and the United States had in the preceding twenty years grown unpleasantly similar:

> Our military complexes are too large, are too closely entwined with our industrial might, and consume too much of the research effort and the national income. Both of us are more willing to give military aid to underdeveloped countries than the food, fibre and peaceful hardware that they need; both of us are madly security conscious, pouncing on weaker nations, making them shape up our way; both of us do these things in the name of goodness. We cry democracy and freedom of speech; they cry communism and freedom from financial exploitation.[66]

But American imperialism, in Rice's analysis, was not confined to the ruling circles alone: it had created such a moral obtuseness that ordinary Americans could no longer recognize atrocity, even when it was thrust into their faces, as it was by the slaughter of villagers at My Lai by American soldiers (not to mention the routine slaughters of Vietnamese civilians which never made the headlines).[67] Moreover, he saw the brutal hand of American imperialism at work around the world. When the revolutionary Che Guevara was killed in Bolivia, Rice proclaimed: "Guevara was hunted down like a dog by American equipment, betrayed by American money, and finished off by American counter-insurgency experts or their pupils. We seem to have learned how to suppress revolution in Latin America."[68] When Marxist Salvador Allende was elected president of Chile, Rice asserted that this would be the test case of whether America had learned anything from Vietnam.[69] (Allende was permitted to take office, and was later reelected, only to be overthrown and killed in a military coup with U.S. connivance.) Rice was now having second thoughts about Israel, and said: "I used to say that Israel represents the glory and flower of the West, the Free World; alas that tough little country represents the sin of the West along with the glory, the colonization along with the progress." To which he added: "I am not a liberal; I am a radical."[70]

When George Romney, who had previously supported the American war effort in Vietnam reversed himself, after a fact-finding mission, and claimed he had been "brainwashed" by the generals there, Rice was sympathetic:

Romney, in all truth, has put his finger on an ugly fact of life. We have all been brainwashed. I do not mind admitting that I was successfully brainwashed during the whole course of American foreign policy since World War II; and, if the Vietnam mess had not turned so sour, I might ever have realized what was done to me.

In Communism we have an enemy who, we have been taught, is pure evil endowed with unhuman tenacity, deception and skill. It is all right to hate the devil, and Communism has been made into a devil substitute.

"To contain Communism is to do good even if the methods of containment be sloppy, cruel, destructive and devious." Like many others, I accepted that proposition, and I thought I was virtuous and farsighted because I rejected the idiocies of the extreme right.

However, I did not reject the idiocies of the modern position, nor was I sufficiently aware of the idiocies and mental atrocities of the prevailing military- diplomatic establishment, and I did not realize how completely our whole public posture is shot through with lies and concealment.

I was an innocent about the CIA and thought that their victories in Iran and Guatemala, for instance, were the legitimate victories of local forces, and that they advised rather than purchased their allies. I thought it perfectly proper for us to ring Russia with bases and load the seas around her with nuclear submarines while resisting and condemning as evil her counter moves.

Like everyone who has ever made an act of faith in a con artist, I ignored, or explained away, all flaws in the running cover story which our authorities present as truth and fact. Now, I do not believe anything that they say, and I look behind every statement, be it specific or general.[71]

It is certainly clear that Rice was now rejecting much of his early liberal optimism about the American establishment, that he felt the scales had been stripped from his eyes and he was no longer being "suckered" as he had been for many years. But this still leaves open the question of what sense to make of his renewed claim to be a "radical." In the terms in which I have been pursuing the discussion here, several conclusions seem to be warranted. First, his preference (at least most of the time) for legal and peaceful tactics continued to mark him as a reformer, whereas his occasional resort to civil disobedience and his private advocacy of violence suggested the rebel. Secondly, some of his allies were indeed rebels or even revolutionaries, but Rice's interactions with them tended to be based on and emphasize their more moderate side. Thirdly, his deepening analysis of American imperialism created a certain revolutionary potential. But it was counterpoised by his unwillingness to participate in the sort of coalition-building that might have been able to challenge the imperialism he opposed, as also by the continuing absence in his writings of any revolutionary theory on what to do about imperialism (not even the guilds of the popes that he had briefly advocated in the 1930s showed up in the 1960s).[72] Thus, although Rice had evolved somewhat into a rebel in the 1960s, he never approached being a revolutionary. Perhaps the claim of "radical" made a bit more sense than it had in the 1930s, but it was still likely to strike many observers as unconvincing.

This dubiousness of Rice's claim, at least in the view of seasoned political observers, was neatly exemplified in an incident growing out of his address to a mostly youthful audience at Moratorium Day in Pittsburgh in October 1970. There he said, "I have been a radical all my life." This brought a letter from an older observer, William Shaffer, who recalled Rice's Red-baiting days of working against the UE, and invited him, "Prick your own conscience, Father, for that pastiche of fascism which might lie just below the surface." Rice replied, in a letter he insisted was not for publication, that Shaffer was partly right, and he elaborated:

> In the past few years my moods have shifted with regard to the UE: sometimes I have the feeling that I made a terrible mistake and did grave harm; at other times I feel that it was probably right to fight the tight red machine. Definitely I did wrong in not fighting for certain victims of the McCarthyite purges even if they were Stalinists.[73]

For Rice to become a radical, in any very meaningful sense of that term, would have involved not only changing his mind on certain issues, but doing battle with his own history as well. Even in the 1960s, he was not prepared to reject that history wholesale.

As a remarkable epilogue to a remarkable decade, Rice opted in 1971 to run for political office. It was as if he had decided to offer all his critics in Pittsburgh the opportunity to place formally on his forehead their stamps of disapproval. He had been urged by a young peace and race activist, John Seidman, to make a run for one of the four seats on the Pittsburgh city council up for election in May of that year, and in late February Rice announced his candidacy.[74]

Immediately his broadcasts on WWSW ceased, as did his two-hour Sunday afternoon phone-in program on WJAS, where he had for the previous two years enjoyed roasting and being roasted by a sometimes vitriolic listenership. On May 15, three days before the election, his term on the Pittsburgh diocesan Board of Consultors expired, and was not renewed by Bishop Leonard. Some time after the election, his 15-minute WWSW broadcasts would resume, but the talk show was over for good. He would become a consultor again after a lapse of three years.[75]

Thus was Rice, almost from the first moment of his candidacy, thrust abruptly out of the public limelight. By the time of the election, as it turned out that year, there was not much limelight for any of the candidates: newspaper workers in Pittsburgh went out on strike and stayed out most of the summer. But Rice's campaign staff (considered the youngest and most energetic of any of the Council candidates' staffs),[76] had in Rice a candidate who was already well known, with an amazing 90–95 percent name recognition in Pittsburgh. The contest was a primary election, with good chances for those four candidates who won it to win again in the general elections in November. Because it was a primary, a small turnout could be anticipated — probably about one-third of the party faithful, and probably the most faithful at that. These party loyalists would be selecting four candidates out of a field of twenty-eight.

All in all, then, the Rice campaign found itself in a rather anomalous position. Where most campaigns had to concentrate on getting name recognition for their candidate, Rice already had that — too much of it, if anything. There was little likelihood of his being slated by the Democratic Party, so he never even asked for an endorsement.[77] With the newspapers on strike, there were only limited means for publicizing the candidate anyhow: radio spots and ads on public transit vehicles. this was fine, because there were only limited funds to be spent — around $12,000.[78] So the outcome was going to hinge much less on events in the campaign than on what voters, particularly Democratic loyalists, thought of the Rev. Charles Owen Rice.

A proper campaign, nevertheless, was planned and executed. Rice, as might be expected, raised the sorts of issues that would in turn raise eyebrows if not blood pressures. He argued that church-owned land should no longer be exempt from taxation. He wanted to abolish the vice squad, stop arresting marijuana users and pushers, and go after heroin instead. As to public transit, he opposed the multi-million dollar Skybus proposed for Pittsburgh.

On urban redevelopment, he said the city would almost be better off if none of it had ever occured. As to the elderly, he suggested that "heartbreak hotels" (where some elderly lived in exchange for their Social Security checks) ought to be regulated, but not routinely put out of business. In Pittsburgh's Hill District a for-profit hospital was proposed, which Rice vehemently opposed. This cost him the support of a key financial backer, as he learned later. Regarding the police, Rice offered the opinion, at a hearing before the Council on one of their complaints, that they were "too touchy and easily hurt for mature people." Most of the fifty police officers in attendance thereupon rose and walked out of the meeting.[79] Later, Rice's campaign workers would have inordinate difficulties with police who would stop them from posting handbills, or scrape the posters down when they found them afterward.[80]

Perhaps the most dramatic event during the campaign was one only marginally related to it: a right-wing extremist named Charles Lawrence was arrested in Akron, Ohio, with ten sticks of dynamite, which he allegedly had intended to use to blow up Holy Rosary church, because of Rice's activities in programs involving blacks. Apparently an FBI informant had relayed the information, which was transmitted both to the Akron police and to Rice. Said Rice, with relief: "I'm not a big fan of J. Edgar Hoover, but the FBI certainly knows what it's doing."[81]

Like many another dark horse candidate, Rice convinced himself that victory was out there waiting for him.[81] But when election day finally came, he finished well out of the money — in seventh place, with 12,199 votes (one for every dollar spent, noted Rice), whereas the four winners had around twenty thousand votes apiece.[83] To be sure, Rice had drawn a relatively inauspicious position on the ballot (18th out of 28). To be sure, seventh place out of twenty-eight could have been worse. To be sure, the time may not have been ripe for a priest to run for office. (Rice later reflected that for him the time never was ripe: in earlier days when he had been better liked, David Lawrence would never have heard of his running for office.) But given Rice's enormous recognition by voters and especially by the more politically astute voters, it was hard to interpret the results as anything but a repudiation. This was the more true when the results were analyzed closely: Rice had done well in most black and some Jewish precincts, but ran worst in the white, blue-collar, union enclaves. The election, in brief, was telling Rice what he already knew: the white, middle-class, and union constituency, whose hero he had once been, had now decisively rejected him.[84]

This rejection came close on the heels of a much more serious loss. Rev. Patrick Rice, who had been ill for over two years, entered the hospital a week after his brother's declaration of candidacy. After a two-month struggle in which he remained lucid to the end and refused any measure that would merely prolong his life without improving his condition, he died on May 15 — the day Rice's term as a diocesan consultor ended, and three days before his electoral defeat. Rice was now alone in the world, more so than he had ever been before.

EIGHT

Keeping the Faith

IN MID-1971, RICE WENT INTO THE DEEPEST and most difficult period of depression in his life. His brother was dead, Rice himself had been repudiated by the voters and simultaneously removed from the airwaves from the inner circle of advisors to the bishop. The war he had opposed with all his strength dragged on, with no real end in sight. Black militance in Homewood had collapsed, and Holy Rosary parish seemed to be following a similar course. Years later, comparing this period of his life with other bad times — when he and Pat had been brought back from Ireland and thrust into the urban world of Pittsburgh, or when he had been "exiled" from Pittsburgh, sent up the river — Rice had to rank 1971 as the lowest of all the low points. If it was not quite a depression in the clinical psychiatric sense, his condition certainly involved the loss of that insatiable appetite for life and activism that had characterized all his earlier years.[1]

Then, as the days and weeks gathered into months, the depression slowly lifted, the fog dispersed. There was no single, dramatic event that pulled Rice out of his brooding; life simply went on and the wounds healed. Rice went about his daily rounds with the returning zest of a successful survivor.

"Survivor" is, in fact, a tempting label to apply to him for the portion of his life that stretched from 1971 onward. He had survived the deaths of many close friends and relatives of his own and even later generations, outlived many of his allies and enemies from earlier battles, and was now in a position to tell the stories of many tumultuous decades from his own unique point of view. In all these senses Rice was indeed a survivor.

And yet he did more than merely survive, as he passed the 70-year mark in 1978 and moved toward octogenarian status in 1988 still in good health and sometimes feisty disposition. Having what he called a "radical" point of view by the 1960s, he continued forcefully to expound that viewpoint — frequently to the outrage of his readers in the pages of the *Pittsburgh Catholic* — even when the U.S. political climate turned more conservative in the 1970s and much more so in the 1980s. Even though his admirers (and certainly his detractors) would have understood if in his seventies he had confined his social commentary to the lines of his weekly column, Rice continued to find occasions to march in picket lines, to demonstrate, and in other ways to work vigorously for social change. And both his words and his actions made increasingly clear to the observers of this apostle of contradiction what had been implicit in his career all along: whatever other commitments he had, he was always first and foremost a loyal son of the Roman Catholic Chruch in its institutional manifestation. Thus the 1970s and 80s were years when Rice not merely survived, but staunchly kept the faith.

The survival of Holy Rosary parish, at least in its earlier and more glorious form, was clearly open to doubt in the early 1970s. Rice later pointed out that the Holy Rosary he had inherited from Msgr. Carlin had been but a shadow of its earlier self, when in the early postwar years it had been the "cathedral" of Homewood, teeming with some four thousand white Catholic families on their way up the socio-economic ladder.[2] But at least the shadow Rice had inherited in 1966 had about twelve hundred families still, a vigorous, racially integrated parochial school, and was able to pay its bills.

By the mid-1970s, Rice had only the shadow of a shadow. Only two hundred families remained parishioners. The school continued, but its enrollment was now entirely black (unlike the parish, which remained racially mixed) and Rice now wondered whether those students had been well served by departing from the traditional regimen of Catholic education for the open-school concept. Rice had staked the bulk of the parish treasury on innovation at the school, had gotten far less support from universities and foundations than anticipated, and now felt his gamble had failed to pay off.[3] His campaign literature had touted the fact that Rice had appointed a black as principal (a succession of blacks, actually), but the fact was that Rice considered the Sisters of St. Joseph, who still remained at Holy Rosary, to be the source of whatever strength the school still had. One consequence of the decade of educational innovation at Holy Rosary was that the school and the parish were now bankrupt, and could be kept open only with a special subsidy from the Pittsburgh Diocese. Rice may well have been facing odds that were too steep for anyone to overcome, but his financial stewardship of Holy Rosary could hardly be called a success.

A story that is illustrative of the "white flight" from Holy Rosary, and of Rice's response to that flight, is the story of a parishioner there who shall remain anonymous. He headed a very well-known and successful business in Pittsburgh, as well as a large, affluent family. A man of conservative opinions, he found much to object to when he and his family came to Holy Rosary in 1973. He thereupon began a correspondence with Rice, taking strong exception to folk Masses (with guitar accompaniment rather than organ), to solicitations in church in support of Cesar Chavez's United Farm Workers, and in general to any form of politics showing up in church bulletins or sermons. Rice responded in deferential tones, dropped the folk Masses, and promised to omit even the few statements of support he had been making for Chavez, unions, and others of his favorite political causes. (Rice, by the way, always insisted that he kept his politics out of his sermons — a contention which at least this listener did not accept.) The last of the above promises apparently was the one Rice was unable to keep. The parishioner in question then grew more demanding and scornful of Rice in his letters, and announced in late 1975 that he and his family would attend another church. Rice thereupon vented on the parishioner the resentments that had been accumulating for two years, accusing him of being a bully, of using his family to manipulate the parish, and, worst, of failing to contribute to the parish as much as a man of his means should. The parishioner replied that his total family's contributions were generous considering his other obligations, and that Rice was ruining the parish. Rice disregarded this rejoinder.[4]

Rice later said that this whole episode illustrated a key philosophy of his: if affluent parishioners insisted on certain things, he would to an extent defer to their wishes, but he would refuse to serve them "on the cheap."[5]

Few parishioners were leaving Holy Rosary with quite the acrimony just described, but many were in fact leaving to migrate to the suburbs. Their places were being taken in Homewood by blacks, few of whom were Catholics. This meant that Rice was saying Mass each Sunday in a cavernous church with very few faithful in attendance. His other priestly work for this declining flock was less challenging than when the parish had been larger. Once more, Rice's great supply of energy — even in his late sixties — was being underutilized. He concluded that after a decade in Homewood, it was time for a change.

He also decided that the action right now was going on in the Catholic Church, in the throes of post-Vatican II changes, but that this period of ecclesiastical rebellion and reform had largely passed him by in his inner city parish and out on the marches and demonstrations of the last decade. So it was time now to return to a mainstream Catholic parish — perhaps one out in the suburbs which he used to ridicule as "slurbs," with their rows of "ticky-tacky houses" lining the landscaped greenery.

In 1976 a choice parish opened up in Castle Shannon, Pennsylvania, where the pastor had become ill. St. Anne's was attractive to Rice not only because it was a vigorous, mainstream parish, but because of some sentimental connections as well. His beloved mentor, Phil Murray, had been a parishioner there; Murray's remains lay in the cemetery, and a bell tower erected in his honor by the USWA tolled the hours — somewhat erratically, as it happened. Rice asked his old friend Bishop Leonard for the assignment, and Leonard acceded. Holy Rosary was entrusted to a black pastor, Rev. David Taylor, and Rice was transferred to St. Anne's effective May 15, 1976.[6]

I have noted that as early as 1960 Rice had been rethinking his anticommunist work of the late 1940s. But the years from the late 1960s to the late 1970s were the period when he finally repudiated his anticommunist past almost (but not quite) completely, was reconciled with many of his adversaries from that period, and in the process adopted many of the positions they had taken and on which he had strenuously fought them.

The earliest of these reconciliations took place in 1966 when the UE, then a shrunken remnant of its former self, held its national convention in Pittsburgh. As James Matles, the Secretary-Treasurer of the UE, tells it, UE president Albert Fitzgerald shortly after arriving in the city got a call from Rice, who said, "Fitzie, you are suprised to hear from me. I read the news that your convention is in town and I'm calling to wish you well." Rice went on to say that he regretted the losses the UE had suffered over the years.

When Fitzgerald suggested that Rice's regrets came some twenty years too late, Rice said, "even twenty years is not too long for a man to change his mind." Fitzgerald recounted their conversation at the convention, and said to the assembled delegates, " I forgive him and I suppose you do, too."[7]

In the 1970s Rice was reconciled not only with labor leaders who had been accused of being communists, but with members and officer of the CPUSA itself. Arnold Johnson was a communist of about Rice's age who had been active in the New Mobilization against the Vietnam war effort. The House Internal Security Committee (HISC), successor to HUAC, in 1970 subpoenaed Johnson in order to investigate the degree of communist presence in the "New Mobe," and Johnson declined to answer questions. This led to his being indicted for contempt. Norma Spector of ACLU invited Rice and William Patterson of CPUSA headquarters, to cochair a Committee to Protest the Indictment of Arnold Johnson. Rice accepted, worked with Patterson from 1971 to 1973, flew to Washington to spend a day with Johnson while legal proceedings were underway, and issued statements saying "We need more men like Arnold Johnson," and "If they can jail Arnold Johnson they can put me in jail." Some of Rice's shocked readers considered this last idea to be quite a good one.[8]

A little later, a somewhat similar cause united Rice with Steve Nelson, who as CPUSA leader in Pittsburgh had been imprisoned — to Rice's evident satisfaction — in the early 1950s. The event that brought them together was the arrest in Spain of the Carabanchel Ten, a group of workers and one priest who were arrested by the Franco regime for attempting to hold a trade union meeting — an illegal activity for which they stood to be sentenced to as long as twenty years in prison. Nelson, as a veteran of the Abraham Lincoln Brigade in the Spanish civil war and now a leader of the Brigade's veterans' group, became active in the defense of the Carabanchel Ten. His son Bob Nelson, now a student at Pitt, wrote to Rice to enlist his support. Rice replied with a statement condemning the Spanish government's action and saying of the priest in the group: "The things that he is being jailed for, without trial, and for which he will be tried and possibly convicted — because that's the way I understand things go there — are things which we find perfectly legal in the United States, we have not been deprived of them yet."[9] The appeal helped in reducing the participants' jail term drastically, as Franco died and his authoritarian regime came to an end. Rice and Nelson (now an ex-communist who had left the CPUSA in the wake of Nikita Khrushchev's revelations of Stalin's excesses) both found satisfaction in their cooperation.

Some of Rice's former adversaries had in the intervening years been modifying their allegiances and political positions, but he seemed to have changed more. Back in the 1940s, for example, the twin litmus tests of loyalty to the CIO had been advocacy of the Marshall Plan and opposition to the progressive Henry A. Wallace third-party presidential candidacy, and the trial of Cardinal Minds-zenty in Hungary had fanned the fires of anticommunism to a white heat. But now, Rice had come around to seeing the Marshall Plan as the Left had then: a step toward international hegemony for the United States in postwar Europe. He certainly would not boggle at a prospective third-party candidacy; indeed, he some-times had difficulty stomaching the presidential choices preferred by the Republicans and Democrats.[10] And even on the trial of Mindszenty, though still regarding it as a "disastrous Red mis-take," he noted that "we did not get the Russian side of the matter," that Mindszenty apparently fought the Nazis less vehe-mently than he did the communists, and that his record in resist-ing the Nazi extermination of Hungarian Jews was not altogether clear. He advocated that the Mindszenty affair and Mindszenty himself be permitted to cool off, a position that brought bitter protest from some Catholic Hungarian-Americans.[11]

Perhaps Rice's most explicit and extensive recantation of his Red-baiting days came when he published an article in 1977 en-titled "The Tragic Purge of 1948." His general thesis was that he had overestimated the strength and the potential strength of com-munists in American labor, and hence had gone off on an ill-considered crusade. In this aricle, he made a number of other fascinating admissions: (1) he had cooperated with the FBI up to 1941 (and much longer, in fact); (2) Phil Murray used the Wallace issue as a weapon the Left had given him, but would have found another one had the Wallace issue not been handy; and (3) "when the Communistic unions were supporting Soviet Union positions in the Cold War they were closer to reason than to treason." He concluded: "I wasted a lot of time on a crusade that did more harm than good."[12]

All the above may sound like quite a thorough repudiation of his anticommunism, but it should be noted that it was less than total. Rice would say repeatedly that he wished there were still a "strong Left" in American unions, but a minority Left, which would leaven the mass of conservative American unionism.[13] Yet his fear in the 1940s had not been of a leftist minority, but of a possible *majority*. Suppose (this is quite a supposition, of course) that the Left were again to bid for leadership of all American labor; would Rice prefer to allow the struggle to run its course, or should it be decided by extraordinary interventions like his own of the 1940s? In his writings and interviews he never addressed himself to this precise question, perhaps because he never answered it in his own mind.

By the late 1970s, Rice reached septuagenarian status, an age often associated with both respect and credibility regarding past events. One of the more interesting uses that he seemed to make of this status was that of giving testimony about his friends and enemies, whether still living or already departed. Even to his adversaries he was generous; to his friends he was rather more than generous.

For example, some of his allies were getting into trouble with the law, and Rice was always willing to help them out as a character witness. In 1977 Sam Begler who had been Rice's ally from the early days with the Laundry Workers, and more recently was in charge of patronage for Pennsylvania Governor Milton Shapp, was nominated to become a Pennsylvania Turnpike commissioner. The nomination ran into trouble, however, when Begler was accused of irregularities in the patronage job, and of having certain gangland connections. Rice was the only witness to testify in favor of Begler's appointment. But that proved to be insufficient and the nomination was torpedoed.[14]

Another good friend of Rice's, who was in even more serious trouble in 1981, was Cyril Wecht, Democratic Party official and coroner of Pittsburgh. Wecht stood accused of various malfeasances in office, and, if convicted, could have lost his right to practice both as a physician and as an attorney. Rice testified in the trial, which found Wecht not guilty.[15]

Finally, Tom Nolan, an ally from the anticommunist campaign in District 6 of the UE, who had become a prominent (and to Rice a distressingly conservative) state senator, was indicted on charges growing out of the practice of "ghost" employment with the state for certain political operatives. Rice again testified for the defense.

His chief consideration in these cases seems to have been less with the legal guilt or innocence of the accused, in what he regarded as politically motivated proceedings, than with the duty of standing up for old friends. That duty, as he saw it, he performed.[16]

A sadder but perhaps more dignified duty waited to be performed as various figures from Rice's activist years passed away. He memorialized Bouie Haden, the lion of Homewood, with a funeral service and burial from Holy Rosary, although Haden was not a Catholic.[17] In Robert Lowell he eulogized a self-described "lapsed Catholic" who had stood beside him at the Pentagon in 1967, and he hoped that Lowell's brave antiwar resistance, as well as his poetry, would be remembered.[18] Toward the end of 1978, Rice marked the deaths of two famed radio priests, both of whom he had had occasion to oppose: Charles E. Coughlin and Fulton J. Sheen.

As to the former, Rice had come to regret his silencing as being opposed to the best interest of truth.[19] After burying Bill Hart in late 1982, Rice recalled their hectic days together in the early steel strikes, and Hart's later rebellions within the USWA (not mentioning, interestingly, their ACTU work together). He prayed that Bill be admitted at the pearly gates, but not without expressing some doubt about Bill's ability to settle down for a heavenly rest.[20]

In 1984, Rice marked wistfully the passing of his first and most admired editor at the *Pittsburgh Catholic*, John Collins,[22] and of his respected senior partner in the founding of the CRA, Msgr. Carl P. Hensler.[23] The death of House of Hospitality stalwart, Charles Francis Barrett, prompted Rice to recall how Barrett, happening upon a convention of Rotarians, had had "George F. Babbitt" paged repeatedly, wondering whether the Rotarians had gotten the dig.[24] Late in 1985, Rice bade a "fond farewell to three good men": Msgr. Paul Bassompierre, Rice's successor at the House of Hospitality, Rev. John Jacob Hugo, retreat master to Dorothy Day and the Catholic Worker Movement in its formative years, and James Groppi, priest-activist from the 1960s.[25] The death that probably affected Rice most was not that of any of the abovementioned men, but of the woman who had been the early inspiration of his life as an activist: Dorothy Day. When she died in late 1980 at the age eighty-three after several years of illness, Rice brooded. His column of tribute to her concluded: "Dorothy Day was unique. Faithful, strong, beautiful inside and out. She would make a wonderful saint."[26]

During the 1970s and 80s, Rice not only continued to battle for the causes that had been familiar to him over the decades, but took up new issues as well. Generally his commitment to the newer causes was less strong than that to the older ones, and was hardly ever expressed in deeds as opposed to words. Nevertheless, these new concerns represented some striking changes or at least a marked flexibility in a person in his sixties and seventies.

The most obvious issues in this category, for Rice, were those of the women's liberation movement and the Equal Rights Amendment. No movement of the latter part of the twentieth century posed more problems for Rice, ideological and personal, than the call to liberate women from the subordinated economic and social status traditionally assigned them. He had grown up in Irish Catholic families in Ireland and the United States where the assumption that women's role was in the home and rearing young children was so pervasive that it never needed to be articulated. Even his aunt and later stepmother Jennie, who had worked in a factory before marrying, had left that job to follow Michael Rice to Pittsburgh and there stay home to raise his two children, Pat and Charlie. Then Rice had dedicated his adult life to the Catholic Church, which institutionalized the subordinate status of women by allowing them to serve as nuns but not as priests and of course not in the hierarchy.

In his years working for the advancement of labor unions, Rice and many of his associates often regarded women employees as less than genuine workers because they were earning "extra" income, and hence were harder to organize and more dubious supporters when push came to shove at contract negotiation time. As late as his years at Holy Rosary when he was attempting an autobiography, Rice had boasted that in a steel strike in 1959, he had been able to "help quell a women's revolt" of wives who wanted their husbands to go back to work.[27]

Finally, Rice, who had won his kudos debating for the Catholic position on birth control under Bishop Dearden, was vehemently opposed to abortion on demand, which soon became associated with the women's liberation movement. Thus there was very little in his background that prepared him, in his sixties and seventies, to become an advocate of women's liberation; it may even be suprising that he moved as far as he did in the direction of advocating economic equality for women.

It was during his first and only campaign for office, in 1971, that Rice signed on as an advocate of women's economic rights. Excerpts from his column on the matter indicate both the struggle he had undergone in arriving at this position, and the numerous qualifications with which he hedged it even at the beginning:

> It has taken a long while for me to grasp the reality that women are oppressed and exploited and that this is not a necessary condition of human nature . . . . Questions nag at one: can we discard the exploitation and oppression and let women take their rightful position without destroying the family and the Church among other things? . . . . I am conscious of the danger of sounding smug and condescending to the women who are deeply committed to the struggle . . . . In the past I have deserved the appellation of male chauvinist, as have most of my brother males, but I am no longer proud of the characterization . . . . It has been hard for me to adjust because I have been so content in my priestly stronghold of male dominance . . . . I still am not sure about women priests . . . . On some matters I have not changed and will not change. Test tube babies and casual couplings will not ever get my vote. Abortion on demand need not be a condition of woman's freedom.[28]

Thus did Rice come out in favor of economic equality for women, flatly oppose abortion, and remain nervous about the implications of most other sex role changes the movement seemed to him to be advocating. From then on he consistently supported ERA[29] and expressed disappointment with Catholic women's groups that opposed it.[30] He also spoke out against rape and against the courtroom harassment of rape victims, urging that justice be equally strict regardless of the racial identity of rapists or victims.[31]

On the other hand, he spent more effort attacking abortion than he did supporting all other women's issues combined. Indeed, he refused to treat abortion as a feminist question at all, insisting instead that it was a transcendent issue.[32] Early in the 1970s he supported the political struggles of prolifers,[33] but by 1973, at the time of *Roe vs. Wade*, he declared the political and legal battle against abortion lost.[34] Later he became progressively more disenchanted with the prolife movement when it adopted a series of conservative positions on other social issues (like school busing), which he found offensive.[35] But he never changed his own vehement opposition to abortion, and indeed outraged some of his allies in the ACLU around election time in 1980 when he sought to prevent the distribution of prochoice literature on the sidewalks outside St. Anne's and other Catholic churches after Mass on Sundays.[36]

A case that focused on the question of abortion rights and Church authority occurred in 1983 when a Mercy nun, Sister Agnes Mary Mansour, was ordered by Pope John Paul II to leave her order because she had taken a job for a state welfare agency that distributed funds for (among other things) abortions for poor women, because she refused to denounce that practice. (Interestingly, the member of the hierarchy assigned to deal with the Mansour affair would shortly thereafter become the next bishop of Pittsburgh — Anthony Bevilacqua.) Rice expressed sympathy with religious like Mansour — intelligent, competent women who had stayed with the Church when many others left — but he still came down on the side of the pope.[37] When Geraldine Ferraro ran for vice-president in 1984, taking the position that although she personally opposed abortion still she would not seek to outlaw it, Rice's was one of the voices raised from within her church asking her to "clarify her stand."[38]

On issues of sex role changes beyond the question of equal economic opportunity for women, Rice remained cool and often only half-serious. He proclaimed that out of his well-known love for the English language and its mother country, he would refuse to be addressed or to address another male as "chairperson," but if women wanted to be called chairpersons, so be it.[39] He was "pessimistic" about prospects for the equal treatment of female athletes.[40] When he again took up the question of female priests in 1977, he said he would not mind having *one* on his staff, but he feared what would happen if the cook quit and all the male clerical eyes turned to the female priest.[41] Two years later he was forced by Sister Elizabeth Carroll, R.S.M., to take the question more seriously in debate, and he came out with the judgement that the psychological effect of women priests on the Catholic Church would be "disastrous."[42]

Clearly, Rice's preoccupation with women's issues aside from ERA and abortion was not a major one. The "danger of sounding smug and condescending," which he had thought to put behind him in 1971, kept popping up again, in some of the passages cited above and his slighting references to "the Lib."[43] He never did become a true advocate of women's liberation, but he did take the major step of championing economic equality for women.

Among the other causes for which Rice was an advocate in the 1970s and later were those of homosexuals, farm workers, native Americans, immigrants, and the environment. Of homosexuals, he insisted that it was unjust of society to harass and punish them for a sexual orientation which they had not chosen, that to see them as "virulently dangerous" even in teaching positions was a "misapprehension" (heterosexual males, he argued, were allowed to teach female students), and that the Catholic archdiocese of New York had made a mistake in opposing a city ordinace guaranteeing the civil rights of homosexuals.[44] As noted earlier, Rice promoted Cesar Chavez's United Farm Workers, and he continued to support it against takeover efforts by the Teamsters.[45] As to native Americans, Rice was glad to see some of them taking up initiatives once more in the 1970s and throwing off "deadly apathy." He offered them the advice that "confrontation can do little but good for the Indian."[46] Illegal immigrants from South America, Central America, and Mexico could not be stopped by any attempt at sealing U.S. borders, he thought. And he rejoiced to say that one day they would make the land theirs.[47]

But the land might by then be uninhabitable. Rice criticized the pollution that big companies willingly caused, and was particularly fearful that attempts to create a nuclear-powered society could not only kill persons near and far, but reach into generations yet unborn. He feared the alternative that big businesses would export this pollution and potential devastation, along with dull, low-paying jobs, to Third World nations, which appeared eager to have them.[48]

There were times during these years when violence and even murder intruded harshly into Rice's life, sometimes coming very close to Rice himself. At Holy Rosary, the daughter of an associate was murdered by a mentally retarded black teenager in an attempted rape. At St. Anne's, a talented young organist was killed by three young white males, just for kicks.[49] But probably no murder was more deeply disturbing to Rice himself than that of his longtime friend, Jock Yablonski. Yablonski had been a mine worker and then an official in the United Mine Workers [UMW]. Rice had known him well, and had officiated at Jock and Margaret's wedding in 1939 in the little chapel at the House of Hospitality.

Thirty years later, Yablonski had become a power to be reckoned with in the UMW, which was still ruled over by the aging A.W. "Tony" Boyle. Yablonski decided to challenge Boyle for the union presidency, and even in an election in which suspicions of a dishonest count were rife, came close to winning. Shortly thereafter, at his home one night, Yablonski, along with his wife and his daughter, was murdered in what appeared to be a professional killing. Rice now officiated at the funeral of that same couple he had wed thirty years previously.

Much as he disliked the autocratic regime of Tony Boyle's UMW, Rice rather doubted that the murder was connected with the union at all.[50] But the official investigation indicated otherwise and by late 1972 Rice confessed himself "shaken" to find the trail of evidence leading to some high-ranking in UMW officials. Reflected Rice: "I have probably been too tolerant toward trade union leaders and what they do to hold power."[51] But he was in for an even greater shock when Boyle himself was indicted for ordering the assassination, convicted, and imprisoned under a life sentence. By 1976, when Boyle was a resident of the Western Pennsylvania State Penitentiary, Rice spoke pityingly of the suffering the elderly Boyle would undergo there, "whatever he did."[52]

The fact of the matter was that Rice could not convince himself that Boyle was guilty. When Boyle's original conviction was voided and Boyle released pending retrial, Rice flatly announced in his column, "Tony Boyle isn't guilty,"[53] and around the same time offered to testify on Boyle's behalf. Unfortunately for Boyle, Rice's belief in his innocence was based on gut feelings rather than hard evidence, and Rice was not called as a witness. Boyle was convicted again, and returned to prison. But Rice remained convinced that Boyle was innocent.[54]

On a lighter note, although occasioning some remarkable displays of vitriol between two kindred spirits, was a running feud Rice conducted during the 1970s and 80s with fellow priest-columnist Andrew Greeley. In 1972 these two disagreed over whether Irish and other Catholic ethnics were more liberal and racially tolerant than other Americans. Greeley, a sociologist and opinion researcher at the National Opinion Research Center (NORC), used interview data to conclude that they were; Rice relied on his own experience to conclude that they were not. In the process, Rice remarked that Greeley's studies were of dubious value; Greeley riposted that Rice was anti-intellectual and arrogant.[55] Rice later took Greeley to task for his "waspishness" in attacking the Berrigans,[56] and for what Rice considered his unfair characterizations of liberation theology exponents as "romantics" and "faddists,"[57] and concluded that Greeley himself was becoming a reactionary.[58]

Although frequently commenting that Greeley was a fine journalist, who should be retained even if some Catholic papers were dumping him,[59] Rice continued to attack Greeley's studies when they reached conclusions with which Rice did not agree. When one such study attributed the decline in the Catholic Church in America to Pope Paul's encyclical on birth control (*Humanae Vitae*), Rice denounced opinion research as a "soft science," arguing that persons do not respond logically or accurately in interviews, and asked how Greeley knew that 23 percent, rather than 24 or 25 percent of those interviewed held a given opinion.[60] (Clearly Rice had not taken the trouble to inform himself on probability theory or other basics of opinion research.) When Rice in 1981 attacked another NORC study, James S. Coleman's second study on integration and public schools, Greeley shot back that although many persons commented on books they had not read (Rice had read only a summary of the report in the *New York Times*), only priests had the arrogance to expect such pronouncements to be taken seriously.[61] Rice replied frostily that Greeley himself was a "study in arrogance."[62]

Rice also criticized Greeley for conducting "dull" feuds in his column, although it should be noted that Rice attacked Greeley more often than Greeley responded.[63] But in 1983, when Greeley retired from column writing to devote his energies to authoring novels instead, Rice regretted his adversary's departure. He teased Greeley about the steamy novels his pen might produce, and queried: "Was it really no fun bashing and being bashed?"[64]

There runs through all of Rice's years and particularly through his writings in the 1970s and 80s a fascination with political power, how it is acquired, how exercised. Rice found by the 1980s that sheer celebrity no longer held the attraction for him that once it had. As a young man, he had delighted in the company of the famous and the powerful; as an older man he could hardly care less, he said.[65] Yet his preoccupation with prominent politicians continued in his writings; if anything, the portion of his columns devoted to dissecting presidents, labor leaders, and other power holders increased over the years.

Rice would often criticize politicians who once in office abandoned their early idealism in favor of the conservative sort of policies that would keep them there. (Pennsylvania Governor Richard Thornburgh was one of Rice's favorite targets for this kind of thrust.) And yet Rice himself, in his one relatively minor and unsuccessful run for office, had found himself sorely tempted to tone down some of his own positions in order to get votes he needed.[66] After that, he grew rather more sympathetic with those politicians who had to court the voters and prospective campaign donors not merely as an avocation but for a livelihood. He worked out a fairly tolerant and pragmatic set of standards for judging politicians: we should not expect them to be on the right side all the time or even most of the time; we should not expect them to keep all their promises or even most of them; but we should oppose them strenuously when their major policies are manifestly foolish, dangerous, or malevolent. (It will be readily evident how such a set of standards be consistentl with the support of political allies who are less than simon-pure.)

Rice's commentaries on presidential politics during the 1970s and 80s offer a convenient window which to see his particular standards of political responsibility at work. Richard Nixon he had found offensive during his first term in the presidency, both for his prosecution of the war in Vietnam and for his antilabor policies. Thus Rice attended the counterinaugural in 1973 to oppose Nixon's second term from the outset.[67] When the Watergate investigation began to heat up, Rice's reaction was hardly that of agonized hand-wringing: he said it was again a pleasure to read the newspaper and watch television news![68] Thereafter Rice vacillated from fears for the presidency itself,[69] to a cynical view that in Watergate nothing was changed,[70] to the conviction that the White House was a "scary" place in the latter days of the investigation,[71] to a final indifference with which he declared himself "unawed" by Richard Nixon's ultimate departure from power.[72]

For Gerald Ford, Rice expressed contempt when he became the unelected vice-president after Spiro Agnew's resignation from that office under indictment. Rice said, in the midst of the Watergate affair, that it would be preferable to have Nixon serve out his term "rather than have the nation fall into the hands of a limited and insensitive man such as Gerald Ford, who will be Nixon redivivus."[73] He never revised this judgement.

Among prominent national politicians in the 1970s and 80s, Rice's clear favorite was Sen. Edward M. Kennedy. Rice had been "reluctantly" charmed by John F. Kennedy, and his hopes for peace and justice had been dashed by Robert F. Kennedy's assassination in 1968, but it was the youngest of the brothers who impressed Rice the most by his consistent championing of social justice and his strength of character in bearing up under intense pressures. Rice did not agree with Kennedy on all issues: the Irish Republican Army was a case in point. But he reacted with sadness when Kennedy withdrew from the 1976 presidential race:

Kennedy is one of the few powerful men with both attractiveness and principles. There are other reasons: in addition to power, charm and convictions he has a pinch of pragmatism and several sorts of courage.[47]

When Kennedy was back on the campaign trail in Pittsburgh in 1980, Rice commented:

Seeing Kennedy campaign and sensing the enthusiasm he evokes in all sorts of people, one listens to what he has to say and finds that it makes sense; this man is in touch with reality.[75]

In the meantime, Rice had puzzled over Jimmy Carter, finding the choice between him and Ford an unappetizing one in 1976,[76] by turns praising him for his good intentions, especially on human rights, and criticizing him for a poor performance,[77] and being driven into support for Carter only by the appearance of Ronald Reagan from the right wing of the Republican Party. Of Reagan he said after the 1980 election that he had believed that "this great land in a time of troubles would not, could not, choose a 70-year-old retired actor for its glorious leader. — It could not, eh?"[78] From that point on, Rice proceeded to flay Reagan (two years Rice's senior) in his columns without honeymoon or much letup at all. Even when Reagan was reelected by a convincing margin in 1984, Rice found it nearly impossible to find anything good to say about him. When the "Irangate" affair began to heat up in 1987, Rice suggested, as Hamlet had put it, "Let the great axe fall."[79]

Among the new issues in the 1980s that preoccupied Rice were the growing threat of nuclear devastation and the role being played by U.S. military power in Central America. As to the threat of nuclear war, Rice decided that despite his own strenuous opposition to abortion, nuclear weapons posed a still greater moral evil:

What can be a more grave evil than abortion, the killing of the innocent unborn? . . . Nuclear war is the greatest evil that we can imagine because it means the killing of countless innocents, born and unborn, and it means the possible destruction of life itself, human life anyway.[80]

Rice himself was not an activist on the nuclear weapons issue, but he did rise to the support of others who defied the law to oppose the nuclear arms race. Thus he defended the actions of

Pittsburgh housewife, Molly Rush, when she joined with the Berrigan brothers and others who broke into a General Electric plant where Minuteman missiles were being manufactured. He argued that not Molly Rush but the "merchants of death" should be languishing in jail, because: "The vile and crazy arms race threatens not only the destruction of the world but, in the meantime, its impoverishment."[81]

In Central America, Rice became more and more convinced that the United States was throwing its military might around in the shameless way of an international bully, and much of this even before the election of Ronald Reagan. When Archbishop Oscar Romero, spokesman against governmental oppression in El Salvador and U.S. military aid to that regime, was slain while celebrating Mass, Rice editorialized that he had likely been killed by Cubans trained by the CIA and with CIA support.[82] The American invasion of Grenada in 1983 enjoyed widespread popular support in this country, but not with Rice:

> Will it ever sink in on the American public that this was a shameful episode. We are an enormous nation and we pulled a sneak attack on a tiny island, the smallest nation in the hemisphere. We did a Pearl Harbor number, negotiating as we prepared to strike.[83]

And further:

> We have not only overpowered Grenada but enslaved it. There is every sign that we intend to control that tiny spot permanently, both directly and through our local allies.[84]

As confrontation heated up between the Reagan administration and the Sandinista government in Nicaragua, which had succeeded in driving from power the Somoza government the United States had earlier installed there, Rice proclaimed:

> That this little backward country was able to overthrow an American-backed dictator, and has for four years managed to survive in the face of so much that has been thrown against it by us and our friends and clients will amaze history . . . . Even if we succeed by open invasion in overthrowing the Nicaraguan experiment in democracy, the seed will have been sown and it will be the beginning of the end of American control.[85]

There is a fascinating parallel between Rice's opposition to what he saw as American imperialism in Central America and his opposition to British imperialism in Ireland. Alongside his columns condemning U.S. adventures south of the border were even more frequent pieces supporting the efforts of the Irish Rebuplican Army in Ireland. Although as was noted earlier the Rices of Bellurgan had been anti - *Sinn Fein* at the time of the Rising in 1916, Rice's father and Uncle Joe had converted him to the rebel cause when he returned to America, and that conversion had proved permanent.

The rebel cause, after a sustained war of insurrection and internecine killings during which the twentieth century got its first look at modern guerilla warfare, had gained a limited independence in the Irish Free State led by Eamon De Valera. Chief among the limitations was the exclusion of the six-county Northern Ireland, or as much of the country as British and Orangemen leaders could reasonably gerrymander with a Protestant majority. There Catholics found themselves in a subordinate status, the victims of official and unofficial discrimination in jobs, housing, and a host of other areas. The Irish Republican Army found itself in business again.

When Rice had vacationed in Ireland in 1930, he had established his first link with *Sinn Fein* and the illegal Irish Republican Army through one Frank Ryan. This link had become operative in 1938 (CRA days) when Sean Russell of the Irish Republic Army contacted Rice on a fund-raising tour of the United States. Some funds from the Irish Sweepstakes were to be used for guerrilla operations by the Irish Republic Army, and Rice estimated that his help and his contributions gave him a proprietary interest in a bomb that was subsequently detonated in the British House of Commons. No one was injured, and Rice remained proud of his cooperation.[86]

There were years when the cause of Irish independence throughout the whole island was quiescent, and Rice's statements on the topic were likewise. But when the movement, now cast in parallel to the black civil rights movement in the United States, gathered a new head of steam under Bernadette Devlin in the late 1960s, Rice was supportive. He described Devlin as "a fiery little socialist who would like to end the Protestant-Catholic row by uniting all poor and workers of whatever religious persuasion," but cautioned the more militant elements, "I do not believe that guns are the solution to anything."[87] If that was indeed his position, it had hardly been a very consistent one.

As the conflict turned once more into a bloody and protracted one, Rice wrote about the situation in Ireland more often than any other single topic throughout the 1970s. He strongly supported not only the Catholic side, but the militant Irish Republican Army and the Provisionals, at a time when most prominent Irish Americans were growing cool or silent on that struggle.

By the 1980s, although privately regretting the Marxist sectarianism of the Irish Republic Army and now preferring the Irish National Liberation Army (and its political arm, the Irish Republic Socialist Party), [88] Rice in his columns was espousing the cause of the Irish Republican Army, even to their dreadful deaths in H-Block of Long Kesh Prison. He charged that the British had convicted Irish Republican Army men with torture, forced confessions, and "Kangaroo courts." He insisted that it was wrong to treat these political prisoners as common criminals and to force them to dress accordingly in prison garb. Thus he sympathized with their going " on the blanket" — that is, wearing only blankets and smearing their own excrement on the cell walls in protest of their treatment.[89] When a hunger strike led to the death of Irish Republic Army soldier Bobby Sands, Rice criticized not only the British and Margaret Thatcher, but also prominent Irish-American politicians who would not speak up on behalf of the Irish Republican Army, and who conspired to keep their spokesmen out of this country.[90]

How could a priest devoted to spreading God's peace also be devoted to an army that frequently resorted to killing and destruction as its means of achieving its goals? Perhaps a large part of the reason is exemplified in a story that Rice heard from his grandmother, about an event from her own girlhood, and which he repeated in his column over seventy-five years later:

> It was Ireland, the year 1850, and Ellen Rice, my grandmother, who remembered, was seven years old. Her father had died of cholera the year before, and her mother with four young children was struggling to survive. She was managing chiefly through the heroic efforts of her small son Patrick [Rice's great-uncle], who plowed the fields, although he was so small that his head was bobbing up and down between the shafts as he guided the plow. Then came word that the dread Mauleverer [a land agent known for serving eviction notices] was on his way to clear the whole townland of its tenants and toss them on the road. No wonder the mother had her children kneel down to thank God for deliverance and pray for the deliverers, the men who had assassinated Mauleverer, twelve miles to the north, near Crossmaglen.[91]

Although authorities and the Catholic hierarchy condemned the local bogmen for murder, and although his grandmother respected church authority, Rice added, deep down she knew that the killing was justified — with a sort of implicit theory of "just war." And Rice himself has never wavered in his commitment to the Irish Republican Army in its quest for full Irish independence of Great Britain, nor has he ever experienced regret about that commitment.[92]

Although it is true, as noted earlier, that many causes Rice advocated in his advanced years he advocated mostly in writing rather than in action, still there have been numerous occasions in the 1980s when he took to picket lines or marches just as he had in the 1930s and 1960s. There were also occasions for him to discover new dimensions of his own activist past, particularly when he explored government files compiled on him over the years. And there were some social issues during these years where he was able to play a policy-making role, even if largely in the minority.

An example of his picketing during his seventies was the day in 1981 when the University of Pittsburgh had American U.N. ambassador Jeane Kirkpatrick as its commencement speaker and recipient of an honorary doctorate. To protest her support of the government in El Salvador and a recent meeting she had had with the military of South Africa, Rice and two hundred protesters picketed outside the graduation ceremony at Pittsburgh's Civic Arena. Said Rice to the assembled picketers: "We should be proud we did not let this wretched woman come here and receive an honor — an honor literally dripping with blood — without a protest."[93]

It had been only a bit earlier that Rice had utilized the Freedom of Information Act to obtain some of the files compiled on him over the years by the FBI. As he leafed through the documents had been able to pry loose from the government, it must have become clear to Rice that people whom he had considered his allies had been informing on him in the 1960s — for example, a woman who had allegedly been involved with Rice on various racial matters, told the FBI in 1967 that he habitually spoke "without thought or planning," and that he had recently been "under the influence of alcohol" when announcing his intention to participate in a march on Mount Lebanon. More generally, KDKA, the radio station on which he had made that announcement, routinely had made reports to the FBI on Rice's activities, he concluded.[94] Rice also reflected that in the early days he had used the FBI and the FBI had used him, [95] and that during the later days of his civil rights and antiwar activism, "They missed a lot. "[96] But by the time all the cards had been turned over, or as many of the cards as the government would deal out, it was clear that several big brothers had been watching him closely over the years, whether he had realized it or not, and whether he had been uncooperative or cooperative.

An area about which Rice had been concerned for most of his years as a priest, and in which he was finally able to play something of a policy-making role in his later years, was that of prisons. He had become a familiar figure inside prisons in Pennsylvania from the early 1940s, when the House of Hospitality had served as a halfway house for ex-convicts, with as many as fifty former prisoners paroled at one time to the custody of Rice. From these beginnings, Rice had developed a firsthand familiarity with prisons, prisoners, and prison culture, which would last throughout his career. Year in and year out, for example, he maintained a voluminous correspondence with prisoners, many of whom had no other contact with the outside world, and some of whom wrote not only highly intelligent prose, but rather good poetry as well.[97]

Readers of Rice's columns could, as a result of his immersion into prison life, get some viewpoints strikingly at odds with conventional wisdom about crime and punishment in America. Rice argued, for example, that most street crime was rooted in the migrations of the poor, in their isolation (particularly when elderly), as well as in the American "me-philosophy" and the nation's growing industrial mechanization and resultant alienation. Against such forces, argued Rice, police, prisons, and guns were no solution.[98] Eighty percent of convicts were quite harmless, he insisted, and minor criminals were in fact punished more severely than major criminals, the worst of whom ended up with some measure of control in prisons. Sentences in the United States were longer than in any other country, and this nation had more persons in prison than any other society in the world.[99]

Although such a system could never really "work", he argued, some things could be done to make it more reasonable: status offenders could be segregated from true juvenile criminals, and marital visiting rights would help to preserve families and cut down on homosexuality in prisons.[100] But, most fundamentally, he argued that American corrections treated crime less as a problem to be solved than as an industry to be managed, to the greatest profit and convenience of those who had power in it: attorneys, judges, police, wardens, and the like. He sometimes sympathized with prison guards, whom he saw as often being in the same boat as the convicts, but he feared being shot "mistakenly" by guards if he ever were caught amid a prison disturbance.[101] He remained cool to the idea of "rehabilitating" as opposed to punishing criminals, because he thought the hypocrisy of proceedings to determine whether or not an inmate had been rehabilitated simply gave to those in charge of the industry another tool with which to control convicts' behavior.[102].

The first opportunity Rice got to play a policy-making role in corrections, albeit only in an advisory capacity, came when Pennsylvania Governor Milton Shapp in 1973 appointed him to a special commission to recommend a state policy with respect to the death penalty — then under review as a result of a United States Supreme Court decision holding state death penalty statutes then on the books unconstitutional. The Rice of the 1970s was strongly opposed to capital punishment, quite unlike the Rice at the time of the Rosenberges' trial and executions. He argued now that the death of a convict accomplished neither deterrence, because most killers were not reflective but emotional types, nor retribution, because calculating killers and especially the professional ones were not apprehended. The commission went along with this viewpoint, and recommended flatly against the death penalty, making no exceptions whatever. Shapp upheld this position when he vetoed a death penalty bill passed by the legislature. It passed over his veto, but Shapp routinely used the pardon power to prevent any executions during his administration.[103]

Rice continued to write against the death penalty, pointing in particular to the differential with which it had been applied to black and white convicts, and predicting (correctly, as it turned out) that when the United States Supreme Court permitted new death penalty statutes to become operative, the earliest executions would perforce involve whites.[104] Even when his own organist at St. Anne's was killed "for kicks" by several youths who boasted about the crime, Rice did not change his mind on capital punishment.[105].

Another platform for expounding his ideas about crime and punishment came with his appointment in 1975 to the Allegheny Regional Planning Commission, part of the Governor's Justice Commission, which was then being funded by Federal Law Enforcement Assistance Administration [LEAA] dollars. Of the thirty-nine members, Rice was the only clergyman and soon emerged as the head of the commission — to the considerable chagrin of Democrats and police officers who found his very presence there objectionable. Yet once in the chair, Rice got along well enough with the police representatives, who agreed with him that LEAA monies should not be used exclusively for brick-and-mortar sorts of projects.[106] Rice was able to use the periodic reports of the commission to promote his own views on crime and corrections, but he had to divide his time between this and fighting off efforts by Mayor Pete Flaherty and later the Congress to cut off funds for the body. These attempts succeeded by the end of 1980, when the commission (now a mere "advisory committee") went out of business.[107]

Perhaps the best publicized of Rice's stints on corrections bodies, however, was that on the Allegheny County Prison Board, the body exercising review over the corrections system in Allegheny County. In 1983, after what he described as "many frustrating months" on the prison board, Rice was finally able to report one victory. He had made a motion to relieve the perennial over-crowding at the prison simply by releasing, every time a new and dangerous prisoner was admitted, one prisoner being held on a nonviolent charge for lack of bail money. To his surprise, the motion picked up a second and passed by unanimous vote.[108]

But Rice's presence and maverick conduct on the board apparently became annoying enough to County Commissioner Barbara Hafer that she had him removed the following year. Rice crowed in 1985 that "La Belle Dame Sans Merci" seemed to have been more jinxed by his departure than she had been inconvenienced by his presence, in that she now faced a series of threats of prosecution, resignations and firings in the prison she was trying in effect to run without a truly independent board.[109] But Rice continued, whether in a policy-making role or not, to raise one of the few voices heard speaking on corrections issues on behalf of the prisoners themselves.

Of all the causes that brought Rice back into an activist role in the 1980s, the oldest and arguably the most central to his life was that of organized labor and particularly of the Steelworkers. This re-newed activism is the more striking because of what had been Rice's progressive disenchantment with labor unions and union leaders over the decades of his career. It was noted earlier that much of organized labor rejected Rice and his various causes by the late 1960s; in the 1970s, he seemed to be rejecting much of labor, or at least the established hierarchies of the international unions. He followed a clear pattern with the Steelworkers, the Mine Workers, the Teamsters, and others of supporting the challengers rather than the incumbents in union elections and other tests of strength. More privately, he expressed the sentiment that the noble days of the union movement were gone, perhaps never to return. [110]

What seems to have arrested Rice's slide into complete cynicism about labor unions was the gradually dawning fear that their very survival, amid the crises of late capitalism that overtook the United States in the 1980s, might be in question. The steel mills, auto plants, and other centers of U.S. Industrialism had for decades been providing relatively good wages for workers and good profits for investors, whereas reinvestment into the modernization of those facilities had been in the short-term interest of neither side. Few had stopped to realize that the strength of American industrialism rested in part on the absence of sharp competition from the other advanced countries of the world, devastated as they had been by World War II. But by the later 1970s that competition was intensifying as the newer, more efficient facilities and techniques of European and Japanese steelmakers and automakers began making serious inroads not only into the international market, but into the domestic U.S. market as well.

Faced with the immediate loss of sales and the longer-term need for reinvestment, automakers and steelmakers turned to massive layoffs, plant shutdowns, and frequently a strategy of disinvestment in outmoded production facilities in the United States in favor of facilities in other countries with a cheaper labor market, or in favor of alternative means of turning a profit. Rapidly shrinking unions were offered the unappetizing choice between wage and benefit give-backs to the company, or plant closings. The accession of Ronald Reagan to political power in 1981 only aggravated the existing crisis for many unions, for the federal government now seemed to embark upon union-busting as a matter of policy. Amid such troubled times, unions once more needed whatever allies they could find.

Rice's own recognition of the crisis seems to have come in stages. Back in 1967, when asked about the future of American labor and in particular of the Steelworkers, he had replied complacently: "Oh, the Steelworkers will remain strong and the labor movement will remain strong."[111] By 1972 he was warning about the prospects for unemployment in Pittsburgh, one of the oldest and therefore most decayed industrial centers in the nation.[112] Five years later, in more general terms, Rice warned that "trade unionism in the U.S. is not so strong as I had been thinking that it was; really it is in some danger."[113] He wished there were more young labor priests and intellectuals to take up the stagnant cause of labor as there had been in the 1930s (there were some, and they were significant, he later added)[114] but he was not yet pushing the panic button.

That happened largely in the 1980s. Rice watched in mounting anger and disbelief as the automobile industry went into a depression and as the steel industry set a course of disinvestment in steel and in America,[115] or used tax breaks and profits to go on a binge of corporate takeovers,[116] sometimes casting to the wolves even moderately profitable industrial enterprises (and of course their employees).[117]

These developments finally jolted Rice out of his self-distancing from organized labor, and back into an activist prolabor role in his seventies. After watching and commenting as U.S. Steel closed a number of unprofitable major plants, including one at Youngstown that shut down despite workers' offers to take over the plant and operate it at a profit,[118] Rice became active in promoting the use of eminent domain by local authorities to acquire rights to plants (which would otherwise be sold for scrap) and turn them over instead to workers' groups. Thus he joined an informational picket line with steel activist Ron Wiesen at Homestead in 1980, and in language reminiscent of his CRA days referred to the danger of transferring blue collar jobs to Third World nations as "radical capitalism at its worst."[119]

An even more regrettable closing, from Rice's point of view, was that of the relatively profitable Crucible Steel in Midland, Pennsylvania. There, Rice and other activists with the Tristate Conference on Steel, like Staughton Lynd, spoke to the town in favor of eminent domain proceedings.[120] But both the townspeople and the local union were cool to the idea, and the facility was subsequently sold off and closed. At Weirton Steel in 1982 the movement for worker ownership scored a success and kept the mill alive in Weirton, West Virginia.

Rice next intervened in the issue when Mesta Machine at Homestead, the manufacturer of much of the heavy machinery used by other industries in the region, underwent bankruptcy. Ron Wiesen this time had used his clout as president of a large steel local to be elected to the city council of West Homestead, Pennsylvania, which had attempted eminent domain on the treatened Mesta works. Rice and other partisans of Tristate now joined in a demonstration outside the bankruptcy proceedings to insist that the fate of employees and the community should be considered along with financial stakes of creditors and stockholders. Rice commented that this was a "just and reasonable request but in the context of law and precedent, radical."[121]

Thereafter, other members of the clergy from the Pittsburgh area joined with Ron Wiesen and with his tactician Charles Honeywell, a disciple of Saul Alinsky, to form the Denominational Ministry Strategy and the Network to Save the Mon/Ohio Valley [DMS/ Network], and to use increasingly dramatic means to bring the plight of workers along the Monongahela and Ohio valleys to the attention of those corporate and financial leaders whose indifference, they argued, was sealing the fate of their workers. These methods included press conferences, calls on depositors to withdraw their money from Mellon banks, the spraying of skunk oil in major downtown department stores, and attempts to confront power holders at the churches where they worshipped.

Rice never chose to join with DMS/Network, and his attitude toward it seemed to vacillate between criticism and support. He applauded when Lloyd McBride threw the influence of the USWA behind the Mellon boycott,[122] correctly predicted that Charles Honeywell rather than Mellon Bank would be made the "problem" in the public mind,[123] but confessed when DMS invaded the Shadyside Presbyterian church that "Alinskyism leaves me cold."[124] He nevertheless wrote admiring pieces on pastors John J. Gropp and David Roth (incarcerated for defying his bishop's order to quit his church, and concluded that if Charles Honeywell could command their loyalty there must be more to him than mere Alinskyism.[125]

Rice even went so far as to draw a parallel between the struggle of DMS/Network and that of the Irish Republican Army.[126] At the outset of 1985, he noted with apparent gratitude that his own Tristate Conference on Steel was getting rather better press now, due to its being placed in comparison with DMS/Network.[127] Thus did Rice remain, if not at the cutting edge of activism on behalf of steel and steelworkers, at least an important force within those activist ranks.

It was noted at the outset of this biography that many observers of Rice over the half-century of his career have had a difficult time getting a clear fix on the man and his positions. He has appeared successively or to different observers as priest, radical, labor priest, hawkish patriot, Red-baiter, radical reborn, and archconservative. But to Rice's own way of thinking, there was never any question as to his primary identity or his deepest loyalty: he was a priest, loyal to his church.

If evidence of the primacy of this commitment were needed, it was provided anew in the 1980s, particularly when any apparent conflicts would occur between other causes that Rice espoused and the institutional well-being of the Catholic Church. It was on the side of the church that Rice would come down, time and time again.

Thus, although Rice had striven to be as sympathetic as possible with the struggles and even the tactics of DMS/Network, that sympathy all but evaporated when the group decided to pay one of its visits to St. Paul's cathedral in Pittsburgh. Rice was doubly embarrassed because the announcement came just when a column of his appeared with a favorable review of the group. He quickly insisted that Catholic Masses should not be subject to the kind of interruptions Protestants had experienced at their services (he later apologized for the implied derogation of those services), revised his estimate of the DMS/Network prospects, and threw in some gloomy projections for Ron Wiesen himself:

> If he [Wiesen] is unwise enough to participate in disruption of the Mass he may find his own labor union members quite displeased. Frankly his post as union president will be in jeopardy. . . . As for the rebelling organization: it has some of the characteristics of a cult but it seems doomed to be a tiny one, elitist in its own way. . . . Their lack of a popular base will eventually do them in.[128]

If this apparent about-face appeared to be a sudden and startling one (Rice did modify his seeming condemnation a little later)[129], it was very much in line with a pattern that he had exhibited all the years of his activist life: he would support and even participate in the challenging of any authority, save Catholic Church authority. Similarly, he had been a staunch advocate of unions, but not of priests' unions (not even of priests' associations, which were much less than unions). He was cool toward unions of teachers in parochial schools, although the news that nuns had crossed one of their picket lines during a strike "made me sick."[130]

Rice had good liberal credentials on most issues of free expression, but not when prochoice advocates wanted to hand out leaflets in front of his church. He was himself a maverick thinker of many issues, but when a "maverick" theologian like Hans Kung came into conflict with the Vatican, Rice sided with the pope.[131] The same was true of Rice's attitude toward theologian Charles E. Curran of Catholic University, who was in hot water with Rome.[132] When Pittsburgh prelate Anthony Bevilacqua created a furor by declining to wash the feet of women at Holy Thursday ceremonies, and was accused in the press of currying favor with the Vatican on the women's issue, Rice retorted that this was a "low blow."[133] Only when Archbishop Raymond Hunthausen of Seattle was partially suspended from his episcopal duties (and replaced, interestingly, by Bishop Donald Wuerl, soon to become bishop of Pittsburgh), did Rice grouse that archconservatives had gotten to the Vatican in order to can Hunthausen, an opponent of nuclear weapons (Hunthausen was later reinstated).[134] On other occasions too numerous to mention, Rice was both an exponent of the approved Catholic position on an issue and a defender of hierarchical authority, not only against attacks from without, but also against the tides of democratization within the church.

The only major church issue on which Rice permitted himself to be at variance with church authority was that of priestly celibacy. But even here, though he advocated in the 1980s that the church move toward ordaining married men, he advocated doing so only by steps, and first in remote mission countries where priests were not otherwise available.[135] And this stood in contradistinction to the ordaining of women priests, to which he seemed to remain opposed.

On *social* issues, however, Rice had repeatedly taken the hierarchy — usually the American Catholic bishops but sometimes implicitly the papacy — to task for a failure to take strong moral stands on issues of the day. Thus in the 1960s he had rebuked the bishops time and again for their failure to condemn as aggression the U.S. involvement in Vietnam. But by the 1980s when the U.S. bishops were considering a statement on nuclear weapons that criticized not only their use but even their possession and deployment for purposes of deterrence, Rice was jubilant. In a column headlined "U.S. hierarchy in finest hour," he asked:

> Would it be total insufferability for one to exult in the fact that one's own bishops have caught up with one? I suppose it would, so I shall just

exult a little, along with proclaiming how proud I am of these wise and brave men of God.[136]

His exultation, however, would not remain unalloyed. As the bishops' statement went from its first draft in 1981 to its third version by 1983, there intervened developments he considered ominous and amendments he found unfortunate. Representatives of the Reagan administration and the United States military lobbied first the U.S. bishops (unsuccessfully) and then the Vatican. Opus Dei, which Rice characterized as "that secretive, powerful, creeping and shadowy organization beloved of Pope John Paul" was active on the issue.

The principal architect of the statement, Cardinal Bernardin, was summoned to the Vatican. Rice recounted: "He said it was no big deal and that the American bishops' bold stand was supported. Not really, as it turns out."[137] Thus the third draft disassociated itself from the nuclear Freeze movement feared by the Reagan administration, and from pacifism. Its stand on deterrence became, in Rice's opinion, "meaningless," and on the demand for a no-first-strike pledge by the United States, it "waffled shamefully." Rice continued:

> Even more disturbing is the slip into cold war rhetoric toward the Soviet Union, laying the blame for nuclear build up and uneasiness on the "history of the conduct of Soviet Power." This, from the hierarchy of the nation which developed Atomic power and which alone used that power to deliberately kill human beings.[138]

Although Rice had not given up on the bishops, and although he hoped that a new and different draft might yet be approved (no such later draft ever was), he seemed to be relearning the lesson that even the voice of the hierarchy could be modulated by power as well as by truth.

When the bishops began circulating a draft of their next letter, this one on the American economy, Rice was more nuanced in his praise, and more hesitant to predict the final outcome to what appeared to be their strong critique

> of prevailing economic and political orthodoxy in America: The bishops' letter, while not so strong as I would like it to be, is firmly grounded in true Christian principles and has a nobility about it contrasting with the

ignobility of the criticisms. . . . One hopes they will not be intimidated when they get to the final draft, but will be even more forthright. After all, they are not so strong as the Pope has been in his condemnation of capitalism and materialism.[139]

Thus did Rice alternate between criticism and support of the bishops on social issues, siding with the hierarchy of his church on virtually every ecclesiastical issue, and remaining as much the loyalist within his church as he was the critic outside it. It was perhaps this combination of churchly conservatism with social criticism that had enabled him to remain a clerical *Catholic* activist through the many years of his career.

At about the time Rice was on the one hand working to persuade public opinion of the value of eminent domain in projected steel plant closings, and on the other hand being removed from the County Prison Board for his activism there, two items appeared in the *Pittsburgh Press* that contained what he labeled a "shocking untruth" about himself: that he was semiretired. He retorted as follows.

ME?! Semi-retired? From what? I am still full-time active pastor of St. Anne's, I write this column, accept speaking engagements, and do about as much as I ever did in everything appropriate, lawful, moral and non-fattening.[140]

That was at age seventy-five. But two years later Rice decided to retire formally, reasoning that "it is better to walk to the exit than to be carried or pushed."[141] Administration, he had found, had become a chore, whereas priesting was still fun. He said he still loved to preside at Mass, preach short sermons, visit the sick, and offer consolation at funerals. Weddings were rather more tiresome, because "virtually all brides are late." And he summarized his principal shortcoming as pastor under the heading of counseling:

Counseling has not been my strong suit, because people talk too long and repeat themselves. If for nothing else, I shall do a "bit" in Purgatory for impatience. Totally available, take all phone calls, see everyone, but not for long. A good pastor should be a better listener.[142]

Apparently, then, the poor Wee Charlie who had not been able to sit still for very long in the classroom in Ireland had not changed all that much in his subsequent seven decades of life.

On June 15, 1986, Msgr. Rice formally retired as pastor of St. Anne's parish. But there was rather less than met the eye in this retirement: he stayed on as pastor emeritus (he had expressed distate for the idea of moving to a retirement home for priests), keeping up many of his earlier rounds of duties. He continued to publish his weekly column, which showed no signs of becoming less controversial, and he pledged that "in my active retirement I shall be more involved than ever in the labor struggle, in prisons, racial justice, anti-war and similar good causes."[143] His life had changed, but it went on much as it had before.

Robena, PA mine disaster, December, 1962.
Consoling waiting families and miners.

Teach-in at Pitt on Viet Nam War, 1965.

March to the U.N. Building, April 15, 1967. Mrs. Spock, Benjamin Spock, Martin Luther King, Charles O. Rice.   *– Pittsburgh Catholic*

Press conference, New York City, August 29, 1967. Preparing for march on Pentagon. Back row, Dave Dellinger. Front row, Charles O. Rice, H. Rap Brown, Abby Hoffman, Dave Greenblatt, Dick Gregory.

March on Pentagon, October 21, 1967. Front left, Robert Lowell. Beside Charles O. Rice to right, Benjamin Spock and Mrs. Spock.

Accepting draft cards illegally, December 4, 1967.

Addressing anti-war rally, Pittsburgh, November, 1969.

Leading peace and justice march, 1970.

Rev. Charles O. Rice delivers homily at Yablonskı funeral, January, 1970. Washington, PA.

Chatting with a worker against Pittsburgh skyline, 1982. *– J. L. Alexandrowicz*

NINE

A Preliminary Assessment

I TURN FINALLY, AND NOT WITHOUT RELUCTANCE, to the task of interpretation and assessment. To attempt to evaluate the historical significance of anyone who has played an important part in his or her times is to run the risk of being too critical, too sympathetic, or too simplistic given the complexity of the subject matter. In the case of Charles Owen Rice, the inherent hazards of biography are exacerbated by the extraordinary length and diversity of his public life, the internal contradictions manifested in that career, and the newness of scholarly study of him. Permit me to elaborate.

Rice's public career of a half-century, as I have noted repeatedly, sometimes appears to consist of a series of contradictions, each more startling than the one before. The "radical" young priest who did battle for the CIO turns into the wartime superpatriot and postwar Red-baiter supreme, then reemerges as a self-proclaimed radical redivivus in the 1960s. The "flophouse father" famed for extending the charity of Christ and bowls of soup to the poor and homeless, Rice also graced the golf links and dined alone. The opponent of violence in war, capital punishment and abortion, he opposed clemency for the Rosenbergs and said he helped to buy bombs for the IRA and rifles for black militants. The liberal proponent of unions, the right of dissent, and equality for women, he opposed unions of parochial school teachers, most dissent within the church, and the ordination of women. Even in the 1980s, when he flayed corporate decision-makers in steel and autos who closed down American plants and exported jobs abroad, Rice often drove to his next podium or press conference in his Swedish-made Volvo (later his Mercedes).

Some of these contradictions were only apparent ones and, as we have seen, could be explained by a more careful reading of Rice's own viewpoints. Others had to do with what he regarded as deep-going changes of viewpoint on social issues or political groups that he experienced in his long life. Still others make more sense when we taken into account his very different approaches to matters civil and ecclesiastical. Still others had to do with human foibles which Rice share in at least as fully as the next person, and so on. But there are times when I despair of ever "explaining" Rice to the reader in the sense of finally resolving each and every one of the contradictions which his life presents. So the assessment of Rice offered here will not pretend to offer a definitive understanding of this highly complex man, but only to evaluate or raise critical questions about certain aspects of his public significance.

Additionally, the tentative nature of the interpretation offered here results in part from the fact that scholarship into Rice's life is still in its early stages and promises to be nearly as controversial as Rice himself. Earlier published accounts of Rice have tended to be either minor notations by scholars or fulsome accounts by journalists. Those scholars who have made Rice into a mere footnote to the McCarthy era have not had the opportunity to study the much greater scope of his activism, in that era alone, that today can be gleaned from the Rice Papers. Journalists, on the other hand, have generally relied on interviews with Rice himself and his selective (even inventive) recollection of the past — hence, for example, the whole business of the "exile theory" of the 1950s. Both of these approaches are limited and misleading and must now be abandoned.

Other researchers with access to the Rice Papers are today active in the field, and their accounts of Rice will likely differ in major ways from the one offered here. Rice continues to play a role in the researches, and not just as an interview subject. One biographer, for example, has charged that Rice has destroyed unflattering documents from his FBI file, and attempted to derail the publication of her study. As more researchers enter the fray, and as new viewpoints and resources are brought to bear, the diversity of evaluations of Rice's life will surely grow. The assessment offered here, then, is one against which future writers may wish to test their own findings, and which they may feel compelled to qualify or reject.

Having strewn the way liberally with complaints and disclaimers, I will now proceed to examine critically three significant aspects of Rice's life: Rice as a thinker, as an activist, and as a clerical activist. They are arranged, as will be seen, in ascending order of importance.

[RICE THE THINKER]

It is of course impossible to separate neatly anyone's actions from his or her thoughts: human thought and action exist only in a profound mutual interdependence so that each is virtually impossible without the other. Yet among significant historical figures, some are most appropriately remembered for the distinctive ideas they contributed to their cultures, irrespective of whether or not they themselves were distinguished for acting upon those ideas (Baruch Spinoza or Immanuel Kant for example). Others are remembered for the actions of their lives, whether or not they ever elaborated much in the way of a body of thought with which to explain or defend those actions (Franklin Roosevelt or Benito Mussolini). Still others make their mark on history by combining their blueprint for action with the action itself (Vladimir Lenin or Adolph Hitler). Within these categories, Rice will take his place as a man of action, rather than a man of ideas or even a man of both ideas and action.

This is not to deny that in his weekly columns and other writings Rice was a witty, provocative and frequently insightful writer. Dealing with a startling variety of topics, he was able for many years to inform, entertain, inspire or outrage a similarly varied readership.

But he never went much beyond the format of the 15–to–18 column inches of print or the occasional somewhat longer article. It is even comparatively rare that one finds a topic that Rice treated in as many as two or three successive installments of his columns. Most columnists or journalists have in a drawer someplace a book-length manuscript which they have been worrying for years, trying to whip it into the shape of a more complete exposition of their view of the world than they can convey in their ordinarily brief formats. Not so Rice. The only longer piece he seems to have put much effort into was an attempt at his own autobiography and even this reads much more like a disjointed series of weekly columns than a coherent account of his life. Whether Rice's creative powers were limited by the procrustean bed of the weekly column, or whether the weekly column along with the 30-minute radio program and the still briefer Sunday sermon matched the full scope of his powers of concentration, the result remains the same: a large body of writings, in search of some principle of internal coherence.

The point is not merely to complain against Rice's chosen format of expression. Week-by-week, issue-by-issue writings are, after all, ideally suited for reaching and influencing a considerable number of readers — many of whom might never sit down to read ponderous tomes containing elaborate expositions of writers' social theories. Better then to set forth the theory in bite-sized chunks, relating them to whatever are the issues of the day.

The point, rather, is that Rice did not appear to *have* any very consistent theory of society or social action at all. His writings over the years, like his actions, seemed not merely to be related to the issues and passions of the day, but to be driven by them. When one surveys the whole, one gains the impression not of one consistent underlying philosophy, but of numerous disparate and even contradictory philosophies, all incompletely digested. The social critique by the American radical Pettigrew furnished the syntax for anti-corporate rhetoric, but no corresponding base for revolutionary action. The distinctive American personalism of Peter Maurin and the Catholic Worker Movement Rice espoused in the abstract but abandoned as soon as he opened the doors of the House of Hospitality. Pacifism and war resistance were likewise advocated briefly but jettisoned, as soon as the Roosevelt Administration moved toward engagement in World War II. Principled anti-communism gave way to nearly mindless Red-baiting. Rice's later "radicalism" offered no real alternative vision of a modern society for post-corporate times. The social theories of the popes are sufficiently broad in their parameters and indistinct in their details that Rice has been able to operate within their limits without elaborating any comprehensive theory of his own. Rice's writings, then, were hardly a steady compass which pointed always in the same direction. At best they served as a barometer of the changing intellectual styles of the day.

Rice's lack of a consistent, overarching social theory is related to another, perhaps less obvious absence in his writings: originality. This may appear anomalous, because his readers no doubt found his columns to be highly original, particularly when they treated familiar social issues with quite unfamiliar information or analyses. Whether the headline story dealt with Grenada or Lebanon, prison riots or labor-management struggles, Rice could generally be counted upon to offer information not found in the daily papers and a slant quite different from the established one. Readers' reactions ranged from awe to skepticism regarding the implied range of Rice's expertise on the affairs of the world. Yet Rice himself was frank enough to admit on at least one occasion that his grasp of the subjects he discussed came as much from his reading as from his personal experiences, and more from skimming through reviews and digests of articles than from personally acquired competence in a variety of areas.[1] On some subjects, of course, he laid claim to a certain degree of expertise, based on his own life experience: labor, the ghetto, prisons, and Ireland. For the rest, his facts and his viewpoints were largely derivative from and dependent upon what he was reading at the time he wrote. Whether he had the background to distinguish what was more reliable from what was less so in what he read, rather than pick out sources that were just ideologically congenial, is another question. But Rice's voracious reading, costing him many hundreds of dollars per year in magazine subscriptions, at least allowed him to pepper his readers with facts and opinions which they would have encountered in the established media only much later, if at all.

Yet if Rice's lifetime experiences and his reading often allowed him to steal a march on public opinion and the mass media, still they provided him with no crystal ball. Among the phenomena he ruefully admitted having failed to foresee, even when they loomed on the horizon, were the outcomes of various labor insurgencies, the agony of American steel and autos, and the election of Ronald Reagan. At least in this sense, he was no prophet.

A final charge against Rice the thinker that must be taken into our accounting is the charge of anti-intellectualism. This was brought by, among others, his fellow priest-columnist, Andrew Greeley. Rice was accused, and fairly enough, of criticizing books he had not read, condemning whole disciplines he never studied, and pronouncing on court cases he had not heard. In other matters, like that of William Shockley, he went so far as to condemn even the uttering of thoughts with which he vehemently disagreed. Rice in these cases seemed to prefer not to have ideas survive or perish of their own merit in the free-for-all of intellectual scrutiny and competition, but to have them scratched from the competition in the first place. This note of intellectual authoritarianism did not characterize all of Rice's writings — more typically he enjoyed "bashing and being bashed" by other writers. But the willingness to rush to judgment without bothering to hear the evidence surfaced often enough in Rice's pronouncements to raise doubts about their reliability. (Much the same, of course, might be said of many other writers who are required to produce a column every week.)

Rice, then, was not primarily a thinker or an intellectual. He neither elaborated his own theory of social action nor consistently followed anyone else's. His writings were typically derivative rather than original. Finally, enough evidence of anti-intellectualism emerged in his life and writings to make some observers uneasy.

Some of these charges are serious enough, and these short-comings have affected adversely other aspects of Rice's life. But it can be replied that Rice never really represented himself as an original thinker and that his writings in fact clearly presented him as an apologist instead. It would hardly be fair, in this view, to condemn him failing to be something other than what he was.

What was he then? In the early days of the CRA, when Msgr. O'Toole and Fr. Hensler were delivering themselves of learned lectures on Catholic social principles, the junior Fr. Rice was busy inciting their young listeners to demand action on those principles, and designing an attention-grabbing name for the organization. Leaving to others the tiresome task of charting the course, he was preparing to set out on the march. A half-century later, the remarkable thing was how little this had changed.

[RICE THE ACTIVIST]

If Rice was not much of a theoretician, he was always a remarkable tactician. In one era after another, one cause after another, Rice's fellow activists time and again turned to him to formulate and execute the plans that would rally the troops, attract the media, and infiltrate or overwhelm the opposition. From the Soho-Gazzam evictees and the CRA to the ACTU, numerous union insurgencies, black militants, anti-war protesters, and those fighting disinvestment in steel, the charge given to Rice was usually the same: show us how to translate our ideas into effective action. And this is where Rice excelled. He was the planner, the organizer, the showman, the orator and the point-man who took the ideas formulated by others out into the glare of publicity and the heat of opposition. Sometimes his causes were victorious, sometimes vanquished. But never did they fail for lack of trying or timidity of approach.

In fact, so effective was Rice as an organizer, a publicist and a battler, that in his struggles there was frequently rather less than met the eye. His enemies would sometimes be daunted by the fearful opposition that had arisen against them, only to discover later that the storm consisted of the one-man whirlwind of Rice, and perhaps a few helpers.

It is only when we see his writings an an extension of or a distillation from his activism that they truly begin to make sense. Rice's column began as another tool to fight for organized labor and against the Communist Party. Over the years the lists of allies and opponents changed extensively, but the use of the column to attack the opposition and encourage the allies continued (except when they grew too complacent and needed to have their own flanks nipped). Even in the 1980s, when Rice was in the forefront of fewer activist causes, his columns continued to recall and reflect the battles of yesterday and apply their lessons as Rice saw fit. Thus his writings are perhaps best understood as the ongoing memoirs of an activist rather anything else.

I must note, by the way, how absolutely crucial to Rice's activism was the presence of some specific *enemy*. Whether the enemy was an insensitive federal bureaucracy, or Reds presumably intent on controlling organized labor, white construction unions denying opportunity to blacks, or corporate boards of directors engineering the demise of American labor, Rice was always at his most effective when he could point the finger of blame at some clearly definable individual or group, and arouse opposition accordingly. Generally adverse social conditions or the inherent contradictions of modern life were never nearly so useful. In fact, it can be pointed out that sometimes he had to practically invent the enemies or at least endow them with surrealistically ominous characteristics. His diatribes against leftists in the UE were perhaps the most striking examples of this approach, but by no means the only ones.

But if Rice attained his greatest historical significance as an activist, the key question for us to ask here is: what kind of activist? It has been argued above (chapters 2 and 7) that while Rice termed himself a "radical" in the 1930s, he in fact acted as a liberal, prolabor reformer in that era; and that his renewed claims of radicalism in the 1960s were accompanied by an activism which combined reformist and rebellious elements, but not revolutionary ones. Now, surveying five decades of Rice's activist life, there seems little reason to alter that characterization.

In defending this conclusion, I wish to draw strong distinctions on the one hand between Rice's allies and Rice himself, and on the other hand between his rhetoric and his actions.

Both in the 1930s and in the 1960s Rice opted to ally himself with those who could realistically be called revolutionaries: the Catholic Workers in the 1930s, and in the 1960s the Students for a Democratic Society [SDS] and other militants. In the Catholic Worker ideal of Christian perfectionism in social action, in SDS and some members of the Chicago Seven one can find not only social agitation but the blueprint for a new society. But Rice, while he worked at least briefly with revolutionaries, was never one of their number. He never had any revolutionary theory, either his own or anyone else's. However much he may have been attracted to their example, he never seemed to look to them for a blueprint for post-capitalistic society. The blueprints he followed, as we shall see, were much more modest than the personalism of the Catholic Worker Movement or the Port Huron Statement of Tom Hayden and SDS.

Others of those whom Rice admired or cooperated with clearly pursued a rebellious course of social activism, and suffered official repression as a predictable result. Bouie Haden, Stokeley Carmichael and many anti-war protesters of the 1960s brought to their activism a willingness and sometimes a seeming preference to engage the government with illegal or violent methods. However much Rice defended these actions in his writings, it must be recalled that he testified at the trial of the Chicago Seven that he himself would have nothing to do with violence. He said that he privately advised blacks to use illegal tactics to gain attention, but he almost always kept his own actions legal. His relationship with Bouie Haden seemed to smack as much of cooptation as cooperation. He counselled antiwar and civil rights protesters about using illegal protest behavior, but that was not the same as breaking the law himself. Once he agreed to participate in civil disobedience at the Pentagon, but did not get arrested. And when push came to shove in the antiwar movement, with the Weathermen preparing to go underground, Rice moved in another direction toward NPAC which preferred to treat Vietnam as one isolated issue, using large, legal demonstrations.

As noted earlier, the clearest example of Rice's willingness to engage in illegal behavior came in the course of his work with draft resisters. He helped young men to surrender or burn their draft cards, but never burned one of his own (presumably he didn't have one). He may have exposed himself to prosecution as an accessory to draft resistance, but in fact was never prosecuted. The FBI, even with its massive file on Rice, never opted to proceed against him, although it was pursuing and prosecuting other priest activists, who subsequently served federal prison sentences. Probably the closest Rice ever came to being indicted was the time he called J. Edgar Hoover a punch-drunk old man!

In the 1980s as the Wiesens, Roths, and Honeywells of DMS/ Network moved to confront the corporate power of steel companies in the personal lives of corporate officials, Rice said he sympathized with their plight but kept his distance.

So if we measure Rice's record not by his words or by the deeds of his associates but by his own deeds, we discover that he does not come much closer to being a rebel than a revolutionary.

That leaves us with the category of reformist — which, as it turns out, is quite adequate to describe not just some parts but nearly the whole of Rice's career as a social activist. In the 1930s when he represented homeowners who wanted more money for their soon-to-be-bulldozed houses, or unionists who sought recognition and collective bargaining agreements, his demands were clearly ones that the government could — and in fact did — grant. Even in the 1960s when he espoused the causes of legal and economic equality for blacks and an end to American military involvement in Vietnam, nothing in his demands was beyond government capabilities. These latter struggles were rather more protracted, and Rice's writings tended to become more impassioned as his frame of mind grew more exasperated and his feelings more alienated. But the reach of his rhetoric should not obscure the fact that his own actions in pursuit of his goals were rarely or never violent or illegal, and never brought upon him any form of punishment from civil authorities.

The operative sources of inspiration for Rice's activism appear, in the last analysis, to have come not from revolutionaries or rebels but from reformers of American capitalism like Msgr. John A. Ryan, Phil Murray and the CIO, and moderate anti-war coalitions like NPAC. The CIO of Phil Murray was already becoming less threatening to U.S. capitalism as Rice came on board, having given up earlier demands for worker control of the workplace. When it fudged on its determination to organize all the unorganized, and concentrated instead on good wages, hours, and benefits for its own portion of the workforce, it was less threatening still. And when its leftist element had been excised with Rice's help and the organization itself reunited with the AFL, it was less accurate to speak of the CIO as being rebellious or even reformist, rather than a sort of junior partner of the establishment. By the 1960s, when Rice took his marching orders from the suave and liberal Bishop Wright (certainly not from the Black Panthers), he also eschewed united front activism in favor of NPAC's single-issue approach to the Vietnam War. In the 1980s his opposition to corporate disinvestment in steel and autos led him to propose the novel but perfectly legal and essentially reformist measures of eminent domain proceedings and worker ownership of plants otherwise slated to be closed.

If Rice's own political activism is best described as reformist, the agenda underlying that activism is best described, despite his frequent protestations to the contrary, as liberal. The contemporary liberal is distinguished from the radical on the one hand whose revolutionary vision of society demands the overthrow of capitalism, and on the other hand from the conservative who wants to preserve capitalism as is or to strengthen it by reducing governmental influence on the marketplace. The liberal wishes to preserve and to humanize capitalism by a variety of economic and social reforms implemented by the government. Those economic measures enumerated in Ryan's *Reconstruction of the Social Order*, with more recent additions like equal opportunity for blacks, women and gays, supplemented by a growing disenchantment with the global projection of American economic and military strength, provide a reasonably representative listing of the reforms advocated by contemporary American liberals. These are, of course, precisely the causes which Rice advocated, in season and out, for most of his public life.

Not only what he wrote, but what he did, for the most part fit comfortably within the parameters of liberal reformism: his wartime post as rent regulator, his anticommunist crusade and his role as arbitrator of management-labor disputes, all exemplified his willingness to make New Deal liberalism work without moving on toward the socialist or New Testament transformation of society. In the 1960s he may have been somewhat ahead of other mainstream liberals in advocating black equality or opposing American militarism abroad, a bit behind them in advocating economic equality for women. But these are essentially matters of nuance, and hardly justify his rejection of the liberal label. Even in the 1980s, Rice's advocacy of eminent domain/worker ownership of plants scheduled for closing, an American variant of "lemon socialism," may yet prove congenial enough to American capitalism, and was at any rate in sharp contrast to the activism on the same issue of Ron Wiesen, Charles Honeywell and David Roth.

Rice often said of American workers in general and steelworkers in particular that they saw American capitalism as quite a good thing and at most wanted to modify it a bit so that it worked better, rather than scrapping it. This carried with it an implied distinction from his own presumably more radical viewpoint. Yet if we examine his deeds as opposed to words, reality as opposed to mystique, and the absence even in Rice's writings of any comprehensive alternative to contemporary capitalism, we can conclude that his description of steelworkers applied almost equally well to himself.

Rice's own insistence that he was a "radical" can be read as a reflection of his increasingly critical questioning of certain myths about American society or the international uses of American power. But as the conservative and anti-revolutionary position of American power in the world today has become more apparent, many other Americans who are hardly radicals have come to share in the same sort of questioning. Or his preference for the "radical" label can be construed as reflecting his feeling since the 1960s of alienation from mainstream politics and politicians, another fairly widespread current trend. But in the realm of political action as opposed to attitude, that label is hardly accurate.

[RICE THE PRIEST ACTIVIST]

Our discussion to this point of Rice's social activism has had to it an obvious incompleteness: we have hardly adverted to the fact that whatever he did, he did it as "a Roman Catholic priest in good standing," as he was often wont to say. Yet his clerical status and the Roman collar that he wore made an enormous difference both in the nature and in the consequences of his activism.

He received much greater visibility as an activist priest than he would have as a layman, and seemed to have a correspondingly greater impact on his listeners and readers. Had a *Mr.* Charles Rice been telling steelworkers back in the 1930s that they should join the CIO, this would have had far less influence than did the *Rev.*

Charles Rice telling Catholic laity, in days when they looked to the Church for more guidance than they do today, that unions and the CIO had the blessing of the pope and indeed that it was their duty as good Catholics to join a union. His ability to tilt American Catholic unionists, up to and including Phil Murray, against their leftist coworkers was based precisely on his claim to speak for the Catholic Church, locked in combat with the atheistic materialism of the communists. In the 1960s, when the audiences to which he addressed himself on issues of war and race were not necessarily Catholic, Rice's impact on them was correspondingly attenuated. Yet it was again the clerical garb and the ancient religious tradition it represented that put Rice at the head of the march and on the speakers' podium, rather than back in the ranks. And throughout all his years of writing, it was of course his clerical status and the pages of the *Pittsburgh Catholic* that provided him with a regular forum. Other examples could be multiplied, but the point is clear: Rice's attainments as a social activist cannot be separated from, and would have been highly improbable without, his priestly status.

But of course that status brought with it constraints as well as opportunities. We have seen Rice repeatedly explaining to local bishops why he should be given leave to speak at labor events within their dioceses — and not always obtaining the needed permission. At a practical level, Rice's pastoral assignments generally did not leave him the time or the opportunity to plunge full-time into social causes — although he was able to make remarkably effective use of what time he had.

But most of the restrictions on Rice growing out of his priestly status seem to have been ones that he very consciously chose at the outset of his career and reaffirmed over and over as the years passed. That is, he opted for highly conservative positions on nearly every theological issue and question of church discipline. Aside from a bit of liturgical experimentation at the House of Hospitality back in the 1940s, and the diffidently-offered suggestion in the 1980s of allowing some priests to marry, Rice consistently lined up on the conservative, pro-hierarchy side of virtually every ecclesiastical question. Even twenty years into the Vatican II era, he hankered for the earlier days when priests not only wore clerical garb, but even used the old-fashioned *linen* Roman collars rather than the more recent plastic facsimile.[2]

On the one hand, this conservative orientation led to many of the more striking inconsistencies we have had occasion to notice, when Rice abandoned in ecclesiastical affairs what seemed to be his strong convictions on secular matters. On the other hand, it may have been precisely Rice's ecclesial conservatism that gave him rather more leeway than other priests had to take strong positions on social issues — for example, his condemnation of what he viewed as the U.S. Catholic Bishops' too-timid stance on the war in Vietnam, and their backing down on the moral issues of the nuclear arms race.

Rice's distinctive model of priestly social activism becomes clearer when compared with those of others who followed similar yet divergent paths. Rev. Charles F. Coughlin was another Catholic priest who reached greater heights of fame than Rice as a radio preacher and advocate of social causes. But his anti-Semitism and his general outspokenness brought him into conflict with the hierarchy, and he was effectively silenced. Rice, who observed the fate of Coughlin, always managed to get along well enough with the local bishop that he never underwent any comparable treatment ("exile theory" to the contrary notwithstanding).

Revs. Raymond Dietz, Adelbert Kazinsky and James Renshaw Cox were, as we noted, earlier examples of "labor priests" in whose footsteps Rice followed. Rice and his age cohort of labor priests extended the earlier priests' advocacy of unions to include the industrial unionism of the CIO. Rice personally advanced clerical involvement into the issues of race and war in the 1960s, being the most prominent Catholic priest-activist to bridge the two eras.

James Groppi and the Berrigan brothers Daniel and Philip emerged in the 1960s as priest advocates of black rights and opponents of U.S. militarism. Clearly committing themselves to civil disobedience, they brought down the wrath of government — and frequently of the local bishop — upon themselves, amassing among them numerous and sometimes extended periods of incarceration. Another priestly ally of the Berrigans, who himself served time in prison for his activism, once explained the difference between his initial approach to priestly social activism and the conversion that he underwent because of the Berrigans' example:

> So you go into Harlem and you say, "How can we look good? How can we have a mission to Harlem?" You know, so the people will say, boy, the Catholic Church is really on the ball in Harlem. That's the way you thought. It's people like the Berrigans who said, the hell with that! What do we care how we look? You know there are people who are dying,

starving, and what are we going to do about them? And that sounds very simple, but that's a real drastic change in the whole way you look at things. And once you start to look at things that way you start to get yourself in a lot of trouble.[3]

Rice never got himself into that kind of trouble, remaining a priest in good standing with the institutional church when Groppi and Phil Berrigan withdrew from it and Daniel Berrigan continued to have troubled relations with the hierarchy and his religious order.

Likewise in the 1980s Lutheran minister David Roth in Pittsburgh, over the plight of unemployed steelworkers, chose a course of activism that confronted corporate decision-makers in their private lives and at their churches. This choice of tactics brought Roth into conflict with legal authorities and his hierarchy alike — who combined to remove him from his congregation and to defrock him. Rice, while expressing admiration for Roth and his allies, grew more distant when they turned their attention to Catholic churches. Needless to say, Rice never imitated Roth's approach.

Another line of comparison which is useful to recall at this juncture is that between Rice and Dorothy Day, Peter Maurin and other members of the Catholic Worker Movement. The latter were of course laity rather than priests. But they dedicated their lives to a literal application to modern social conditions of the New Testament principles of love and compassion, within the context of Roman Catholicism. Rice, albeit with the same loyalty to the Catholic Church, never felt called to and never practiced the same sort of voluntary poverty the Catholic Workers did. Underlying these differences in personal practice were differing concepts of what Jesus demanded of his followers. The Catholic Worker Movement insisted on a literal following of the Sermon on the Mount and other expressions of Christian perfectionism. Such a very intense practice of Christianity has usually turned out to appeal to only a relatively small number of people, so that the Catholic Worker Movement can be referred to as a "sect." Rice adhered to the more conventional Christian notion of "church," which posits that the more difficult demands of Christ were only "counsels of perfection" for the few rather than requirements for all believers. The church, then, could encompass a much larger body of believers, with a great diversity of life styles, from whom far less was demanded. And it was to this notion of Catholicism, as a large, not necessarily terribly fervent body of believers, governed in matters of faith and morals by the visible church hierarchy, that Rice devoted his loyalty. If he never took his social activism to the same degree as did Dorothy Day or Peter Maurin, Daniel Berrigan or David Roth, this may have been due on part to his less perfectionist interpretation of the New Testament and the church.

Evaluating Rice specifically as a *priest* activist, there are two aspects of his record which seem to raise particularly troublesome questions. The first of these arises from occasions when he appeared to use ethically dubious or repugnant means to attack his antagonists; the second comes from what appears to be a pattern of allowing others to take the most serious consequences of his activism. Both of these are related to his clerical status.

I have noted, particulary during his Red-baiting years, the charges made against Rice of resorting to unfair or immoral tactics. Even allowing that some of these charges were exaggerations or inventions, it remains clear enough that he sometimes made severe personal accusations against his enemies — both in public, which they at least had the opportunity to deny, and in private when he delated people to government officials on charges unrelated to breaking the law. Such behavior became particularly troublesome when, speaking as a Roman Catholic priest, Rice alleged that various of his opponents who said they were Catholics were in fact "bad Catholics." Sometimes, as in the cases of Mooney and Durkin of the Office Workers, these charges seemed to be made with little or no familiarity with their personal lives. Moreover, such charges, in the context of the American Catholic Church of the 1940s and 50s, were powerful enough not merely to weaken an individual's political position, but also to ruin his or her standing in the parish or community.

In the very early days of the CRA, Rice had distinguished between Christian and communist social activism in that while Christians must choose morally good means to advance their cause, and must embody the love of Christ for all, communists believed that the end justified the means and so might resort to all sorts of lies and tricks. "Choose your enemies well," goes an old saw, "because you will grow to resemble them." Rice's conduct in battle sometimes raised the question: was he exhibiting more of the love of Christ for all, or the use of unsavory tactics he condemned in his opponents?

The second question raised by Rice's clerical activism is whether his clerical status served him as a convenient shield from many of the consequences of his advocacy and actions, thus imparting to his social activism a certain tinge of irresponsibility. When he exhorted strikers to keep the picket line going, that might mean the loss of jobs or income to them, but not to him. When he inveigled against leftist unionists to throw them out of a union and out of a job, they could never retaliate with the same measure against him. When he encouraged dissident unionists to stand up against union leadership, if that strategy backfired they might become unemployed or worse, but he would escape unscathed. If he helped blacks buy guns, it was not he who was shot as a result. When he counselled young men to burn their draft cards, some of them ended up in prison but he never did. And after a march on the Pentagon, when other marchers languished in jail and went on a hunger strike, Rice could return to the rectory that night for a warm meal and his regular round of priestly duties. So the question arises of whether Rice was a responsible activist, or an irresponsible one.

There was no obvious way out of this dilemma, if dilemma he ever sensed it to be. Presumably Rice did not feel called to the level of commitment of a James Groppi or a Daniel or Phil Berrigan, who did not merely inspire others who ended up in jail, but went there themselves. Yet he was equally disinclined to follow the example of other socially concerned priests and simply leave the activism to others. So he continued to be an activist, but one who never suffered very much for that activism. It was like his boyhood in Ireland, when he was better at starting fights than at finishing them.

At base, the above questions arose ineluctably from the fact that Rice had two commitments in his life which, while they were not mutually exclusive, were not 100 percent compatible either. One commitment was to a variety of socially progressive causes; the other was to the well-being of the Roman Catholic Church. So it is to the social involvement of the Catholic Church, especially in America, that I now turn to round out my evaluation of Rice as a priestly activist.

During the years when Rice was preparing for the priesthood and serving as a young priest, the Catholic Church was still wrestling with the question of whether to adapt at all to the new environment of the modern world. In 1864 Pope Pius IX's *Syllabus of Errors* had stated that it was "false to teach that the Roman pontiff can and ought to reconcile himself with progress, liberalism, and modern civilization."[4] This setback to liberal Catholics in America had been followed in 1899 by Leo XIII's much more specific condemnation of those errors he associated with the church in America, under the title of "Americanism." In a letter entitled *Testem benevolentiae* addressed to Cardinal Gibbons of Baltimore he condemned such practices as dialogues with heretics, downplaying the supernatural or the need of the faithful for external guidance, and the modifying of religious doctrine in order to attract converts. Gibbons had responded that these were errors indeed, but had "nothing in common with the views, aspirations, doctrine and conduct of the Americans."[5]

More to the point, the challenge to the Catholic Church in America was whether it was willing and able to forego the privileged position it had held from ancient times in Europe, and to adjust to the American climate where the separation of church and state was constitutionally mandated, religious diversity flourished, and error presumably had the same right to be expressed as truth. Critics like Blanshard, as noted in Chapter 1, doubted that the authoritarianism of Roman Catholicism could subsist in American soil without undermining the democratic culture and institutions here.

American Catholics were to some extent prevented, at least temporarily, from facing these tensions by the fact that many of them lived in big-city Catholic "ghettoes," further subdivided along ethnic lines and serviced by a variety of national-origin parishes. This was particularly true of the Pittsburgh diocese. But during Rice's priestly ministry the ghettoes began to be depopulated of Catholics — and re-populated, as in the case of Holy Rosary parish, with mostly non-Catholic blacks. The white Catholics moving out to suburbs like Castle Shannon would find themselves in a more heterogeneous environment.

It was the American Jesuit theologian, John Courtney Murray, who provided the theological justification for Catholic adaptation to the United States, arguing that Catholic natural law teaching actually underlay the Founders' framework for a liberal and pluralistic society. This recasting of the Catholic stance vis-à-vis modern society would finally triumph at Vatican II. But in the meantime ordinary Catholic laity and clerics like Rice had already been forging ahead into the practice of Catholicism amid diversity.

Rice may be said to have adapted remarkably well to these cultural changes, and even to have been near the forefront in some cases, winning wide acceptability for himself and his message inside the Catholic milieu and outside it (even though he was usually at his most effective with Catholic audiences). The Catholic triumphalism that characterized his early years imperceptibly gave way to greater respect for other religious traditions and to involvement in ecumenism as early as the 1950s. A good liberal and card-carrying member of the ACLU, Rice could not fairly be accused, as Blanshard had once accused Irish Catholics *in globo*, of threatening the democratic culture of America.

Yet there was always the line Rice drew between civil and religious questions, so that his acceptance of the liberal values of individual freedom, toleration of diversity, and the like stopped short of the church doors — and of the sidewalk in front of those doors, when it came to the abortion issue. Thus his support for political democracy and religious freedom was always somewhat limited and conditional.

After the 1985 Extraordinary Synod of Bishops in Rome, the Vatican's propensity to restrict personal freedoms in line with religious authority, more than American Catholics are inclined to do, surfaced in the issue of academic freedom in Catholic colleges. The Vatican insisted that freedom of expression at such institutions must be subject to the control of the local bishop, while some U.S. bishops winced at the thought of trying to implement such a rule. The question of individual freedom vs. church authority, although more limited now than it had been previous to Vatican II, still had not gone away.

Another set of questions the Church faced during the twentieth century had to do with social involvement, and these were altogether central to Rice's activist career. Should the Church involve itself in social questions at all, or should it merely preach to the faithful a supernatural message of salvation in the next world that did not relate to social and political problems in this one? And if it were going to pronounce on social issues at all, should the church align itself with the dominant groups and institutions in society, or give voice to the needs of the poor and powerless? These questions were less theological than practical ones, in that *Rerum Novarum* in 1891 and *Quadragesimo Anno* in 1931 already provided the justification for the church's intervention into social questions, and on the side of the masses of people against the spirit of organized greed too often displayed by modern capitalism. But in practice the Church in Europe had lost much of the working class by appearing to be too closely aligned with existing aristocracies and entrenched wealth, and the same could have resulted in America if some church forces of conservatism here had had their way.

Perhaps the greatest significance to Rice's career was that he insisted that this must not be allowed to happen again. Thus he helped move the Catholic Church in America toward the side of the working class from the 1930s, toward the aid of beleaguered blacks in the 1960s, and toward opposition to dangerous American militarism from the 1960s onward. I say "toward." Members of the American Catholic hierarchy are no more deaf than are other church leaders to the blandishments and occasionally the threats of those who hold political and economic power. And the average American Catholic is susceptible enough to the prejudices within American society, and prone enough to confound loyalty to church and state, sometimes following both with more enthusiasm than critical reflection. Despite these tendencies, the U.S. Catholic Bishops have moved into a habit of challenging civil power, and Catholic laity have themselves become much more questioning of that power than they were fifty years ago. These changes can be attributed in some part to activist priests like Rice.

A more specific social question, but perhaps the gravest one facing the human race today, is that of war in the age of nuclear weaponry. The Catholic Church, as early as the time of Emperor Constantine, abandoned its earlier absolute pacifism to advocate the "just war" theory. This theory, distinguishing between immoral wars of aggression and moral ones of defense, always allowed sufficient subjectivity of interpretation that opposing kings and nations could engage in wars against each other, with both sides' troops being solemnly blessed by their respective hierarchies in a presumably "just" cause, and then sent out to kill one another. Rice's fulminations against the Germans and Japanese during the World War II, and his refusal then to see in the "just war" theory any basis for Catholic pacifism, certainly mirrored this mentality.

But Rice and many others began to become more critical of the motivations and the deeds of their civil leaders during the Vietnam War era. As this occurred, doubts also surfaced about the viability of the "just war" theory itself. Rice himself modified it in the case of Vietnam to embrace the principle of selective conscientious objection. Meanwhile Vatican II had seen a comparable shift away from exclusive reliance on "just war" theory to approve total pacifism as well. The U.S. Catholic Bishops questioned in 1968 whether U.S. participation in the war in Vietnam was just, and concluded in 1972 that it was not.

Regarding nuclear weapons these bishops, sometimes with Vatican backing, have condemned the nuclear arms race and the concept of total war, and, without insisting on unilateral disarmament, have raised pointedly the question of whether the mere possession of vast nuclear stockpiles, targeted as they must be against noncombatants as well as soldiers, and in a sense against the whole future of the human race, is not a moral evil in and of itself. That the Catholic bishops of the nation that has led the nuclear arms race should take such a stance is an altogether extraordinary event, and one not at all predictable just a few years earlier.

In all these social issues in which the Catholic Church in America and the world involved itself, Rice was a participant. Sometimes operating as a compass pointing the direction, sometimes as a barometer reflecting the changes which had occurred, he continued to serve the church with all of its grandeur and all of its faults, never seeming to entertain (at least not in public) the slightest notion of disloyalty to that institution.

More recently, however, other changes have begun to make themselves felt within the church — changes Rice has neither led nor adapted to, but has resisted. Liberation theology, growing out of the struggles of various peoples around the world, returned to the New Testament to find a Christ who championed the "little people" in their struggles against the powers of that day. Liberation theology translated those struggles to today, when third world peoples fight to be free of military dictatorships, international corporate capitalism, and indeed of those who cooperate with the generals and the bankers. Abandoning the traditional search for a "third way" between capitalism and communism, these fighters proclaim that one must either be with the oppressed or against them. Liberation theologians find in the struggles of campesinos against landowners and the military a justifiable use of force. Within the church, they insist that the Holy Spirit does not speak exclusively through the pope or the hierarchy, but also through local groups of people engaged in the struggle to free themselves and to make society more truly Christian.

In more advanced countries including the United States, some Catholics no longer feel themselves constrained by the hierarchy's teaching on subjects like birth control, the ordination of women, or abortion, but insist that there exists a variety of viewpoints within the church, all of them deserving of a respectful dialogue.

This seemed to be where Rice got off. Modern trends that began with a call for liberation were one thing, but when they ended up by challenging the very foundations of power within the church, that was quite another. Rice never discussed Liberation theology in his columns to any great extent. He was not a participant in dialogues between Marxists and Christians. And it probably remained as true as when he first said it in the 1960s that Rice did not involve himself in the recent Catholic revolution because he did not know where that revolution was going.

To summarize this preliminary assessment of Rice, we can say that he was an insightful commentator and doughty apologist, but not a systematic or original thinker about the social issues he has addressed. He was a highly effective battler for numerous liberal reformist causes, and sometimes a law-defying rebel, but never a revolutionary. Although he allied himself at times with secular and Christian radicals, he always stopped short of the revolutionary outlook or personal commitments that would have made him one of their number. He was a churchman first and a social activist second, a fact which has both underlined his occasional seeming failures to observe high ethical standards of conduct and contributed to the appearance of a certain degree of irresponsibility in his activism. But his loyalty to the church, combined with his engagement on social issues, together with the similar efforts of other Catholic clergy and laity, helped to move the American Catholic Church towards much greater involvement in American social and political life than was the case a half century ago. Whether the church will move further on the tides of forces like Liberation theology remains to be seen and would likely have to occur in any case without Rice's support. But it is safe to say that Rice played a significant role in bringing the American Catholic Church as far as it has come today.

And how — if at all — to assess Rice the individual? Casual observers, depending mostly on their own ideological preferences, will doubtless continue to admire, even revere him, or to condemn him altogether. But perhaps those who have taken the time to examine Rice's days and ways somewhat more closely will conclude, in the lexicon of traditional spirituality, that while Rice never was a saint, he always strove to be on the side of the angels — and succeeded more often than most of us do.

Notes

Introduction

1. *Pittsburgh Catholic*, Feb. 3, 1984; Jan. 10, 1986; July 11 through Aug. 1, 1986; May 20, 1988; Feb. 27, 1987.

Chapter 1

1. Throughout this chapter, materials relating to Rice's own early recollections of his life are based on interviews with him conducted by me from November 1981 to July 1983, additional written reflections prepared by Rice for this biography, and Rice's own unpublished autobiographical manuscript written between 1968 and 1970 and still in Rice's personal possession.

2. Charles Owen Rice was generally called "Charlie" by his relatives in the U.S. and by his mother's family in Ireland. But to the Dundalk Rices he was always known (perhaps after his oldest uncle there) as "Owen," a name pronounced in that corner of the world as if it had but one syllable.

3. Blanshard, *The Irish and Catholic Power: An American Interpretation* (Boston; Beacon Press, 1953). Although Blanshard's personal observations and research of Irish Catholic culture date from a later time than the boyhoods of Charlie and Pat there, most of the characteristics stressed by Blanshard seem to have remained similar; if anything, they were *more* pronounced in the earlier period.

4. Ibid., p. 3.

5. Ibid., pp. 110–138.

6. Ibid., pp. 110–138.

7. Ibid., pp. 139–167.

8. Rice, autobiographical MS (unpublished).

9. Blanshard, *The Irish*, pp. 168–202.

10. Charlie and Pat were never caught up in the Gaelic revival in Ireland, although one or two of their uncles did spend some time "up in the mountains" learning that ancient language.

11. Rice, autobiographical MS (unpublished).

12. Willard Glazier, *Peculiarities of American Cities* (Philadelphia, 1884), p. 55.

13. Robert I. Vexler, *Pittsburgh, 1682–1976*, p. 55.

14. Richard F. Pettigrew, *Imperial Washington: The Story of American Public Life from 1870–1920* (originally published in 1922; republished by Anno Press and *The New York Times*, 1970).

15. Ibid., p. 7.

16. Ibid., pp. 10–11.

17. Ibid., p. 131.
18. Ibid.
19. Ibid., p. 186.
20. Ibid., p. 248.
21. Ibid., p. 333.
22. Ibid., pp. 394–95.
23. Ibid., p. 392.
24. *Quadragesimo Anno*, translated as "Reconstructing the Social Order," in *Seven Great Encyclicals* (Paulist Press, 1939), section 45.
25. Ibid.
26. Ibid., section 46.
27. Ibid.
28. Ibid., section 47.
29. Ibid.
30. Ibid., sections 72–74.
31. Ibid., section 75.
32. Ibid.
33. Ibid., section 53.
34. Ibid., sections 92–94.
35. *Rerum Novarum* (1891), translated as "On the Rights and Duties of Capital and Labor," in *The Church Speaks to the Modern World*, ed. Etienne Gilson (Doubleday, 1954), section 32.
36. Ibid., section 17.
37. Ibid., section 18.
38. *Quadragesimo Anno*, sections 111–122.
39. Douglas P. Seaton, *Catholics and Radicals* (Bucknell University Press, 1981), pp. 15–16.
40. *Quadragesimo Anno*, sections 31–36.

Chapter 2

1. Alan Brinkley, *Voices of Protest: Huey Long, Fr. Coughlin and the Great Depression* (New York: Knopf, 1982), p. 240.
2. Ibid., p. 229.
3. Ibid., pp. 228–29.
4. Ibid., pp. 227–28.
5. Ibid., p. 235.
6. Ibid., p. 185.
7. Ibid., p. 223.
8. Ibid., pp. 218–222.
9. Ibid., pp. 8–81, passim.
10. Ibid., pp. 131–132.
11. Ibid., pp. 265–268.
12. Charles E. Curran, *American Catholic Social Ethics: Twentieth-Century Approaches* (University of Notre Dame Press, 1982), pp. 37–43.
13. Ibid., pp. 50–62.
14. Ibid., pp. 71–84.
15. William D. Miller, *Dorothy Day: A Biography* (Harper and Row, 1982). See also his *Harsh and Dreadful Love*. See Dorothy Day's autobiographical

writings, including *The Eleventh Virgin* (Albert and Charles Bons, 1924), *From Union Square to Rome* (Preservation of the Faith Press, 1938), and *House of Hospitality* (Sheed and Ward, 1939).

16. For a sampling of *Catholic Worker* articles, see Thomas C. Cornell and James H. Forest (eds.), *A Penny a Copy; Readings from The Catholic Worker* (MacMillan, 1968).

17. Mel Piehl, *Breaking Bread: The Catholic Worker and the Origin of Catholic Radicalism in America* (Philadelphia: Temple University Press, 1982), pp. 70–73.

18. Curran, *American Catholic*, pp. 138ff.

19. Piehl, *Breaking Bread*, pp. 134ff.

20. Curran, *American Catholic*, p. 149.

21. Piehl, *Breaking Bread*, p. 108.

22. It has since been renamed Carlow College.

23. Rice, autobiograhical MS (unpublished).

24. Rev. T. Blantz interview with Rice, 1977 (unpublished).

25. T. William Bolts, "Pittsburgh's Labor Priests in the 1930's" (unpublished MS), p. 11.

26. Ibid., pp. 1–2.

27. Author's interview with Rice, March 22, 1982.

28. "Priests, Pickets and Pickle Workers," *Time*, June 28, 1937, pp. 62–63.

29. Author's interview with Rice, March 22, 1982.

30. Rice Papers at Hillman Library Special Collections, box #6; Rice's recollections of the early days of the Catholic Radical Alliance, compiled for an article in the *Pittsburgh Press* in 1973.

31. Author's interview with Rice, March 22, 1982.

32. Rice, autobiographical MS (unpublished).

33. Verbatim texts of these lectures, some of them in the form of catechismlike questions and answers, and apparently distributed to all participants, have been preserved in the Rice Papers (box #6, folder #1) and form the basis for the account here. Individual authorship of the lectures is possible to ascribe in some cases, not because of the documents themselves, but because of contemporaneous reports in the *Pittsburgh Catholic*.

34. Ibid.

35. Ibid.

36. Ibid.

37. Ibid.

38. *Pittsburgh Catholic*, April 22, 1937.

39. Rice Papers, box #6. This particular document, while undated, bears the Catholic Radical Alliance heading, with the organization's earliest address of 3221 5th Ave.; it is probably almost contemporaneous with the events described.

40. Author's interview with Rice, March 23, 1982.

41. Ibid.

42. "Priests, Pickets and Pickle Workers," *Time*, June 16, 1937, p. 62.

43. Author's interview with Msgr. Hensler, August 14, 1984.

44. Author's interview with Rice, March 22, 1982.

45. Ibid.

46. Michael Phelan, "Catholics Under Radical Banners," in Rice Papers, box #6 (journal and date unidentified).

47. Day, *House of Hospitality*, p. 428.

48. Ibid., p. 260–267.

49. Douglas P. Seaton, *Catholics and Radicals* (Bucknell University Press, 1981), p. 53.

50. *Pittsburgh Catholic*, July 1, 1937 (Cox comment quoted from the *Pittsburgh Post Gazette*, June 28, 1937).

51. *Social Justice*, July 5, 1937.

52. *Pittsburgh Catholic*, July 1 and Aug. 12, 1937.

53. Rice to O'Connell, Sept. 7, 1937; Rice Papers, box #25.

54. Rice to Gibbons, ibid.

55. Gibbons to Rice, Sept. 8, 1937; ibid.

56. Rice Papers, box #27.

57. Ibid.

58. Ibid., Sept. 11, 1939.

59. *Pittsburgh Catholic*, Dec. 2, 1937.

60. Ibid., July 28, 1938.

61. Ibid., Dec. 23, 1937 and Jan. 26, 1939.

62. See Lawrence Sullivan letters (undated) to Rice, Rice Papers, box #21.

63. *Pittsburgh Post Gazette*, Jan. 27, 1939.

64. *Time*, Feb. 26, 1940, p. 54.

65. Rice to author, November 8, 1983.

66. Sullivan to Rice (undated), Rice Papers, box #21.

67. Notes prepared by Rice for a *Pittsburgh Press* writer in 1973; Rice Papers, box #6.

68. See *Pittsburgh Catholic*, 1939–41, passim.

69. Author's interview with Rice, March 23, 1982.

70. Dorothy Day, *House of Hospitality*, pp. 142–149.

71. Ibid., p. 59.

72. Ibid., p. 266.

73. Donald Powell, reprinted in Cornell and Forrest, *A Penny* (n. 16, above), pp. 29–31.

74. Seaton, *Catholics* (n. 49, above) passim. See also Rice's columns in the *Pittsburgh Catholic* for 1941 and 1942, passim.

75. Rice Papers, box #6.

76. Ibid.

77. Author's interview with Rice, March 23, 1982.

78. Radio address July 15, 1941, as reported in the *Pittsburgh Catholic*, July 17, p. 16.

79. Miller, *Dorothy Day* (n. 15, above), p. 332.

80. Ibid., pp. 343–344.

81. Ibid., p. 345.

82. Day, *House of Hospitality*,p. 115.

83. Miller, *Dorothy Day*, p. 344.

84. *Pittsburgh Catholic*, March 21, 1940.

85. Ibid., March 23, 1941.

86. The discussion here is an adaptation of one in Theodore Lowi's *American Politics: Incomplete Conquest* (Holt, Rinehart and Winston: 1976), pp. 695–98.

Chapter Three

1. See Rice Papers, box #21.
2. Ibid.
3. In fairness, such statements overlooked the network of prominent politicians and businessmen whom Rice had engaged in fund-raising efforts, and by late 1945 the House of Hospitality received a check for $1,000 from Mrs. Clifford Heinz.
4. Rice Papers, box #27.
5. Author's interview with Rice, March 23, 1982.
6. Broadcast, Feb. 22, 1942. Typewritten manuscripts for this and all other broadcasts cited are to be found in the Rice Papers, box #27.
7. Ibid., Rice Papers, box #27, April 26, 1942.
8. Ibid., Sept. 27, 1942.
9. Ibid., Oct. 25, 1942.
10. Ibid., Aug. 18, 1943.
11. Ibid., Dec. 26, 1983.
12. Ibid., April 12, 1943.
13. Author's interview with Rice, May 21, 1983.
14. Broadcast, June 14, 1942; Rice Papers, box #27.
15. Ibid., July 5, 1942.
16. Ibid., July 4, 1943.
17. Ibid., Oct. 10, 1943.
18. E.g., broadcast for Dec. 6, 1942; Rice Papers, box #27.
19. Ibid., Nov. 22, 1942.
20. Ibid., April 11 and August 8, 1943.
21. Ibid., April 11, 1943, April 15, 1945 and June 10, 1945.
22. Ibid., Sept. 19, 1943.
23. Ibid., Apr. 22, 1945.
24. Ibid., July 25, 1943.
25. Ibid., Nov. 28, 1943.
26. Ibid., Feb. 20, 1944.
27. Ibid., March 11, 1945.
28. Ibid., Aug. 12, 1945.
29. Ibid., June 14, 1942.
30. Ibid., Jan. 30, 1944.
31. Ibid., Oct. 1, 1944.
32. Ibid., Nov. 22, 1942, June 6 and 20, 1943, Aug. 14 and Nov. 26, 1944.
33. Ibid., Sept 24, 1944.
34. Ibid., Aug. 5, 1944.
35. Ibid., Jan. 14, 1945.
36. Ibid., March 17, 1944 and May 13, 1945.
37. Ibid., Nov. 19, 1944.
38. Author's interview with Rice, Marci 23, 1982.
39. Rice Papers, box #12.
40. Ibid.
41. Ibid.
42. Author's interview with Rice, March 23, 1982.
43. In a fascinating epilogue to the SGHOTPA affair, Hovde was nominated in 1949 to become president of Queens College in New York, but was vetoed Mayor O'Dwyer under pressure from the conservative

Catholic *Brooklyn Tablet* because of Hovde's alleged left-wing and anti-Catholic affiliations. Rice, then at the height of his anticommunist crusading, took time out to defend Hovde and attack the *Brooklyn Tablet* — to no avail.

44. The official story at the time had it that Zimmerman resigned in order to take a full time job with the OPA, but a curious memo from Rice a few months later alleged that Zimmerman "was successfully sabotaged and railroaded into [the] Army by certain elements who tried to smear him as a Communist, which charge was untrue" (Rice Papers, box #21).

45. Rice Papers, box #11.

46. Ibid.

47. Ibid.

48. Author's interview with Rice, March 23, 1982.

49. Rice to Guffey, June 1, 1942; Rice Papers, box #21.

50. Rice Papers, ibid. This memo also contains the reference to Zimmerman's having been "railroaded."

51. Author's interview with Rice, March 23, 1982. David J. O'Brien, in *American Catholics and Social Reform; The New Deal Years* (Oxford University Press, 1968), p. 55, points out several other examples of priests who were New Dealers, including John A. Ryan on the NRA Industrial Appeal Board and Francis Haas on the National Labor Board and the Labor Advisory Board of the WPA.

52. Tally McKee, "Radical for Christ," *Catholic Digest*, June 1946, p. 56.

53. Graves to Casgrain, June 9, 1942; Rice Papers, box #21.

54. Rice Papers, box #16.

55. Author's interview with Rice, March 23, 1982.

56. Rice Papers, box #21.

57. Ibid. It is of course possible that Guffey's assessment of Rice's committee was drawn from Rice's own memo or talks with Rice.

58. Ibid.

59. Ibid.

60. *Pittsburgh Press*, Aug. 4, 1942.

61. Rice to Murray, Aug 10, 1942; Rice Papers, box #16.

62. Rice Papers, box #21.

63. *Labor Today*, Nov. 26, 1943.

64. Rice Papers, box #21.

65. Author's interview with Rice, March 23, 1982.

66. Rice correspondence with Murray, 1941–46, Rice Papers, box #16.

67. Author's interview with Rice, March 23, 1982.

67a. "After she died it all came together. Undoubtedly ____-____ [Unnamed OPA official] gave her some small break and she was mistakenly grateful to me. I met ____-____ years later and found this out. At the time, I didn't know it, you see." Author's interview with Rice, July 1, 1983.

68. Ibid., July 1, 1983.

69. Rice Papers, box #14a.

70. Ibid. Note the critique by Douglas P. Seaton (discussed in the next chapter) that Catholic "labor priests" in fact displayed their false colors when they ended up becoming arbitrators who were not unacceptable to management (Seaton, *Catholics and Radicals* [Bucknell University Press: 1981]).

71. Author's interview with Rice, May 21, 1983.

72. Ibid.

73. Ibid.
74. Proceedings in Rice Papers, box #14a. Carolyn Burkhart is referred
to in some of the records as Alice Burkhart; subsequently her last name
appears as "Hart." Years later she would be expelled from the CPUSA
(*Daily Worker*, Aug. 1, 1948).
75. In UE File on Rice, Hillman Library Special Collections.
76. Rice Papers, box #14a.
77. Author's interview with Rice, May 21, 1983.
78. Ibid.
79. Sigmund Diamond, article on James Carey and the FBI, forthcoming
in a festschrift for Professor Yeshoshua Arieli of the Hebrew University in
Jerusalem.
80. Michael Harrington, "Catholics in the Labor Movement: A Case
History," *Labor History*, I:3 (Fall 1960), pp. 257–58.
81. FBI file on Charles Owen Rice, obtained by Rice through the
Freedom of Information Act and kept in Rice's personal papers.
82. Author's interview with Rice.
83. FBI file on Rice.
84. Rice Papers, box #10.
85. Ibid.
86. Ibid.
87. *Pittsburgh Post Gazette*, Feb. 26, 1946.
88. Rice Papers, box #10.
89. *Pittsburgh Post Gazette*, April 12, 1946.
90. Rice Papers, box #10.
91. Ibid.
92. Interview with Ronald L. Filippelli, The Pennsylvania State University United Steelworkers of America Oral History Project, April 5, 1967, p. 6.
93. Ibid.
94. Rice Papers, box #10.
95. *Pittsburgh Post Gazette*, Oct. 5, 1946.
96. Ibid., Oct. 14, 15 and 16, 1946.
97. Ibid., Oct. 18, 1946.
98. Ibid., Oct. 21, 1946.
99. Rice Papers, box #10.
100. Author's interview with Rice, Nov. 27, 1981. Rice's friend at
WWSW, manager Frank Smith, also left around this time, so that Rice was
put, in his own words, "under a blanket."
101. Author's interview with Rice, Nov. 27, 1981.
102. Rice Papers, box #21.
103. *Pittsburgh Press*, Oct. 29, 1946.
104. Author's interview with Rice, March 23, 1982.

Chapter Four

1. David Caute, *The Great Fear: The Anti-Communist Purge Under Truman and Eisenhower* (New York: Simon and Schuster, 1979).
2. Ibid., pp. 17–18.
3. Ibid., pp. 217–219.
4. Ibid., p. 185.
5. Ibid., p. 54.

6. Ibid., pp. 17, 21.

7. Ibid., p. 216.

8. Ronald Schatz interview with Rice, May 10, 1977, quoted in his *The Electrical Workers* (University of Illinois Press, 1983), p. 183.

9. See, for example, his column in the *Pittsburgh Catholic*, Nov. 30, 1961.

10. Author's interview with Rice, March 23, 1982.

11. Religious News Service News Release, October 15, 1938. Rice Papers, box #11a.

12. Author's interview with Rice, March 23, 1982.

13. *Labor Leader*, March 14, 1938.

14. Author's interview with Rice, March 23, 1982.

15. Ibid., March 24, 1982.

16. Ibid., March 23, 1982. and Filippelli interview, April 5, 1968, pp. 2–4.

17. *Labor Leader*, Jan. 10, 1945, and July 21, 1949.

18. Author's interview with Rice, May 21, 1983.

19. Ibid., March 24, 1982.

20. Daniel Guerin, *100 Years of Labor in the U.S.A.* (London: Ink Links, 1979), pp. 173–74.

21. Author's interview with Rice, March 24, 1982.

22. An interesting example of this support came in 1945 when Murray issued an attack on Spain's Franco for his suppression of labor unions. Despite considerable support by the American Catholic hierarchy for Franco, Rice defended Murray's position. See his broadcast, Dec. 10, 1945.

23. Rice Papers, box #16.

24. Ibid.

25. Author's interview with Rice, May 21, 1983.

26. *Pittsburgh Catholic*, April 1, 1948.

27. Author's interview with Rice, June 7, 1983.

28. Ibid.

29. *Pittsburgh Catholic*, April 1, 1948.

30. Ibid., April 8, 1948.

31. Ibid., April 15, 1948.

32. *New York Herald Tribune*, Jan. 30, 1966.

33. *Pittsburgh Catholic*, April 22, 1948.

34. Author's interview with Rice, June 7, 1983.

35. *Pittsburgh Catholic*, Sept. 16, 1948.

36. Ibid., Aug. 26. 1948.

37. Ibid., Jan. 13, 1949.

38. *Daily Worker*, April 21, 1949, p. 10.

39. Author's interview with Rice, June 7, 1983.

40. Rice Papers, box #18.

41. Ibid.

42. Ibid.

43. Author's interview with Rice, June 7, 1983.

44. "An American Inquisition," ABC News Closeup, June 23, 1983.

45. Rice Papers, box #21.

46. *Pittsburgh Catholic*, July 22, 1948.

47. Ibid., Sept. 9, 1948.

48. Rice Papers, box #21.

49. Ibid., box #25.

50. Author's interview with Rice, March 24, 1982.

51. Ibid.

52. *Labor Leader*, April 30, 1947.

53. Ibid., July 25, 1947.

54. Michael Harrington, "Catholics in the Labor Movement: A Case History," *Labor History*, I:3 (Fall 1960), p. 239.

55. FBI file on Rice, obtained by the author through an FOIA request. While Rice himself had obtained portions of his file through a similar request, by the time I was reviewing it, numerous pages seemed to be unaccountably missing. My own request to the FBI for the portion of his file prior to 1966, for which Rice gave his consent, resulted in the receipt of 13 file pages, along with notification that 42 other pages had been withheld, and one entry on Rice destroyed by the Bureau in 1958. Hence the conclusions to be drawn from this source must be tentative, a fact complicated by Rice's own inability or reluctance to recall certain events from this chapter in his life.

56. Ibid.

57. Rice's FBI dossier, Sept. 26, 1947, as reported by Sigmund Diamond, article on James Carey and the FBI, forthcoming in a festschrift for Professor Yeshoshua Arieli of the Hebrew University in Jerusalem.

58. Michael Harrington, *Catholics*, p. 259. See also Sigmund Diamond.

59. *Pittsburgh Catholic*, Oct. 2, 1941. Rice's hounding of Bridges was so continual that it led me to ask him (June 7, 1983) whether he had ever cooperated in bringing federal charges against Bridges. His answer: "The FBI was after Bridges anyhow; they didn't need me."

60. Ibid., Feb. 26, 1942.

61. Ibid., May 21, 1942.

62. Ibid., June 25, 1942.

63. Ibid., Sept. 25, 1947.

64. Ibid., Nov. 20, 1947. The statement was viewed by the UE leadership and local 601 as proof of Rice's antilabor animus.

65. Ibid., Oct. 2, 1947.

66. Ibid., Oct. 23, 1947.

67. Ibid., Nov. 13, 1947. He would continue to plug Riesel's column; e.g., Feb. 17, 1949; Oct. 13, 1949; Dec. 1, 1949.

68. Ibid., Aug. 23, 1947.

69. Ibid., Nov. 27, 1947.

70. Ibid., Dec. 11, 1947.

71. Ibid., Sept. 4, 1947.

72. Author's interview with Rice, March 24, 1982.

73. *Pittsburgh Catholic*, Dec. 18, 1947.

74. Ibid., Dec. 25, 1947.

75. Ibid., Jan. 29, 1948; Feb. 25, 1948; Sept 9, 1948; Oct. 11, 1948.

76. Ibid., Nov. 11 and 18, 1948.

77. Ibid., April 29, 1948; June 17, 1948; Nov. 11, 1948.

78. Ibid., Aug. 26, 1948.

79. Ibid., Oct. 14, 1948.

80. Ibid., Sept. 30, 1948.

81. Ibid., Oct. 7 and 14, Nov. 4, Dec. 16 and 23, 1948.

82. Ibid., Aug. 12, 1948, and March 25, 1949.

83. Ibid., Mar. 11, 1948; June 2, July 28, and Nov. 10, 1949.

84. Ibid., May 13, 1948.

85. Ibid., Jan. 13, Dec. 1, Dec. 8, 1949.

86. Ibid., Aug. 11, 1949.

87. Ibid., Oct. 20, 1949.

88. Ibid., Dec. 12, 1949.

89. Ibid., Oct. 20, 1949.

90. Broadcast, June 18, 1949.

91. Ibid., March 4, 1949.

92 James J. Matles and James Higgins, *Them and Us; Struggles of a Rank-and-File Union* (Englewood Cliffs, N.J.: Prentice-Hall, 1974), p. 52, and Schatz, *Electrical Workers*.

93. Matles and Higgins. *Them and Us*, pp. 103–104.

94. Ibid., pp. 131–133.

95. Ibid.

96. Ibid., p. 213. Michael Harrington comments that "the party-lining of many UE leaders was established beyond any doubt" ("Catholics"), p. 260.

97. Author's interview with Rice, March 24, 1983.

98. Ibid.

99. Matles and Higgins, *Them and Us*, p. 161.

100. *Pittsburgh Catholic*, Aug. 23, 1947.

101. Ibid., July 29, 1948.

102. Ibid., Jan. 29, 1948.

103. Ibid., Nov. 11, 1948.

104. Author's interview with Rice, March 24, 1982, and May 21, 1983.

105. *Pittsburgh Catholic*, Aug. 8 and 15, 1948, for example.

106. In correspondence with the director of a testimonial dinner for Murray in Harrisburg, Rice said, "I regard it as one of the high spots of my life that I was partaking in this magnificent testimonial to a great leader" (Rice Papers, box #16).

107. Matles and Higgins, *Them and Us*, pp. 192–94.

108. Ibid., p. 201.

109. Ibid., p. 193.

110. Ibid., pp. 188–90.

111. *Pittsburgh Catholic*, Dec. 18, 1947, and Jan. 1, 1948. Schatz argues convincingly that the Rank and File were little more than younger, less skilled workers anxious to enjoy the perquisites of union office — until Rice provided them with the leadership, the brains, and above all the anti-communist issue that would ultimately win out in Local 601. Schatz, *Electrical Workers* (n. 8, above), pp. 193–194. (Schatz mistakenly refers to Rice, who was a member of the diocesan clergy, as a Jesuit, p. 183.)

112. *Pittsburgh Catholic*, June 26, 1947.

113. Ibid., Oct. 30, 1947.

114. Ibid., Jan. 1 and Aug. 19, 1948.

115. Ibid., Jan. 15, 1948.

116. Ibid., Oct. 30, 1948.

117. Ibid., Jan. 20, 1948.

118. Ibid., Aug. 19, 1948.

119. Ibid., March 18, 1948.

120. Ibid., April 15, 1948.
121. Letter to the author, March 9, 1984.
122. Memorandum of UE District meeting Jan. 29 and Jan. 30, 1948.
123. "The Weigand Case," District 6, undated, p. 6.
124. *Pittsburgh Catholic*, June 3, Sept. 30 and Dec. 9, 1948.
125. Author's interview with Rice, March 24, 1982; see also Filippelli interview with Rice, April 5, 1968, (n. 16, above), p. 16.
126. FBI field report, quoted by Diamond.
127. *Pittsburgh Catholic*, April 22 and June 24, 1948.
128. Ibid., April 28 and Oct. 13, 1949.
129. Ibid., Dec. 9, 1948.
130. Ibid., Oct. 14, 1948; April 8, 1949; and Schatz, *Electrical Workers*, p. 210.
131. Author's interview with Rice, March 24, 1982.
132. "The Huntington Story," UE District 6, Jan. 3, 1949.
133. Ibid., p. 9.
134. *Pittsburgh Catholic*, Sept. 23 and Dec. 16, 1948.
135. *Pittsburgh Catholic*, April 8, 1949. Author's interview with Rice.
136. *The Worker*, April 10, 1949.
137. Ibid.
138. *Pittsburgh Catholic*, April 8, 1948.
139. *Saturday Evening Post*, July 15, 22, and 29, 1950.
140. Author's interview with Rice, June 29, 1983.
141. *Pittsburgh Catholic*, June 23, 1949.
142. Ibid., June 9, 1949.
143. "Trade Union Cannibalism," District 6, Jan. 20, 1949.
144. Harrington, "Catholics," pp. 250–52.
145. *Labor Leader*, Jan. 17, 1949.
146. *Pittsburgh Catholic*, Aug. 11, 1949.
147. UE Papers, Local 601, box #6.
148. "Congressman Admits Fr. Rice-ACTU Rank-and-File Planned Un-American Attack," District 6, Aug. 4, 1949.
149. "UE Pres. Fitzgerald Blasts Un-American Attack on UE," UE National Office, Aug. 3, 1949.
150. Letter to the author, March 9, 1984.
151. *Pittsburgh Catholic*, Aug. 18, 1949.
152. Ibid., Aug. 25, 1949.
153. Ibid., Sept. 22, 1949.
154. Matles and Higgins, *Them and Us*, p. 195.
155. James Caldwell Foster argues persuasively that the purges resulted in 1949 primarily from Murray's changing perceptions of the limits on acceptable political disagreement within the CIO (*The Union Politic; The CIO Political Action Committee* [University of Missouri Press, 1975], p. 93).
156. Matles and Higgins, *Them and Us*, p. 203.
157. *Pittsburgh Catholic*, Nov. 10, 1949.
158. Ibid., Nov. 17, 1949.
159. Ibid., Dec. 9, 1948.
160. Documents of UE 601 and District 6, from which this argument is abstracted, are in the collected papers of the UE at the University of Pittsburgh Archives of the Industrial Society, box #6. Included are a flier,

"A Dual Outside Movement," March 20, 1947; three pamphlets prepared in 1949: "The Weigand Case — According to ACTU Plan," "Trade Union Cannibalism," and an annotated (by UE 601) version of Rice's "How to Decontrol Your Union of Communists." Much the same critique informs attacks on Rice and the ACTU published in the CPUSA *Worker*, e.g., "Parish Census Bares ACTU 'Underground,'" Oct. 7, 1947, p. 5; "The Real Meddlers in CIO Unions," June 5, 1947; "ACTU Takes to Stormtrooping," June 16, 1948, p. 8; "Father Rice Dons Coughlin's Mantle," Jan. 30, 1949, p. 7; and "ACTU Ignores Pay Proposals at Westinghouse UE Meeting," March 3, 1949. A lecture on ACTU contained in *Pravda* in 1950 and excerpted in translation in *Labor Leader*, Sept. 30, 1950 (Don Capellano Column), argued that the ACTU was most active in progressive unions, least so in reactionary ones, and had as its objective the weakening of the labor class — the only class that might effectively oppose the forces of reactionism (government and hierarchy) then pushing the Marshall Plan. See also Daniel Guerin, *100 Years* (n. 20, above).

161. Author's interview with Rice, June 7, 1983.
162. Rice Papers.
163. Author's interview with Rice, June 7, 1983.
164. Harrington, "Catholics," pp. 259–60.
165. Author's interview with Rice, June 7, 1983.
166. *The Worker*, Jan. 30, 1947, p. 7.
167. *Labor Leader*, Dec. 22, 1949.
168. *Pittsburgh Catholic*, Jan. 27, 1949.
169. Letter from WWSW station manager, Rice Papers, box #28.
170. Author's interview with Rice, June 7, 1983.
171. *The Worker*, Jan. 6, 1949, p. 7.
172. Ibid., June 16, 1948, p. 8.
173. Letter from Charles Newell to Bishop Boyle, Rice Papers, box #8.
174. George Morris, "'Parish Census' Bares ACTU Underground", *Daily Worker*, Oct. 7, 1947, p. 5.
175. "The Huntington Story," UE Papers, box #6.
176. *The Worker*, Oct. 7, 1947, p. 5.
177. Douglas P. Seaton, *Catholics and Radicals* (Bucknell University Press, 1981), passim. Despite his generally thorough documentation throughout, Seaton makes two unsupported statements about Rice, which turn out to be false. One is that Rice was a member of the Pennsylvania State Labor Relations Board (pp. 142, 174); in fact, Rice did not serve on that body, although he did a fair amount of labor arbitration over the years. The other, more interesting, allegation (p. 120) is that Rice was the pseudonymous "Don Capellano" whose column ran in the *Labor Leader* from 1943 to 1951. Rice has flatly denied this (Author's interview with Rice, June 7, 1983). There seems little reason why he would wish to deny this report if true, and close reading of the column suggests that the author (if there were only one) lived in New York City rather than Pittsburgh.
178. Author's interview with Rice, June 7, 1983.
179. Charles E. Curran, *American Catholic Social Ethics: Twentieth-Century Approaches* (University of Notre Dame Press, 1982), p. 171.
180. Matles and Higgins, *Them and Us*, p. 258.

Chapter Five

1. William Serrin, *New York Times*, June 7, 1982, p. A–16.
2. See *Time*, March 14, 1949, pp. 63–64 and March 21, 1949, p. 68.
3. Douglas P. Seaton (*Catholics and Radicals* [Bucknell University Press, 1981] pp. 244–45) in fact uses this incident as the epitaph for an ACTU which he believes had by now lost all credibility.
4. Serrin, n. 1, above. This version of the story shows up time and again, for example, in the *New York Times*, Jan. 10, 1970, p. 20; in Rice's autobiographical manuscript (unpublished); in an interview with Rev. Thomas E. Blantz C.S.C., 1977 (unpublished); in Rice's interviews with me, March 23, 1982; in the *National Catholic Reporter*, Sept. 3, 1982, pp. 1 and 8; in *The Chicago Tribune*, Aug. 31, 1986.
5. *Pittsburgh Catholic*, March 10, 1949.
6. Despite a search through the massive Rice Papers, neither Rice nor I nor any other researcher I know has been able to come up with the alleged quote. See my letter to Rice, Sept. 8, 1982, and Rice's letter to me, Nov. 23, 1982. Rice associate and later director of organizing for AFL-CIO, Alan Kistler, says he remembers Rice making the remark but cannot recall where or when (my interview with Kistler, March 1, 1984). It should be noted that Rice has continued to repeat this story for years after it was revealed to be without a basis in the record.
7. Author's interview with Rice, March 23, 1982.
8. Ibid.
9. Broadcast, July 1, 1951.
10. In a broadcast Nov. 30, 1952, he noted that he had been living at St. Brigid's for a year and a half.
11. Ibid.
12. Author's interview with Rice, March 23, 1982.
13. *Pittsburgh Catholic*, May 8, 1952.
14. Author's interview with Rice, March 23, 1982.
15. *Pittsburgh Catholic*, June 12, 1952.
16. Author's interview with Rice, March 23, 1982.
17. *Pittsburgh Catholic*, Aug. 21 through Dec. 18, 1952. Virtually every week's column had Rice's reports on developments at Liberty.
18. Ibid., Aug. 21, 1952.
19. Ibid., Sept. 18, 1952.
20. See Correspondence, "Dearden," in Rice's private papers at St. Anne's.
21. See n. 4, above.
22. Author's interview with Rice, March 23, 1982.
23. Rice, who regarded Murray as one of the few great men and teachers he had met in his lifetime, would attempt both a book and a film on Murray's life, neither of which came to fruition (my interview with Rice, March 23, 1982 and Rice Papers, box #16).
24. Ibid. Rice in his autobiographical manuscript referred to Dearden as a "rigid and cold-blooded bishop."
25. Broadcast, Aug. 27, 1950.
26. See Steve Nelson, James R. Barrett and Rob Ruck, *Steve Nelson,*

American Radical (University of Pittsburgh Press, 1981), pp. 298–340.
  27. Rice Papers, box #17.
  28. *Pittsburgh Catholic*, Jan. 17, 1952. See also Nelson et al., *Steve Nelson*, pp. 303–304.
  29. Letter to Edward J. McHale, March 12, 1953; Rice papers, box #17.
  30. Broadcast, Feb. 22, 1953.
  31. Ibid., Nov. 11, 1945.
  32. Ibid., June 7, 1953.
  33. Ibid., June 21, 1953.
  34. *Valley Daily News*, Dec. 11, 1953.
  35. Rice Papers, box #15.
  36. Broadcast, July 26, 1953.
  37. Author's interview with Rice, March 23, 1982.
  38. Ibid.
  39. Ibid.
  40. Ibid.
  41. Rice Papers, box #25.
  42. Author's interview with Rice, March 23, 1982.
  43. Letter to the author, March 22, 1984.
  44. Author's interview with Rice, March 23, 1982.
  45. Rice Papers, box #28.
  46. Author's interview with Rice, March 23, 1982.
  47. Ibid.
  48. Broadcast, Jan. 25, 1959.
  49. Author's interview with Rice, March 23, 1982.
  50. Ibid., March 24, 1982.
  51. The first "Charles Owen Rice Column" appeared in the *Pittsburgh Catholic* on April 9, 1959.
  52. Rice Papers, box #24.
  53. Ibid.
  54. Ibid.
  55. Ibid.
  56. Ibid., box #17.
  57. Ibid., box #25.
  58. Ibid., box #24.
  59. Ibid., box #15.
  60. Ibid., box #25.
  61. Author's interview with Rice, March 24, 1982.
  62. Rice Papers, box #14a.
  63. Ibid., box #24.
  64. Broadcast, June 4, 1964.
  65. Rice Papers, box #15.
  66. Rice Papers, box #19.
  67. Ibid.
  68. Author's interview with Rice, June 7, 1983.
  69. Rice Papers, box #13.
  70. *Pittsburgh Catholic*, May 7, 1964.
  71. Rice Papers, box #13.
  72. Ibid.
  73. *Pittsburgh Catholic*, March 25, 1965.

74. Ibid., July 17, 1964.
75. Author's interview with Rice, June 10, 1983; *Pittsburgh Catholic,* March 25, 1965.
76. Author's interview with Rice, March 24, 1964.
77. *Pittsburgh Catholic,* Nov. 12, 1964.
78. See letter of Anthony Venneri, President, USWA Local #1904, to *Pittsburgh Catholic* editor, Jan. 7, 1965.
79. *Pittsburgh Catholic,* Nov. 26, 1964; Jan. 14, 1965; Feb. 18, 1965.
80. Ibid., May 27, 1965.
81. Rice Papers, box #23.
82. Ibid., box #25.
83. Ibid.
84. *Pittsburgh Catholic,* May 7, 1959; Aug. 31, 1961; Nov. 30, 1961. The last of these, a eulogy of John Duffy after his premature death when he, his wife, and one of their five children perished on a Los Angeles highway, contained Rice's revelation that Philip Murray had financed Duffy's years of anticommunism in UE District 6.
85. Michael Harrington, "Catholics in the Labor Movement; A Case History," *Labor History,* I:3 (Fall 1960), pp. 231–63.
86. *Pittsburgh Catholic,* May 7, 1959.
87. Ibid., Dec. 20, 1962.
88. Ibid., March 20, 1952.
89. Ibid., Sept. 19, 1963.
90. Ibid., March 11, 1965.
91. Ibid., Feb. 18, 1960.
92. Broadcast, Jan. 23, 1960.
93. *Pittsburgh Catholic,* May 5, 1960.
94. C. Wright Mills, *The Power Elite* (Oxford University Press, 1956). See also G. William Domhoff, *Who Rules America?* (Prentice-Hall, 1967), and other works cited by Domhoff.
95. *Pittsburgh Catholic,* Oct. 8, 1959.
96. Ibid., Feb. 8, 1962.
97. Ibid.
98. Ibid., Aug. 9, 1962.
99. Ibid., Aug. 13, 1964.
100. Ibid., Oct. 29, 1959.
101. Ibid., June 4, 1964.
102. John Deedy, "Crusader for Social Justice," *Ave Maria,* Oct. 5, 1963, p. 6.

Chapter Six

1. Broadcasts, Oct. 6 and 13, 1955.
2. Ibid., Sept. 29, 1957.
3. Ibid., Feb. 12, 1956; Sept. 7 and 21, 1958.
4. Author's interview with Rice, June 1, 1983. One night police officers there arrested a white girl for dating a black athlete and brought her to Rice on the miscalculated expectation that he would give her a sermon on the moral evil of interracial dating. Rice instead sermonized the surprised

officers to the effect that they should mind their own business. A delegation of black athletes later stopped by the rectory to thank him.

5. *Pittsburgh Catholic*, March 10, 1960; April 20, 1961; June 20, 1963.

6. Ibid., Feb. 21, 1963.

7. Ibid., May 23, 1963.

8. Ibid., Dec. 26, 1963.

9. Ibid., May 14, 1964.

10. Ibid.

11. Ibid., Dec. 26, 1963.

12. Author's interview with Rice, July 1, 1983.

13. "The innocence of U.S. Steel," *Commonweal*, July 24, 1964, pp. 505–506.

14. Rice Papers, box #17.

15. *Pittsburgh Catholic*, Dec. 16, 1965.

16. Author's interview with Rice, March 24, 1982.

17. Ibid., March 24, 1982, and June 10, 1983.

18. Ibid.

19. *Pittsburgh Catholic*, Jan. 20, 1966.

20. Ibid., May 15, 1966.

21. Ibid., Aug. 11, 1966.

22. Ibid., Sept. 15, 1966.

23. Ibid., Jan. 27, 1966.

24. Author's interview with Rice, April 10, 1983. See also *Pittsburgh Catholic*, March 24, 1966, and "The Bishop's Hair Shirt," *The Nation*, April 11, 1966, p. 411.

25. *Pittsburgh Catholic*, April 21, 1966.

26. Rice Papers, box #1.

27. *Pittsburgh Catholic*, Dec. 19, 1969, and author's interview with Rice, March 24, 1982.

28. Rice Papers, box #6.

29. Ibid., box #7.

30. Ibid., box #21.

31. Ibid., box #11.

32. Ibid.

33. Ibid., box #11a.

34. Ibid.

35. Ibid.

36. Ibid., boxes #11a and 11b.

37. Ibid., box #11a.

38. Ibid., boxes #16 and 17.

39. Ibid., box #17.

40. Author's interview with Rice, March 24, 1982.

41. Rice Papers, boxes #18 and #18a.

42. Ibid., box #20.

43. Ibid., box #11a.

44. Ibid., box #23.

45. Author's interviews with Rice, March 24, 1982 and June 10, 1983. See also Rice Papers, box #11a.

46. Ibid.

47. Ibid.

48. *Pittsburgh Post Gazette*, July 30, 1974 (published at the time of Haden's death).
49. Broadcast, Aug. 3, 1974.
50. Author's interview with Rice, March 14, 1982.
51. *Pittsburgh Catholic*, Jan. 19, 1967.
52. Ibid., May 4, 1967.
53. *Ave Maria*, May 29,1967, pp. 24–25.
54. *Pittsburgh Catholic*, Jan. 12, 1967.
55. Rice Papers, box #18b. Author's interview with Rice, June 10, 1983.
56. Rice Papers, box #18b.
57. Ibid., box #6.
58. *Pittsburgh Catholic* June 29, 1967.
59. Rice Papers, box #11a.
60. *Pittsburgh Catholic*, April 20, 1967.
61. Author's interview with Rice, March 24, 1982.
62. *Pittsburgh Catholic*, May 4, 1967.
63. Rice Papers, boxes #18b and #11a. Author's interviews with Rice, March 24, 1982, and June 10, 1983.
64. Ibid.
65. Ibid.
66. *Pittsburgh Catholic*, Aug. 31, 1967.
67. Ibid., March 30, 1967.
68. Rice Papers, box #7.
69. *Pittsburgh Catholic*, Nov. 1, 1968.
70. Ibid., Jan. 12, 1968.
71. Ibid., March 15, 1968.
72. Ibid., May 24, 1968.
73. Ibid., April 5, 1968.
74. *Pittsburgh Post Gazette*, April 10, 1968. Author's interviews with Rice, Mar. 24, 1982, and June 10, 1983.
75. *Pittsburgh Catholic*, April 12, 19, and 26, 1968.
76. Ibid., July 12, 1968.
77. Author's interviews with Rice, March 24, 1982 and June 10, 1983.
78. *Pittsburgh Catholic*, Oct. 18, 1968.
79. Ibid., Feb. 16, 1966.
80. *Pittsburgh Catholic*, June 28 and July 19, 1968; Olbum letter to the editor, July 12, 1968.
81. Ibid., Aug. 30, 1968.
82. Ibid., Oct. 18, 1968.
83. Author's interview with Rice, March 24, 1982.
84. Ibid.
85. *Pittsburgh Catholic*, Oct. 18, 1968 and Dec. 19, 1969.
86. *Pittsburgh Post Gazette*, Nov. 6 and 7, 1968.
87. *Pittsburgh Catholic*, July 11, 1969.
88. Rice Papers, box #11a.
89. Ibid., box #20.
90. Ibid., box #6.
91. Author's interview with Rice, March 24, 1982.
92. Ibid.
93. *Pittsburgh Catholic*, May 2, 1969.

94. Ibid., Sept. 19, 1969.
95. Ibid., Oct. 9, 1970.
96. *Pittsburgh Press*, Dec. 16, 1970.
97. *Pittsburgh Catholic*, Feb. 17, 1966.
98. Author's interview with Rice, March 24, 1982.
99. *Pittsburgh Catholic*, Aug. 15, 1969.
100. Ibid., Sept. 5, and 26, and Oct. 10, 1969.
101. Author's interview with Rice, March 24, 1982.
102. *Pittsburgh Catholic*, Sept. 5, 1969.
103. Ibid., Feb. 13, 1970.
104. Author's interviews with Rice, March 24, 1982 and June 10, 1983.
105. Rice's private papers at St. Anne's, Wright letter to Rice, May 24, 1968.
106. Ibid., Rice letter to Wright, May 28, 1968.
107. Ibid.
108.*Pittsburgh Catholic*, Feb. 13, 1970.
109. Rice's private papers at St. Anne's, Rice letter to Wright, May 22, 1968.
110. Author's interview with Rice, March 24, 1982.

Chapter Seven

1. Quoted by Bill Rodd in "Charles Rice — Priest and Politician," *Pittsburgh Forum*, April 30, 1971, p. 8.
2. Author's interview with Rice, March 24, 1982.
3. *Pittsburgh Catholic*, July 9, 1959.
4. Ibid., Aug. 25, 1960.
5. Ibid., Sept. 6, 1960.
6. Ibid., April 27, 1961.
7. Ibid., Oct. 5, 1961.
8. Ibid., May 7, 1964; March 25 and April 8, 1965.
9. Ibid., Feb. 6, 1964.
10. Broadcast, Jan. 23, 1960.
11. *Pittsburgh Catholic*, Jan. 26, 1961.
12. Author's interview with Rice, June 10, 1983.
13. *Pittsburgh Catholic*, Feb. 28, Oct. 31, 1963.
14. Ibid., Jan. 16, 1964.
15. Ibid., June 6, 1965.
16. Ibid., April 22, 1965.
17. Ibid., July 1, 1965.
18. Ibid., Sept. 30, 1965.
19. Ibid., Oct. 28, 1965.
20. Rice Papers, box #24.
21. *Pittsburgh Press*, March 27, 1966.
22. *Pittsburgh Post Gazette*, July 12, 1966.
23. Rice Papers, box #23.
24. *Pittsburgh Press*, Nov. 5, 1966.
25. Rice Papers, box #23.
26. Ibid.

27. Ibid.
28. Ibid.
29. *Pittsburgh Catholic*, Oct. 26, 1967.
30. Rice Papers, box #23.
31. Ibid.
32. Ibid.
33. *Pittsburgh Press*, Dec. 6, 1967.
34. FBI file on Rice, Dec. 8, 1967.
35. Ibid.
36. Rice Papers, box #9.
37. Ibid.
38. *Washington Post*, March 9, 1970.
39. Rice Papers, box #9.
40. Ibid.
41. Ibid.
42. Author's interview with Rice, March 24, 1982.
43. Rice Papers, box #23.
44. *Butler Eagle* (Butler, Pa.), March 10, 1967.
45. Rice Papers, box #23.
46. Author's interview with Rice, March 24, 1982.
47. E.g., *Pittsburgh Catholic*, Jan. 20, 1970.
48. Rice Papers, box #23.
49. Interview with Ronald L. Filippelli in the Penn State University United Steelworkers of America Oral History Project, Oct. 17, 1967. Quoted with permission.
50. Rice Papers, box #23.
51. Ibid.
52. FBI file on Rice, April 21, 1967.
53. Author's interview with Rice, March 24, 1982.
54. *Pittsburgh Catholic*, Dec. 6, 1967.
55. Rice to White (in Taiwan), Aug. 4, 1966; Rice Papers, box #23.
56. Author's interview with Rice, March 24, 1982. See also *Pittsburgh Catholic*, Aug. 9, 1967, Jan 2 and Feb. 12, 1971.
57. Author's interview with Rice, March 24, 1972.
58. Ibid., June 27, 1983.
59. *Newsday*, Aug. 29, 1967.
60. Rice FBI file.
61. Rice to NPAC, Oct. 7, 1971, Rice Papers, box #24.
62. Author's interview with Rice, March 24, 1982.
63. Ibid., June 27, 1983.
64. *Pittsburgh Catholic*, Jan 3, 1969.
65. Ibid., April 24, 1970.
66. Ibid., Sept. 6, 1968.
67. Ibid., Dec. 5, 1969.
68. Ibid., Nov. 3, 1967.
69. Ibid., Sept. 25, 1970.
70. Ibid., Aug. 7, 1970.
71. Ibid., Sept. 14, 1967.
72. He would briefly take up the notion again in 1985, when U.S. trade

losses prompted at least one sociologist to advocate similar industrial councils to make American industry more competitive (*Pittsburgh Catholic*, April 12, 1985).

73. Shaffer to Rice, Oct. 16, 1969; Rice to Shaffer, Oct. 17, 1969; Rice Papers, box #24.
74. *Pittsburgh Catholic*, Feb. 26, 1971.
75. Author's interview with Rice, March 24, 1982.
76. Bill Rodd, (n. 1, above), p. 7.
77. Author's interview with Rice, June 29, 1983.
78. Ibid.
79. *Pittsburgh Post Gazette*, April 7, 1971.
80. Rice Papers, box #18a.
81. *Pittsburgh Post Gazette*, March 18, 1971. See also FBI file on Rice, March 18, 1971.
82. Letter to campaign donor, Rice Papers, box #18a.
83. *Pittsburgh Catholic*, May 21, 1971.
84. Author's interview with Rice, March 24, 1982.

Chapter Eight

1. Author's interview with Rice, March 24, 1982.
2. *Pittsburgh Catholic*, May 7, 1976 and March 23, 1984.
3. Author's interview with Rice, July 1, 1983.
4. Rice Papers.
5. Author's interview with Rice, July 1, 1983.
6. Ibid., March 24, 1983. Cf. also *Pittsburgh Catholic*, May 7, 1976.
7. Matles, *Them and Us* (Chap. 4, n. 92), p. 259.
8. Rice Papers, box #8.
9. Ibid., box #22
10. E.g., *Pittsburgh Catholic*, Oct. 8, 1976.
11. Ibid., July 5, 1974.
12. *Blueprint* (newsletter of L. J. Twomey, S.J., New Orleans), Feb. 1977; in Rice Papers at St. Anne's.
13. Ibid.
14. Rice Papers at St. Anne's, newsclipping April 17, 1977.
15. Ibid., May 5, 1981.
16. Author's interview with Rice, July 1, 1983.
17. *Pittsburgh Catholic*, Aug. 2, 1974.
18. Ibid., Sept. 30, 1977.
19. Ibid., Nov. 2 and Dec. 28, 1979.
20. Ibid., Nov. 26, 1981.
22. Ibid., Dec. 28, 1984.
23. Ibid., Nov. 30, 1984.
24. Ibid., Jan. 3, 1986.
25. Ibid., Dec. 20, 1985.
26. Ibid., Dec. 12, 1980.
27. Rice autobiographical manuscript (unpublished).
28. *Pittsburgh Catholic*, April 2, 1971.
29. Ibid., May 9, 1975, and Feb. 11, 1977.
30. Ibid., May 9, 1975.

31. Ibid., April 5, 1974.
32. Ibid., May 9, 1975.
33. Ibid., Dec. 15, 1972.
34. Ibid., Feb. 9, 1973.
35. Ibid., Aug. 6, 1976.
36. Rice Papers at St. Anne's, newsclipping Nov. 13, 1980.
37. *Pittsburgh Catholic*, June 3, 1983.
38. Ibid., Sept. 14, 1984.
39. Ibid., Jan. 11, 1974.
40. Ibid.
41. Ibid., April 8, 1977.
42. Ibid., Dec. 14, 1979.
43. E.g., ibid., April 5, 1974.
44. Ibid., June 28, 1974.
45. Ibid., June 5, 1973.
46. Ibid., April 13, 1973.
47. Ibid., Jan. 21, 1977.
48. Ibid., April 13, 1977.
49. Ibid., Jan. 11, 1980.
50. Ibid., Jan 16, 1970.
51. Ibid., Nov. 17, 1970.
52. Ibid., April 23, 1976.
53. Ibid., March 25, 1977.
54. Author's interview with Rice, July 1, 1983.
55. Greeley in the National Catholic Review, Nov. 17, 1972; Rice, ibid., Dec. 22, 1972; and in the *Pittsburgh Catholic*, Feb. 2, 1973.
56. *Pittsburgh Catholic*, July 20, 1970.
57. Ibid., April 25, 1975.
58. Ibid., July 25, 1975.
59. Ibid., Sept. 12, 1980.
60. Ibid., April 9 and 16, 1976.
61. Greeley, ibid., Sept. 1981.
62. Ibid., Sept. 25, 1981.
63. Ibid., July 25, 1975.
64. Ibid., Jan. 14 and 21, 1983.
65. Author's interview with Rice, July 1, 1983.
66. *Pittsburgh Catholic*, March 24, 1982.
67. Ibid., Jan. 26, 1973.
68. Ibid., April 27, 1973.
69. Ibid., June 1, 1973.
70. Ibid., Aug. 3, 1973.
71. Ibid., Nov. 2, 1973.
72. Ibid., Aug. 30, 1974.
73. Ibid., Dec. 3, 1973.
74. Ibid., Oct. 11, 1974.
75. Ibid., April 8, 1980.
76. Ibid., Oct. 8, 1976.
77. Ibid., March 18 and June 3, 1977; June 2 and 16, 1978; Aug. 10, 1979; May 2, 1980.
78. Ibid., Nov. 11, 1980.

79. Ibid., March 6, 1987.
80. Ibid., Aug. 22, 1980.
81. Ibid., Sept. 26, 1980.
82. Ibid., April 4, 1980.
83. Ibid., Oct. 28, 1983.
84. Ibid., Jan. 13, 1984.
85. Ibid., Oct. 26, 1984.
86. Author's interview with Rice, March 24, 1982.
87. *Pittsburgh Catholic*, July 3, 1970.
88. Author's interview with Rice, June 29, 1983.
89. *Pittsburgh Catholic*, Nov. 17, 1980.
90. Ibid., May 8 and 15, and July 10, 1981. See also Nov. 28, 1980.
91. Ibid., March 15, 1985.
92. Author's interview with Rice, March 24, 1982.
93. *Pittsburgh Post Gazette*, April 27, 1981, p. 5.
94. *Pittsburgh Catholic*, Jan. 13, 1978.
95. Ibid., Jan. 6, 1978.
96. Ibid., Jan. 13, 1978.
97. Rice Papers, "Prison Correspondence," passim.
98. *Pittsburgh Catholic*, March 28, 1975.
99. Ibid., April 6, 1979.
100. Ibid., Jan. 6, 1978.
101. Author's interview with Rice, March 14, 1982.
102. *Pittsburgh Catholic*, Feb. 28, 1975.
103. Ibid., March 9, 1974; July 9, 1976.
104. Ibid., Oct. 22 and Dec. 24, 1976; June 8, 1979.
105. Ibid., Jan. 11, 1980.
106. Author's interview with Rice, July 1, 1983.
107. Rice Papers at St. Anne's, newsclippings, 1974–80.
108. *Pittsburgh Catholic*, May 13, 1983.
109. Ibid., Mar. 22, 1985.
110. Author's interview with Rice, March 24, 1983.
111. Ronald L. Filippelli interview with Rice, Penn State University, United Steelworkers of America Oral History Project, Oct. 17, 1967.
112. *Pittsburgh Catholic*, Dec. 8, 1972.
113. Ibid., May 27, 1977.
114. Ibid., Feb. 20, 1987.
115. Ibid., May 22, 1981.
116. Ibid., Nov. 27, 1981; Jan. 22, 1982.
117. Ibid., Aug. 6 and Sept. 3, 1981.
118. Ibid., March 28, 1980.
119. Ibid., July 18, 1980.
120. Ibid., Sept. 3, 1982.
121. Ibid., May 6, 1983.
122. Ibid., June 10, 1983.
123. Ibid., June 17, 1983.
124. Ibid., May 18, 1984.
125. Ibid., May 25 and Nov. 16, 1984.
126. Ibid.
127. Ibid., Jan. 18, 1985.

128. Ibid., Jan. 25, 1985.
129. Ibid., March 1, 1985.
130. Ibid., Sept. 13, 1985.
131. Ibid., Jan. 18, 1980.
132. Ibid., Sept. 5, 1986.
133. Ibid., April 4, 1986.
134. Ibid., Oct. 17, 1986.
135. Ibid., July 23, 1982.
136. Ibid., Dec. 13, 1981.
137. Ibid., April 15, 1983.
138. Ibid.
139. Ibid., Jan. 4, 1985.
140. Ibid., Oct. 12, 1984.
141. Ibid., April 18, 1986.
142. Ibid.
143. Ibid.

Chapter Nine

1. *Pittsburgh Catholic*, April 24, 1981.
2. Ibid., Nov. 29, 1985.
3. Robert Cunnane, in *Witness of the Berrigans* eds. Stephen Halpert and Tom Murray (Doubleday, 1972), p. 49.
4. Pope Pius IX, *"Syllabus Errorum,"* in *Church and State through the Centuries*, eds. Sidney Z. Ehler and John Morrall (London: Burns and Oates, 1954), p. 285.
5. See Thomas T. McAvoy, *The Americanist Heresy in Roman Catholicism* (Notre Dame, Indiana; University of Notre Dame Press, 1963).

Index

A-bomb, 73, 109, 143, 154, 207
ABC television, 103
Abel, I. W., 151–152, 181
Abortion, 217, 232–234, 239, 260, 280
Abraham Lincoln Brigade, 202, 228
ACTION Housing, Inc., 174, 175, 181–182
Adult Education Institute, 140, 146
Agnew, Spiro T., 212, 238
Aggiornamento, 147
Alinsky, Saul, 103, 189, 249
Allegheny County Democratic Party, 30
Allegheny County Prison Board, 246
Allegheny Regional Planning Commission, 245
Allegheny-Ludlum Steel, 145
Allende, Salvador, 218
Allis-Chalmers, 114, 119
Amalgamated Meatcutters Local, 46
American Arbitration Association, 82, 145, 152
American Civil Liberties Union, 36, 112, 228, 233, 277
American Federation of Labor [AFL], 86, 88, 97–98, 112–113, 129–130, 191, 213, 269
American League Against War and Fascism, 48
Americanism, 276
Americans for Democratic Action [ADA], 149
Anticommunism, 49, 57, 63, 65, 70, 93, 100, 102–127, 144, 227, 229, 263
Anti-Semitism, 17, 35, 53, 69, 73
Anti-war movement, 267
Arbitration, 83
Association of Catholic Trade Unionists [ACTU], 45, 50–51, 93, 99, 105–108, 111, 117–121, 123, 126–133, 137, 141, 144, 148, 152–153, 231, 265
Atlantic City, 97
Atomic Energy Commission, 111
Ave Maria, 156

Ballinger, Amy, 83
Bassompierre, Paul, 231

Barr, Joseph, 171, 181, 192
Bay of Pigs, 201
Begler, Sam, 83, 231
Belloc, Hilaire, 39
Bellurgan, 8–14, 16
Berdyaev, Nicholas, 39
Bernardin, Cardinal, 252
Berrigan, Daniel, 272–273, 275
Berrigan, Philip, 272–273, 275
Berrigans, 236, 240
Bevilacqua, Anthony, 234, 251
Bilbo, Theodore, 34
Birmingham, Alabama, 170
Birth control, 147, 178, 232, 237
Black Construction Coalition, 192–193
Black Panthers, 174, 269
Black Power Center, 188, 190
Blanshard, Paul, 4, 5–6, 7–9, 276, 277
Blawnox, Pa., 143
Bloy, Leon, 39
Bonus March, 66
Boyle, Hugh C., 23, 60, 72, 78–79, 90, 132, 136, 142
Boyle, A. W. "Tony", 235–236
Bridges, Harry, 98, 101, 104, 108, 111
Brooklyn Tablet, 144
Brooks, Daniel, 80
Brotherhood of Locomotive Engineers, 107
Brotherhood of Sleeping Car Porters, 183
Browder, Earl, 94, 108
Brown, 168
Brown, H. Rap, 205, 216
Buckley, William, 182
Buddhists, 202
Burkhart, Carolyn, 83–85, 131–132
Burkhart, Logan, 83

Cambodia, 212
Capital punishment, 245, 260
Capitalism, 25, 31, 35, 40, 44–45, 68–69, 110–111, 154, 267, 268–269, 277, 279
Carabanchel Ten, 228
Carey, James B., 85, 113–114, 125–126, 127

Carlin, Henry, 170–171, 225
Carmichael, Stokely, 168, 172, 176, 182
Carnegie Hall, 121–122, 207
Carroll, Sr. Elizabeth, 234
Carson, Sir Edward, 11
Carter, Jimmy, 239
Casgrain, A. E., 79–80
Castle Shannon, Pa., ix, 227, 276
Castro, Fidel, 153, 201
Catholic Interracial Council, 174, 183,
  189, 193
Catholic Radical Alliance, [CRA], x,
  xii, 40, 43, 45–50, 52–54, 55, 57–65,
  68–69, 72, 89, 90, 98, 105, 120, 139,
  146, 199, 231, 248, 265, 274
Catholic University of America, 42
Catholic Worker, The, 24, 38, 43, 50, 55,
  60, 64, 152–153
Catholic Worker Movement, xiii, 35,
  37, 40, 45, 50, 53–54, 57, 58–61, 64,
  67–68, 139, 231, 263, 267, 273
Caute, David, 92–93
Central America, 235, 239–240
Central Intelligence Agency [CIA],
  130, 219, 240
Chavez, Cesar, 226, 235
Chessman, Caryl, 154
Chesterton, Gilbert, 39
Chicago Seven, 267
Chile, 218
China, 66, 204
Christian Brothers, 1
Christian Front, 35
Christian Left, 96
Church in the Modern World, 210
Churchill, Winston, 116
CIO Political Action Committee, 109,
  117
Citizens Against Slum Housing
  [CASH], 174
Civil disobedience, 267
Civil rights, 112, 152, 193–196, 267
Civil Service, 79
Civil Service Commission, 79
Class warfare, 26
Cleveland, 207, 212
Cold War, 92, 116, 201
Coleman, James, 237
Collective bargaining, 31
Collins, John, 231
Colodny, G. Robert, 202
Cominfil, 85
Committee to Defend America
  by Aiding the Allies, 63
Commonweal, 24, 37, 156, 170
Communism, 60–61, 78, 89, 102–105,
  133–135, 153, 154, 156
Communist Party, 32, 59, 85, 266
Communist Party of Italy, 96
Communist Party, U.S.A.
  [CPUSA], 92–93, 96, 99–101,
  107–108, 111, 113, 115, 121–122,
  131–132, 142, 217, 228–229
Communists, 84–86, 92, 96–97,
  101–105, 106, 108–120, 127, 137, 144,
  146
Community Action Against Poverty
  [CAP], 174, 176, 180–181
Congress of Industrial Organizations
  [CIO], x, xii, 17, 35, 41, 42, 48, 49,
  68–69, 80, 85, 86, 88, 97–101, 104,
  108–110, 112–117, 119, 123, 124–131,
  133, 229, 260, 268–269, 270–271, 272
Connolly, James, 12–13
Conscientious objection, 208, 211
Constantine, 278
Copeland, Charles, 124
Coraopolis, Pa., 83
Coughlin, Charles E., 35, 36, 48, 51,
  131, 231, 272
Council on Race and Religion, 196
Cox, James R., 41–42, 48, 51, 55, 184,
  272
Crucible Steel, 249
Cuba, 153, 201, 203
Curran, Joseph, 100, 109, 127
Cvetic, Matt, 122–123, 143
Czechoslovakia, 96, 218

Daily Worker, The, 32, 94, 101
Davis Act, 76
Davis, Rennie, 205, 216
Day, Dorothy, xiii, 37, 50, 54, 56, 59,
  60–62, 64, 65, 72, 139, 211, 231,
  273–274
Dearden, John, x, 136, 138–139,
  141–142, 147, 171, 232
Deedy, John, 156
Dellinger, David, 205, 216
Demilitarized zone [DMZ], 200, 203
Democratic Party, 197, 214
Denominational Ministry
  Strategy/Network [DMS/Network],
  249–250, 268
Depression, 29–30, 32–34, 43, 67–68, 71
De Valera, Eamon, 74, 241
Development of Peoples, 210
Devlin, Bernadette, 241
Dewey, John, 32
Diem, Ngo Dinh, 200–203
Dien Bien Phu, 200
Dies Committee, 99, 113

Dietz, Raymond, 41, 272–273
Distributism, 39
Dominican Republic, 203
Domino theory, 203
Donelli, Buff, 23
Dostoyevski, Fyodor, 39
Dow Chemical, 207
Draft, 215
Draft resistance, 208–209, 268
Dresden, 73
Duffy, John, 106, 108, 114–115, 117, 118–121, 123, 124, 126, 127, 128, 129, 130
Duggan, Robert, 187
Dulles, John Foster, 200
Dundalk, Ireland, 13–14, 16
Duquesne Light, 86–88, 90, 154
Duquesne University, xiv, 21–23, 42, 102, 105, 136, 138–139, 140, 189, 212
Durkin, James, 100–101, 103, 274

Eby, Kermit, 131
Eight-hour day, 269
Eisenhower, Dwight D., 142, 200–201
El Salvador, 240, 243
Elitist School, 155
Eminent domain, 269, 270
Emspak, Frank, 98, 113, 118
End Poverty in California (EPIC), 33
Equal Rights Amendment (ERA), 67, 232–234
Erie, Pa., 114, 120, 123
Evans, George E., 76
Executive Order 9835, 116

Fair Rent Committee, 76–78, 80–81
Fairmont, W. Va., 114, 120, 123, 127
Farm Equipment (FE), 109, 126, 132
Farm-Holiday Association, 33
Farm-Labor Political, 33
  Federation, 32
Farm workers, 234
Farmer-Labor Party, 33
Fascism, 95
FBI file on Rice, 85, 261
Federal Bureau of Investigation [FBI], 84–86, 93, 106–107, 112, 117, 122, 132, 167, 174, 197, 208, 229, 243–244, 261
Federal Law Enforcement Assistance Administration [LEAA], 245–46
Ferlo, Jimmy, 202
Ferraro, Geraldine, 234
Fiok, Judge, 191
Fitzgerald, Albert, 100, 113, 118, 125, 227–228

Fitzpatrick, Mike, 117, 118, 124
Fitzpatrick, Thomas, 107, 117, 122
Flaherty, Pete, 246
Flournoy, Nick, 189, 196
Ford Foundation, 174
Ford, Gerald, 238
Fordham University, 138
Forever Action Together [FAT], 174, 185–186, 189
FORWARD, Grassroots, 174
France, 92
Franco, Francisco, 228
Freedom of Information Act, 243
Free Speech Movement, 155
Furfey, Paul H., 39, 53

Gallagher, Dan, 140
General Electric, 113, 240
General Motors, 113
Geneva Accords, 200, 203
Germany, 63, 92, 181
Giap (General), 200
Gibbons, Cardinal, 51, 276
Gill, Eric, 39
Gladstone, William, 11
Goldwater, Barry, 203
Graves, W. B., 79
Great Britain, 74
Greeley, Andrew, 236–237, 264
Greenlee, "Doc" (Charles), 178, 182–183
Greece, 218
Grenada, 240, 263
Gropp, John J., 249
Groppi, James, 172, 196, 231, 272–274
Guatemala, 219
Guevara, Che, 218
Guerin, Daniel, 97
Guffey, Joseph F., 78–79
Guild, 44

H-Block, 242
Haden, Bouie, 176, 177–179, 181–183, 184, 185–186, 188, 189, 231, 267
Hafer, Barbara, 246
Haiphong, 212
Halifax, Lord, 97
Hanley, Ed, 145
Hanoi, 212
Harrington, Michael, 106, 130, 152–153
Harrisburg, 170
Hart, William, 106, 128, 129, 140, 144–145, 152, 231
Hathaway, Clarence, 94
Hayden, Tom, 267
Haywood, Alan, 17

Headstart, 175
Healey, Patrick, 83
Heinz, H. J., 46–49, 96, 98
Heinz strike, 76
Henderson, Leon, 80
Hensler, Carl P., 42, 43, 45, 47, 49, 60,
 86, 146, 231, 265
Hetzell, 79–80
Hillman Library, xiv, 103
Hillman, Sidney, 82, 98
Hines, Billy, 191
Hiroshima, 73, 207
Hitler, Adolph, 63, 73, 96, 262
Hoffman, Abby, 205
Hoffman, Julius, 216
Hogan, William (Rev.), 138
Holy Rosary parish, 170–173, 175, 176,
 178, 179, 183, 186–191, 224–227, 231,
 232, 235, 276
Homestead, Pa., 248
Homewood, xii, 171–179, 180, 181,
 182, 184, 186–190, 193–196, 208, 224,
 225, 227, 231
Homewood-Brushton Alliance [HBA],
 175
Homewood-Brushton Chamber of
 Commerce [HBCC], 175
Homewood-Brushton Citizens'
 Renewal Council [HBCRC], 175
Homewood-Brushton Civic
 Improvement Association [HBCIA],
 175, 182
Homewood-Brushton Health Center,
 178
Homosexuals, 234–235
Honeywell, Charles, 249, 268, 270
Hoover Administration, 31
Hoover, J. Edgar, 106, 112, 213, 222,
 268
House Internal Security Committee
 [HISC], 228
House of Commons, 241
House UnAmerican Affairs Committee
 [HUAC], 89, 111, 113, 124, 125, 127,
 128, 153–154, 228
House of Hospitality, (see St. Joseph's
 House of Hospitality)
Hovde, Bryn, 76
How to Decontrol Your Union of
 Communists, 102–105, 126
Hugo, John, 231
Humanae Vitae, 237
Humphrey, Hubert H., 188
Hungary, 96
Huntington, W. Va., 120

Immaculate Conception Church
 (Pittsburgh), 30
Immaculate Conception Church
 (Washington, Pa.), 147, 170
Immigrants, 235
Imperialism, 129, 217, 218, 219, 240–241
Independent Association of Employees
 of Duquesne Light and [5]
 Associated Companies, 86–88
India, 201
Indonesia, 199
Institute of Management-Labor
 Relations, 105, 136, 138
International Brotherhood of Electrical
 Workers [IBEW], 88
International Christian Federation of
 Trade Unions [ICFTU], 131
International Union of Electrical
 Workers [IUE], 85, 104, 126, 127,
 130, 154
Iran, 219
Ireland, 2, 3–7, 8, 9, 10–15, 18, 23, 74,
 214, 224, 241
Irish National Liberation Army, 242
Irish Republican Army [IRA], 23, 238,
 241, 242, 243, 249, 260
Irish Republican Brotherhood, 12, 13
Irish Republican Socialist Party, 242
Irish Sweepstakes, 241
Irish Transport Workers' Union, 12
Irish Volunteers, 12
Iron Curtain, 116
Israel, 151, 201, 218
Israel Bonds, 151
Italy, 92

Japan, 92
"Jim Crow", 167, 182
John XXIII, 147
John Paul II, 234
Johnson Administration, 203
Johnson, Clyde, 107
Johnson, Lyndon B., 200, 203, 205, 207,
 212
Jones & Laughlin Steel, 48
Just-war theory, 36, 53, 243, 278–279

KDKA, 52, 147, 213, 243
Kant, Emmanuel, 262
Kazinsky, Adelbert, 41, 272
Kelly, Dave, 206
Kennedy Administration, 168, 201
Kennedy, Edward, 238–239
Kennedy, John F., 146–147, 201, 203,
 238

Kennedy, Robert, 238
Kent State University, 212
Kerner Commission Report, 184–185
Khrushchev, Nikita, 229
King, Martin Luther, 168, 169, 180, 185, 186, 207
Kirk, Raymond V., 105
Kirkpatrick, Jeane, 243
Kistler, Alan, 42, 58, 108, 213
Knights of Columbus, 55
Knights of Labor, 26
Koestler, Arthur, 94
Korea, 93, 142, 203, 204, 217
Korean War, 127
Ku Klux Klan, 17
Kung, Hans, 251

LEAA (see Federal Law Enforcement Assistance Administration)
Labor Day, 146, 148, 192–193
Labor Leader, 95, 106, 123, 131
"Labor Priest", x, 41–42, 50, 192, 250
Labor priests, 27, 248
Labor schools, 43, 93, 120
LaFollettes, 18, 33
Laissez-faire, 31
Lappan, Thomas, 42, 45–46
Larkin, James, 12–13
Latin America, 203, 218
Latrobe, Pa., 24
Laundry Workers International Union, 83–84
Lawrence, Charles, 222
Lawrence, David, 87, 89, 149, 151, 222
League for Independent Political Action, 32
Lebanon, 263
LeBlanc, Paul, 202
Lee, Bridget, 81–82
Lemon socialism, 270
Lenin, 262
Lenz, William, 42, 54, 56, 58, 195
Leo XIII, 276
Leonard, Vincent, 189, 227
Lewis, John L, x, 97, 98, 108
Lewis, Katie, 97–98
Liberation theology, 279–280
Liberty Bakery, 140, 174
Lincoln, Abraham, 199
Litchfield, 202
"Literary Varieties", 150
Loney, Stan, 118
Long, Huey, 34
Long Kesh Prison, 242
Losbough, Bernard E., 181

Lowell, Robert, 207, 231
Loyalty Order, 116, 127
Lynd, Staughton, 248
Lyons, Daniel, 212

MacLeish, Archibald, 32
MacNeill, Eoin, 12, 13
Malaya, 204
Malcolm X, 168
Management-Labor Relations Institute, 105, 136, 138
Mansour, Sr. Agnes Mary, 234
Marijuana, 221
Maritain, Jacques, 39
Marshall Plan, 99, 110, 217, 229
Martin de Porres Society, 57, 58
Mater et Magistra, 210
Matles, James J., 113, 118, 126, 135, 227
Maurin, Peter, xiii, 37–40, 50, 54, 59, 68, 263, 273–274
Mayoral Campaign (Pittsburgh), 220, 221
McBride, Lloyd, 249
McCabe, William, 107
McCarthy, Joseph, 127, 144, 261
McCarthyism, xiii, 93
McCollester, Charles, xiv
McDonald, David, 134, 145, 151–152
McIlvane, Donald, 183, 184, 189, 214
McKissick, Floyd, 182
McLaughlin, Frank C., 79, 80
McNabb, Vincent, 39
McPeak, C. Howard, 81
Mellon banks, 249
Mellons, 187
Mesta Machine, 248
Mexico, 235
Meyers, George, 95
Midland, Pa., 248
Mills, C. Wright, 154
Mindszenty, Cardinal, 96, 146, 229
Minh, Ho Chi, 199, 200, 203
Minimum wage, 36
Molotov-Ribbentrop Pact, 96
Monte Cassino, 73
Montgomery, Harry, 142
Mooney, Bernard, 100–101, 274
Moratorium Day, 220
Morlion, Felix A., 150
Mounnier, Emmanuel, 39
Mount Lebanon, 243
Mount Mercy College, 40–41
Mueller, George, 86–89
Mumford, Lewis, 32

Murray, Phil, x, xii, 80, 81, 93, 97–99, 101, 108, 114, 115–117, 119, 124, 126, 131, 142, 153, 177, 227, 229, 268, 271, 276
Musmanno, Michael, 142, 143, 212
Mussolini, Benito, 150, 262

Nagasaki, 73
National Association for the Advancement of Colored People [NAACP], 149, 168, 170, 175, 179, 184
National Labor Relations Board [NLRB], 47, 88, 109, 116
National Liberation Front (Vietnam) [NLF], 216
National Maritime Union, 100
National Mobilization, 205
National Opinion Research Center [NORC], 236, 237
National Peace Action Coalition [NPAC], 216, 217, 268–269
Native Americans, 234, 235
Natrona, Pa., 136, 138, 139, 140, 141–142, 144, 146–147, 150, 169
Nazis, 63, 73, 96, 203, 206, 229
Negro Educational Emergency Drive [NEED], 175
Neighbors in Need, 175, 176, 179, 196
Nelson, John, 120, 123
Nelson, Steve, 142–143, 202, 228–229
New Deal, xi–xii, xiii, 18, 24, 30–31, 34, 35, 36, 62, 66, 69, 70, 79, 214, 269
New Left, 154
New Mobilization, 213, 216, 228
Newell, Charles, 85
Newspaper Guild, 96
Nicaragua, 240
Nixon, Richard M., 144, 188, 209–212, 238
No-first strike pledge, 252
Nolan, Tom, 118–119, 123, 127, 128, 129, 230
North American College in Rome, 42
North Vietnam, 203
Northern Ireland, 211, 241
Nuclear Freeze Movement, 252
Nuclear war, 239
Nuclear weapons, 202, 239, 251, 272, 278–279

Ochs, Paul, 207
Office of Economic Opportunity [OEO], 180

Office of Price Administration [OPA], 77–78, 80–81, 85, 90
Ohio Conference on Action for Peace, 208
Olbum, David, 187
O'Reilly, Frank M., 109
Orlemanski, Casimir, 85
Olson, Floyd B., 33
"On the Condition of Labor", xii
O'Toole, George B., 42, 43, 44, 45, 46, 47, 54, 60, 265
Opus Dei, 252
Ordination of women, 251, 279
Our Sunday Visitor, 102, 104

Pacem in Terris, 210
Pacifism, 57, 61–62, 72, 252, 263, 278
Palestinians, 151
Panama, 203
Parnell, Charles Stuart, 10, 11
Passavant Hospital, 170
"Pastor of the Poorest", 56
Patton, George, 73
Paul VI, 210
Pearl Harbor, 72, 78
Pegler, Westbrook, 108
Peguy, Charles, 39
Penn State University, 138
Pennsylvania Public Utilities Commission, 173
Pentagon, 207, 214, 267, 275
Personalism, 37–39, 60, 267
Pettigrew, Richard F., 19–21, 25, 72, 263
Pittsburgh Area Religion and Race Council, 174, 175, 176
Pittsburgh Area Students for Peace, 207
Pittsburgh Catholic, xi, 42, 54, 58, 104, 107–108, 111, 136–138, 141, 148, 151, 152, 156, 172, 187, 203, 225, 231, 271
Pittsburgh City Council, 181
Pittsburgh Defense Council, 76
Pittsburgh diocese, 23, 27, 42, 53, 136–137, 146, 174, 184, 186, 226, 276
Pittsburgh Hospital, 182–183
Pittsburgh Housing Association, 56
Pittsburgh Housing Authority, 75
Pittsburgh Post Gazette, 23, 170
Pittsburgh Press, 207, 253
Pius IX, 275
Pius XI, 24, 26
Pius XII, 143, 147, 156
Planned Parenthood, 178
Poblich, George, 107

Poland, 63, 73, 96, 134
Pollution, 235
Port Huron Statement, 267
Potsdam, 74, 92
Powell, Adam Clayton, 180
Powers, Gary, 201
Pravda, 128
Pressman, Lee, 85, 98, 109, 115
Price Control Act, 76–77
Priestly celibacy, 251
Priests' unions, 250
Prisons, 245–246
Pro Deo, 150–151, 152
Progressive movement, 67
Progressives, 125
Progressive Party, 33
Prolife movement, 233
Proudhon, Pierre, 39
Provisionals, 242
Puerto Rico, 201

Quadragesimo Anno, 24, 36, 277
Quill, Mike, 99–100, 127

Racism, 167–169
Randolph, A. Philip, 183
"Rank-and-File", 118, 125
Rarick, David, 145
Reagan Administration, 252
Reagan, Ronald, 194, 239, 240, 247, 264
Reaganism, 133
Redmond, John, 11
Reinhold, A. H., 58, 62–63
Religious Agency for Human Renewal [RAHR], 175–176, 178, 188–189, 196
Reno, Milo, 33
Rent Control, xiii, 77–78, 80–81, 89–90, 146
"Rent Czar", 70, 74, 76, 78, 80, 82, 86, 90, 169
Rerum Novarum, 24, 36, 277
Reuther, Walter, 109, 116, 126, 128, 131, 213
Ribbentrop Pact, 62
Rice
  Anna, 1–2
  Barney, 8
  Cock Rices, 10, 11, 13
  Eleanor, 16, 17
  Ellen (grandmother), 2, 242
  Ellen (sister), 2
  Grandfather Patrick, 8, 10
  Great Uncle Patrick, 3, 15, 242
  Ida, 16

Jem, 2, 12
Jennie, 2, 10, 16, 232
Joseph (cousin), 15
Joseph (uncle), 11, 16, 17, 241
Maggie, 2, 6
Matt, 2
Michael, 1–2, 6, 16–17, 30, 232
Owen, 2, 9, 38
Paddy, 2
Patrick, 2, 3, 7, 10, 11, 15, 16–18, 21, 72, 146, 214, 223, 232
Peter, 6, 140, 142
Sarah, 2, 6, 15
Riesel, Victor, 106, 109
Robinson, 98
Roe vs. Wade, 233
Romero, Oscar, 240
Romney, George, 218–219
Roosevelt Administration, 34, 199, 263
Roosevelt, Franklin D., 24, 31, 41, 62, 69, 70, 73, 76, 110, 262
Rosemonde, John W., 78, 81
Rosenbergs, Ethel and Julius, 143–144, 154, 260
Roth, David, xi, 249, 268, 270, 273, 274
Rubin, Jerry, 205
Rumania, 96
Rush, Molly, 240
Ruttenberg, Harold J., 85
Ryan, Frank, 241
Ryan, John A., 35–36, 53, 68–69, 268, 269

Saigon, 200
Saladna, George E., 151
Sandinistas, 240
Sands, Bobby, 242
Saturday Evening Post, 122
School busing, 233
Scott, John, 173
Scully, Cornelius D., 76
Seaton, Douglas P., 132–133
Seidman, John, 220
Selective Service, 208–210
Seton Hill College, 54
Shapp, Milton, 230, 245
Share Our Wealth Plan, 34
Sharon, Pa., 120, 123, 127
Sheen, Fulton J., 51, 231
Shockley, William B., 185, 264
"Silent majority", 210
Sinclair, Upton, 33
Sinn Fein, 12, 13, 14, 18, 241
Sisters of Charity, 55, 182
Sisters of Mercy, 40

Sisters of St. Joseph, 225
Smith Act, 108, 111, 121
Smith, Al, 18
Smith, Rev. Francis, 138, 139
Smith, Nate, 192
Social Security, 31, 36
Socialism, 25, 26, 36, 74
Socialist Party, 32
Soho-Gazzam Homeowners and
  Tenants Association [SGHOTPA],
  74–76, 78, 169, 265
Solidarity, 134
Somoza government, 240
South Africa, 243
Southern Christian Leadership
  Conference [SCLC], 168
Southern Tenant Farmers' Union, 32
Soviet Union, 20, 61, 63, 68, 73–74, 92,
  96–97, 116, 119, 134, 135, 143, 146,
  148, 150, 200, 218, 229, 252
Spanish Civil War, 49, 61–62, 202, 228
Spellman, Francis, x, 137, 138, 139,
  140, 211
Spinoza, Baruch, 262
Spock, Benjamin, 182, 198, 207
Spring Mobilization, 182, 205, 207, 216
St. Agnes, 30, 40, 54, 74–75
St. Anne's church, ix–x, 227, 233, 235,
  245, 253–254
St. Brigid, 138, 139
St. Francis House of Hospitality, 64
St. Joseph's Parish, 138, 142, 146
St. Joseph's House of Hospitality,
  52–60, 64, 70–71, 78, 82, 89, 90, 106,
  136, 138, 139, 169, 171, 183, 195,
  231, 235, 244, 263
St. Joseph's Labor Day Award, 183
St. Mary's, Pa., 120, 127
St. Paul's Cathedral, 206, 250
St. Regis Church, 124
St. Vincent de Paul Society, 42, 45–46,
  55, 186
St. Vincent Seminary, 24, 29, 120, 183,
  189
Stalin, Josef, 229
Statement on Social Reconstruction,
  24, 35–36, 68, 269
Steelworkers' Organizing Committee
  (SWOC), 49
Stock Market Crash, 29
Student Non-violent Coordinating
  Committee [SNCC], 172, 176
Students for a Democratic Society
  [SDS], 267

Sullivan, Lawrence, 42, 57, 64, 106,
  108
Syllabus of Errors, 275
Syndicates, 26
Synod of Bishops, 277

Taft-Hartley, 87, 109–110, 111, 116,
  118, 124, 125, 126, 140
Talmadge, Herman, 34
Teamsters, 104, 235, 247
Terrace Village, 76
Testem benevolentiae, 276
Thatcher, Margaret, 242
Third-world nations, 235, 248
Thomas, Norman, 32
Thornburgh, Richard, 237
Time, 24, 47
Townsend Plan, 33, 41
Trafford, Pa., 124
Transport Workers Union [TWU],
  99–100
Tristate Conference on Steel, 248–249
Truman Administration, 199
Truman, Harry S., 87, 111, 116–117,
  142
Turner, Mildred, 120–121, 130, 132
Turtle Creek, Pa., 114

U.E. District 6, 114, 117–119, 120–121,
  123, 126–127, 128, 130
U.E. Local 601, 83, 85, 108, 111, 114,
  117, 118, 119, 122, 124–125, 128, 132,
  154
U.E. Local 610, xiv, 114, 117, 123
U.E. Local 613, 114, 123, 132
U.E. Local 638, 118, 132
U.E. Members for Democratic Action
  [UEMDA], 123–124, 125–126
Uncovic, Nick, 141
Unemployment compensation, 31, 36
Union Switch and Signal, 114
United Auto Workers [UAW], 109,
  116, 119, 123, 126, 132, 153
United Electrical, Radio and Machine
  Workers of America [UERMA or
  UE], xii, 93, 100, 104, 106, 107, 108,
  110, 111, 112–115, 116–119, 126–127,
  135, 154, 227, 266
United Farm Workers, 226, 235
United Mine Workers [UMW], 104,
  235–236, 247
United Movement for Progress [UMP],
  176, 178, 181–183, 185, 188
United Oakland Ministry, 208

United Office and Professional Workers of America (UOPWA), 101, 103, 104
U.S. Catholic Bishops, 134, 251, 272, 277–279
United States Steel, 138–139, 170, 177, 192, 248
United States Supreme Court, 47, 73, 142, 168, 245
United Steel Workers of America [USWA], 104, 105, 116, 124, 128, 134, 144–145, 151–152, 181, 212–213, 227, 231, 246–247, 249
University of California, Berkeley, 155
University of Pittsburgh, 30, 40, 103, 111, 150, 169, 202, 208, 243
Urban League, 176, 180
U.S. Catholic Conference, 35

Vatican, 73, 134, 148, 150, 189, 251, 252, 277, 279
Vatican II, 58, 147, 156, 210, 227, 271, 276, 277, 278
Vida, Ernest, 124
Viet Cong, 204
Vietnam, xi, 152, 198–205, 214–220, 228, 238, 251–252, 268
Volk, Ed, 19

Wallace, George, 179, 180, 188
Wallace, Henry, 110, 116, 131, 229
Walter, Ernest, 124
War on Poverty, 180
Washington, Pa., 147, 149–150, 152, 167, 169–170, 179, 205
Watergate, 238
Weathermen, 267
Wecht, Cyril, 230
Wehofer, Sam, 140

Weiner, David, 149
Weirton Steel, 248
Welfare, 31
West Penn Hospital, 96
Westinghouse, 113, 114
Westinghouse Air Brake Company [WABCO], 107, 114
Whiskey Rebellion, 66
White flight, 226
White, Frank J., 214
Wiesen, Ron, 145, 248–249, 250, 268, 270
WIIC-TV, 206
Wilmerding, Pa., 123
Wilner, Al, 47, 76
Wilson, Woodrow, 18, 19, 92
Winston, Henry, 121–122
WJAS, 41, 77, 221
Women's liberation, xii, 232–234
Worker, The, 122, 128, 130–131
Worker ownership, 270
World Federation of Trade Unions [WFTU], 131
World War I, 15, 20, 72
World War II, xii, 36, 60, 61, 70, 72, 76, 82, 86, 92, 96, 97, 113, 128, 130, 142, 183, 199–200, 247, 263
Wright, John, 148–149, 150, 167, 171, 175, 177, 179, 180, 188, 189, 193, 195, 269
WWSW, 52, 53, 70, 89, 150, 154, 220, 221

Yablonski, Jock, 235–236
Youngstown, Ohio, 248
Yugoslavia, 96

Zimmerman, Morris, 77